HOW YOU CAN SUCCEED AT PROTECTING YOUR LEGACY

How Great Philanthropists Failed &
HOW YOU CAN SUCCEED AT PROTECTING YOUR LEGACY

Martin Morse Wooster

Fourth edition, revised and enlarged, of
The Great Philanthropists and the Problem of 'Donor Intent'

CAPITAL RESEARCH CENTER
WASHINGTON, D.C.

CAPITAL RESEARCH CENTER

Published in the United States of America

By Capital Research Center
1513 Sixteenth Street, NW
Washington, DC 20036

The previous editions of this book were published under the title *The Great Philanthropists and the Problem of 'Donor Intent.'*

Library of Congress Cataloging-in-Publication Data

Names: Wooster, Martin Morse, 1957- author.
Title: How great philanthropists failed & how you can succeed at protecting your legacy / Martin Morse Wooster.
Other titles: Great philanthropists and the problem of "donor intent" | How great philanthropists failed and how you can succeed at protecting your legacy
Description: Fourth edition, revised and enlarged. | Washington, D.C. :
  Capital Research Center, [2017] | "The previous editions of this book were
  published under the title The Great Philanthropists and the Problem of
  'Donor Intent.'." | Includes bibliographical references and index.
Identifiers: LCCN 2017048716 | ISBN 1892934043 (pbk. : alk. paper)
Subjects: LCSH: Philanthropists--United States. | Charities--United States. |
  Family foundations--United States. | Charitable uses, trusts, and
  foundations--United States.
Classification: LCC HV91 .W6265 2017 | DDC 361.7/6320973--dc23 LC
record available at https://lccn.loc.gov/2017048716

Printed in the United States of America

Book cover designed by Colby Pastre

DEDICATED TO THE MEMORY OF

ANDREW CARNEGIE

HENRY FORD

HENRY FORD II

JOHN D. MacARTHUR

J. HOWARD PEW

JOSEPH N. PEW

JOHN D. ROCKEFELLER SR.

Contents

🌀

Part I: Undermining Donor Intent

Part II: Preserving Donor Intent

Part III: Practical Considerations

Foreword

By the time the third generation becomes involved with running a foundation, the memory of the founder has often become dimmed. His or her aspirations, motivations, and vision are often no longer compelling. Donor intent may have been appropriate for grandpa, but it doesn't apply to his grandchildren.

Unfortunately, this scenario has been repeated too many times in the history of American philanthropy.

Philanthropic institutions will experience a major inflow of new funds during the coming decades. Those who made their money after World War II will reach maturity, and their estates will be passed to their heirs and to foundations. How will those funds be spent? Is it important to donors who created new wealth that their gifts be used in accordance with their political and philosophical beliefs?

Donors should be aware that clear violations of donor intent—even when that intent is explicitly stated in binding documents—have occurred. The Pew Charitable Trusts, the Buck Trust, the Barnes Foundation, and the DeRancé Foundation have all explicitly violated detailed donor intent statements. The Ford Foundation, the John D. and Catherine T. MacArthur Foundation, the Rockefeller Foundation, the Carnegie Corporation of New York, and others do not follow the spirit of their donors' intent. But in these cases the donors did not leave clear mandates of their wishes.

Some foundations regain a lost respect for their donors, but there are not many. The most notable ones are the William H. Donner Foundation and the Buck Trust.* Except for the Barnes and the DeRancé foundations and possibly the Donner Foundation, all these abrogations are characterized by a shift away from traditional forms of charity to left-wing advocacy and from a respect for free markets to redistributive political action.

i

So donor beware. How can someone who wants to create a foundation ensure that his or her wishes will be followed decades from now? What's to prevent trustees, relatives, and lawyers from disregarding, changing, or reinterpreting a donor's intentions to fit their own plans for the money?

Martin Morse Wooster answers these questions in the course of his fascinating survey of the founding fathers of American philanthropy and the great institutions of wealth and generosity they created. He shows how our system of free enterprise and limited government released the entrepreneurial energies of these people, giving them incentives to use their wealth for the benefit of others. He describes the plans and actions of famous entrepreneurs—the Rockefellers, Carnegies, Fords, and others less well known—who created vast new wealth and then pondered what would become of it after they died.

But this is also an instructive and cautionary tale for our time. It is a story about how those who were brilliant in the marketplace often failed to understand the very different outlooks of the trustees and foundation executives they entrusted to handle their fortunes.

There is a world of difference between those who can earn great wealth and those who are bequeathed great wealth—and then find themselves responsible for spending someone else's money. Martin Wooster's recommendations should be carefully considered by those who wish to avoid the pitfalls of modern philanthropy.

—W. J. Hume
Jaquelin Hume Foundation
San Francisco, California

---

* Since this foreword was written, the Daniels Fund has joined this noble group. See chapter fourteen—*Editor.*

Editor's Preface:
How to Use This Book

If you're a scholar of philanthropy, read every word in this book. If you're a busy donor, let me save you time by spoiling the plot: You lose.

That is to say, this book shows that most of the time, donors do *not* secure their legacy. They do not see their own intentions for their own wealth—usually earned by the sweat of their own brow—respected. It is hard to arrange your charitable giving in a way that results in your intentions being carried out in the long run.

Men of amazing entrepreneurial genius, like Andrew Carnegie, John D. Rockefeller, and Henry Ford, built commercial empires larger than the world had ever seen; they produced astronomical returns on investment and were rarely tricked out of their money in business deals. But when they turned to giving that money away, they failed. And as Martin Morse Wooster so finely reports in this book, many other persons of somewhat smaller wealth have also had their charitable plans go awry.

Wealthy and prestigious colleges, Wooster documents, have treated donors shamefully. The donors' own staff and assistants have betrayed the vision of the men and women who gave them the money they now abuse. Even family members have utterly disregarded how their ancestors wanted the fruits of their labor to be used. Billions upon billions of dollars that were earned in the American marketplace by titans of industry are now in the hands of treacherous philanthropic elites who use that wealth to attack the very system that generated it.

So if you're a donor contemplating how to structure your giving, I suggest you skim some of the detailed history in Part I of this book, which lays out the leading horror stories of American philanthropy. Then you may want to skim more slowly through

Part II, where Wooster tells the stories of luckier families, who have achieved better results through careful planning and hard work.

Lastly, you should focus your attention most keenly on the final chapter, which features practical advice based on the histories in Parts I and II—because you must face the brutal fact that it is not easy to give well, even while you're living. After you're gone, the odds of successful giving are stacked even higher against you.

Scholars of philanthropy, on the other hand, will want to savor every word of Wooster's fascinating history, which unearths so many little-known details of this critical aspect of American giving. Perhaps those scholars will also have a pang of guilt at their own neglect of this topic, because only four books have ever been written on this history: namely, the first, second, third, and now fourth edition of this work.

— Scott Walter
President
Capital Research Center

Acknowledgements to the Fourth Edition (2017)

This new edition shows what happened to the foundations I write about in this book between 2007-2017. It includes new case studies on the Daniels Fund and the Packard Foundation, as well as substantially expanded sections on the MacArthur and Barnes Foundations. The result is about 45,000 words of new material.

A chapter on the problems of establishing foundations in perpetuity abridges and updates *Should Foundations Live Forever? The Question of Perpetuity*, published by the Capital Research Center in 1998. The original edition should be consulted for more extensive case studies of some of these term-limited foundations.

This book was edited by Ellen Wilson Fielding and Scott Walter. It was researched at the McKeldin Library at the University of Maryland and the Library of Congress.

For the section on the Packard Foundation, I benefited from interviews with Christopher DeMuth and the late Peter Flanigan. Denise E. Elson and Nicholas Siekierski at the Hoover Institution assisted me with requests for pertinent material on Herbert Hoover's dealings with David Packard. Spencer Howard at the Herbert Hoover Presidential Library also provided many useful documents.

For the chapter on the Daniels Fund, I conducted interviews with Sen. Hank Brown, Linda Childears, the late Bob Coté, and Steve Schuck.

At the Hilton Foundation, Pat Modugno was very helpful in ensuring my understanding of the foundation's history was accurate. He also provided documents about the foundation's efforts to support donor intent.

Gay Clyburn, Mike Glyer, John J. Miller, Nancy Piwowar, and Matt Westmoreland provided additional assistance.

Acknowledgements to the Third Edition (2007)

This third edition shows what happened to the foundations I write about between 1998-2006. It includes a new section on the Robertson Foundation case (which was not a problem in 1998), and a substantially expanded section on the Barnes Foundation. In addition, a great many more electronic databases (including searchable files of the *New York Times* and the *Washington Post,* as well as America: History and Life, which indexes historical journals) allowed me to deepen my knowledge of foundation history. As a result, this third edition includes about 20,000 words of new material.

This book was edited by Robert Huberty. Research for the book was done at the Library of Congress and the McKeldin Library at the University of Maryland.

Herb Berkowitz and Jennifer Berkowitz, public relations specialists for the Robertson family, went beyond the call of duty in providing documents showing the intentions of Charles Robertson. Thanks to Gay Clyburn and Ann Whitfield of the Carnegie Foundation for the Advancement of Teaching, Michael Hartmann of the Bradley Foundation, and Patrick Modugno of the Conrad N. Hilton Foundation for their help in making sure I was accurate. F.H. Buckley assisted me with the legal research.

Acknowledgements to the Second Edition (1998)

This new edition shows what happened from 1994-1999 to the foundations I originally wrote about in 1993. It includes new information about almost every foundation I analyzed, as well as substantial new primary material on the Pews and the MacArthurs. In addition, it incorporates much from "Undermining Donor Internet: Four Case Studies," *Alternatives in Philanthropy,* November 1995, and two paragraphs from "The MacArthur Fellowships: The Oscars of the Multicultural Elite," *Philanthropy, Culture & Society,* January 1996. Other new material about the great philanthropists was uncovered through a search of scholarly material published in the past four years. This second edition has about 12,000 words of new material.

As with the first edition, the book was edited by Daniel T. Oliver and supervised by Robert Huberty. Research for the book was performed at the Library of Congress, the McKeldin Library at the University of Maryland, the library at the Foundation Center's Washington, D.C. office, and the Rockville, Maryland public library.

Acknowledgements to the First Edition (1994)

This book owes its inspiration to Tim Ferguson and Willa Johnson. In fall 1989, Tim Ferguson, then the editorial features editor at the *Wall Street Journal,* read an issue of the Capital Research Center's *Alternatives in Philanthropy* I had written on the Ford Foundation. He suggested I write an op-ed on what happened to the fortunes of Andrew Carnegie and John D. MacArthur. Like all good editors, he identified a subject that a writer would find interesting, and if it were not for him, I would not have begun my exploration of the problems of donor intent.

In January 1993, I had a meeting with Willa Johnson where I first proposed doing an article on donor intent. She suggested a book instead, and by the end of the meeting we had a contract and I had become a CRC visiting fellow. Thank you, Willa, for your suggestions, your inspiration, and your patience.

Research for this book was done at the Library of Congress, the McKeldin Library at the University of Maryland, and the library in the Foundation's Center's Washington, D.C. office. Special thanks to the Foundation Center's series *The Literature of the Nonprofit Sector,* an invaluable research tool that provided a great many citations for articles and books I might otherwise have missed.

At the Capital Research Center, Daniel T. Oliver did a fine job of editing this book. My research on the Buck Trust was aided by earlier research done by Philip Marcus and Robert Davis.

Several staff members at foundations and corporations provided useful information, particularly Elizabeth Locke at the Duke Endowment, Patrick Modugno at the Conrad N. Hilton Foundation, and Claire Sheehan at TIAA-CREF. Kim Dennis of the Philanthropy Roundtable made several helpful suggestions. Other suggestions, articles, or advice were provided by James Bowman, Charles Hamilton, Sean Haugh, and Rodger Morrow.

INTRODUCTION

American Philanthropy and the Problems of Donor Intent

Mr. Rockefeller's method of giving away money impersonally on the basis of investigation by others is careful and conscientious; but it must have cut him off almost completely from the real happiness which good deeds ought to bring the doer, the happiness of giving personally not only one's money, but one's sympathy and labor. He has already done an enormous amount of good, and is going to do much more for many years to come. We all wish that he had got more joy out of it.

> — *Charles W. Eliot, Harvard University president and Rockefeller Foundation trustee[1]*

When you die and come to approach the judgment of almighty God, when you stand before St. Peter in supplication at the gates of heaven, what do you think he will demand of you? Do you for an instant presume that he will inquire into your petty failures and your trivial virtues? ...No! No indeed! He will brush all these matters to one side and he will ask but one question: "How did you do as a trustee of the Rockefeller Foundation?!"

> — *Frederick T. Gates, philanthropic adviser to John D. Rockefeller[2]*

    In 1900, most forms of philanthropy in the United States were locally based. Most of the major national charities either did not exist or were very small. When Clara Barton was ousted as president of the American Red Cross in 1904, the organization's annual budget was only $2,730.

By 1925, the philanthropic world had greatly changed. Large organizations had been created by Andrew Carnegie and John D. Rockefeller. Major national charities, including the American

Cancer Society, National Urban League, and National Association for the Advancement of Colored People had also been established. The American Red Cross had grown from a small decentralized charity to a giant nonprofit that collected and spent $400 million during World War I. Increasingly, the typical philanthropy was a large organization with general—and often vague—goals, rather than a small charity with narrow aims.

Most historians treat the creation of large philanthropies as an important advance. Historians Barry D. Karl and Stanley N. Katz argue that large foundations were able to "play a major role in preparing the way for the modern state. For by supporting research and thereby influencing the choice of social policies, the philanthropists were [able to shape] governmental action in what was increasingly identified as the private sector."[3]

But with the growth of large foundations, the problem of donor intent increased. As historian Kathleen D. McCarthy notes,

> neither the donor's motives nor the donor's decisions were beyond question after the turn of the century. Instead, growing ranks of professionals worked to systematize the benevolent impulse and channel it towards responsible ends. Science, rather than simple good will, infused the philanthropic ethos of the Jazz Age. In the process, donors were increasingly asked to pay for projects they often could neither touch nor comprehend, deferring to the wisdom of reformers and managers of every stripe and hue.[4]

This chapter examines several social trends in the late nineteenth and early twentieth centuries that helped to inspire the increasingly widespread ideal of the "disinterested donor"—the belief that donors should calmly leave their fortunes to trained "professionals" to be distributed in ways favored by those professionals. These trends include the rise of "social engineering," the advent of modern fundraising, the creation of community foundations and the massive increase in requests for charity.

ℰ The Rise of Social Engineering

As Marvin Olasky shows in his historical overview of American philanthropy, *The Tragedy of American Compassion,* until about

1900, most charity in the United States was provided by local organizations that dealt directly with the poor. As the nineteenth century progressed, however, some charity leaders came to believe that national organizations could better deal with the administration of charities. By 1900, Olasky writes, some poverty-fighters "were beginning to suggest that a central organization, based on the most scientific methods of poverty-fighting, might need to have the power to dominate charity distributions and push others to comply with them."[5]

At the same time, anti-poverty crusaders began to emphasize fighting the alleged causes of poverty rather than merely alleviating symptoms. Instead of working with poor persons on an individual basis, ensuring that they re-entered the work force, charity workers increasingly focused on such abstractions as the presumed causes of homelessness and hunger.

A 1906 report by the Charity Organization Society (COS) of New York reviewed 25 years of poverty-relief efforts, concluding that past methods were no longer feasible. "The result to the community in eliminating and diminishing some of the more important causes of pauperism is of infinitely greater value than could have been brought about by the same amount of effort and the same amount of money expended for the relief of individual suffering." The COS therefore "deliberately determined, without neglecting in any way its duty in the relief of individual cases of poverty, to lay emphasis on the field of removing or minimizing the causes of poverty, and to firmly establish and extend these forms of work by organizing them into a department for the permanent improvement of social conditions."[6]

❧ The Russell Sage Foundation

In the philanthropic world, the trend toward fighting the presumed causes of poverty is best exemplified by the Russell Sage Foundation, created in 1907. Russell Sage was a prominent investment banker of the 1890s. As historian Joseph J. Thorndike Jr. notes, Sage apparently had no charitable impulses, preferring to hoard his wealth rather than spend it. Though he was a millionaire, he routinely walked in order to save streetcar fare. When he died in 1906, he unconditionally left his fortune of $65 million to his widow, Margaret Olivia Sage. The result, says Thorndike, is that he "would certainly have been horrified at what happened...."[7]

At first Mrs. Sage tried to help those in need. But after receiving 20,000 requests for help in six months, she decided to create an endowment as a memorial to her husband. She asked the advice of Robert W. de Forest, a long-time president of the Charity Organization Society of New York. De Forest, after consulting with like-minded friends, presented a set of ten options to Mrs. Sage, including building houses for the poor, offering the poor insurance, and subsidizing stores that sold goods at a small profit. But the best way to honor Russell Sage, de Forest suggested, was to create a "Sage Foundation for Social Betterment."

Mrs. Sage, however, worried that a foundation might run out of things to do. What if the problems of the poor were solved? De Forest replied that "with the constant change and shift of social conditions, ...the future may develop other and greater needs for philanthropic action than any which are now apparent." He even addressed the problem of donor intent by saying that Mrs. Sage's intentions "should be sufficiently elastic in form and method to work in different ways at different times."[8]

This belief was generally applauded by the press. *Charities and the Commons,* the leading journal of the charity movement, saluted the new foundation in a 1907 editorial, saying it had "a field of activity that the most enthusiastic would not call cramped or small.... Centuries hence, if the Sage Foundation is still in existence, its managers will not be tied down to any outgrown subject of inquiry or relief."[9]

But the Russell Sage Foundation dispensed with "outgrown subjects" early. Within a month of its incorporation, the board of directors declared that it would "not attempt to relieve individual or family need." Helping individuals would mean that "there would be no money left" for the "peculiar function of eradicating causes of poverty."[10] Instead, the foundation would give money to study poverty and also help create a nonprofit movement by funding *Charities and the Common* (later titled, *The Survey*), a publication roughly equivalent to the Council on Foundations' *Foundation News & Commentary* in our time.

❧ The Advent of Modern Fundraising

The Sage Foundation's grants and its emphasis on centralized philanthropy helped ensure that by 1915 charities in the United

States were largely national organizations that addressed general concerns. Nonprofits created between 1900 and 1916 included the Boys Clubs (1906), Federal (later National) Council of Churches (1908), National Association for the Advancement of Colored People (1909), Boy Scouts of America (1910), Camp Fire Girls (1912), American Cancer Society (1913), Girl Scouts (1915), and National Parent-Teacher Association (1915). By 1922, these groups were joined by the National Association of Travelers' Aid Societies, Girls Clubs, Jewish Welfare Board, Child Welfare League of America, American Federation of the Blind, Big Brothers and Big Sisters, and National Alliance of Legal Aid Societies.[11]

Such large charities were also strengthened by the perfection of fundraising techniques between 1900 and 1910. Historian Scott Cutlip credits three men with systematizing and perfecting fundraising: YMCA leaders Charles Sumner Ward and Lyman Pierce, and Harvard fundraiser Abbott Lawrence.

Ward and Pierce created the "campaign clock," in which large sums of money were raised in short periods of time. Their first campaign in 1905, was a 26-day effort to raise $80,000 for the Washington, D.C. YMCA. They were the first fundraisers to hire publicists and convince a prominent business (the Woodward and Lothrop department store) to buy advertisements urging support of charities. They also invented the fundraising dinner in which prominent individuals paid large sums to support a charitable cause.[12] Abbott Lawrence's contribution was to create the long-term campaign, first used in 1904 to raise funds for Harvard University. His techniques generated $2.5 million for Harvard, and by 1915, they had been copied by dozens of institutions nationwide.

Fundraising transformed the nonprofit sector so drastically that by 1917 Ward had successfully launched his first national campaign and raised over $114 million for the American Red Cross between June 18, and June 25, 1917. Americans were bombarded by editorials, lantern slides, streetcar signs, banners, and continued exhortations to give. President Woodrow Wilson proclaimed the event National Red Cross Week and semi-nationalized the organization, declaring it the nation's official relief agency. Americans for the first time "saw what large sums could be attained through the intensive fundraising campaign hitherto used only at the community level for charity or a civic or church building."[13]

While such techniques increased the pressure on average Americans to give, the appeals to wealthy donors were even greater.[14] One study commissioned by Mary Harriman (widow of the railroad magnate and mother of diplomat Averell Harriman) found that she received 6,000 requests in 1910 and 1911 for aid totaling $267 million. This was at a time when national giving was $270 million.[15] Given the mountains of mail many rich donors received, it was reasonable for them to create foundations to insulate themselves from grantees.

But the temperament of the times went further than this. William H. Allen, the director of the New York Bureau of Municipal Research (which conducted the study of Harriman's giving), believed that misinformed donors could cause great damage. He denounced "the dead hand," meaning a donor's legacy gift that outlived its times. He thought far worse, however, "the sympathetic live hand which from misinformation and lack of efficiency standards invites insincerity, evasion, waste, incompetence and incompleteness in the use of its gifts. Energy can be deadened by riches and freedom, as well as by restrictions."[16]

Allen opposed unrestricted gifts, saying that "history proves that they frequently encourage sloth, extravagance, indolence, disregard for social needs…in institution after institution in this city [New York] unrestricted legacies go regularly to make up deficits in current accounts instead of perpetuating the giver's interest."[17] But he also opposed restricted gifts (i.e., donor intent), saying that these "frequently outlive their usefulness; cannot change with changes in social conditions; handicap societies in time of need; frequently result in carrying coals to Newcastle and putting bounty on wolf scalps when all wolves are exterminated except those specially reared for the bounty."[18]

Allen believed that if trustees of a foundation could show that the intentions of the donor "no longer exist or are otherwise met by funds of this or other agencies," they should be free to use funds for any purpose whatsoever 20 years after the donor's death.[19] "Every city needs experts on will making, not only to draft unbreakable wills but to submit unquestionable needs," he added. "There is room for a new profession of consulting experts on will making and large giving."[20] He also called for a national clearinghouse to review all requests for aid, separate "worthy" from "unworthy" requests, and forward the worthy ones to suitable donors.

❧ The Creation of Community Foundations

The ideas of Allen and like-minded individuals were instrumental in creating community foundations. These were intended to eliminate the "dead hand" problem by giving unbiased experts authority to "scientifically" decide how small fortunes, pooled into a large fund, should be used. When the Cleveland Foundation,[21] the first community foundation, was created in 1914, one of the city's newspapers noted that most fortunes went to "weak children— the weaker for having had too much money when young...it is almost as unwise for the man of wealth to endow a charity. He doesn't know how soon the charity may become obsolete and his money serves only to pension useless hangers-on." But a community foundation, the paper opined, was more admirable, as it had "representatives of the public having a continuously freshened say as to how it is to be used. Obviously that is better than having it spoil heirs or galvanize dead or dying charities or pile up power in the hands of entrenched trustees suffering from fatty degradations of the soul."[22]

Allen's views, and the creation of community foundations, indicate the climate of opinion that led to a widespread repudiation of donor intent early in this century. But Allen and his compatriots failed to answer one question. If "experts" would separate worthy from unworthy requests, and if strong donor intent would lead to the use of legacies for unnecessary purposes, why should donors create foundations in the first place? If donors believed their wishes would likely be repudiated or ignored after their deaths, why should they create foundations? This is the subject of the next chapter, which considers the Rockefeller legacy.

PART I

UNDERMINING
DONOR INTENT

1

The Rockefeller Legacy

The immense fortune which is to be left to the [Rockefeller]
foundation is to be left without any restriction, except that it
is to be devoted to the well-being of the human race. And not
Rockefeller himself, but the unborn generations of the future,
will determine how the money is to be expended.... In the
Rockefeller Foundation there is not a sentence, nor a word,
which will tie down the people of the twenty-first century.
— Herbert N. Casson (1910)[1]

The philanthropic careers of John D. Rockefeller (1839-1937) and John D. Rockefeller Jr. (1874-1960) offer an illuminating example of the problems of donor intent.

John D. Rockefeller was a devout Close Communion Baptist. He believed that helping the less fortunate was a necessary part of life. As biographers John Ensor Harr and Peter J. Johnson note, "there was no question that Rockefeller's exclusive motivation for giving was his religious conviction and the old-fashioned concept of stewardship, not the expiation of guilt or the buying of public favor."[2]

Early in his philanthropic career, Rockefeller gave small gifts of between $50 and $500. But as his wealth exceeded the $5 million mark in the 1880s, he was increasingly burdened by requests. In 1891, he hired Frederick T. Gates, a fellow Baptist, to assist in his philanthropic and business concerns. Gates' first task was to shield Rockefeller from those who wanted part of his fortune. "Neither in the privacy of his home nor at his table, nor anywhere else, was Mr. Rockefeller secure from insistent appeal," Gates wrote in his memoirs. "Nor if asked to write were solicitors willing to do so. If in New York, they demanded personal interviews. Mr. Rockefeller was constantly hunted, stalked, and hounded almost like a wild animal."[3]

Gates swiftly put an end to this. He also found that many Baptist groups Rockefeller funded were deemed unworthy of support by Baptist headquarters. He consequently convinced Rockefeller to practice "wholesale" rather than "retail" philanthropy: instead of giving to individual churches, Rockefeller supported Baptist headquarters or mission boards.

"Wholesale" philanthropy did not mean that Rockefeller was unconcerned with how his money was spent. While he did not try to control the activities of his benefactors, he did seek to ensure that they were financially sound. One early recipient was the University of Chicago.[4] When its president William Harper refused to cut expenses to balance the school's budget, Rockefeller summoned him to his office, where John D. Rockefeller Jr. told him that the school would receive no more money until it balanced its books. Only when Harper left the school and his successor pursued more frugal policies did grants to the university resume.[5]

In addition, Rockefeller was adamant that his charity not be used to promote dependency. "The most perplexing issue for Rockefeller was how to square philanthropy with self-reliance," notes his latest biographer, Ron Chernow. "His constant nightmare was that he would promote dependence, sapping the Protestant work ethic.... He dreaded the thought of armies of beggars addicted to his handouts."[6] As early as the 1880s, Chernow observes, Rockefeller discussed with his brother Frank whether to contribute to a veterans organization in Cleveland. Rockefeller wondered whether such a contribution would be useful, since he did "not want to encourage a horde of irresponsible, adventuresome fellows to call on me at sight for money every time fancy seizes them."[7]

❧ The 'Tainted Money' Controversy

After 1900, Rockefeller expanded his philanthropic concerns to other Protestant churches. In early 1905, he gave $100,000 to the American Board of Commissioners for Foreign Missions to promote Congregationalism overseas. Though not himself a Congregationalist, his lawyer, sister-in-law, and Frederick Gates (who had switched churches) were members, so Rockefeller felt no hesitancy in contributing.

But the Congregational Church's moderator, Rev. Washington Gladden, vigorously protested. Rockefeller's gift was "tainted money," acquired "by methods as heartless, as cynically iniquitous as any that were employed by the Roman plunderers or robber barons of the Dark Ages. In the cool brutality with which properties are wrecked, securities destroyed, and people by the hundreds robbed of their little, all to build up the fortunes of the multi-millionaires, we have an appalling revelation of the kind of monster that a human being may become." Gladden added, "Is this clean money? Can any man, can any institution, knowing its origins, touch it without being defiled?"[8]

For a few months in 1905, "tainted money" was the issue of the day. The *Chicago Tribune* ran a cartoon featuring a prim pastor pointing to a portly man about to contribute to a collection plate. A sign hanging on the plate said, "ONLY HONESTLY ACQUIRED MONEY ACCEPTED." The caption read, "Wait a Minute! How Did You Get That Dollar?" The phrase was even used in vaudeville routines: "Sure it's tainted," the joke went. "Tain't yours and tain't mine."[9]

But the Rockefeller gift had not come to the Congregationalists by whim or chance. The Foreign Missions Board, it soon became known, had been corresponding with the Rockefellers since 1902, and both John D. Rockefeller Jr. and Frederick Gates had talked with representatives before the grant was made. In fact, the Foreign Missions Board had asked for $163,000 to fund ten proposals, four of which the Rockefellers had rejected. "I never had any question whatever regarding the propriety and even duty of soliciting help for the needy institutions and work of the Board from Mr. Rockefeller, as from other people of means who are members in good and regular standing of Christian churches," wrote James D. Barton, the Foreign Missions Board's secretary.[10]

❧ The Rockefeller Legacy

The tainted money episode, however, greatly damaged Rockefeller's reputation. Senator Robert La Follette (R-WI) charged that Rockefeller was "the greatest criminal of the age," while President Theodore Roosevelt called him one of the "malefactors of great wealth" who had to be tamed. The Memphis, Tennessee, *Appeal* compared Rockefeller to Captain Kidd, the pirate. Rockefeller was particularly vulnerable to such assaults because he would not cooperate with writers who wanted to say good things about him.

He believed that posterity would show his business dealings to be ethical and just, and that he therefore needed no favorable press. Further, he was a very private man. Unlike Andrew Carnegie, who wrote several books and took part in the issues of the day, Rockefeller wrote very little and usually responded to public criticism with silence.[11]

Continued attacks gave Gates an opening. He had for some time been needling Rockefeller to dispose of his fortune. As early as 1896, he warned, "Your fortune is rolling up, rolling up like an avalanche! You must distribute it faster than it grows! If you do not it will crush you and your children and your children's children!"[12] Because of the tainted money episode, most denominations, at least for a time, refused to accept Rockefeller money. This meant that much of Rockefeller's charity had to be redirected.

❧ Rationale for the Rockefeller Foundation

On June 3, 1905, Gates wrote Rockefeller a letter that would change the history of nonprofits. "I have lived with this great fortune of yours for nearly fifteen years. To it, and especially its uses, I have given every thought. It has been impossible for me to ignore the great question of what is to be the end and use of all this wealth. You have not made me the confidant of your thoughts in this, which neither surprises nor grieves me..."

"Two courses seem to me open," Gates continued.

> One is that you and your children, while living, should make final disposition of this great fortune in the form of permanent corporate philanthropies for the good of mankind. It seems to me that either you and those who live now must determine what shall be the ultimate uses of this vast fortune, or at the close of a few lives now in being it must simply pass into the unknown, like some other great fortunes, with unmeasured and perhaps sinister possibilities.

"To me, of course, beyond decent provision against want for the unborn who may come after, this great fortune should be dedicated to and legally secured for the service of mankind by those who live," Gates added.

It seems to me that any other course than this is morally indefensible... If you and Mr. John [D. Rockefeller] Junior are, therefore, to discharge this trust while you live, there is only one thing possible to be done, and that is to provide legally incorporated endowment funds under competent management, with proper provision for succession, which shall be specifically devoted to the promotion of human well-being.[13]

After listing ideas for several such funds, including one for higher education, one for medical research, and one for "the promotion of fine arts and refinement of taste," Gates concluded, "these funds should be so large that to become a trustee of one of them would make a man at once a public character. They should be so large that their administration would be a matter of public concern, public inquiry, and public criticism. They should be so large as to attract the attention and the intelligence of the world, and the administration of each would command the highest expert talent."[14]

Gates' letter was followed on June 21, 1905, by a letter from John D. Rockefeller Jr., who told his father that "Mr. Gates' letter to you seems to me a powerful and unanswerable argument ... and I endorse it most heartily."[15] In 1906, he made another suggestion to his father that he create "a large trust fund to which you would turn over considerable sums of money to be devoted to philanthropy, education, science, and religion."[16]

But not until 1909 did John D. Rockefeller give $50 million in Standard Oil Company stock to an organization to be known as the Rockefeller Foundation. As part of the deed of trust, Rockefeller said, "I direct said trustees as soon as can advisedly be done, to apply to the Congress of the United States, or to the legislature of such state as they deem advisable, for a suitable corporate charter."[17]

❦ The Ill-Fated Congressional Charter

In his memoirs, Frederick Gates explains that one of the reasons for a government charter was to restrict John D. Rockefeller's ability to use his fortune.

As a private American citizen he could use his means in any amount anywhere in the world for any lawful purpose. Indeed, the charter, in so far as he used it, would restrict his liberty rather than enlarge it, for it would take away from him altogether and place in the hands of an independent and self-perpetuating board the distribution of the funds contributed to it. But on the other hand, Mr. Rockefeller personally was mortal, the charter would be immortal, and confer on his philanthropies the priceless boon of perpetuity, besides securing for them through competent Trustees a higher and broader efficiency than any single intelligence, however able, could compass.[18]

This, however, does not explain why Rockefeller sought a congressional charter rather than a more easily obtainable state charter. There were two reasons for this. First, as historian Raymond B. Fosdick notes, most nonprofits at the time sought national recognition, including most of the organizations created by Andrew Carnegie, the Russell Sage Foundation, and such scholarly enterprises as the American Academy in Rome and the American Historical Association. "To Mr. Rockefeller's advisers, therefore it seemed appropriate to follow the same course."[19]

Second, however, these advisers had devious motives. A congressional charter would provide an impetus for placing the Rockefeller Foundation under "nonpartisan" control, ensuring not only that Rockefeller's wishes need not be followed but also that they would be irrelevant. Rockefeller's lawyer, Starr Murphy, told a Senate committee that

> ...it is eminently desirable... that the dead hand should be removed from charitable bequests and that the power to determine to what specific objects that should be applied should be left in the hands of living men who can judge of the necessities and the needs in the light of the knowledge which they have as contemporaries, and not that they shall find their hands tied by the will of the man who *is* long years dead. The wisdom of living men will always exceed the wisdom of any man, however wise, who has been long since dead.[20]

Rockefeller believed the passage of a congressional charter would be simple; after all, the General Education Board, a Rockefeller charity that helped Southern black students, had easily obtained one in 1903. Moreover, the chief sponsor of the effort, Senator Nelson Aldrich of Rhode Island, was John D. Rockefeller Jr.'s father-in-law. But neither Rockefeller nor his advisers foresaw intense opposition from those who distrusted anything Rockefeller might do. A federal lawsuit that would ultimately force the Standard Oil Company to divide into five parts was wending its way through the courts, and there was great suspicion that Rockefeller's efforts to acquire a charter were part of a nefarious scheme.

When Aldrich introduced the charter bill in 1910, opposition swiftly formed. Attorney General George Wickersham wrote to President William Howard Taft, saying a charter would give the trustees of the Rockefeller Foundation

> ...absolute control of the income of $100,000,000 or more, to be expended for the general indefinite objects described in the bill, [which] might be in the highest degree corrupt in [their] influence. The medieval statutes against mortmain were enacted to prevent just such perpetuation of wealth in a few hands under the cloak of such a charitable purpose as this.... It was not without much reason that the English common law and English statutes required bequests for charitable purposes to be definite and specific in their terms. Such legislation was the result of experience with the indefinite charities which the monastic and other medieval institutions erected, and which were the occasion of so much scandal and corruption....

Moreover, Wickersham noted, the Rockefeller Foundation's statement of purpose, including "the acquisition and dissemination of knowledge" and the "promotion of any and all of the elements of human progress," was so vague that one could not "imagine anything that might not be made to fall within one of these purposes." President Taft's reply was succinct, expressing firm opposition to the charter. "I agree with your characterization of the proposed act to incorporate John D. Rockefeller.[21]

Aldrich's bill passed the Senate Judiciary Committee in 1910 but went no further. Aldrich then allowed amendments that would have limited the foundation's endowment to $100 million; required that the foundation spend interest from its endowment rather than reinvest it; prohibited the foundation from investing more than 10 percent of its endowment in stocks; and barred a new trustee from joining the foundation if a majority of the following persons disapproved: the President of the Senate, the Speaker of the House of Representatives, and the presidents of Harvard, Yale, Columbia, Johns Hopkins, and the University of Chicago. Had Congress authorized a charter with these amendments, the Rockefeller Foundation could well have become a quasi-governmental organization along the lines of the Smithsonian Institution.

Rockefeller also tried to advance the charter through covert diplomacy. On April 25, 1911, Senator Aldrich, John D. Rockefeller Jr., and the younger Rockefeller's wife, Abby Aldrich Rockefeller, lunched at the White House with President Taft. To ensure that the lunch was secret, Rockefeller Jr. and his wife went through a side entrance, and their presence was not recorded in official White House guest books. Writing to his mother, Laura, the younger Rockefeller said that President Taft was "most agreeable and kindly" and that the president opined that the charter would not pass until the Standard Oil antitrust case was settled (which happened a few months afterwards).[22] But the private presidential luncheon did little good. The charter bill was introduced again in 1911, 1912, and 1913. It passed the Senate Judiciary Committee again in 1913, but was never reported out of committee in the House. After Congress adjourned in 1913, Rockefeller went to the New York state legislature, which quickly passed a bill giving the Rockefeller Foundation a state charter.

ℰ The Rockefeller Foundation's Early Years

Shortly before the creation of the Rockefeller Foundation, Jerome W. Greene, the foundation's first secretary, circulated a memorandum that asked, "How shall the Trustees of the Rockefeller Foundation keep responsive to the will and intelligence of the people through future generations?" Greene wished to create a "Public Council" comprising one person from each state who would be nominated either by the state university or a leading private institution. Although his idea was never tried, these advisors would have represented "better than anyone else,

10

the wisdom and good will of the community in matters affecting the general well-being."[23]

Pressure to dilute the Rockefeller Foundation board by adding new "independent" members continued. "It is very important to add to the number of Trustees of the Rockefeller Foundation persons of independent position, and known to the country, or at least to the State of New York, as publicists, philanthropists, and educators," Harvard University president Charles W. Eliot wrote to Jerome Greene in 1915. "The fundamental criticisms of the Socialists and Labor-leaders can be met in no other way."[24]

According to historian Robert E. Kohler, Rockefeller Foundation trustees split into two factions. The liberals, including Jerome Greene, Starr Murphy, medical researcher Abraham Flexner and former commissioner of police Arthur Woods, wanted the foundation to address "criminology, alcoholism, drug addiction, feeblemindedness, venereal disease, family structure, incomes policy, and delinquency." They were opposed by Frederick Gates and others, who believed the foundation should deal with less partisan scientific and medical issues. Gates called Greene's proposal "scatteration," as it would give many small grants rather than a few large ones.[25]

Kohler also notes that Gates and Greene disagreed on who would control the foundation. Gates foresaw Rockefeller's descendants as wielding control, while Greene believed professional middle managers would predominate. Significantly, neither side seemed to believe that John D. Rockefeller's ideas or principles would matter. By 1914, many foundation trustees and employees were looking for ways to exclude Rockefeller from the foundation's affairs. One incident in particular helped contribute to that effort.

❧ The Ludlow Massacre

In October 1913, the United Mine Workers of America launched a strike against Colorado Fuel and Iron, a company controlled by the Rockefellers since 1912. On April 20, 1914, after a seven-month standoff, private guards and members of the Colorado National Guard surrounded the strikers' camp and began firing. At one point, a tent was set ablaze, and the smoke caused two women and 11 children trapped in a cellar below to die of suffocation. The remaining strikers began to attack Colorado Fuel and Iron property. Ten days later, President Woodrow Wilson ordered other National Guard units into the area to suppress the uprising.

The "Ludlow Massacre" quickly became a *cause célèbre* for the Left. Novelist Upton Sinclair picketed John D. Rockefeller's home, and in New York City, four members of the Industrial Workers of the World, a radical union, died when a bomb exploded prematurely in their apartment. As historian Priscilla Long notes, "it was generally believed that the bomb had been intended for the Rockefeller townhouse."[26]

The Rockefellers reacted swiftly. John D. Rockefeller Jr. (a member of the Colorado Fuel and Iron board of directors) went to Colorado, where he met with prominent union organizers, including Mary Harris "Mother" Jones.[27] The Rockefellers also hired Ivy Lee, one of America's first public-relations specialists, to deal with the aftermath. They also made a fatal mistake by involving the Rockefeller Foundation in the Ludlow affair.

John D. Rockefeller Jr. had long been interested in public policy, believing the foundation should be involved in nonpartisan research on public issues. He decided that a study of the Ludlow incident might lead to better relations between labor and management. On the advice of Jerome Greene and Harvard University president Charles Eliot, he decided to interview W. L. Mackenzie King, a Canadian politician and industrial relations specialist.

Mackenzie King was at first hesitant, fearing that working for the Rockefellers might jeopardize his career in Canada's Liberal Party. But in December 1914, he accepted a five-year grant with a salary of $12,000 a year, which could be cancelled at any time if the Liberals, then out of power, made a comeback.[28] At the time, Mackenzie King was not just a liberal but a radical. Historian H. M. Gitleman notes that on April 6, 1917, he toasted America's entry into World War I with Raymond Fosdick, who later became president of the Rockefeller Foundation and its historian as well as John D. Rockefeller Jr.'s biographer. After denouncing John D. Rockefeller Jr.'s opposition to a Wilson Administration proposal to boost income-tax rates on wealthy Americans, Mackenzie King and Fosdick "agreed that in the not too distant future the state would act to level out all of the great fortunes. Before the evening was out, they concluded that socialism was inevitable and desirable, that workers would one day own the factories in which they toiled, and that society would take proper title to all natural resources."[29]

12

The mere fact that the Rockefeller Foundation had appointed someone to study Rockefeller businesses was ammunition for Rockefeller's foes. No enemy was more vigorous than Frank Walsh, chairman of the U.S. Commission on Industrial Relations, a federally funded agency that investigated labor-management relations. On January 27, 1915, John D. Rockefeller Jr. testified before the commission. The hearing included an audience that, according to historian Graham Adams Jr., consisted "chiefly of Single-Taxers, Socialists, anarchists, AFL members," and members of the Industrial Workers of the World.[30]

John D. Rockefeller Jr. charmed them all. Commission member Mary Harriman decided that John D. Rockefeller Jr. was not "a psalm-singing, cold-blooded capitalist," but an "intensely human" person. Even *The Masses*, the leading leftist journal of the day, said the younger Rockefeller was "apparently frank," "gentle," and "Christianish."[31]

But Frank Walsh was not through with the Rockefellers. He believed the commission should go beyond "challeng[ing] the wisdom of giving public sanction and approval to the spending of a huge fortune through such philanthropies as that of the Rockefeller Foundation," and that "the huge philanthropic trusts, known as foundations, appear to be a menace to the welfare of society" since they enabled the wealthy "to become molders of public thought" and to influence public policy.[32] At the hearings, Walsh grilled both Ivy Lee and Mackenzie King about their involvement with the Rockefellers. When the U.S. Commission on Industrial Relations was terminated, Walsh formed a nonprofit to criticize the Rockefellers.

Eventually, the Ludlow affair subsided. Colorado Fuel and Iron formed a union to give workers more benefits. Mackenzie King completed his report and returned to Canada, where he eventually became Prime Minister in the 1930s and 1940s. He and John D. Rockefeller Jr. remained close friends for the rest of Mackenzie King's life. However, the Rockefellers' image had been further scarred.

❧ The Rockefellers Relinquish Control

In 1916, John D. Rockefeller transferred his fortune to his children. John D. Rockefeller Jr. was given most of the estate that did not go to the Rockefeller Foundation or other Rockefeller charities. Nearly all the younger Rockefeller's advisors were liberals or leftists, and they continually urged him to abandon the stalwart confidence in free markets that his father had.

After John D. Rockefeller Jr. testified before the U.S. Commission on Industrial Relations, Mackenzie King wrote that

> when it is remembered that Mr. Rockefeller, Jr. is at present only administering his father's affairs and is not free to act of his own responsibility in complete measure, when further, it is remembered that it has been his father's friends ... who have been his immediate advisers, the progress which has been made by him toward a modern, progressive outlook is remarkable indeed. What is particularly satisfying about it is the circumstance that every bit of it is based on conviction. He has said absolutely nothing that he does not with his whole heart and mind believe."[33]

Raymond Fosdick also helped persuade the younger Rockefeller to abandon the principles of his father. As historian Robert Kohler notes, Fosdick "worked hard to wean Rockefeller, Jr. away from the family's hidebound conservatism."[34] By 1921, Fosdick's brother, noted left-wing theologian Harry Emerson Fosdick, wrote to Fosdick praising him for helping the younger Rockefeller replace "old Tory" board associates of the elder Rockefeller with more liberal ones.[35] Indeed, John D. Rockefeller Jr. became his own man after the Ludlow Massacre, and he was heartily approved by liberals. His first significant act after taking control of the Rockefeller fortune was to serve as head of a committee that temporarily combined seven major nonprofits—including the YMCA, Young Women's Christian Association (YWCA), Jewish Welfare Board, Salvation Army, and National Catholic War Council—in a huge charity devoted to the war effort. He was also active in a failed effort to amalgamate existing Protestant denominations into an interdenominational "Church of the Living God."[36]

As biographers John Ensor Harr and Peter J. Johnson note, the main lesson John D. Rockefeller Jr. learned from the Ludlow episode was to erect a firm wall between the Rockefeller Foundation and the Rockefellers' personal affairs.[37] Though he continued to be a Rockefeller Foundation trustee, he personally repudiated the family's interest in the foundation. Likewise, the Ludlow Massacre severed the elder Rockefeller's associations with the foundation. Though he was a trustee until 1922, he never attended a board meeting, having delegated this task to his son.

When John D. Rockefeller gave the initial grant of $100 million to the Rockefeller Foundation, it was given with a stipulation he called "founder's designations." "It is a condition of this gift that from the income of the Foundation the sum of Two Million Dollars ($2,000,000) annually, or so much thereof as I shall designate, shall be applied during my lifetime to such specific objects within the corporate purposes of the Foundation as I may from time to time direct."[38] But under pressure from his son, Rockefeller rescinded this clause on July 29, 1917, saying that "in view of the increasing demand upon the funds of the Foundation, especially those arising in connection with the great war for human freedom in which our country is now engaged, which have led the Foundation to appropriate a part of its principal, as well as all of its income, I hereby release the conditions."[39]

Rockefeller did, however, make one last effort to assert his will. In 1919, he wrote to his lawyer, Starr Murphy.

> I could wish that the education which some professors furnish was more conducive to the most sane and practical and possible views of life rather than drifting, as it does, in cases, toward socialism and some forms of Bolshevism. It seems to me that some influences ought to be brought to bear upon the universities and colleges with reference to the textbooks which, from my standpoint at least, are calculated to lead astray and do harm rather than good.

Murphy was aghast. Having helped create the Rockefeller Foundation to block Rockefeller's wishes, he was determined to stop Rockefeller's plan. "The placing of limitations upon ... academic freedom must be left to the trustees and faculties of the institutions," Murphy wrote. "[As] it would be extremely unwise for any donor to attempt to place limitations on the character of the teaching which shall be given in an institution to which he contributes, it is hardly less objectionable for him to make the determination as to whether or not he will give to any particular institution dependent upon that matter ... I have sufficient faith in the truth," Murphy added, "to believe that in an atmosphere of freedom it will ultimately vindicate itself."[40]

Though Rockefeller lived 18 years after this exchange, he is not known to have asserted his wishes again. He spent the rest of his life in quiet retirement, allowing Ivy Lee and other public-relations people to remold his image. The Rockefellers eagerly took the advice of Lee and his associates. If the John D. Rockefeller of 1915 was a ruthless capitalist who held the world in octopus-like tentacles, the Rockefeller the press portrayed in 1925 was a kindly eccentric who delighted in giving dimes to children. The favorable publicity, however, was won only by severing John D. Rockefeller from the philanthropies he created.

John D. Rockefeller Jr. took one more step to distance the family from the Rockefeller philanthropies. In the early 1920s, he greatly expanded the trustees of the Rockefeller Foundation board. While trustees of the foundation in 1920 were mostly Rockefeller friends, business associates, and family members, by 1925 many had retired. (Frederick Gates retired from the board in 1923.) Their successors were leading businessmen and scholars. From the early 1920s onwards, note Harr and Johnson, the board "could be compared favorably at any time with the Cabinet of the U.S. president—and indeed many trustees later served as Cabinet members."[41]

But there was a crucial difference between the Rockefeller Foundation board and the President's cabinet. While the President can dismiss cabinet members, John D. Rockefeller Jr. abdicated his role as leader of the foundation. The board was free to act without regard for the sources of wealth that made the foundation possible. Indeed, a main reason John D. Rockefeller Jr.'s sons, John D. Rockefeller 3rd, Nelson, Laurence, Winthrop, and David, created the Rockefeller Brothers Fund in 1941 was to reassert ties between the Rockefeller family and the charities John D. Rockefeller Jr. had created.

ℰ The Problem of Donor Intent Is Solidified

By 1925, the wealthy donor had two main types of foundations from which to choose: those created by John D. Rockefeller (as discussed in this chapter) and Andrew Carnegie (see chapter three).

In both cases, donor intent was ignored, either because, in the Carnegie Corporation's case, the donor had run out of ideas for disposing of his wealth, or in the Rockefeller Foundation's case, the donor had chosen not to assert his will. Not surprisingly, most foundations after 1925 distanced themselves from the sources of their wealth.

Yet two major donors of the 1920s did assert their wishes and manage to ensure that these were preserved. Tobacco magnate James Buchanan Duke structured the indenture of the Duke Endowment so it could only be broken by a massive legal effort. Further, he was a regional donor who limited his charity to North and South Carolina (see chapter twelve). Likewise, Julius Rosenwald, a long-time Sears, Roebuck executive and a prominent liberal philanthropist of the 1920s and 1930s, also asserted his wishes, though by different means. Long a critic of foundations that outlived their donors, Rosenwald in 1928 gave the Julius Rosenwald Fund $20 million worth of Sears, Roebuck stock on condition that the fund cease to exist within 25 years of his death:

> I am not in sympathy with this policy of perpetuating endowments and believe more good can be accomplished by expending funds as Trustees find opportunities for constructive work than by storing up large sums of money for long periods of time. By adopting a policy of using the Fund within this generation, we may avoid those tendencies toward bureaucracy and a formal or perfunctory attitude toward the work which almost inevitably develop in organizations which prolong their existence indefinitely. Coming generations can be relied upon to provide for their own needs as they arise.... [In] accepting the shares of stock now offered, I ask that the Trustees do so with the understanding that the entire fund in the hands of the Board, both income and principal, be expended within twenty-five years of the time of my death."[42]

In two articles in the *Atlantic Monthly*, Rosenwald explained his reasons for imposing "term limits" on foundations. Narrowly imposing one's wishes on the future meant the creation of philanthropies that out-lived their usefulness, such as an endowment given to Bryn Mawr College that protected students against hunger by giving them baked potatoes. But it was also true, Rosenwald argued, that organizations with vague charters could quickly succumb to institutional hardening of the arteries, becoming preoccupied with self-preservation rather than the purpose for which they were created. "I think it is almost inevitable that as trustees and officers of perpetuities grow old they become more concerned to conserve the funds in their care than to wring from those funds the greatest possible usefulness," Rosenwald wrote. "That tendency is evident already in some of the foundations, and as time goes on it will not lessen but increase. The cure for this disease is a radical operation. If the funds must exhaust themselves within a generation, no bureaucracy is likely to develop around them."[43]

Rosenwald also argued for what today might be called a marketplace of ideas in philanthropy. A donor with a worthy notion, he said, would have that notion funded by others. Yale University was begun with an initial endowment of 600 pounds and a few hundred books. John Harvard created Harvard University in 1638 with a legacy of 300 books and 750 pounds. But these institutions thrived, Rosenwald said, because "they were recognized to be meeting a human need, and this recognition has been expressed in financial support generation after generation.... Real endowments are not money, but ideas.... Desirable and feasible ideas are of much more value than money, and when their usefulness has once been established they may be expected to receive ready support as long as they justify themselves."[44]

The employees of the Julius Rosenwald Fund accepted Rosenwald's conditions. In fact, they spent the money faster than Rosenwald asked. The Rosenwald Fund terminated in 1948, only 15 years after Rosenwald's death.

Since then, few philanthropists have followed Rosenwald's example. Not until John M. Olin created the Olin Foundation in 1953 was a major foundation organized with a term limit. Rosenwald himself prophesied that few philanthropies would follow his example because trustees of perpetual foundations with vague charters could easily ignore the wishes of their founders.[45]

In short, by 1925 the problems of donor intent were firmly established. As the following chapters grimly reveal, the conflicts between donors and the philanthropies they created would harden, not weaken, over time.

2

The Ford Foundation

How firm a Foundation, we saints of the Lord.
We've built on the faith of our excellent Ford.
We've laundered and lightened the Trustees' Report.
And left for California,
And left for California,
And left for California,
The place to resort.

How firm the Foundation has been for E.C.A.
And for Hutchins, for Davis, what those boys get ain't hay.
What more can we do than for them we have done?
Way out in Pasadena,
Way out in Pasadena,
Way out in Pasadena,
We bask in the sun.

How firm a Foundation, we've Funds by the score.
Have you an idea? We'll establish one more.
We smile through the smog; (some say that we smirk);
Out here in Pasadena,
Out here in Pasadena,
Out here in Pasadena,
The funds do the work.

How fine a Foundation; we are for peace;
We live peaceful lives, and we hope wars will cease.
We've heard mankind cry, and we've answered the call;
We're out in Pasadena,
We're out in Pasadena,

We're out in Pasadena,
Away from it all.

How firm a Foundation; we've three times the dough,
And ten times the brains that any other can show.
The hell with Rockefeller, and Carnegie, too.
We've left for California,
We've left for California,
We've left for California,
The hell with you.
         — Robert Maynard Hutchins, associate
         director, Ford Foundation (1952)[1]

The extremities to which the millionaire is reduced by this closing
up of old channels of bequest are such that he sometimes leaves
huge sums to bodies of trustees "to do good with," a plan as
mischievous as it is resourceless; for what can the trustees do but
timidly dribble the fund away on charities of one kind or another?
         — George Bernard Shaw, "Socialism for
         Millionaires" (1896)

The Ford Foundation provides one of the grandest and best-known examples in philanthropic history of the abandonment of donor intent. Yet its story repays careful attention, because the blame for the tragedy lies partly on the donors' shoulders.

In judging whether the Ford Foundation violates donor intent, one must assess the intentions of two men: Henry Ford (1863-1947) and his grandson, Henry Ford II (1917-1987). (Edsel, son of the first Henry Ford and father of the second, died before he could wield control of the Ford fortune. In this family, power passed from grandfather to grandson.) The two men were quite different. Henry Ford never outgrew his agrarian background, while Henry Ford II was a pillar of the Establishment who attended Hotchkiss and Yale (though he left Yale without receiving a degree).

The evidence suggests that the Ford Foundation routinely violates every charitable principle of Henry Ford, and in a lesser way, those of Henry Ford II. In his last years, even Henry Ford II, who was certainly not conservative, railed against "the liberals" who had seized control of the foundation.

The conventional history of the Ford Foundation is that Henry Ford left no instructions on how his money should be used, thus leaving the trustees free to do whatever they pleased with his fortune. According to foundation historian Waldemar Nielsen, who worked for the Ford Foundation for many years, when Henry Ford died in 1947, four lawyers, supervised by Maurice N. "Tex" Moore (brother-in-law of Henry Luce), combed Ford's personal and corporate papers and "were unable to find a single sentence or a single note from old Henry expressing any interest in, or ideas about, his philanthropy."[2]

It is true that Ford left no explicit instructions on how his money should be spent. But his philosophy of charity was very clear, and he consistently expressed it throughout his life. His views were simply ignored by those who staffed and led the Ford Foundation.

❧ George Bernard Shaw's 'Socialism for Millionaires'

According to William Greenleaf, author of the most extensive study of Henry Ford's charity, Ford gave $37,641,627 during his lifetime. This was not as much as Andrew Carnegie, who gave $325 million, John D. Rockefeller, who gave $600 million, or John D. Rockefeller Jr., who gave $400 million. But Ford nonetheless donated one-third of his income to charity, and was far more generous than most Americans of his generation.

Greenleaf notes that between 1922 and 1936, millionaires in America on average gave less than five percent of their incomes to charity; Ford's annual donations, however, were in excess of 15 percent of income. Nearly two-thirds of this was not only *not* tax-deductible, but subject to a surtax. "As gauged by outlay in ratio to taxable income," Greenleaf wrote, "the record speaks well for Ford's intentions and performance as a donor."[3]

According to Greenleaf, Ford derived his philosophy of charity from "Socialism for Millionaires," an 1896 essay by George Bernard Shaw. Shaw warned that the millionaire should not try to help the poor directly. Giving money to "the utterly worthless, the hopelessly, incorrigibly lazy, idle, easy going good-for-nothing," Shaw believed, "would soon exhaust the resources of even a billionaire. It would convince the most sentimental of almsgivers that it is economically impossible to be kind to beggars."[4]

Shaw illustrated this point by describing how he once offered to pay someone two pounds to copy a book in the British Museum's reading room. He first offered the job to a former teacher "whose qualifications were out of date, and who, through no particular fault of his own, had drifted into the reading-room as less literate men drift into Salvation Army shelters." The teacher, more interested in leisurely reading than work, sub-contracted the job to someone else, who hired someone else, who then hired "the least competent and least sober female copyist in the room, who actually did the job for five shillings, and then turned it into a handsome investment by making it an excuse for borrowing endless sixpences from me from that time to the day of her death."[5]

Instead of direct aid, Shaw advised the rich to support large projects that government was unwilling to assume.

> I confess I despise a millionaire who dribbles his money away in fifties and hundreds, thereby reducing himself to the level of a mere crowd of ordinary men, instead of planking down sums that only a millionaire can. The millionaire should ask himself what is his favorite subject? Has it a school, with scholarships for the endowment of research and the attraction of rising talent at the universities? Has it a library, or a museum? If not, then he has an opening at once for his ten thousand or his hundred thousand.[6]

☙ Henry Ford's Philosophy of Giving

These ideas guided Henry Ford throughout his life. He created philanthropies that outlived him and still honor his wishes. Ford N. Bryan, the most authoritative historian of the Ford family, says that Henry Ford began contributing small amounts to charity as early as 1908. By 1910, Ford was a steady contributor to causes such as the Anti-Cigarette League of the United States and Canada. He also served on the board of Detroit's Protestant Orphan Asylum.[7]

But his major works were the Henry Ford Hospital in Detroit and two related efforts in Dearborn, Michigan—Greenfield Village and the Edison Institute (now the Henry Ford Museum). The Henry Ford Hospital is still one of Detroit's leading hospitals, and millions of visitors flock to Greenfield Village each year to see the historic houses that Ford collected and reassembled.

Throughout his life, Ford was besieged by requests for aid. As early as 1914, after he introduced one of the nation's first profit-sharing plans, swarms of people lined up outside his house. By 1915, he received 200 letters a day for aid; by 1924, the number had climbed to 10,000 a week, and a team of private secretaries sent out over fifty form letters in response.[8]

Ford often gave money spontaneously to poor people he met during his travels. But he always refused to give to organizations he could not directly control. He would not give to community chests, the predecessors of the United Way, and he consistently opposed any form of charity that might reward idleness.

In *Today and Tomorrow* (1930; co-written with Samuel Crowther), Ford explained at length his views on charity.

> We hold that it is part of our industrial duty—that is, part of our service that supports the wage motive—to help people to help themselves. We believe that what is called being charitable is a particularly mean form of self-glorification—mean because, while it pretends to aid, it really hurts. The giver to charity gets a certain cheap satisfaction out of being regarded as a kind and generous man. That would be harmless enough in itself were it not that the recipients *of* charity are usually destroyed—for once you give a man something for nothing, you set him trying to get someone else to give him something for nothing.

"Charity creates non-producers, and there is no difference at all between a rich drone and a poor drone," Ford added. "Both are burdens on production. It will easily take a generation to wipe out the effects of the dole upon the peoples of Europe."[9] In a 1924 interview, he said,

> I believe in living wages—I do not believe in charity. I believe we should all be producers. Organized charity and schools of philanthropy and the whole idea of 'giving' to the poor are on the wrong track. They don't produce anything. If a railroad had a bad piece of track that wrecked cars every day and piled them in the ditch it would cure nothing to merely build a fine repair shop. The track itself should be fixed. Charity

and philanthropy are the repair shops and the efficiency, however high, does not remove the cause of the human wrecks.[10]

For those who had experienced misfortune and were willing to work, Ford had plenty of jobs at good wages at his plants. He prided himself on taking people that others might have considered hopeless and turning them into productive workers. He routinely hired the disabled. In 1919, nearly 20 percent of his workers had some sort of disability, including one employee who had lost both hands, four whose legs or feet were gone, four who were totally blind, 123 who only had one hand or arm, and 1,560 with hernias.[11]

Former criminals—even violent ones—were routinely hired at Ford plants, and many performed well. Between 1914 and 1920, Ford hired between 400 and 600 convicted criminals, including one convicted of forging the name "Henry F. Ford Jr." on a $15 check.[12] Ford's policy was not to ask for references or a work history, but to judge employees by how well they did on the job. "We do not care anything about references, and a man is kept or discharged solely on his record with us," Ford wrote in *Moving Forward* (1930; also co-written with Samuel Crowther). "The man stands on his own feet and nearly always he becomes a valuable employee once he has gained his self-respect and the knowledge that he is not going to be hounded for anything that he has done in the past."[13]

In memoirs published 30 years apart, two close associates of Ford recalled that Henry Ford, while strongly disliking organized nonprofits, was nonetheless personally very charitable.

In a 1923 memoir, Samuel S. Marquis, employed by Ford Motor between 1917 and 1921, recalled that when he worked for Henry Ford, he tried to keep a total of the amount requested from Ford in donations. He concluded that in his day Ford Motor received about $4 million in requests each year, while Henry Ford was personally asked for $72 million a year. Ministers frequently asked for Ford cars, while one enterprising bishop thought "two carloads of runabouts" a splendid donation for his missionaries. "The entire output of the factory, it often seemed to me, would hardly meet the demand if every request [for aid] were to be granted," Marquis wrote.[14]

"Mr. Ford hates the word charity and all that it stands for," Marquis added. "He gives generously to friends and employees, but it is in recognition of services rendered. He gives neither a stone nor money to the man who asks for bread, but a job." [15]

According to Marquis, Henry Ford was no skinflint. He offered thousands of jobs to workers whom other companies would reject as being too old or too handicapped to enter the labor force. Marquis writes that Ford Motor had employed 1,700 handicapped workers in 1917, and agreed to hire another thousand wounded war veterans "as fast as they come out of hospitals." [16]

In addition, Ford routinely raised the pay of any employee caring for a parent too old to work. "Mr. Ford lifted to the level of self-support hundreds of people who otherwise would be living on the charity of others," Marquis noted. [17]

"Mr. Ford was more benevolent than charitable," observed Charles E. Sorensen, a close associate of Ford for four decades. "Although Ford Motor Company contributed to local charities, Edsel was behind that. Henry Ford took no interest in Community Chest drives or various national drives for special funds. He was interested in families and individuals—in cases in which he could encourage people to avoid or throw off poverty." [18]

Ford and his staff looked hard for families who *truly* needed help—widows struggling to raise a family after their husbands died, or families where husbands were too sick to work. Here Ford would hire one of the children if he or she were old enough to work, or quietly give financial or medical aid if the children were still in school.

In helping these families, Sorensen recalled, Ford "observed how the family members reacted to his help. He expected them to improve their ways of living. He did not call this charity. He was never satisfied that charity could be doled out by a system or that happiness or peace of mind could be bought. He preferred his own way." [19]

Sorensen recounted one case where Ford's aid backfired. One day Ford was driving and saw a tramp on the road. The tramp said he was unemployed and was heading to Detroit "to see that fellow Ford and see if he will give me a job."

Ford invited the man into his car and personally drove him to company headquarters. He then personally escorted the man to Sorensen's office. "Charlie," Ford said, "I found this man looking for work. He seems like a good man. What can we give him to do?"

Sorensen found a job for the man in the paint shop. Ford would regularly meet with the tramp, shaking his hand and telling him he would soon get a raise. Ford quietly put the following note in the man's personnel file: "If this man leaves his job, contact me before paying him off."

Six weeks later, the tramp decided he didn't like his job and quit. Henry Ford walked in during the man's exit interview and saw the tramp screaming because he wasn't being paid quickly enough. "When he saw Ford," Sorensen recalled, the tramp "sailed into him saying, 'I want to get out of this jail.' I don't believe that even then he was sure if it was the real Henry Ford who had picked him up." [20]

ꙮ The Revitalization of Inkster

Ford's belief in self-help also extended to blacks. In 1931, Ford heard of the plight of the largely black city of Inkster, a distant suburb of Detroit. Wracked by the Great Depression, most residents were out of work and heavily in debt. The city was bankrupt and had laid off its police and garbage collectors, and could not even afford to turn on the streetlights.

Ford decided to help by offering not charity but jobs. He hired dozens of residents to work in his factories at six dollars a day, while others were paid a dollar a day to pick up trash, clean the streets, and grow crops. He loaned trucks to pick up garbage and tractors to plow fields. Ford factories crushed slabs of concrete from demolished buildings for use in paving streets and roads.

As biographer Keith Sward notes, "Inkster, in no time at all, became a shining little oasis, immune from the worst ravages of depression." By 1936, Ford had recovered most of his investment. But as William Greenleaf says, his "final achievement was the recovery of usefulness and self-respect by the Inkster residents through their own efforts. This is as Ford would have wanted it." [21]

In May 1932, in the frostiest period of the Depression, Ford ran an advertisement saying that the Inkster experiment was a better way to fight poverty than government welfare. "I do not believe in routine charity," Ford wrote. "I think it a shameful thing that any man should have to take it, or give it. I do not include human helpfulness in the name of charity. My quarrel with charity is that it is neither helpful [nor] human. The charity of our cities is the most barbarous thing in our system, with the possible exception of our prisons." Ford wrote that the residents of Inkster would not have become productive workers "by paying out welfare funds [in] the orthodox manner. The only true charity for these people was somehow to get under their burdens with them and lend them the value of our experience to show them what can be done by people in their circumstances."[22]

❧ 'A Chance and Not Charity'

Given his belief in self-reliance, Ford always told reporters that he planned to use his wealth to create jobs and cars, not a foundation. "Mr. Ford," William L. Stidger, one of his biographers, asked in 1923, "the people want to know what you are going to do with your huge fortune when you die?"

"Why do they want to know?" Ford replied.

"I presume because it is getting to be a habit with wealthy men to do some useful and social thing with the vast sums of money that they accumulate. Take Mr. Rockefeller, he has established the Rockefeller Foundation," Stidger said.

"So they want to know what I'm going to do with my money. Well, you can tell them there is no 'going to do' about it. I am doing it now! I am investing my money in men; every cent of it, and will continue to do so. When people ask me what I am going to do with my money they usually mean what bunch of secretaries or societies I am going to select to dole out my 'charity.' My money is going to keep on going where it is going now—into men," Ford said.

"Then the business itself is to be the Ford Foundation?" Stidger asked.

"That's right. The organization is to be the Ford Foundation. I want that Foundation to be the life-saving opportunity of millions of men and women to be self-supporting and self-sustaining. My old motto, 'A chance and not charity,' will be the spirit of the Ford Foundation. I do not believe in giving folks things. I do believe in giving them a chance to make things for themselves!"[23]

❧ Enemy of the New Deal

Henry Ford's belief in self-reliance and community self-help was coupled with an intense dislike of government. As early as 1925, he told journalist Judson C. Welliver that he worried how inheritance taxes would affect his estate and the Ford Motor Company. "Mr. Ford has never taken much out of his business," Welliver wrote. "He questions whether the Government ought to be more severe with it than he has been.... But some day he will have to relinquish control. When that time comes, the Government will demand the extreme limit of inheritance taxes. To pay them will require liquidating a considerable portion of the estate. The problem will be to take care of the business and at the same time liquidate a sufficient part of it to pay the taxes."[24]

If Ford worried about inheritance taxes in the comparatively benign administration of Calvin Coolidge, he had much more to fear under Franklin Roosevelt. An ardent critic of the New Deal, Ford was the only major industrialist who refused to take part in the National Recovery Act, a system of government-organized cartels that was later declared unconstitutional by the Supreme Court. "Through all of his career the conservative grimoires of the American free enterprise system regarded him with alarm," wrote biographer Garet Garrett. "He was a dangerous maverick, almost a revolutionary, at the least a menace, an anticapitalist capitalist—certainly the last man you could trust to defend the premises with his life. And yet, when the New Deal came, he was the one who had the will and the courage to stand against it, *and he stood alone.*"[25]

In 1935, partly inspired by Senator Huey Long's calls to "share the wealth" and "soak the rich," Congress passed the Revenue Act, which Roosevelt declared would change the tax code to fight "unjust concentration of wealth and power."[26] Under the act, taxes on estates rose to 50 percent of assets over $4 million and 70 percent of assets over $50 million.

The Ford Motor Company had always been a closely held, family-run business. Between them, Henry and Edsel Ford held 96.9 percent of the company's stock. If either died, the estate could pay taxes on that man's share of the Ford Motor Company. But if both died, the tax burden might well mean the end of the family enterprise. Ford's lawyers calculated that if nothing were done, 77 percent of the estates of Henry and Edsel Ford would be consumed by estate taxes, because the value of the two men's estates would be over $10 million, invoking the maximum federal estate tax rate.[27]

Some politicians sided with Ford in his efforts to stop the Revenue Act. In August 1935, Senator Arthur Vandenberg (R-MI) argued that the bill was specifically designed to dismember the Ford Motor Company. "The Ford example seems to have been chosen, even by the authors of the plan themselves, as the most important and challenging clinical test," said Vandenberg. "There need be no speculation as to what will happen to the great Ford industrial enterprise under this proposed tax confiscation. It will be driven into diversified ownership which can come only through enormous ultimate stock sales to the public."[28]

❧ Creation of the Ford Foundation

On January 15, 1936, Henry Ford took the only option he could to preserve family control of the Ford Motor Company. He created the Ford Foundation. The existing Ford Motor Company stock was converted into two types: non-voting Class A common stock, which comprised 95 percent of the total stock, and voting Class B common stock. Ford drafted a will leaving the Class A shares to the Ford Foundation and the Class B shares to his son and grandchildren. Edsel Ford drafted a similar will. The Ford estate was thus divided into two parts, leaving the wealth Ford created to philanthropy and the Ford Motor Company to the family.

Ford did not create the Ford Foundation out of altruism or to restore his reputation. Unlike those who amassed their great fortunes before the Income Tax Act of 1913, Ford was not attacked as a "robber baron" or wicked capitalist. Nor was he seen as a paragon of conspicuous consumption. He lived simply and reinvested most of his profits back into his business. "Much of the public was extremely hostile to the fortunes of Carnegie, Rockefeller, and Mellon, which were largely diverted into endowments and foundations," write Ford biographers Allan Nevins and Frank Ernest Hill. "Comparatively few were hostile to Ford's, which people felt was usefully employed for social purposes just where it stood."[29]

Further, the Ford Foundation was created in great secrecy. Ford never announced its creation. The press found out only when the head of Michigan's corporation and securities division told reporters that Ford's lawyers had filed the necessary papers. These lawyers refused to talk to the press, and only Edsel Ford had anything to say: "The foundation will take care of the various charitable, educational, and research activities that I don't care to do personally. It will be on a small scale and I have no intention of making it larger."[30]

For the first few years of its existence, the Ford Foundation was, in fact, small and inconspicuous. During World War II, the Ford Motor Company reached its lowest ebb. After Edsel Ford's death in 1943, Henry Ford resumed control of the company. But he was in his eighties and ailing. He delegated control to Harry Bennett, a hard-headed union buster whose extraordinary incompetence as Ford CEO caused the value of the company to plummet.[31]

❧ Henry Ford II Rescinds Control of the Foundation

In a power struggle in 1945, Henry Ford II triumphed over Harry Bennett and began a 34-year tenure as chairman of the board of the Ford Motor Company. Two years later, the elder Henry Ford died. Given that both Henry and Edsel Ford were dead, the provisions of their wills took effect, and the Ford Foundation became the wealthiest foundation in America.

From its beginnings, the Ford Foundation was eager to spend money. According to historian Francis X. Sutton, the foundation went $31 million into debt before a single share of Ford Motor stock was acquired by borrowing against the value of the shares it was to receive. In 1948, as the wills of Edsel and Henry Ford were being probated, Henry Ford II signed a statement that he would later regret. He declared that the Ford family would make no effort to use the inheritance of his father and grandfather to control the Ford Foundation. Henry Ford II would be chairman of the board of the foundation and his brother Benson would be a trustee, but their influence would be no greater than that of any other Ford Foundation employee.

The best explanation of why Henry Ford II signed this document comes from testimony he gave before a House committee (known as the "Cox Committee") in 1952.

> We thought that the amount of funds that would be available in this public instrument was of such magnitude that it would hardly be right for one family

to have the decision as to the distribution, in how they should be spent for educational, charitable, and scientific purposes. Further than that, I think it was said, and probably justifiably so, that people who have left their moneys [sic] to charitable organizations so that this trust was so large that the family should not have control of it.

Naturally we want to—we feel that we have an obligation as a family to—carry out to the best of our ability the desires of our forebears, and we intend to do so. I am speaking of my brothers and myself. We intend to do our part as a trustee of the foundation. However, we felt that for the benefit of the whole thing it would be better to have the members and the trustees the same, and also have a majority who were not connected with the Ford Motor Co. or members of our family, so that, if a matter came to the vote within the foundation, we would not have the control.[32]

By signing this document, Henry Ford II ensured that the intentions of his family would be steadily undermined.

☙ The Foundation's Early Years

If Henry Ford was such a firm advocate of free markets and voluntarism, how did the Ford Foundation become such a bastion of the welfare state? Part of the answer lies in the different political views of Henry Ford and Henry Ford II. Some of Henry Ford's views, such as his support of Prohibition, were peculiar. Others, such as his support of traditional dancing, were eccentric.[33] Finally, some of Henry Ford's views, particularly his anti-Semitism, were reprehensible. Nonetheless, he championed free enterprise and fought government intervention.

Though not a leftist, Henry Ford II was moderately liberal. He was what pundits of the 1950s called a "modern Republican," a pillar of the establishment who preferred Dwight Eisenhower to Robert A. Taft, and whose relations with Lyndon Johnson were so friendly that, in 1968, he was appointed to head the liberal National Alliance of Businessmen.

31

Describing Henry Ford II's political views, historian Thomas C. Reeves observes that he was the sort of man

> who had no basic quarrels with the New and Fair deals, who respected academic credentials, who liked Ike (and Adlai), who contributed to *Harper's,* subscribed to *Foreign Affairs,* and read *Time* and *Newsweek,* who professed belief in racial equality, who supported foreign aid and the United Nations, who played prominent (the Far Right frequently used 'conspiratorial') roles in national political conventions, and who was often appointed to positions of authority by both parties.[34]

Henry Ford II supported most of what the Ford Foundation did in its early years. He was, however, bored by some of its activities. In 1951, Paul Hoffman, the Ford Foundation's first president, was leading a discussion about proposed grants to Indonesia when Henry Ford II asked, "My God, where is this place Indonesia that you're talking about? And why in God's name should we be interested in it anyway?" According to Francis Sutton, Hoffman "just shriveled," and was overheard later to say that "he was not going to devote his life to educating this young ignoramus."[35]

In 1952, the feud between Hoffman and Henry Ford II escalated when Hoffman took an extended leave of absence to work on the Eisenhower presidential campaign. During this time, Henry Ford II acted as president of the Ford Foundation, although he wished to leave the post as quickly as possible. "I want to make cars," he told top Ford Foundation executive W.H. "Ping" Ferry.[36] Hoffman, on his return, was forced to resign, and was replaced by Rowan Gaither. The Ford Foundation moved its offices from Pasadena to New York City.

℮ The Legacy of Robert Maynard Hutchins

Hoffman's lasting achievement was the appointment in 1950 of Robert Maynard Hutchins as an associate director. Hutchins was a long-time chancellor at the University of Chicago and a leading authority on education. In 1950, he had Senator William Benton (D-CT) visit Henry Ford II. "I spent an hour and a half at breakfast with Henry Ford II this morning," Benton wrote to Hutchins on February 9.

> He is expecting you to call him and have lunch with him the next time you are in Detroit. You are recommended to join Paul Hoffman in heading up the Ford Foundation but it was felt that you would bring enemies along with you! I assured Henry Ford that no one would have enemies when he had his hands on half a billion dollars. He doesn't seem to realize the enormous impact himself. My own suggestion is that you don't wait too long on a Detroit visit.[37]

From the start, Hutchins and Henry Ford II disliked each other. The aversion appears to have been personal rather than ideological. Hutchins was an originator of the "Great Books" program of liberal education, while Henry Ford II was a Yale dropout. The feud between them was the proximate cause of Henry Ford II's later resignation as chairman of the board of the Ford Foundation.

❧ The Fund for the Republic

Robert Maynard Hutchins chafed while in Pasadena. He wrote satirical poetry about the Ford Foundation, calling it "Itching Palms." But in 1952 the foundation reorganized. Among the changes was the creation of several specialized funds. To study civil liberties, the foundation created the Fund for the Republic with $15 million. Hutchins became its first and only president.

Hutchins was eager to head the organization. "I've got a new job," he wrote to his friend Thornton Wilder. "It's spending $15 million stolen from the Ford Foundation on civil liberties & racial & religious discrimination, if you know what I mean. It's not bad. It's better than the Ford Foundation."[38] As early as August 1951, Hutchins wrote a memo saying he would deal in "unpalatable causes," and offered ways for the Ford Foundation to distance itself from possible controversy.

In an unsolicited memo to the Ford Foundation board, W.H. "Ping" Ferry explained that the Fund for the Republic was

not in conflict with the real interest of the Ford Motor
Company, although it may sometimes prove irritating to
some of its officials, and may embarrass, temporarily,
members of the Ford family. In the long run it will
bring more credit to the Ford name than the easy and
innocuous course of making impressive contributions
to established activities or undertaking programs that
cannot arouse criticism or opposition. Here it should
be remembered that the reputation of the Ford Motor
Company largely centers around Henry Ford's lifelong
preoccupation with experimentation and pioneering
ventures.[39]

Ferry's predictions were to prove radically wrong. In its early
years, the Fund for the Republic, which Hutchins called a "wholly
disowned" subsidiary of the Ford Foundation, saw itself as a bold,
path-breaking venture. As Hutchins declared,

The Fund should feel free to attack the problem
of the freedom of the press; of migrant workers;
of the immigration laws and the McCarran Act; of
loyalty investigations; [of] the House Unamerican
Activities Committee; of conscientious objectors; of
academic freedom and teachers' oaths; of racial and
religious discrimination in all its manifestations, from
lynching to inequality of educational opportunity; of
disfranchisement; of dishonesty in government; of
the liberties guaranteed by the First and Fourteenth
amendments; of the administration of justice, etc.[40]

Hutchins condensed this into a decoration in his office, which
consisted of a sampler embroidered with the words, "FEEL
FREE." During its short life, the Fund for the Republic acted like
a bullfighter waving a red cape at conservatives and daring them to
attack. Among its activities were spending hundreds of thousands
of dollars for a report on Hollywood black-listing, having
Washington Post cartoonist Herbert Block prepare a television
documentary on civil liberties, and hiring political scientist Clinton
Rossiter to write a report on American communism. (Rossiter in
turn hired Earl Browder, former head of the Communist Party

U.S.A., as a consultant. Browder was at the time under indictment for perjury.)

Hutchins continued to pick battles with the Right. In 1953, Los Angeles superintendent of schools Alexander Stoddard won a $35,000 Ford Foundation grant for a pilot program to train teachers which would involve intensive summer institutes and a year's worth of practical training in the classroom to partially supersede traditional teacher training in graduate schools of education. The conservative *Los Angeles Herald and Express* charged that because the Ford Foundation had given money to teacher training programs sponsored by UNESCO, Stoddard was trying "to swing UNESCO and 'One World' back into the Los Angeles school system."

After a month of controversy, the Los Angeles Board of Education voted against accepting the Ford grant. "The patriotism of the Los Angeles school board," Hutchins told *Time*, "was so intense that it developed an X-ray eye that enabled it to see Henry Ford, Benson Ford, Donald David of the Harvard School of Business, and the other men who dominate the Ford foundation as Communist agents."[41]

Conservatives increased their attacks on the Ford Foundation after the Fund for the Republic was created. Columnist George Sokolsky charged that Henry Ford "made nearly all the money in this country, but Paul Hoffman, who is spending that money, seems to be placing [it] in remote bottomless pits and [expending] it for meaningless purposes such as an investigation as to why the world is full of refugees when, in fact, it always has been."[42] The most ardent critic was probably Fulton Lewis Jr., a newspaper columnist and radio commentator. Every night, millions of radio listeners heard Lewis comment on the issues of the day. For three months in 1955, Lewis's nightly topic was the Fund for the Republic.

A typical example of Lewis's critique was a broadcast of August 25, 1955. After describing efforts to distribute liberal publications, including a book by Harvard University's Erwin Griswold, a television interview on book censorship, and 25,000 copies of the *Bulletin of the Atomic Scientists,* Lewis said that

> in all I have read to you, from these projects of the Fund for the Republic, there is not one penny for anything to benefit the farmers of the nation, the man and his wife

who run the corner grocery store and provide jobs for a
couple of other neighbors... nothing about bringing up
healthier kids, or better education, or better salaries for
school teachers and policemen and postmen ... just the
same old lines of agitation from the policy book of the
CIO Political Action Committee and the Americans for
Democratic Action.[43]

Henry Ford II was caught between the Fund for the Republic
and American conservatives. According to foundation historian
Waldemar Nielsen, the foundation's trustees had "gone for the
storm cellar" when the conservative critique began, while Henry
Ford II stood steadfast.[44] But the foundation's critics were not
just complaining—they were launching boycotts of Ford Motor
products. These were actions that Henry Ford II could not ignore.
According to Thomas C. Reeves, Henry Ford II received at least
1,200 letters complaining about the Ford Foundation or the Fund
for the Republic. Historians Leonard Silk and Mark Silk say that
one Ford Foundation officer kept a box with "choice samples of
the intimidating missives," and that after reading some of them at
the Links Club, Henry Ford II was so irritated that he emptied the
box into a fire, leaving the foundation officer frantically grabbing
ashes for scarred scraps of evidence.[45]

Many of these letters were from Southerners bothered by the
Fund's attitude towards race relations. Its "activities have seriously
frightened Ford dealers in this region," Charleston (S.C.) *News
and Courier* editor Thomas R. Waring wrote to Ford Foundation
executive Walter Millis, on July 20, 1956. "[This] may be unfair
but nevertheless is a demonstrable fact."[46] So many Southern Ford
dealers complained that Henry Ford II had a form letter printed
that said, "it is not Ford Motor Company policy to attempt, directly
or indirectly, to influence the personal beliefs of Southerners."[47]

ꙮ Resolution of the Controversy

By 1956 the problem of the Fund for the Republic had been
settled. On November 29, 1955, *National Review* editor William
F. Buckley Jr., wrote to Henry Ford II about the Fund for the
Republic. "What is your own judgment on those activities of the
Fund for the Republic that are at public issue?" Buckley asked. "Do

you believe that the present management of the Fund is faithfully and effectively carrying out the intentions of the Foundation in establishing the Fund?"[48]

A week later Henry Ford II answered Buckley's charges by replying to a letter sent by John K. Dunfey, chairman of the Anti-Subversive Committee of the American Legion's Post 41 in Syracuse, New York. "Despite the fact that I have no legal right to intervene in the affairs of the Fund for the Republic," Henry Ford II wrote, "I have exercised my right as a private citizen to question the manner in which the Fund has attempted to achieve its stated objectives. Some of its actions, I feel, have been dubious in character and inevitably have led to charges of poor judgment. I am satisfied, however, that no public trust can expect to fulfill its responsibilities if it does not respond to intelligent and constructive public criticism."[49]

Henry Ford II's letter was the apogee of the Fund for the Republic controversy. Some of the Fund's more controversial programs, such as the Herblock television project, were canceled, and Robert Maynard Hutchins conducted himself in a less fiery manner. Eventually, the Fund for the Republic became the Center for the Study of Democratic Institutions, an organization that, while still liberal, did little that was controversial, or even interesting. "When the center set up in Santa Barbara in September 1959 it was intended as a near-total change of life," W. H. "Ping" Ferry noted in a 1988 memoir. "We were to become reflective, not active; quiet, not noisy."[50] In fact, the Center's hottest controversy during its 28 years of existence was a 1975 dispute over whether or not Alex Comfort wrote *The Joy of Sex* and *More Joy* while working as a Center fellow, and whether the Center was entitled to royalties.

The Ford Foundation spent years explaining away the Fund for the Republic controversy. Writing in the *Saturday Evening Post* in 1963, Ben Hibbs observed that "today foundation officials speak of the Fund (for the Republic) with marked reticence. 'It did some good,' they say. 'But—,' No further grants were ever made, and officials point out, a bit defensively, that there was never any expressed intent to give the fund any more money. It was, they say, a one-time experiment."[51]

But the Fund for the Republic controversy illuminated the problematic relationship between the Ford Foundation and the Ford Motor Company. Since the Ford Foundation's endowment consisted mostly of Ford Motor stock, and since the foundation had no influence in Ford Motor affairs, it was unable to determine the size of its endowment. Conversely, the Ford Motor Company was often blamed for the activities of a large philanthropic enterprise over which it had no control.

The Ford Motor Company and the Ford Foundation were also often confused in the public's mind. According to a 1957 article in *Holiday,* a California trucking magnate celebrated his daughter's receipt of a Ford Foundation fellowship by buying dozens of Ford trucks; another man in Florida insisted on buying Lincolns in the hope that the foundation would take note and give grants to schools and hospitals in the area. An Indian government official had trouble understanding why he did not have to buy Ford cars and trucks after receiving a Ford Foundation grant.[52]

Other conflicts revolved around the Ford Foundation's television programs. According to *Holiday's* Joe McCarthy, Henry Ford II was "a little put out, to say the least" when he learned that the foundation-subsidized television show *Omnibus* had sold commercials to Willys, one of Ford Motor's competitors. Henry Ford II was enough of a Republican partisan to be incensed when the foundation gave money to a children's television show called *Excursion,* which asked former President Harry S Truman to be a guest.[53]

℮ The Foundation in the 1960s

By 1957, all Henry Ford II could do about the Ford Foundation was complain. In 1956, the nightmare the elder Henry Ford had sought to avoid came true. The Ford Foundation, in the largest stock offering of its time, began selling its Ford Motor shares. Because of New York Stock Exchange prohibitions against selling non-voting corporate stock, the shares were converted into voting-class stock. Although the Ford family was able to retain control of 40 percent of the voting shares, the Ford Motor Company was now a public enterprise.

Leonard Silk and Mark Silk say that Rowan Gaither agonized about how to handle the Ford Foundation's newfound wealth, spending many late-night walks brooding about what to do with the money and then not doing anything. At one point, say the Silks, Ford Foundation trustee Donald David proposed that the foundation give all the money to hospitals and spend itself out.[54]

The board's response to this indecision was to force Gaither out, replacing him with Henry Heald.[55] They then announced that their 1956 grantmaking would include $550 million from the stock sale, including $198 million to private hospitals, $90 million to private medical schools, and $260 million to private liberal arts colleges to be used to raise faculty salaries.

"The purpose of the huge giveaway was unabashedly political," the Silks write. "The hospital grants were deliberately arranged so that there would be some Ford money flowing into every congressional district." (The Silks charged that two of the $250,000 hospital grants had to be recalled after the "hospitals" turned out to be "coyly named whorehouses.") [56] At the same time, Henry Ford II resigned as chairman of the Ford Foundation board of trustees, preferring to concentrate on Ford Motor affairs. With every share of Ford Motor stock sold, his influence on the foundation declined. As president of the Ford Motor Company, he commanded one of the world's largest companies. But as a Ford Foundation trustee, he cast only one of 16 votes.

During the 1960s, the Ford Foundation continued to grow. In a 1969 report, *The Law and the Lore of Endowment Funds,* the foundation addressed the issue of how colleges and universities could ensure that their endowments would grow relatively free of restrictions, thus touching on the problems of donor intent. "The courts in all jurisdictions pay at least lip service to the necessity of observing the donor's intent," authors William L. Cary and Craig B. Bright wrote. "In practice the attempt to ascertain that intent is often an exercise in futility, which ultimately ends with the predilections of the court masquerading as the wishes of a deceased donor who is no longer able to speak for himself."[57] Technically, Cary and Bright's views were not those of the Ford Foundation, but their advice was nonetheless a fair example of what the foundation was receiving.

In the late 1960s, the divorce between the Ford family and the Ford Foundation was completed. In 1967, Detroit suffered a severe riot, and Henry Ford II resolved to rebuild the city. He led an effort to construct the Renaissance Center, a major office building, and hired thousands of unemployed blacks to work in Ford Motor plants. According to Peter Collier and David Horowitz, Cristina Ford (Henry Ford II's wife) urged him to help the Henry Ford Hospital, which was still serving Detroit as it had since the elder Henry Ford created it. However, it was now in a bad neighborhood and needed funds. Henry Ford II's brother Benson asked the Ford Foundation three times for money for the hospital, and was rejected each time. Henry Ford II also asked Ford Foundation president McGeorge Bundy for a grant, but was told, "Giving to hospitals is not part of our program."

Cristina Ford, Collier and Horowitz recount, was outraged. "How can you do this?" she told Bundy. "Do you forget that the old man left three billion dollars to the foundation? He gave it to you instead of to his own children!" Bundy was not persuaded, so Cristina Ford went to Ford Foundation trustee Robert McNamara and told him how bothered she was that the foundation would spend $45 million on a new headquarters building but nothing on one of Henry Ford's favorite charities. McNamara said he would do what he could. Henry Ford II also conducted an intensive lobbying effort. In 1973, the Ford Foundation gave $100 million to the Henry Ford Hospital, but McGeorge Bundy announced that this was a "terminal" grant.[58]

☙ Henry Ford II's Resignation

The Henry Ford Hospital affair further estranged Henry Ford II from the foundation. In October 1976, Henry Ford II's mother died. Three months later, he went to the Ford Foundation trustees meeting and resigned. He had several reasons for doing so, including concern over at least three grants the foundation had made:

- A 1967 grant to the Congress for Racial Equality for a voter-registration drive in Cleveland. Newly enfranchised voters voted en masse for Democrat Carl Stokes, ensuring a narrow victory;

- A 1969 grant to several members of assassinated Senator Robert Kennedy's staff to "ensure their transition into private life." However, several of these people, such as Peter Edelman and Frank Mankiewicz, were resuming law practices and earning up to $500,000 a year;[59]

- A 1974 grant to S. David Freeman, who became chairman of the board of the Tennessee Valley Authority during the Carter Administration, to study problems relating to energy. Freeman's report called for massive controls on oil companies and energy production. "I felt that Freeman was not the fellow to do the study, but they picked him," Henry Ford II told *New York Times Magazine* writer Lally Weymouth.[60]

Henry Ford II was also disturbed by the management practices of McGeorge Bundy. According to Collier and Horowitz, he believed Bundy was an executive very much like Lee Iacocca, who served under Henry Ford II before beginning his checkered career with Chrysler Corporation. Henry Ford II, say Collier and Horowitz, thought Bundy was "a philanthropic analogue of Iacocca—someone devoted to self-aggrandizement and empire-building at the expense of the institution itself."[61] During Bundy's tenure, the Ford Foundation lost a billion dollars of its endowment—a third of its assets—due to a combination of bad investments and massive grant programs.[62] The situation was so dire that in 1974 Bundy told *Time* that he wanted to spend down the Ford Foundation, but was blocked from doing so by his board.[63]

As Waldemar Nielsen notes, the effects of inflation made the loss even greater: "by dint of bad financial and investment management [the foundation] has dissipated almost three fourths of the real value of its assets [since 1970], a loss of something in the order of $6 billion of philanthropic resources measured in current dollars. No disaster of comparable magnitude has ever been recorded."[64]

By late 1976, Henry Ford II had lost patience with the Ford Foundation. "I don't think I can stand this much longer," he told long-time associate Walter Hayes. "This place is a madhouse."[65] Unable to stop the abuses he saw, he could only call attention to them by resigning. In a letter to the trustees, he said, "After 33 years I have come to the point where I have pretty much done all there is to do as a trustee and have said all there is to say." He urged the trustees to have more respect for the free-enterprise system that had created the fortune they were spending. "In effect, the foundation is a creature of capitalism," he wrote, "a statement that, I'm sure, would be shocking to many professional staff people in the field of philanthropy. It is hard to discern recognition of this fact in anything the foundation does. It is even more difficult to find an understanding of this in many of the institutions, particularly the universities, that are the beneficiaries of the foundation's grant programs." He added, "I'm not playing the role of the hard-headed tycoon who thinks all philanthropoids are Socialists and all university professors are Communists. I'm just suggesting to the trustees and the staff that the system that makes the foundation possible very probably is worth preserving."[66]

Accompanying his letter was a cartoon from a 1964 issue of the *New Yorker,* which showed a prim man in a tight suit confronting a subordinate who was throwing currency out an open window. "Just a minute, young man," read the caption. "That's not the way we do things at the Ford Foundation." Henry Ford II personally inscribed the cartoon in a firm, unwavering hand. "To my fellow trustees with warm and high regard. Maybe this fellow has a better idea."[67] For a while, the cartoon hung in the Ford Foundation's lobby. In 1987, a *USA Today* reporter searched the foundation offices for some trace of the Ford family. He found one grainy portrait of Henry Ford in a development officer's suite—the only evidence that the Ford Foundation respected the memory of Henry Ford, Edsel Ford, and Henry Ford II.

After his resignation, Henry Ford II expressed regret for his 1948 decision to abandon control of the Ford Foundation. In a late 1977 interview, he said that if he could live again, he would have divided his grandfather's estate into three parts—one-third for Greenfield Village and the Henry Ford Museum, one-third for the Henry Ford Hospital, and one-third for the Ford Foundation. The foundation would have been only "one-third as big, and therefore it wouldn't have gotten into so many different kinds of things, but nevertheless might have been able to do a substantial job in the meantime."[68]

Additional evidence of Henry Ford II's intentions comes from a series of oral histories that he taped for the Henry Ford Museum in the early 1980s. These tapes were sealed until five years after Henry Ford II's death, and were unearthed by *Detroit News* reporter Jon Pepper, who used them for a multi-part series in 1994. The tapes refer at least twice to the Ford Foundation. "I made a big mistake on the Ford Foundation," Henry Ford II said. "I had the Ford Foundation in my hand at one time. Then I lost it, and lost it on my own volition. I gave it away on my own. I was young, inexperienced, and stupid. I just muffed it. It got out of control, and it stayed out of control. And now it's gone, of course."

In a second passage, Henry Ford II referred to how easy it would have been for the Ford family to ensure that the Ford Foundation did what the family wanted. "It could have been done so easily. It could have been done with a pen—in four seconds. We had three trustees. We could have done anything we wanted. We could have taken the [Ford Motor] stock and given it to any nonprofit company, nonprofit Edison Institute (now the Henry Ford Museum), nonprofit Henry Ford Hospital, nonprofit Fair Lane (Henry Ford's house, now a conference center), nonprofit whatever you want. And done a much better job for the whole family than I did. I did it all on my own and made a horrible mistake. I'll never live it down, and I regret it sincerely. But what the hell can I do about it? I can't do anything about it. Just have to lie and die with it."[69]

In a 1990 biography of Henry Ford II, Walter Hayes, a long-time friend and former Ford Motor vice-president, recalled a 1979 conversation with Henry Ford II. Ford said that if he had not abandoned family control of the Ford Foundation, it would have remained in Detroit with a primary purpose of serving the local area. There would have been national programs, Hayes recalled, but the main goal would have been to aid the needy in Detroit.

Could Detroit's institutions have absorbed all the Ford Foundation's wealth? Would a Detroit-based foundation have done as much good as a global philanthropy? "They couldn't have done a worse job than the one that has been done," Henry Ford II replied, "no matter what they did."[70]

The controversy over Henry Ford and Henry Ford II's intentions was revived in 2006, when Michigan Attorney General Mike Cox announced a probe of the Ford Foundation to see if the foundation was spending enough of its money in Michigan. Because of the foundation's incorporation in Michigan, General Cox claimed that the investigation fell within his oversight.

Patricia E. Moordian, president of the organization that managed the Henry Ford Museum, told the *Chronicle of Philanthropy* that the last grant by the Ford Foundation to the museum was in 1973. She said that the museum "is definitely supportive of the A.G.'s efforts. The need is very, very big in southeast Michigan."[71]

In June 2006, state representatives Andy Dillon and Bill Huizenga introduced a bill in the Michigan state legislature that would require foundations incorporated in Michigan to spend half their grants in the state. The bill would affect not just the Ford Foundation, but also such other large foundations as the Charles Stewart Mott, Kresge, and Kellogg foundations, none of which spent half their grants in Michigan.

Attorney General Cox said he supported the legislation. He told the *Detroit News* that the bill "applies to all foundations so it'll make them all nervous—which is fine with me."[72]

Critics of the efforts said that the actions were a wrong way to enforce donor intent, given the Ford Foundation's vague charter and Henry Ford II's 1948 renunciation. "The Ford experience is an argument for donors to be more careful about setting up their philanthropic organizations, not for government to take control whenever there is a dispute," said *Detroit News* columnist Thomas Bray.[73]

"Whatever its flaws," added *National Review* reporter John J. Miller, the Ford Foundation "is a private institution in a free society. It should not have to endure political shakedowns, even when they come from well-meaning conservatives."[74]

The Michigan Attorney General's investigation of the Ford Foundation quietly ended in the summer of 2007, when Ford agreed to increase its annual contributions to nonprofits in southeastern Michigan to around $25-30 million a year. Ford's spending in Detroit increased after Darren Walker became the foundation's president in 2013. In June 2017, Ford opened a regional office in Detroit, making this the first time the Ford Foundation had an office in Detroit since 1953.[75]

There have been no efforts since the Michigan investigation concluded to force the Ford Foundation to honor the ideals of Henry Ford. The foundation remains a large, liberal organization ideologically opposed to the market-oriented capitalism of its founder.

3

The Carnegie Corporation
of New York

*I note what you say about giving as none knows more about that
than yourself. 'The way of the giver' is hard like that of the
transgressor but you and I don't give for applause, nor to please
any body of men, or any man but ourselves, what we see to be the
good of others, therefore criticism and mean flings don't pierce the
skin and we go on—our own reproach alone we fear—that's my
talisman. If I please myself I'll have to do much better than ever.
Nobody abuses me as keenly as I do myself. I know more faults
in myself than all the outsiders do.*
>   — *Andrew Carnegie, letter to John D. Rockefeller
>   (1903)*[1]

The philanthropic enterprises of Andrew Carnegie (1835-1919)
are both good and bad examples of donor intent. The
organizations Carnegie endowed before 1911—the Carnegie
Foundation for the Advancement of Teaching, the Carnegie
Institute of Pittsburgh (now Carnegie-Mellon University), the
Carnegie Institution of Washington, and the Carnegie Endowment
for International Peace—still reflect Carnegie's wishes. But his
last creation, the Carnegie Corporation of New York (which we
would call a foundation, not a corporation), evolved in a way that
undermined the causes Carnegie supported.

Unlike most entrepreneurs of his day, Carnegie was a prolific
writer, producing four books and scores of magazine articles.
His views remained remarkably constant throughout his life.
A student of the classical liberal thinkers Herbert Spencer and
William Graham Sumner, he championed free enterprise (with

45

the exception of protectionism, which he favored for the United States) and opposed expanding government.

Carnegie's major work, *Triumphant Democracy* (1886; revised 1893), is a 500-page salute to American inventiveness and ingenuity. Carnegie delighted in attacking socialism ("a domain of foreign cranks") and the income tax, which he correctly predicted could only be administered by "a thorough system of espionage and minute examination ... not in harmony with the spirit of free institutions."[2] He was particularly harsh on efforts to establish government welfare. These, he warned, would "foster the idle and improvident at the expense of the industrious and prudent.... Whenever paupers regard charity as a right, they are apt to demand it in cases where they would hesitate to ask for favors."[3]

❧ 'The Gospel of Wealth'

Documents unearthed by David Nasaw, whose biography of Carnegie was published in 2007, showed that Carnegie spent years thinking about what to do with his fortune. In an 1885 letter to British Prime Minister William Ewart Gladstone, Carnegie said that he would give away his fortune during his lifetime. And in an 1887 prenuptial agreement with Louise Whitfield Carnegie, Carnegie stated that "Andrew Carnegie desires and intends to devote the bulk" of his fortune to charity "and said Louise Whitfield sympathises and agrees with him in said desire."[4]

Carnegie explained his philosophy of philanthropy in "The Gospel of Wealth," the famous 1889 essay that also continued his critique of socialism.

> The Socialist or Anarchist who seeks to overturn present conditions is to be regarded as attacking the foundation upon which civilization itself rests, for civilization took its start from the day when the capable, industrious workman said to his lazy and incompetent fellow, "If thou dost not sow, thou shalt not reap," and thus ended primitive Communism by separating the drones from the bees.[5]

"The Gospel of Wealth" was the first essay to recognize the problems of donor intent. Carnegie noted that there were three ways a wealthy person could dispose of his fortune: leave it to his children, leave it to charities, or give it away during his lifetime. Carnegie believed that while giving *some* money to one's children was desirable, giving heirs great wealth would make them soft and indolent. "Wise men will soon conclude that, for the best interests of the members of their families, and of the State, such bequests are an improper use of their means."[6]

Carnegie was also critical of creating charities that outlived a donor's death. "Knowledge of the results of legacies bequeathed is not calculated to inspire the brightest hopes of much posthumous good being accomplished by them," he wrote. "The cases are not few in which the real object sought by the testator is not attained, nor are they few in which his real wishes are thwarted. In many cases the bequests are so used as to become only monuments of his folly."[7]

Carnegie argued that philanthropists should, after deducting expenses for a modest life, give money during their lifetimes. But they should not, he believed, randomly give to people they did not know. The "main consideration" of the philanthropist "should be to help those who cannot help themselves, to provide part of the means by which those who desire to improve may do so; to give those who desire to rise the aids by which they may rise; to assist, but rarely or never to do all."[8] For Carnegie, libraries, hospitals, colleges, astronomical observatories, parks, concert halls, and the like would enrich the lives of many, and were thus worthy objects of philanthropy.

Carnegie expanded on these views in an 1895 address for the dedication of Pittsburgh's Carnegie Library. He reiterated his belief that donors should give during their lifetimes, stating that "the aim of millionaires should be to deserve such eulogy as that upon the monument of Pitt: 'He lived without ostentation, and he died poor.'"[9] But the goal of giving, he insisted, was not to redistribute income. If a rich man divided his fortune equally among the poor, the result would be to increase, not decrease, poverty, since lower-income workers would stop working in order to receive aid. Rather than trying to help the poorest, he argued, it was more important to aid "the vastly more precious class" of "the swimming tenth—the industrious workers who keep their heads above water and help themselves, though sometimes requiring our assistance, which should never be withheld in times of accident, illness, or other exceptional cause, and always deserving our sympathy, attention, and recognition, and the outstretched hand of brotherhood."[10]

❧ Carnegie's Early Philanthropy

Until 1905, Carnegie followed the principles set forth in "The Gospel of Wealth." He either gave communities things they needed, such as libraries and church organs, or created institutions with narrow, specific aims. Frederick Lynch, a New York pastor who worked with Carnegie on peace issues, recalled in a 1920 memoir that even Carnegie's "most intimate friends could seldom persuade him to give large sums to anything in which he was not personally interested or of which he had not made a special duty."[11] On one occasion, a group of friends urged Carnegie to give money to medical research. He responded, "it's a great thing; but that's Rockefeller's sphere. Get him to do it."[12]

In at least one case, Carnegie's aims were impossible to achieve and were altered. In 1906, he became worried about college professors who lacked funds for retirement, and created the Carnegie Foundation for the Advancement of Teaching. This provided free pensions for professors with at least 15 years of service, as well as for widows married to eligible participants for at least 10 years and also for "librarians, registrars, recorders, and administrative officers of long tenure."[13] By 1909, 96 institutions had been informed of their eligibility. Because the pensions were free, historian William C. Greenough notes, everyone wanted one. Even Woodrow Wilson, after resigning from the presidency of Princeton University in 1910 to run for governor of New Jersey, demanded one.

Carnegie began the program with a grant of $10 million. Over the years, the Carnegie Corporation of New York gave the Carnegie Foundation for the Advancement of Teaching another $12 million, and loaned another $15 million. This, however, was insufficient, and in 1918, with Carnegie's approval, the pension program was transferred to the Teachers Insurance Annuity Association of America (TIAA), a newly created for-profit enterprise. Later named TIAA-CREF, this giant insurance company still sells pensions to most of America's college and university professors. But for many years eligible academics and their widows (widowers were apparently not eligible) continued to receive Carnegie pensions, even though the list of potential recipients was sealed in January 1931. The pension program finally ceased in October 2008, when the last eligible recipient died.[14] Since 1918, it paid $87.4 million—substantially more than the $10 million to $15 million Carnegie thought the program would require.[15]

❧ The Carnegie Corporation of New York

The nature of Carnegie's philanthropy began to change between 1905 and 1910, when he created the Carnegie Endowment for International Peace. After nearly two decades as America's leading philanthropist, Carnegie was growing weary of the part. Biographer Joseph Frazier Wall notes that by 1906, "Carnegie was tired of the game," and by 1910, "he was desperately sick of it." As Carnegie wrote to a friend, "The final dispensation of one's wealth preparing for the final exit is... a heavy task—all sad.... You have no idea the strain I have been under."[16]

That strain grew as Carnegie aged. In 1908, Carnegie asked several of his friends, including Harvard president Charles W. Eliot and Columbia University president Nicholas Murray Butler, for suggestions on what sort of organization would be worth an additional $5 or $10 million. Butler's biographer, Michael Rosenthal, noted that while Eliot did not ask for money for Harvard, Butler was blunter. "I know of no other way in which more useful work could be done for the civilization of the United States and of the world than by making it possible for the one great metropolitan University to do the work of leadership and enlightenment which lies ready at hand." In fact, Butler argued, to make Columbia the equal of universities in London, Berlin, and Rome as "a real lighthouse of humanity," Columbia would need, not just $10 million, but "up to twenty millions" of Carnegie money.[17]

49

Carnegie had no interest in giving to university endowments, except for universities that he created. But Butler's proposal contained one clause that $10 million of Carnegie funds could be used to create an institute that could produce "a great body of international opinion which would not tolerate the brutalities and immoralities of war, with all that war meant and involves."[18]

This idea intrigued Carnegie. He was long interested in international peace, and had been a steady contributor to peace societies. Carnegie spent the next two years mulling over Butler's idea. His decision was accelerated in 1909, when textbook magnate Edwin Ginn announced that he would create a peace organization (which eventually became the World Peace Foundation) and endow it with $1 million upon his death.[19]

Ginn's announcement acted as a catalyst for Carnegie to create his own peace organization. He was further spurred to action by his conviction in 1910 that President Taft would sign treaties with Great Britain and France ensuring that all disputes between them and the United States would be submitted to binding arbitration. The move by President Taft, observes Michael Rosenthal, "ignited Carnegie as all the complicated persuasion by Butler and his colleagues had not.... Carnegie's belief that a genuine system of international arbitration could be the key to perpetual peace now seemed not a dream, but an actual political possibility."[20]

As historian Larry L. Fabian notes, Carnegie rewrote the deed of trust for the Carnegie Endowment for International Peace several times, and only agreed to transfer $10 million in United States Steel bonds to the organization when Taft seemed ready to support the arbitration treaties.[21] But the endless negotiations and lobbying involved in creating the endowment wore Carnegie out. He was 73, and still in possession of vast wealth. What was he to do?

On the advice of Theodore Roosevelt's Secretary of State, Elihu Root, Carnegie used $125 million in 1911 to create the Carnegie Corporation of New York. Root's biographer, Philip Jessup, observes that Carnegie went to Root with a plan for a large foundation that would come into existence after Carnegie's death. Root advised Carnegie to create an organization during his lifetime, because the courts could easily declare a posthumous trust invalid, as had happened with the will of presidential candidate Samuel Tilden.[22]

Carnegie gave the Carnegie Corporation only one instruction: to provide pensions for former presidents of the United States and their widows. Otherwise, "I give my Trustees full authority to change policy or causes hitherto aided, from time to time, when this, in their opinion, has become necessary or desirable. They shall best conform to my wishes by using their own judgment."[23]

As Joseph Frazier Wall notes, when Carnegie created the Carnegie Corporation of New York, he "had been forced to abandon almost all of the basic tenets of philanthropy he had expressed in the 'Gospel of Wealth.'"[24] Moreover, he quickly found that his deed was irreversible. Biographer Burton J. Hendrick tells how a few years after the Carnegie Corporation was created, Carnegie wanted to create a similar organization in Great Britain. He tried to transfer $10 million of the Carnegie Corporation's endowment to a new institution. "Carnegie was astonished when the question was raised as to the legality of this step," Hendrick writes. He went to Elihu Root, "who served as a kind of supreme court when points like this were at stake," and was told that his deed could not be altered and that his wishes no longer mattered. (Carnegie, however, used money he had saved for his retirement to create the British organization.)[25]

Fortunately, during Carnegie's remaining years the Carnegie Corporation of New York did not become a bureaucratic hierarchy. According to historian Robert E. Kohler, it "was more like an old-fashioned family charity than a modern foundation,"[26] with Carnegie personally involved in most gifts and with much of the money given to other Carnegie philanthropies. Still, some of Carnegie's instructions were altered or countermanded. In 1918, a year before Carnegie's death, the trustees voted to end pensions for former presidents. (Only William Howard Taft received one.)

Also while Carnegie was still alive, the trustees of the Carnegie Corporation violated his wishes by slowing down and nearly eliminating the library program. As historian Theodore Jones notes, by 1914 it was clear that many communities were misusing Carnegie's funds for libraries. The town of Clarksville, Texas, for example, received a $10,000 grant in 1902 for a library. But by 1905, the librarian was tired of working without pay and left. The town mayor asked Carnegie if he could turn the library into offices, and was refused. Eventually, according to Jones, "tramps moved in and warmed themselves by burning books and bookshelves." In 1910, a local barber tried to buy the long-vacant building for $1,000 but was refused on the grounds that he would have to pay the money directly to Andrew Carnegie."[27]

The Carnegie Corporation decided to investigate, and hired Cornell University economist Alvin Johnson to travel across America investigating how the library funds were used. Johnson found that many libraries were soundly run, but still others were badly managed. In some cities, he found that library board members "thought reading a futile and usually an injurious activity."[28] "I found relatively few towns in which the library had been located where it would be most accessible," Johnson recalled in his memoirs, "and some towns where the library had been located on a practically inaccessible site, to oblige some powerful real-estate owner."[29]

Johnson recalled being summoned to a meeting of the Carnegie Corporation board in November 1916 to discuss his report. He proposed that the corporation eliminate most of the money spent on libraries, divert the funds to training librarians, and tighten procedures by which communities could obtain Carnegie libraries. After Elihu Root read the report, Andrew Carnegie's private secretary, James Bertram, confronted Johnson. "Your proposals, Doctor Johnson, fly straight in the face of Mr. Carnegie's intentions," Bertram said. "He wanted to give libraries to communities and leave the communities absolutely free to manage them any way they might see fit. He abominated centralized, bureaucratic control. That is exactly what you want to introduce. Mr. Carnegie never wanted an unnecessary cent to be spent in the administration of his charities. I have administered the whole huge enterprise of establishing libraries with just one secretary, with a desk in my room. To do what you propose would require twelve secretaries and at least six rooms—a big unnecessary expense."

"Not so huge an expense," Johnson replied, "for keeping track of an investment of fifty millions." "A big expense, and unnecessary," Bertram repeated. "And as for library training, Mr.

Carnegie never believed in it. He believed in having books where anybody could get hold of them. What made him, he used to say, was a private library a philanthropic gentleman opened to him. A librarian's business is to hand out the books. That doesn't require a long, expensive training."[30]

After the board meeting, Elihu Root invited Johnson to his office and explained that the board, with the exception of Bertram, supported Johnson's proposals. "Bertram was in Carnegie's service for years," Root said. "He loved Carnegie, and Carnegie was devoted to him. And we can't do anything to hurt the old fellow, who retires before the year is out. However, as you will see, your recommendations will presently be in force." (At the time of this conversation, Bertram was 44. He remained with the Carnegie Corporation until his death in 1934.)[31]

Unlike Carnegie himself, who as a classical liberal wanted library patrons to see themselves as "joint proprietors" of their local library, the trustees held elitist, "progressive" views in which ordinary citizens needed to be led by "experts." They "envisioned library readers becoming 'clients' of the expert librarians they would hire," explains historian Ellen Condliffe Lagemann.[32] One year later, the Carnegie Corporation board voted to terminate library construction grants except for those already in the pipeline. Of the 1,419 libraries built with Carnegie's money, only six new grants were made after 1917, with the last, to American Fork, Utah, made in 1919. Historian Theodore Jones notes that there is no evidence of Carnegie's reaction to the corporation's decision to terminate the library program.[33]

☙ The Erosion of Carnegie's Views

After Carnegie's death in 1919, the erosion of donor intent at the Carnegie Corporation was slow. The foundation's president, James R. Angell, tried to end all grants to Carnegie philanthropies and, for that matter, to anything except graduate schools. This was too radical, and in reaction Angell was succeeded by Henry S. Pritchett, also president of the Carnegie Foundation for the Advancement of Teaching and the TIAA insurance company. Pritchett, says Kohler, decisively "turned back to tradition"[34] and supported other Carnegie charities, including the bailout of the ill-fated pension program. His successor, Frederick Keppel, however, gradually cut funding to Carnegie charities. Grants to maintain public libraries ended in 1925; to medical programs in 1929; and to scientific research in 1931. In fact, Keppel spent most of his tenure ending old programs without creating new ones. He read all proposals, and "what did not appeal to him went off the desk into the waste basket, what did appeal to him was approved."[35] Consequently, the Carnegie Corporation remained small.

Not until after World War II did the Carnegie Corporation become a large foundation comparable to those created by the Rockefeller family. As the organization grew, it moved steadily away from the beliefs that Carnegie had espoused. As Ellen Condliffe Lagemann shows in her history of the Carnegie Corporation, *The Politics of Knowledge* (1989), the foundation was responsible for many of the ideas of the Great Society. Under the presidency of John Gardner (1955-1965), it specialized in education, and many of the ideas it championed (such as increased educational aid to the poor) were implemented when Gardner left to become Secretary of Health, Education, and Welfare in the Johnson Administration.[36] When Alan Pifer was president (1965-1982), the foundation became, in the words of foundation observer Waldemar Nielsen, "the quintessential liberal, activist, entrepreneurial foundation: more of a combat force than a traditional charity."[37] Under Pifer, it spent millions on grants to the Children's Television Workshop for production of *Sesame Street*. [38] It was also a major supporter of the Children's Defense Fund in its early years, and continues to support the organization.

The Carnegie Corporation quietly forgot Carnegie's belief in free enterprise, limited government, and self-help. In 1977, the foundation issued *All Our Children,* a report that included the following propositions:

- The society we want ... would be a society where a parent would be seen as an honorable calling, a form of work as worthy of public support as the defense of the nation or the construction of superhighways....

- It would be a society where present excessive inequalities of income, power, and dignity were much reduced.

- It would be a society where the rights of parents and children were more adequately represented in the courts and throughout the land.

- It would be, in short, a society that took seriously and had translated into its basic outlooks and policies today's rhetoric that claims children to be our "most precious natural resource" and calls families "the building blocks of our society."[39]

In 1985, 300 representatives of the many Carnegie philanthropies met in Dumfermline, Scotland (Carnegie's European home) to celebrate the Carnegie sesquicentennial. Though the leaders of the organizations talked about Carnegie projects (a telescope in Chile, a genetics program in Washington, D.C.) and were entertained by a Scottish actor impersonating Carnegie, no one, according to a report in the *Chronicle of Higher Education,* discussed Carnegie's support of capitalism, limited government, and voluntarism. Carnegie Corporation president David Hamburg told the *Chronicle* that Carnegie's failure to leave instructions on how the foundation's money should be spent showed "a tone of receptivity to new information and ideas and a sensitivity to changing circumstances. He would have liked that we took the time to fundamentally reconsider what we do, and he would have seen in our new programs a continuing commitment to three major themes that shaped his philanthropy: peace, education, and social justice."[40] Hamburg did not explain how Carnegie supported "social justice"—often a euphemism for government wealth redistribution.

The Carnegie Corporation has continued to be a champion of expanded government in recent decades. Grant recipients include the Children's Defense Fund, National Council of La Raza, National Urban League, and the Council on Economic Priorities. When the Clinton Administration took office in 1993, three members of the Cabinet—Secretary of State Warren Christopher,

Secretary of Health and Human Services Donna Shalala, and National Economic Council chairman (and future Treasury Secretary) Robert Rubin—had served as Carnegie Corporation trustees.[41]

In 1996, Vartan Gregorian, a former president of Brown University and the New York Public Library, became Carnegie Corporation president, and Thomas Kean, former Republican governor of New Jersey, was named chairman of the board of trustees. In an interview with the *New York Times Magazine,* Gregorian explained that, in his view, the Carnegie Corporation should support affirmative action, world peace, and education issues. When asked if foundations could replace government social programs, he stated that, in his view, the foundation's role should be to "stimulate, assist, ask questions, and risk being critical. They cannot replace ongoing, sustained national commitments" by government.[42]

The Carnegie Corporation has also been engaged in an extensive effort to expand the federal government's role in childcare. In 1991, it established the Carnegie Task Force on Meeting the Needs of Young Children. In 1994, the task force issued a report, claiming that America was "beginning to hear the rumblings of a quiet crisis" about childcare, and calling for more state regulation of childcare centers, government subsidies to increase the pay of childcare workers, and developing networks so that childcare providers could receive more state and private grants. In 1996, the corporation gave $175,000 to the National Governors Association to ensure that the states had policies "that promote young children's healthy development and school readiness."[43] (Note that the Corporation's 1977 stress on *parents,* not professional childcare providers, has disappeared.)

In 1999, the Carnegie Corporation decided to commemorate the millennium by awarding $15 million in library grants. None of the money (far less, before adjusting for inflation, than the $56 million Carnegie spent on library construction) went to new libraries, but instead went into the budgets of existing libraries. In Houston, the grants were given to programs designed to reach Latino patrons. The Cleveland Public Library stated it would use the funds for new programs for daycare providers and to provide new library cards for the city's children. These grants, said Carnegie board chairman Thomas Kean, were designed "to highlight the central role of America's public libraries in preparing young people, adults, and newcomers for a new century."[44]

In 2001, the Carnegie Corporation announced it was honoring its founder's legacy by presenting the first annual Andrew Carnegie Medal of Philanthropy. It was unclear how the winners of this prize—Leonore Annenberg, Brooke Astor, Irene Diamond, William H. Gates Sr., David Rockefeller, George Soros, and Ted Turner—upheld Carnegie's faith in limited government and free enterprise. (Astor and Diamond, however, upheld one of Carnegie's principles by running term-limited foundations that spent themselves out of existence.)[45]

In the 21st century, the Carnegie Corporation has continued to award the Carnegie Medal of Philanthropy. It has also added other prizes, including:

- The Andrew Carnegie Medals for Excellence in Fiction and Nonfiction, co-sponsored with the American Library Association, and launched in 2012. The winners in 2017 were Colson Whitehead for *The Underground Railroad* for best novel and Matthew Desmond for *Evicted* as best non-fiction book.

- The Andrew Carnegie Fellows, launched in 2015, in which 35 professors receive two-year, $200,000 grants. Unlike the MacArthur Fellows, this program is only limited to professors.

- The I Love My Librarian Award, also co-sponsored with the American Library Association, in which ten librarians in schools, public libraries, colleges, and universities win $5,000 prizes and a trip to New York City for an award ceremony. This award was launched in 2008.

- The Academic Leadership Awards, given every two years since 2005, in which the Carnegie Corporation awards four colleges and universities $500,000 grants and gives medals to the heads of these institutions.

Vartan Gregorian said that he still kept a photograph of Carnegie in his office. "Every day," Gregorian said, "I ask him, 'How'm I doing?'"[46]

In 2011, the Carnegie Corporation marked its centennial with lavish celebrations. Vartan Gregorian, who continues as the foundation's president, held an extensive interview with Susan King, a Carnegie vice-president, posted on the foundation's website. Gregorian described the Carnegie Corporation as, "a guardian of a tradition: a guardian of an important mission.... We are not on an ego trip as an institution, we don't have to be the biggest or the most celebrated; we just have to keep Andrew Carnegie's notion about spreading the gospel of wealth, and that's what we are doing."

Gregorian's comments lacked any acknowledgment of Carnegie's vigorous support of limited government, free-market capitalism, and self-reliance, and the notion that philanthropists should help the poor as a way of fighting socialism.

Gregorian reiterated his truncated understanding of what Andrew Carnegie's life and thinking had to offer the Carnegie Corporation and philanthropy in general in a 2011 interview with the *Chronicle of Philanthropy*. When asked why he admired Andrew Carnegie, Gregorian responded, "Because he was short, poor, and without formal education." How did the Carnegie Corporation influence philanthropy? "The Carnegie Corporation was the first one to have an annual report."

Finally, "How has the Carnegie Corporation been faithful to its benefactor's vision?"

Carnegie "believed in progress. He believed that opportunities were not frozen, so he wanted trustees to take advantage of those opportunities. Frankly, he has left such a broad mandate— 'Education, international peace, creation of knowledge'—that gives leeway for anything we wanted to do, but we have respected his wishes in terms of spending the bulk on American institutions rather than foreign institutions."[47] Again, Carnegie's robust and forceful views on philanthropy had completely disappeared from the Carnegie Corporation.

A more critical assessment of Carnegie's philanthropic heirs was provided by Indiana University philanthropy professor Leslie Lenkowsky in *Philanthropy* magazine. "In important ways," Lenkowsky wrote, "the Corporation's work has departed from its founder's vision. Although it remains riveted on curing social and political inequalities, it has come to regard them less as the unfortunate by-product of an otherwise successful and worthy economic system and more as symptoms of fundamental flaws that require substantial changes to the system itself."[48]

The Economist took a different angle in analyzing the Carnegie Corporation, noting that in 2011 both IBM and the Carnegie Corporation celebrated their centennials. Which has done more good for the world?

The magazine argued that while the Carnegie Corporation had a great deal of influence in its first half-century, in the last 50 years IBM had done more good. In part, noted *The Economist*, this was due to IBM's continued growth, as contrasted to Carnegie's relative stagnation. IBM had sales of $200 billion and employed 427,000 people, while Carnegie barely made the list of America's 20 largest foundations. "Because firms sell something that people want, they make the world a better place in ways that charities do not. In particular, companies create what is known as 'consumer surplus'—the difference between the market price and what a consumer would be willing to pay. This surplus benefits society, not shareholders."

"Another reason for Carnegie's relative decline may be that 100 years is too old for a philanthropic foundation," *The Economist* observed. "The absence of an existential threat may have made it too comfortable." IBM faced several crises in corporate history—abandoning personal computers, transforming into a giant consulting company, nearly running out of money twice. "By contrast it is not clear what, if anything, keeps the people in charge of the Carnegie Corporation awake at night. The passage of time saps a foundation of the unique energy of its founder."

"No wonder," *The Economist* concluded, "many of today's philanthropists aim, as Carnegie did, to give away all of their money by the time they die, or at least put a time limit on the lifespan of their foundation after their death."[49]

Those wise words, and the consequences of Carnegie's failure to carry them out himself, should sober any donor today who contemplates his or her legacy. Even Carnegie, almost certainly the most influential donor in American history and by any measure one of the most generous ones, nonetheless did not succeed in ensuring his own legacy.

4

The John D. and Catherine T. MacArthur Foundation

An arch conservative, MacArthur is worried about the power the Federal government has today and is gloomy for prospects for prosperity in the future.

"The liberals have destroyed what makes this country great," he said. "Now the government is telling everyone how to run his business. How much to pay people. How long they will work. It will take over the insurance business altogether—just you wait and see. The peanut farmer [Jimmy Carter] will have it on his platform. Health and casualty insurance will become like the social welfare system—bankrupted, if the truth be known"….

Taking a long draw on his cigarette, he said, "My advice to a young man today? Hell, go on welfare. Why not? Be a playboy. I probably would. The only thing that will save the country is a paper shortage. Then, the government won't be able to print any more money."

> — *Kiki Levathes, reporter,* New York Daily News, *1976*[1]

One difference between God and John D. MacArthur is that God chose to rest on the seventh day. John D. MacArthur hardly rests, at least not on the same day God did.
> — *Tom Burke (1970)*[2]

❧ *Like Carnegie, John D. MacArthur (1897-1978) was a champion* of free enterprise. In 1935, he bought Bankers Life, a bankrupt insurer, for $2,500. He grew the company by selling policies at lower rates than competitors and by being the first insurance company to hire large numbers of part-time and handicapped workers. MacArthur, the sole owner, reinvested most of the profits in real estate in Florida and New York City. When he died, he was one of only two billionaires in America. His holdings included thousands of acres in Florida and 19 office buildings and 6,000 apartments in New York City. (As late as 1992, the MacArthur Foundation was still one of the largest holders of undeveloped land in Palm Beach County, Florida.)

MacArthur's innovative strategies brought him scores of enemies, particularly in government. He fought the Internal Revenue Service (which he loved to call the "Infernal Internal Revenue Service")[3], the Post Office, the Federal Trade Commission, and the insurance commissions of scores of states. At one point in 1951, the Illinois insurance commissioner held what *Fortune* called "a grand inquisition" in which the insurance commissioners of 14 states tried—and failed—to prove that Bankers Life had broken the law.[4]

A typical example of MacArthur's pugnacious form of capitalism came in 1947, when Bankers Life bought Westminster Life Insurance for $325,000. Shortly thereafter the officers of Westminster Life were indicted for mail fraud, and MacArthur's name was added because he allegedly beat up a postal inspector.

> They claimed that I knocked four teeth out of a postal inspector and beat him to a pulp," MacArthur recalled in a 1976 interview with the *New York Daily News*. "What happened was that the inspector wanted to go over the books of Bankers Life as well as those of Westminster Life. I didn't see any reason why he should and blocked his entrance into my office. He insisted and pushed me aside. I pushed him back but unfortunately he fell over a desk and onto a floor.

> When he picked himself up he said, "Perhaps you would like the Grand Jury to investigate your company." I said, "I understand that there are ladies and gentlemen on the Grand Jury—which is more than I can say for the Post Office—and I'd be delighted."

The charges against MacArthur were not dismissed until 1950, when a judge said MacArthur had nothing to do with the alleged crimes at Westminster Life. After the Westminster Life imbroglio,

MacArthur said, "I knew I'd have to fight for my rights and I've never given up since."[5]

All these investigations left MacArthur with an intense dislike of bureaucracy and regulation. He refused to give money to politicians[6] and denounced environmentalists who sought to block development of his Florida properties as "bearded jerks and little old ladies" who "are obstructionists and just throw rocks in your path."[7] "A staunch conservative with political views to suit his nineteenth-century personality," Lewis Beman noted in *Fortune* in 1976, MacArthur "complains that environmental regulations require heavy investments in sewage treatment, buried utility lines, and other improvements." Planners, MacArthur told Beman, "think alligators are more important than people."[8]

MacArthur also quarreled with his son, J. Roderick "Rod" MacArthur (1920-1984). While the elder MacArthur was fairly conservative, Rod MacArthur was liberal and a self-proclaimed "draft-dodger" who spent the Second World War in the ambulance corps. As Joshua Muravchik notes, in 1972 Rod MacArthur organized the Chicago branch of Republicans for McGovern, "although friends doubt that he really was a Republican."[9] In 1984, he received the Roger Baldwin Lifetime Achievement Award from the American Civil Liberties Union—an award given only five times in 60 years. "Rod MacArthur was the kind of guy who harangued total strangers in restaurants about PCB levels in white-fish," Kenneth W. Hope, director of the MacArthur Foundation's fellows program, told the *New York Times Magazine*.[10]

Rod MacArthur spent most of his career starting businesses that failed. In the late 1960s, he founded a company to produce lava lamps just as they were becoming unfashionable. In 1973, however, he created the Bradford Exchange, a successful collectible-plate business. John D. MacArthur, who advanced Rod MacArthur $70,000 for the business, promptly sued, claiming that he owned 51 percent of the company. The senior MacArthur even padlocked the doors of the warehouse where the plates were stored and seized the firm's customer lists and bank accounts. Rod MacArthur took his revenge by breaking into the padlocked warehouse and taking the plates out.

In 1975, Rod MacArthur bought out his father for $100,000 and became owner of the Bradford Exchange. The firm continued to thrive. Rod MacArthur told the *New York Times* in 1977 that his pre-tax profits were $1.6 million in 1975 and $4 million in

1976.[11] Rod MacArthur used profits from the Bradford Exchange as well as Hammacher Schlemmer, a mail-order firm acquired in 1980, to endow the J. Roderick MacArthur Foundation, which supports left-wing causes. After his death in 1984, the companies were passed on to his three children, most notably John R. "Rick" MacArthur (born 1956). According to *Forbes,* Bradford Exchange profits in 1992 were about $20 million, much of which went to the J. Roderick MacArthur Foundation.[12]

(By 2015, the Roderick MacArthur Foundation, in the process of spending itself out of existence, had reduced its assets to $215,000 from an endowment of $15.5 million in 2010.)

ℰ Creation of the Foundation

From the mid-1960s onwards, John D. MacArthur worried about disposing of his fortune. He spent much of his last decade in the coffee shop at the Colonnades Hotel (which he owned), in Palm Beach Shores, Florida.

When Stewart Alsop interviewed MacArthur in 1965, he found the billionaire "lounging against a pillar" at the Colonnades. "I thought at first glance he might be the hotel janitor," Alsop wrote. "The mistake was a natural one, because the hotel is expensive, and most of the guests have a rich look. MacArthur was wearing a baggy old brown sweater, an open-necked white shirt that couldn't have cost more than three dollars, and nondescript slacks. But a second glance suggested that if this man was a janitor, he was no ordinary janitor."[13]

MacArthur delighted in having a beachfront "office" where he would spend his days drinking pot after pot of coffee, barking into a tan telephone, and smoking three packs a day of Super King Winstons. "I can order my day just the way I want it," MacArthur told *Esquire* in 1970. "I like to get up early and have a fried egg, there's somebody here to cook it. If I have to meet with my secretary, or see one of my other men, or even have to talk to *you,* I can do it right here, and it's social, too. Keeps my pulse steady. My calls come right here through the hotel switchboard and they get rid of anyone I don't want to speak to, just like in an office. I hate like hell to be stuck in an office. I like to see people passing by all day, why the hell not?"[14]

Writing in the *New York Times* in 1973, Jon Nordheimer found MacArthur to be "quite possibly the nation's most accessible billionaire." "Women in straw hats and bathing suits trot by his table on the way to the beach," Nordheimer wrote, "passing a steady stream of petitioners and hucksters who line up each day to curry favor from Mr. MacArthur, who sits stone-faced and skeptical between a Silex coffee pot and a telephone."

"This is the greatest racket," MacArthur said. "If I took these guys up to my office [in the hotel penthouse], I'd have to be courteous to them. Here I can just get up and walk off into the kitchen and hide."[15]

MacArthur did not wish to leave his fortune to his children and he was also concerned about estate taxes. So he quietly decided to leave his wealth to two foundations: the Retirement Research Foundation, a small think-tank that analyzes pension programs, and the John D. and Catherine T. MacArthur Foundation. Together, these two organizations received 99 percent of MacArthur's fortune.

Like Carnegie, MacArthur willed his fortune without instructions on how his wealth should be used. It has been commonly assumed, including in previous editions of this book, that MacArthur never publicly explained why he created a perpetual foundation with no restrictions on how its money was to be used. Scholars have relied on the memories of MacArthur's lawyer, William Kirby, who recounted to *Foundation News* in 1982 that MacArthur told him during a meeting at the Colonnades Hotel, "Bill, I'm going to do what I know best. I'll make it [money]. But you people, after I'm dead, will have to learn how to spend it."

Kirby said that at one point he asked MacArthur to "do something big for charities." MacArthur erupted, saying, "Forget it. The hell with it." He then added, "it's not because I'm cheap. Do you have any other client who is going to give as much money as I will? So I'm charitable. If I was going to decide who to give the money to right now, I couldn't sit at this coffee table, because I'd be bothered day and night. They'd all be after me to try and get my money, and I couldn't lead the life I want to lead. So let me alone in peace. Don't worry—you're going to get all the money."[16]

Kirby, who stayed with the foundation until his death in 1990, said that he saw "two beautiful ironies" in the MacArthur Foundation. The first was that MacArthur, well known for his thrift,[17] would leave his money to philanthropy. Second, that a man "who ran the business, a single owner—some would say a tyrant—turned control over completely to us."[18]

However, MacArthur revealed more of his reasoning in a 1976 interview with the *Chicago Tribune*. "What will happen to your money when you die?" asked *Tribune* reporter Carol Oppenheim.

"You know, I was very ill a few years back," MacArthur said, "I was a terminal case—virus pneumonia. I felt I couldn't go to sleep because I wouldn't wake up, and the accountants were telling me that, if anything happened, the government would get 70 percent of everything. Now I got things lined up—about 90 percent will go to a foundation—and when Gabriel blows his horn, which I won't expect will happen this year, we will carry on without MacArthur. I'm sure they'll have my picture in the lobby and that will keep them all straight."

"Have you told the foundation what to do with the money?" Oppenheim asked.

"No," MacArthur said. "I've seen too many people, including Henry Ford, try to administer their estates from the grave. You have changing times. Besides, you lay down rules and people don't follow them. So, I'll trust in the Almighty that my trustees will do more good for the country than I would."[19]

This was the most extensive statement John D. MacArthur ever made about his reasons for giving. MacArthur gave a more typical response to a Canadian television documentary crew in 1976. When asked to describe the John D. and Catherine T. MacArthur Foundation, MacArthur refused, saying, "You will be making me out to be a philanthropist.... I would be a sucker.... It would be open season."[20]

One potential donor who courted John D. MacArthur extensively was Florida State dean Richard Fallon. In 1972 Florida State's theatre department revived *Twentieth Century*, a play written by Charles MacArthur (John D.'s brother) and Ben Hecht in 1932. The play's premiere was attended by John D. MacArthur; Charles MacArthur's widow, Helen Hayes; and Charles's son, James MacArthur (star of *Hawaii Five-O*). Two years later, doctoral student John Irvine discovered *Stag at Bay*, an unpublished play written by Charles MacArthur and Nunnally Johnson in the 1930s. Florida State staged the premiere of *Stag at Bay* in 1974, and the school announced the creation of the Charles MacArthur Center for the American Theatre to continue research on Charles MacArthur's work. John D. MacArthur agreed to donate $75,000 a year to support the center and began extensive interviews with Fallon, including several trips made with MacArthur on his airplane.

Fallon hoped that John D. MacArthur would reward the MacArthur Center with a generous slice of MacArthur's philanthropic legacy. He was bitterly disappointed. The MacArthur Center was not mentioned in John D. MacArthur's will, and as a result, the center disbanded late in 1978. The tapes and transcripts of the many interviews Fallon conducted with John D. MacArthur were kept in storage at Florida State for nearly 30 years until Alice Kriplen had them unearthed for her MacArthur biography.[21]

When the MacArthur Foundation was created, it had six board members: William Kirby, two executives from Bankers Life and Casualty, radio commentator Paul Harvey, Rod MacArthur, and Catherine T. MacArthur. (Catherine T. MacArthur attended no board meetings before her death in 1981.)[22]

Paul Harvey told Joshua Muravchik that in selecting them, MacArthur "knew we mostly feel the same way about things that he did." Said another board member, "We're mostly a bunch of Midwestern businessmen devoted to free enterprise and opposed to more government controls."[23]

❧ Controversy over the Foundation's Course

Between 1979 and 1981, Rod MacArthur fought for control of the MacArthur Foundation. He threatened lawsuits alleging that the board had conflicts of interest, since two members were top executives of Bankers Life. He also charged that the foundation's assets had been mismanaged. "Rod was a forward-thinking guy on the giving side," William Kirby said, "but on this control question we felt that we couldn't give and we wouldn't give."[24]

As a compromise, the board was expanded. The Bankers Life executives appointed two members, former Treasury Secretary William Simon and former University of Illinois president John Corbally. Rod MacArthur nominated two members, scientist Jonas Salk and physicist Murray Gell-Mann. Three other members—former Attorney General Edward Levi, former M.I.T. president Jerome Wiesner, and Gaylord Freeman, former board chairman of the First National Bank of Chicago—were appointed to be neutral members with no ties to Rod MacArthur or Bankers Life. But with these additions, Muravchik notes, "the board was no longer dominated by John MacArthur's associates but by prominent national figures."[25]

Moreover, some of the new members, particularly Wiesner and Salk, were as liberal as Rod MacArthur.

For the next two years, the board engaged in lively disputes over what the MacArthur Foundation would become. "Board members, unable to work together, established separate fiefdoms not only for grant-making decisions but for the complex affair of getting Bankers ready for sale," Brenda Shapiro reported in *Chicago* magazine.[26] While many of these disputes were ideological, others were more personal. Rod MacArthur and William Simon "fought openly," particularly over a $100,000 grant to the U.S. Olympic Committee, an organization Simon chaired at the time. In 1981, according to Shapiro, Simon tried to oust Rod MacArthur, but William Kirby blocked the effort. Shortly thereafter, Simon resigned, ensuring that the MacArthur Foundation would become one of America's largest liberal foundations.

Simon's departure, however, did not end Rod MacArthur's quarreling. He continued to fight with the MacArthur Foundation until his death in 1984. According to John Corbally, the MacArthur Foundation's first president, "for a while the board was devoting only about one-quarter of its meeting time to programs and the rest to litigation." "I recall counting more than 30 lawyers at one board meeting—there literally was not a seat available," added MacArthur Foundation vice-president James M. Furman in a 1987 interview with the *Chronicle of Higher Education*.[27]

Bastion of Liberalism

Today, the MacArthur Foundation is best known for its fellowship program of "genius awards," which gave $103,933,322 between 1981 and 1992. These occasionally went to conservatives, most notably philosopher Leszek Kolakowski and the National Center for Neighborhood Enterprise's Robert Woodson. But for every conservative, a hundred liberals have received the honor. This may be because those who nominate candidates are mostly liberals. As Anne Matthews reports in the *New York Times Magazine,* the list of nominators in 1981 included two conservatives—University of Chicago philosopher Allan Bloom and Woodrow Wilson Center director James Billington—but at least 11 liberals: University of Pennsylvania English professor Houston Baker Jr.; Carnegie Foundation for the Advancement of Teaching president Ernest

Boyer; author Ralph Ellison; author Frances Fitzgerald; critic Alfred Kazin; National Public Radio president Frank Mankiewicz; author Toni Morrison; Equal Employment Opportunity Commission chairman Eleanor Holmes Norton; theater director Joseph Papp; cartoonist Garry Trudeau; and Harvard University English professor Helen Vendler. Since 1981, liberals known to have served as nominators include Children's Defense Fund chair Marian Wright Edelman, historian John Hope Franklin, and biologist Jonas Salk.[28]

In at least one case, a MacArthur Fellowship was awarded to a recipient that John D. MacArthur had personally disliked and whose request for funds he had denied. According to author Denise Shekerjian, at an unspecified time (probably in the 1970s), Patrick Noonan, who later became president of the Nature Conservancy and Conservation Fund, went to MacArthur's Palm Beach coffee shop seeking funds. "You know, Mr. MacArthur, sir ... saving the parklands ... important wetlands ... national heritage ... ecology...." Noonan was swiftly interrupted. "Young man," MacArthur said, "I've never given anything away in my life, and I'm not about to start now." As Noonan left, MacArthur told him to pay for his coffee.[29] (In 1985, Noonan became a MacArthur Fellow, and in 1989, the land Noonan asked MacArthur to donate became the John D. MacArthur State Park.)

According to the *Chronicle of Higher Education,* in 1988 the MacArthur Foundation considered revising its MacArthur Fellows program to include separate fellowships for scientists and for business leaders. Kenneth Hope, former director of the program, told the *Chronicle* that the foundation would probably never recognize a successful capitalist, because "we're competing with other programs that reward people, and prominent among them is the marketplace. There's little case for giving it [a grant] to a millionaire."[30]

The evidence suggests that the MacArthur Fellows Program has gone through three stages. First, under the leadership of Kenneth Hope, the foundation funded liberal activists. Catharine Stimpson's brief tenure (1993-96) shifted funding towards the multicultural race-and-gender left, with essayist and critic Stanley Crouch the only non-liberal. Among the most notorious fellows under her tenure were musicologist Susan McClary, who declared that Beethoven's Ninth Symphony was about "the throbbing music rage of a rapist incapable of obtaining release," and historian

Patricia Nelson Limerick, whose work *The Legacy of Conquest*, as *U.S. News and World Report* columnist John Leo wrote, argued "that the settling of the West was essentially one long spasm of greed, racism, sexism, and violence that isn't over yet."

Leo concluded, "The truth is that the MacArthur Awards, launched in 1981 to reward high achievement and high promise, are not what they once were. The science awards still seem to be given out fairly, but other selections pretty clearly have much more to do with politics than with achievement of potential."[31]

Under the leadership of Daniel Socolow, who oversaw the MacArthur Fellows Program from 1997-2012, grants were no longer given to political activists. Instead, the foundation preferred to give money to tenured academics in endowed chairs. His successor, Cecilia Conrad, has largely continued Socolow's course, while tilting the grants more towards the race-and-gender preferences of Catharine Stimpson.

It's far from clear that the fellows program has done much to encourage "genius" to thrive. In 2005, *Crain's Chicago Business* investigated the MacArthur Fellowships given for literature and found that 88 percent of the fellows wrote their most award-winning works before they received the fellowships. Many winners published little or nothing after receiving their prize, most notably Ernest J. Gaines, author of *A Lesson Before Dying*, who published one book collecting older short stories and essays after winning his MacArthur Fellowship in 1993.[32]

"Many of the people" receiving MacArthur Fellowships, observed Stanley Katz, a professor at Princeton's Woodrow Wilson School, "are the usual suspects, who aren't going to produce much more. The program's track record on unknowns isn't that much better than anyone else's."[33]

Though the fellowship program is probably the best-known part of the MacArthur Foundation, it is a relatively small project. The foundation's educational programs, led until 2001 by Peter Martinez, formerly with the Saul Alinsky Institute, have given millions to education reform proposals, including a ten-year $40-million grant to the Chicago Education Initiative, a major backer of the Chicago school reform program, which seeks to decentralize schools to give parents more say in setting budgets and in hiring and firing teachers. The foundation is also the nation's largest private funder of mental-health research, and has given millions to environmental causes, most notably a $15 million grant in 1982 to create the World Resources Institute, a major command-and-control environmental group.

One of the MacArthur Foundation's more controversial projects is the Peace and International Cooperation Program, (renamed the International Peace and Security Program). which from 1984 to 2017 dispensed $443 million. As Joshua Muravchik reports, grant recipients include the socialist Institute for Policy Studies and three independent organizations created by IPS: the Center for National Security Studies, Center for International Security Studies, and Policy Alternatives for the Caribbean and Central America. Peace grants have also gone to former IPS employees Eqbal Ahmad (once indicted for conspiring to kidnap Henry Kissinger and blow up government office buildings), Todd Gitlin (a University of California sociologist and New Left leader), Daniel Ellsberg, David Cortright, William Arkin, Daniel Siegel, and Jenny Yancey. At least three former Sandinistas—Alejandro Bendana of the Nicaraguan foreign ministry, foreign trade minister Alejandro Martinez, and ambassador Carlos Tunnerman—have received MacArthur Foundation grants since the defeat of the Sandinista government in the 1990 elections. The foundation also gave $55,000 for research on a biography of radical attorney Leonard Boudin, whose daughter Kathy served 22 years for felony murder committed during the Weather Underground's infamous Brinks robbery.

In 2016 the MacArthur Foundation announced that it would shut down the International Peace and Security Program at the end of 2017. Among the grants given under this program in 2015 and 2016 were those to the Chicago Council on Global Affairs ($650,000), the Woodrow Wilson Center ($500,000), and the *Bulletin of the Atomic Scientists* ($450,000).

Under the leadership of Jonathan Fanton, who headed the MacArthur Foundation between 1999-2009, the foundation supported grantees that oppose the death penalty, support increased environmental regulation, support failed public housing programs, and support international bureaucracies. On nearly every issue, MacArthur grantees favored ever-expanding, more intrusive government.[34]

A 2007 profile of the foundation in *Crain's Chicago Business* declared that the foundation was "the 800 lb. guerilla of philanthropy," making grants in 61 countries and with branch offices in India, Mexico, Russia, and Nigeria. Although the foundation continued its domestic programs (including the MacArthur Fellows), it became increasingly focused on international development work, including human rights and environmental issues. "In order to make a difference, you have to focus your time and your money on a few problems in the world," Jonathan Fanton said. "That way you can maximize your impact."[35]

In 2009, former State Department official Robert Gallucci succeeded Jonathan Fanton. Three years later, in 2012, Daniel Socolow ended his career as head of the MacArthur Fellows Program, replaced the following January by former vice president of Pomona College Cecelia Conrad.

Despite changes in personnel, however, the foundation's priorities largely remained the same, promoting the liberal agenda both in the U.S. and overseas. In 2012, for example, during Barack Obama's campaign for re-election to the presidency, the foundation gave grants to nine organizations dedicated to fighting efforts to prevent voter fraud, with the largest grants going to the Common Cause Education Fund ($400,000), the Advancement Project ($300,000), and the League of Women Voters Education Fund ($200,000).[36]

Also in 2012, the MacArthur Foundation donated $500,000 to the Born This Way Foundation, a nonprofit founded by the rock singer Lady Gaga to reduce bullying in the schools. Among the uses of the grant, according to a foundation press release, was a tour bus that "will travel the country to serve as a place where kids can go to feel connected and learn about civic engagement opportunities." The bus was scheduled to accompany Lady Gaga's 2013 concert tour, but no one questioned the idea of Lady Gaga receiving a foundation grant to promote attendance at her concerts.[37]

The MacArthur Foundation is an enormously inefficient one. *Chicago Sun-Times* reporter Cheryl L. Reed found in 2004 that "For every dollar it doles out, the MacArthur Foundation spends another 40 cents for expenses, ranking it first out of the nation's top 10 charitable foundations in its ration of expenses to payout." Reed also discovered that the foundation paid its leading officers very well; in 2002, Jonathan Fanton earned $525,181, while chief financial officer Lyn Hutton earned $764,904. Three other MacArthur Foundation officers—vice president William Lowry, vice president and secretary Arthur Sussman, and general counsel Joshua Mintz—each earned over $350,000. In 2014, the most recent year for which this information was available, Robert Gallucci earned $2.2 million, vice president and chief investment officer Susan E. Manske was paid $1.2 million and $370,000 in retirement contributions, and five other MacArthur Foundation employees each earned more than $500,000.

Paul Harvey, who served on the MacArthur Foundation board from 1978-2002, said that if John D. MacArthur were alive he would have denounced the foundation's extravagance. MacArthur, Harvey said, "would have been exasperated. Embarrassed, frustrated and utterly unsympathetic" to the high salaries paid to MacArthur officials. "He would have loved to bang some heads together."

Rick MacArthur agreed with Paul Harvey, "If my grandfather were alive today, he would have utter contempt for the MacArthur Foundation. There's no question that my father and grandfather wanted the lowest overhead possible."[38]

In 2015, Julia Stasch became MacArthur Foundation president. She had previously been vice-president of the foundation, and had worked for the foundation since 2002, directing MacArthur's American programs. Her earlier experience included several years working as Chicago's housing commissioner and chief of staff to Mayor Richard M. Daley. Stasch was deputy director of the General Services Administration during the Clinton Administration.

Once she became MacArthur Foundation president, the foundation reorganized all of its programs (except for the MacArthur Fellowships) into a group of more limited programs devoted to "big bets" on certain issues. A program designed to limit the spread of nuclear weapons superseded the International Peace and Security Program, for example. In 2015, the foundation announced a five-year, $75 million program to reduce the number of people in prison.[39] Another 2015 effort was a $50 million grant to fight climate change by awarding general operating support to nine environmental groups, including $15 million for the Sierra Club, $10 million for the Nature Conservancy, and $10 million for the Environmental Defense Fund.[40] It added an additional $19 million in climate change grants in May 2017, including $4.5

million to the Climate Policy Initiative for programs about climate change in India and $3 million to Earthworks to help communities document methane pollution.[41]

The MacArthur Foundation's "biggest bet" was a program called "100 and Change," in which the foundation promised to award one grantee a $100 million grant to solve a pressing global problem. As of July 2017 the foundation had narrowed the search to eight semi-finalists but not picked a winner.[42]

The MacArthur Foundation also announced that more of its endowment would be used for program-related investments, or "impact investing." In collaboration with the Chicago Community Trust and the Calvert Foundation, the MacArthur Foundation was a major investor in Benefit Chicago, which began operations in May 2017 with investments in six social enterprises, including Autonomy Works, which provides jobs for people with autism, and Sweet Beginnings, which hires released prisoners and trains them to be beekeepers and involved in other projects involving honey. Individuals could also buy bonds supporting these enterprises through the Calvert Foundation with a minimum investment of $20.[43]

In a 2016 interview with the *Chronicle of Philanthropy*, Stasch said that she could make these dramatic changes in the MacArthur Foundation relatively quickly because "I came up from inside. I wasn't recruited from McKinsey or something like that and I didn't come in and say, 'We're out of business for a year' while I try to understand what we needed to do. I already understood. I was able to accelerate the potential for change within the foundation. I didn't have to build my credibility with the staff."[44]

One thing unchanged about MacArthur is that it continues to be a liberal foundation created by a conservative donor who left no restrictions on how his wealth would be used. Sam Worley made this point in a 2015 profile of Julia Stasch in Chicago Magazine, where he cited the findings of Alice Kriplen, a biographer of John D. MacArthur.

"The tycoon offered no instructions on how the money should be spent," Worley wrote. "In his indifference, MacArthur left behind a neat historical irony: He was politically conservative and by many accounts quite greedy—Kriplen calls him a 'compulsive tightwad'—but the interests of the foundation have tended to be fairly liberal, in every sense of the word. There could hardly be a more liberal grant, for example, than the MacArthur Fellowship."[45]

5

Pew Charitable Trusts

Oil baron Joseph N. Pew, Jr., was an old-time Republican Party boss who despised government regulation and whose oil refinery in Marcus Hook, Pa., emitted noxious fumes that made the town's air almost uninhabitable. The senior executive of Sun Oil in Philadelphia in the '40s and '50s was called many things in his life: humorless, corrupt, Roosevelt-hater. "Environmentalist" was not one of them. But 35 years after his death, a family charity started by Pew is one of the leading funders of the American environmental movement, pumping an expected $22.5 million this year into causes that Pew himself might well have loathed. In particular, the Pew Charitable Trusts played a key role in convincing President Clinton to adopt tough air pollution regulations that the oil industry strenuously opposed. "The founders of Pew would be rolling in their graves if they knew," said Robert Scheffer, a Boston-based consultant to environmental groups.
— *Scott Allen, reporter,* Boston Globe *(1997)[1]*

When I speak of the free enterprise system at its best, I mean when it is entirely free—free from monopoly, private or governmental; free from government control or intimidation; free from trade agreements which result in price or production control after the matter of the cartel systems of Europe.
— *J. Howard Pew (1938)[2]*

With the possible exception of the Barnes Foundation, the foundation that has committed the gravest violation of donor intent is the Pew Charitable Trusts. The Pews believed in free markets, limited government, and traditional virtues. They practiced their charity quietly, without any desire for publicity or fame. The professional philanthropists who succeeded them believe in self-promotion, big government, and communitarianism.

The Pew family's wealth came from the Sun Oil Company, commonly known as Sunoco. Sun's founder, Joseph N. Pew Sr. (1848-1912), had participated in the Spindletop oil strike in Texas in 1901, and he was one of the few independent oil refiners who would not be bought out by Standard Oil. By the 1930s, Sun Oil had become a major oil producer and refiner as well as a manufacturer of oil tankers for itself and its competitors.[3]

The Pews were also active shipbuilders. Sun Shipbuilding and Dry Dock, a division of Sun Oil (later Sunoco), was launched in 1916 to build tankers to carry oil from Sun's Texas oilfields to its Pennsylvania refinery. The company became a major supplier of ships to the military in both world wars. In World War I, the company supplied American forces with three minesweepers and six oil tankers. In World War II, Sun Ship built 285 ships for the military, including 40 percent of all the oil tankers used by the U.S. in the war. In addition, Sun Ship repaired 1,500 ships damaged in combat. Sun Ship built its last ship in 1979; the shipyard was sold by Sun Oil in 1982.[4]

All the Pews were Republicans. But as Sun Oil historian August W. Giebelhaus notes, "some ... took more active political roles than others."[5] The two most politically energetic children of Joseph N. Pew Sr. were Joseph N. Pew Jr. (1894-1963) and his brother, J. Howard Pew (1882-1971).

ℰ Champions of Free Enterprise and Traditional Charity

Joseph Pew was a corporate lobbyist who led the successful effort to overturn FDR's National Recovery Act. In the late 1930s, he began to purchase magazines, including the *Farm Journal* and *Pathfinder*, a rural news weekly, which he transformed into market-oriented publications opposed to government growth.

Joseph Pew's political activity was not limited to words. When the New Deal began, according to a 1939 article in *Fortune*, Pew decided to visit the state Republican Party in Philadelphia. "Mr. Pew had visualized the Republican party as occupying sizable, busy offices, something on the order of a large corporation. Instead he found an office deserted except for a handful of underlings.... His business friends, even those who were substantial contributors, couldn't tell him where the Republican party was, but assured him that it must be where it had always been."[6] Pew spent $1 million to revitalize the Pennsylvania Republican Party and $200,000 more to help Arthur James take the governorship in 1938.

He also sought to influence national politics. "The Republican Party stands today where the Continental Army stood at Valley Forge," Pew said in 1940, "and if Haym Salomon and Robert Morris could empty their purses to keep that army alive, so can we."[7] By 1940, after failing to secure the Republican presidential nomination for Robert Taft over Wendell Willkie, Pew had come to regard the New Deal as "a gigantic scheme to raze U.S. businesses to a dead level and debase the citizenry into a mass of ballot-casting serfs."[8] A 1944 article in the *New Republic* called him the leading "Roosevelt-hater" in the United States, a man whose "rabid antipathy to the New Deal" was far more virulent than that of any member of the Mellon or DuPont families.[9] Pew's fundraising for Republican presidential candidate Thomas Dewey in 1944 was the subject of a speech by Democratic National Committee chairman Robert E. Hannegan, who denounced Pew as "one of the wealthy group of little-known, power-hungry men whose steady stream of money dominates the Republican party."[10]

Joseph's brother, J. Howard Pew, was president of Sun Oil during the Great Depression. He was less active politically, but his many speeches in defense of free enterprise are among the most eloquent ever written by an American corporate executive. "The competitive enterprise system," he said in 1945, "has given us the highest standard of living ever achieved by any country at any time in the world's history."[11] Pew supported many causes but refused to contribute to any organization he believed leftist, including those that favored government welfare. He thought most seminaries were too radical and gave millions to create the Gordon-Conwell Theological Seminary "to turn out the kind of ministers he sought."[12]

By all accounts, J. Howard Pew presented himself in public as a grim and austere man who, in the words of *Institutional Investor* reporter Jack Willoughby, "believed in stiff-backed Christianity, small-town individualism, and local philanthropy." "He was always the chairman of the board, stiff and distant," Pew's grandson, George Black, told Willoughby. "I don't think I ever saw him out of a three-piece suit."[13] One anonymous source told *Fortune* in 1941 that J. Howard Pew was so grim that he looked "like an affidavit all over."[14]

It is important to note the connection between J. Howard Pew's views on economics and theology. The clearest expression of his theological outlook appears in a 1954 debate among members of the National Council of Churches. At the time, Pew was chairman of the National Lay Committee, which advised the Council on public questions. At one point, Bishop William C. Martin said many Christians disagreed with Pew's support for limits on government. Citing Christ's teaching that "Ye shall know the truth, and the truth shall make you free," Pew answered, "Socialism, Welfare-State-ism, Government intervention, or any other term used to describe Collectivism enforced by the power of Government, appears to be directly antithetical to the above ideals." "Jesus depended on the power of persuasion," Pew continued. "He did not coerce individuals. He saw clearly that attitudes of the heart cannot be changed by coercion, by law and penalty. He depended entirely on the persuasive power of his mission. When Christians lose faith in the message of Jesus and seek to reform society by the power of the state, they are in effect appealing from God to Caesar; they are trying force because they have lost faith in the power of their religion."[15]

Pew continued to critique the Presbyterian Church for the rest of his life. In 1960, for example, he said that delegates to the Presbyterian Church annual convention should not "meddle in secular affairs" by endorsing collective bargaining and birth control and opposing capital punishment. Such positions, Pew said, were contrary to "natural law and the freedom and rights guaranteed by the Constitution" as well as being pronouncements that "frequently coincide with Communist objectives."[16]

As part of his theological grantmaking, Pew generously funded *Christianity Today*. As the magazine's first editor, Carl F.H. Henry, recalled in his memoirs, Pew was a member of the *Christianity Today* board from 1955 until his death in 1971. He was actively involved in selecting as editor first Henry, in 1956, and then Harold Lindsell, in 1968. His two-year, $200,000 grant in 1955 ensured that the magazine was successfully launched. Not only was Pew the largest single donor, but also the Pew Freedom Trust was the only major foundation to give money to the magazine until the Lilly Endowment began to donate in the mid-1960s.

But Henry recalled Pew as a donor who wanted to place strong strings on his grants. Although the editors of *Christianity Today* were theologically quite conservative, they did not want the magazine to take stands on political issues. Pew was highly suspicious of the magazine's refusal to take political stands. At one point he demanded that the proofs of each issue be sent to him and that he have some sort of veto power over the magazine's content. The magazine's editors successfully resisted Pew's demand.

Pew was a highly visible donor. Before *Christianity Today* launched in 1956, the *Presbyterian Outlook* charged that he had contributed $400,000 to the magazine—twice as much as he actually gave. Henry also said that as the magazine's first issue appeared, "reports" (which he did not specify) "circulated that Pew had founded *Christianity Today* to get revenge on the National Council of Churches." The Rev. Billy Graham, one of the magazine's founders, called on Pew to respond to these charges by resigning from the magazine's board. The other board members, who said Pew could stay on "as long as he was not the magazine's sole or dominant source of support," outvoted Graham.[17]

Pew was also a generous contributor to conservative and libertarian organizations. "There seems little question that Mr. J. Howard Pew of Philadelphia is one of the biggest contributors to Rightist causes," noted Anti-Defamation League of B'Nai B'rith officials Arnold Forster and Benjamin B. Epstein in the 1964 book *Danger on the Right*, "quite apart from the support provided such organizations by him and his family." They noted that the Pew family were the major donors to the Christian Freedom Foundation, a pro-capitalist Christian organization. They also said that Pew contributed to the Foundation for Economic Education, Americans for Constitutional Action, and the John Birch Society, although they provided no evidence that Pew was active in the Birch organization.[18]

In the 1940s, the Pews began to create several trusts to administer their estates. There would eventually be seven, and some had typically vague charters. The Pew Memorial Trust, created in 1948, was designed to "help meet human needs through financial support of charitable organizations or institutions in the area of education, social services, religion, health care, and medical research."[19]

The J. Howard Pew Freedom Trust, created in 1957, was different. Pew specifically instructed that it be used to "acquaint the American people" with "the evils of bureaucracy," "the values of a free market," and "the paralyzing effects of government controls on the lives and activities of people" and "to inform our people of the struggle, persecution, hardship, sacrifice and death by which freedom of the individual was won." Such "forms of government" as "Socialism, Welfare stateism [and] Fascism ... are but devices by which government seizes the ownership or control of the tools of production."[20]

Like Henry Ford, the Pews appear to have created trusts to retain control of the family company while avoiding inheritance taxes. The Pews willed 45 percent of Sun Oil stock to their estates while retaining 55 percent—enough to ensure family control of the enterprise. This tax-avoiding move ensured that the Pew Trusts would become very large. Nearly all of J. Howard Pew's $100 million estate went to the Freedom Trust. Joseph N. Pew left $30 million from his $36 million estate; Mabel Pew Myrin (1889-1972) willed $84 million of her $88 million estate; and Ethel Pew (1884-1979) left $59 million of her $61 million estate to charitable causes.

Moreover, there's some evidence the Pews worried about the Tax Reform Act of 1969, which altered the rules governing foundations. One provision of the Act required that foundations disburse annually at least six percent of their assets. But soon thereafter, Congress reduced the payout rate to five percent. According to a report in the *New York Times*, Rep. Herman Schneebell (R-PA) introduced the bill changing the payout rate on behalf of the Pews and the Kellogg Foundation. At the time, Sun Oil and Kellogg Company dividends were less than six percent, and this meant that the assets of the foundations would be sure to shrink in a bear market.[21]

ℰ Radical Restructuring

Until the late 1970s, the Pew Trusts were devoted to two causes: charities in the Philadelphia area, which received the largest share, and conservative and libertarian projects. In 1974, for example, the Trusts' largest contributions were to the University of Pennsylvania ($2.8 million), Lankenau Hospital in Philadelphia ($1.1 million), Grove City College ($1.1 million), Children's Hospital in Philadelphia ($1 million), *Christianity Today* ($500,000), and Presbyterian University of Pennsylvania Medical Center ($500,000). The Trusts also donated $435,000 to Gordon-Conwell Theological Seminary, $320,000 to the American Enterprise Institute, and $300,000 to the Christian Freedom Foundation.[22]

As the Trusts' founders died, however, few members of the family were willing to take part in managing them. This ensured that there would be changes in the recipients of Pew gifts. At the same time, the number of Pews steadily increased, as the great-grandchildren and great-great-great grandchildren of founder John Pew came into their inheritances. "With at least 1,000 third-, fourth-, and fifth-generation descendants of John Pew," the *New York Times*'s David Diamond noted in 1981, "dispersed throughout the country, the family no longer functions as a cohesive clan."[23]

Some change occurred during the presidency of Robert Smith, a former Sun Oil vice-president who served as administrator of the Pew Charitable Trusts from 1972 to 1977 and president from 1977 to 1986. Smith began giving money to Ivy League schools and "mainstream social agencies."[24] In 1979, the Pew Memorial Trust issued an annual report for the first time, showing its assets (which, of course, didn't include the other six trusts) at $890.2 million, making it the nation's second-largest foundation at the time.[25] Smith also cut off funds to conservative causes. As Lucinda Fleeson noted in a 1987 *Philadelphia Inquirer* article, Smith began slashing grants to conservatives as soon as he became president in 1977, "and by 1980 they had all but disappeared."[26]

Smith left the Pew presidency in 1986 under mysterious circumstances. "The reasons for Smith's swift departure remain closely guarded," Lucinda Fleeson noted in her 1987 article, stating that they had something to do with the board receiving a report by Wharton School professor Edward H. Bowman that harshly criticized Smith's management.[27]

Smith's successor as Pew president was Thomas W. Langfitt, who had joined the Pew board in 1980. A neurosurgeon who had spent much of his career at the University of Pennsylvania Medical School, Langfitt continued the Pew Charitable Trusts' radical transformation under his presidency. In his first two years as administrator, Langfitt fired 95 percent of the trusts' staff. In 1988, he hired Rebecca Rimel, a self-described "high school cheerleader turned executive feminist," as executive director of the foundation. Rimel became president of Pew in 1994. According to the *Chronicle of Philanthropy*, Rimel's main goal was to increase "access and justice for disadvantaged groups in our society."[28]

Shortly after assuming the Pew presidency in 1986, Langfitt called for placing the Pews' principles "within the context of the world in the late twentieth century." The trusts now would espouse "empowerment of the individual" and "preservation of our American heritage."[29] Langfitt also advocated "more government funds" for welfare, hoping that "public and private agencies [would] join hands [in the 1990s] to provide the human and financial resources needed to empower people."[30]

❧ Disregarding Donor Intent

By 1991, Roger Williams reported in *Foundation News* that the Pew Charitable Trusts had "eliminated almost all of their right-wing grantmaking and embraced a broad range of projects, including some that manifestly oppose the business interests the old Pews held inviolable." He added that many grants would "send the late J. Howard Pew and Joseph N. Pew, Jr. spinning in the family crypt."[31] In an interview with *Town and Country,* Rimel explained her political beliefs. "If we could reinfuse the idealism of the Sixties into our work, it could get the country out of this morass of feeling that problems are insoluble. We have to assume that if we're committed, innovative and thoughtful, there's nothing we as a country can't solve."[32]

In September 1990, Pew had sold 18 million shares of Oryx Energy, a company spun off from Sun Oil, for $968 million. Pew also exchanged 7 million voting shares of Sun Oil stock for nonvoting ones with a higher dividend. The move meant Pew's grants would increase by $25 million in 1990 and $35 million in 1991.

Pew solved its 1990 surplus by paying its 1991 grants six weeks early. They increased their staff from 77 to 100 to handle the extra funds and hired what they called a "dream team" of five consultants to come up with new ideas. All of the consultants, including well-known television commentator Bill Moyers, Harvard education professor Harold Howe II, and Judge Leon Higginbotham Jr., were prominent liberals. The consultants proposed five major grants. Pew then hired more consultants to evaluate the "dream team" proposals, and ultimately expanded existing programs to handle the surplus.[33]

An analysis of Pew grants by the *Philadelphia Inquirer* showed that the amount given to Philadelphia institutions fell from 56 percent of total grantmaking in 1980 to 23 percent in 1991. The

Trusts have also ended gifts to many of the Pew family's favorite charities. Mabel Pew Myrin willed her home and 350 surrounding acres in Chester County, Pennsylvania, to create Camphill Village at Kimberton Hills, a place for developmentally disabled people to live and work. When her granddaughter, Karin Myrin sought a grant from the Pew Charitable Trusts, she found that the Pew staff often would not return phone calls. "There's been such a turnover of staff at Pew that a lot of them don't even know my name," she told the *Philadelphia Inquirer.*[34]

In fact, few members of the Pew family are now involved with the Pew Charitable Trusts. According to Lucinda Fleeson, the Pew heir "who was closest philosophically to the trust founders," John G. "Jack" Pew (a cousin of Joseph and J. Howard Pew), found himself consistently outvoted at Pew board meetings and was forced to resign.[35] The family member most involved in the trusts is R. Anderson Pew, a great-nephew of Joseph and J. Newton Pew. His notion of the purpose of the Pew Charitable Trusts is expressed in a 1990 interview with the *New York Times.* According to reporter Kathleen Teltsch, he professed to be "mystified" by the idea that the Pews were conservative, because "Our Aunt Harriet Pew in Civil War days ran an underground railroad helping slaves from Parker's Landing in Virginia. You can't get much more liberal than that."[36] (Harriet Pew had no involvement in creating the Pew Charitable Trusts.)

Perhaps the Pew Charitable Trusts most directly violate the beliefs of the Pew family by making grants in the area of energy exploration and development. As Dan Rottenberg of *Town and Country* reports, the trusts have supported environmentalists who favor restrictions on oil drilling in the Alaskan wilderness. This strikes directly at the source of wealth that made the Pew Charitable Trusts possible.

Rebecca Rimel summed up her views of the Pew family in a 1991 interview with *Foundation News.* She praised the family for having "humility, a quiet style, a conviction that one doesn't dictate through grants." Nonetheless, she said, "the political ghosts" of the Pews "are gone."[37] In a 1993 interview with the *Chronicle of Philanthropy,* she noted that half the members of the Pew board are either Pew family members or people "who knew the donors and are familiar with the donors' wishes."[38]

In a letter to the author, Rimel stated that the Pew Charitable Trusts board still follows the wishes of their founders. "The Trusts' four founders were, as you describe, conservative in their thinking," Rimel wrote, "but they were also passionate in their commitment to hospitals, churches, schools, universities, and organizations that encouraged civic engagement and democratic principles. The Trusts today have not wandered from these founding precepts. As time has passed, they have necessarily shaped their giving to accommodate evolutionary changes in society. To the extent the Trusts have changed, it is in a way that the founders would likely have saluted."[39]

Readers may judge whether Rimel's statements are accurate by the account of Pew Charitable Trusts activities in the 1990s set out in the succeeding paragraphs. Politically, both Rimel and her staffers describe themselves as non-ideological. Thomas Langfitt, in a 1997 interview with *National Journal,* describes the Pew board as having "no ideological bias," adding that there was ideological bias on the board in the past, presumably because it was conservative.[40] (These claims are echoed in the Trusts' entry in Wikipedia.) In an interview with the *Washington Post,* Paul C. Light, director of Pew's public policy program, claimed that he was a moderate who gave money to both the left and the right.[41]

But an analysis of Pew Charitable Trusts giving done for the Capital Research Center by Robert Lerner and Althea Nagai found that the Trusts gradually increased spending on liberal causes and decreased it for conservatives. In 1981, the Trusts gave $2.4 million to conservative organizations; by 1993, they had eliminated all grants to the right, although they did give $150,000 in 1994. By contrast, spending on liberal causes and organizations steadily increased. In 1986, the Trusts gave three times as much money to the left as to the right; by 1994, liberals were receiving 40 times as much Pew Charitable Trusts money as conservatives.[42]

These spending patterns have continued. In 1996, for example, the Trusts' public-policy program did give $237,500 to the American Enterprise Institute to support a project by AEI fellow Norman Ornstein (a non-conservative) for work on campaign-finance reform. It also gave $300,000 to the Hudson Institute "to strengthen nongovernmental research institutes in the Baltic States." But in the name of J. Howard Pew, the Trusts also gave money to such liberal groups as the Brookings Institution ($150,000), the Center for Responsive Politics ($660,000), the League of Women Voters Education Fund "in support of the Money + Politics: People Change the Equation Project" ($450,000), and Rock the Vote Education Fund ($660,000). Despite the severe restrictions in the Pew Freedom Trust indenture, the Pew Trusts also began to give money to radical environmental groups, including the Tides Center ($245,000) and the Environmental Information Center ($770,000).[43]

In line with the last-mentioned grants, the Pew Charitable Trusts also continues to be a major funder of environmental programs. Green groups who received 1996 grants include the American Conservation Association ($267,500), the Environmental Information Center ($2.4 million), Green Seal, the National Audubon Society ($300,000), the Natural Resources Defense Council ($375,000), the Pesticide Action Network North America Regional Center ($225,000), the Sierra Club Legal Defense Fund ($200,000), the Tides Center ($1.3 million), the Wilderness Society ($800,000), and the World Wildlife Fund ($100,000). Most gravely from the point of view of donor intent, the Pew Charitable Trusts in 1996 gave $550,000 in the name of Joseph N. Pew to the Henry A. Wallace Institute for Alternative Agriculture, even though Wallace, vice-president between 1941 and 1945 (and a communist fellow-traveler) was a man Joseph N. Pew undoubtedly despised.[44]

In a two-part series published in the *Philadelphia Inquirer* in 1996, Stephen Salisbury found that The Pew Charitable Trusts had been transformed from a locally oriented, thinly staffed conservative foundation to a large bureaucracy eager to conquer the world. "No longer an insular conservative family affair designed to dole out money," Salisbury wrote, "the foundation is a full-blown bureaucracy working to influence organizations and events, both inside government and out."[45]

Former Pew grantees charged that the foundation had become increasingly hostile to the organizations that it funded. "Pew is so focused in pursuit of its goals that in many cases, the very organizations it says it wants to aid have become restive and even hostile," Salisbury wrote. "Many local arts officials feel Pew is less interested in funding cultural organizations than in preserving the sanctity of their own programs. They cite, for example, the foundation's recent decision to bar operating support to any organization reporting a deficit."[46] One of the organizations cut off was the Philadelphia Orchestra, which was denied Pew grants in 1996 and 1997 because it ran a deficit.[47]

In the mid-1990s, Pew began to fund organizations that agreed with its particular agenda in order to create the illusion of a massive groundswell for a particular cause. As we will see, this occurred with Pew's support of civic journalism in the 1990s, voting reform in 2005, and "net neutrality" in 2010. Salisbury, however, found this Pew method in place as far back as 1996. "With big-ticket, broad impact programs, Pew launches a full-frontal assault on each problem."[48]

Among other activities of the Pew Charitable Trusts in the 1990s:

- It divested its endowment of all Sun Oil stock, reducing its share of Sun Oil common from 24.1 percent in 1993 to nothing as of August 1997.[49]

- It undertook a major effort to re-shape the environmental movement, giving more money to environmentalists than to any other single donor. "We're not purists. We believe that people ought to be able to cut down trees," Rebecca Rimel told the *Baltimore Sun* in 1997. "But it ought to be done in a sustainable way. That way, there are jobs, trees, owls—everybody wins."[50]

- Under the leadership of Joshua Reichert, former director of the Veatch Foundation and a former employee of Cesar Chavez, Pew money created four organizations, most notably the Environmental Information Center.[51] In 1995 and 1996, the Environmental Information Center bought advertisements denouncing "the new Congress" as "bedding down with corporate polluters." (The Center claimed that because the advertisements did not specify "The Republican Congress" and because they ceased before the 1996 primaries, they were non-partisan.) [52]

- Many environmentalists, however, questioned Pew's methods. For example, green groups in the Pacific Northwest opposed to logging on government property strongly objected to Pew's opinion that there should be a limited amount of logging in state-owned property.

- Levinson Foundation executive director Charlotte Talberth discussed Pew's methods in an interview with the *Philadelphia Inquirer*. "'What does Pew do?' Levinson said. 'They come into a region. They are by far the biggest pot of money anyone has ever seen. They put the pot on the table and invite the 20 or 30 people they know to come to the table. And everyone figures out what Pew wants them to say.'"[53]

- Pew has given millions in support of the "civic journalism" movement. In 1993, it created the Pew Center for Civic Journalism, headed by Ed Fouhy, a former producer for NBC News. According to *Philadelphia Inquirer* reporter Stephen Salisbury, Rimel's interest in civic journalism began with a lengthy conversation in 1993 with James K. Batten, then CEO of Knight-Ridder, a newspaper chain that at the time owned the *Inquirer*. "What interested Rimel was the notion that Pew could leverage its own broader attempts to strengthen social and political engagement by funding civic-journalism projects," Salisbury reported.[54]

Under the program, Pew gave money directly to newspapers and other for-profit enterprises, a move other foundations did not follow until after the 2007-09 recession, when newspapers were far more open to foundation grants. (To ensure that Pew money did not violate federal law that prohibits nonprofits from giving money to for-profit enterprises, Pew supported the Tides Center, which then funded newspapers.) According to Alicia Shepard writing for Capital Research Center, Pew money was used to pay for polls, hold town meetings, and conduct focus groups. Between 1994-1997, Pew gifts paid for 34 projects in 24 cities, involving 22 newspapers, 24 television stations, and 20 radio stations.[55]

One of the recipients of Pew money for "civic journalism" programs was the Hackensack, New Jersey *Record*. The newspaper took $140,000 of Pew money and $100,000 of its own funds to create "Campaign Central," which featured polls, transcripts of speeches by politicians, and fact-checking analyses of campaign commercials. Forums were also held where "ordinary citizens" asked politicians questions.

A post-election analysis of the project by *Hackensack Record* public affairs editor David Blomquist and Rutgers political scientist Cliff Zukin found no evidence that "Campaign Central" changed anyone's minds. Fewer than 20 percent of the newspaper's readers remembered reading any article in Campaign Central. Nor was there any evidence that the section resulted in more people voting or talking about politics. In fact, 42 percent of the readers had no idea who the two candidates running for the Senate in New Jersey—Democratic Sen. Robert Torricelli and Republican Dick Zimmer—were.

In an article in *Columbia Journalism Review*, New York University journalism professor Edwin Diamond reported that Pew blocked Blomquist and Zukin from presenting their findings at the American Association for Public Opinion Research convention, stating that they needed more time to review the paper. Pew eventually published it, but inserted a lengthy preface arguing that the experience of one grantee proved nothing about whether "civic journalism" was worthwhile and blaming the failure of the project on "a heated television-saturated campaign."[56]

Pew cut off funding to its Center for Civic Journalism in 2002, and the civic journalism movement died shortly thereafter. "Civic journalism began to decline around 2003 and not coincidentally with the sunsetting of the Pew Center for Civic Journalism," noted University of Wisconsin (Madison) journalism professor Lewis A. Friedland in an interview published in 2010.[57]

- As part of its effort to promote "civic engagement," Pew sponsored the National Commission on Civic Renewal, headed by former Georgia Democratic Senator Sam Nunn and Heritage Foundation fellow William Bennett. The commission created an "Index of National Civic Health," which determined that Americans were 25 percent less civic in 1996 than in 1972. Among the commission's recommendations were boycotts of shows featuring "violence, sexual license, and the pursuit of immediate, intense sensation that a decent civic life seeks to moderate." It also endorsed community development corporations, charter schools, the character education movement, and voluntary national testing.[58]

- Pew also founded Americans Discuss Social Security with a $10 million grant. The organization produced advertisements with different views on Social Security reform and plans to conduct polls and sponsor a book on Social Security by Rudy Abramson, a former *Los Angeles Times* reporter.[59]

- Allied with the "civic journalism" movement was a Pew-funded campaign led by former *Washington Post* reporter Paul Taylor to provide free airtime for political candidates. In May 1998, Taylor formed the Alliance for Political Campaigns, which lobbied television stations to "donate" more time for campaign commercials and speeches. Other nonprofits that received money in the $7 million campaign were the Annenberg School of Communications at the University of Pennsylvania and the Campaign Management Institute at American University, which planned to work with 200 campaign consultants to "improve" their campaign advertisements. Pew also gave money to ten state organizations to lobby state television stations for more coverage of statewide races.[60]

- Another Pew effort to influence the press was a $1 million grant to the University of Maryland, which produced a report in July 1998 charging that newspapers were neglecting state politics. The report contended that 27 state capitols had fewer reporters covering them in 1998 than in 1996, and only 14 states had more press coverage.[61]

- In the fall of 1996, a subcommittee of the Republican-controlled Pennsylvania state legislature denounced the Pew Charitable Trusts' health care activities as evidence the Trusts were "purchasers of public policy." It charged that the Trusts, in alliance with the Robert Wood Johnson Foundation, "are providing grants as 'seed money' to state, county, and local governmental bodies to develop new or to expand existing government programs, all without the informed consent of the General Assembly.... It is one thing to seek change, it is quite another when changes in public policy are influenced by the offering of public money to state governmental institutions."[62]

- In May 1998, Rebecca Rimel appeared at a Planet Hollywood restaurant in Washington, D.C., for a news conference with rap singer Chuck D., associated with Rock the Vote, and former "Melrose Place" television star Andrew Shue, founder of the group Do Something. She announced that the Trusts would give both groups a total of $4.7 million to get more young people to vote. These votes, Rimel explained, were "a health plan for our ailing democratic heart."[63]

ℰ Moving Still Further from Donor Intent

In the 21st century, the Pew Charitable Trusts has traveled even further from its founders' philosophy, goals, and activities, all while denying that they were doing so. Rebecca Rimel, for instance, has addressed the issue of donor intent several times. In an August 2000 interview in *Philanthropy*, she described J. Howard Pew as "a man of strong convictions and his successors on the board are following in his footsteps by having strong convictions." She claimed that "the only person on the board since its founding" (whom she did not name) said:

> we could not have known what he [Howard Pew] would or would not have done in current circumstances. But he was fiercely independent, he had very strong ideas and he believed that everything he did should be toward the public good and the public interest, and that it should prepare citizens to self-govern in the future. If you apply that standard, we are totally in sync with his intent and interests on individual program areas that were not even around when he was alive.[64]

Rimel expanded on these ideas in an April 2001 speech to the American Philosophical Society. "The law recognizes that circumstances change over time," Rimel said. "It gives what lawyers call 'an affirmative duty' to find a way to continue to honor donor intent, and it assumes that honoring donor intent is a dynamic process. The Pew Trusts believe in our stewardship of our donors' intent. It is through our current work that we honor that intent."[65]

Under Rimel's rule, foundations honor donor intent by doing... well, whatever *they* feel like doing. It is hard to see how the Pew Trusts' feel-good liberalism in any way honors the Pew family's commitment to limited government and traditional virtue.

The Pew Trusts took two further steps to distance itself from its founders. First, in July 2003, they announced that they would partially secede from the Glenmede Trust. The Glenmede Trust split into two parts—a nonprofit entity, which continued to manage the $3.8 billion Pew Trusts endowment, and the original trust, which would continue to be a private bank for the Pew family and other wealthy customers. As of 2003, Glenmede had $13 billion in assets and served 1,300 customers, each of whom had to have at least $3 million in investments.[66]

Next, in November 2003, Pew announced that it would transform itself from a grantmaking foundation into a nonprofit organization that would largely fund entities that it created. The Internal Revenue Service allowed such a change because, although nonprofits are supposed to obtain funds from a variety of sources, the IRS declared that the seven trusts were, under the law, seven separate foundations.

This move freed Pew to spend as much as 20 percent of its budget on lobbying (previously, as a private foundation, it had almost no legal capacity to lobby), and also allowed it to raise money for other organizations (as we will see in the discussion of the Barnes Foundation). Pew also no longer had to pay out five percent of its assets as grants each year. As a public charity, Pew also saves millions of dollars a year it previously paid in excise taxes.

Rebecca Rimel told the *Wall Street Journal* that Pew would "build a wall" between organizations that were nonpartisan, including its polling activities, and more partisan advocacy groups. "We are going to be even clearer in the future that we value both" advocacy and nonpartisanship, Rimel said, "but they are separate."[67]

The "wall," however, seemed both before and after Pew's change in status to be quite porous (if it existed at all). In fact, Pew has become increasingly interested in advocacy. Among recent activities in the years immediately before and after the change to nonprofit status:

- In 1999, Pew announced that it was going to spend as much as 40 percent of its budget on a "national cultural policy." It said it would establish a center in Washington that would conduct polls, hold conferences, and issue reports about the arts.

Historian Dan Rottenberg pointed out that Pew was pouring 40 percent of its arts grants into the failed arts center while it was slashing grants to arts organizations in Philadelphia.[68] In the end, the proposed Pew arts center was never created.[69]

- Pew continued to pour tens of millions of dollars into the environment each year. "With its deep pockets and focus on aggressive political advocacy, Pew is not only the most important new player but also the most controversial among opponents in industry," *New York Times* reporter Douglas Jehl noted in 2001. Jehl found both conservatives and liberals opposed to Pew's efforts to place the environmental movement under the command of Pew environmental director Joshua Reichert. "I don't think you make social change on the basis of paid staff in Washington and paid ads anywhere," Sierra Club executive director Carl Pope told Jehl.

From the other side of the political spectrum, Jehl reported Rep. Helen Chenoweth-Hage's (R-Idaho) statement in a 2000 Congressional hearing that Pew's efforts to close the national forests to economic activity showed how communities near these forests "are being crushed by an inaccessible and faceless movement wielding great power and influence."[70]

- Pew also poured millions into trying to influence the 2004 election. It donated $9 million to the New Voter Project, which sought to register 265,000 18- to 24-year-old voters in Colorado, Iowa, Oregon, Wisconsin, New Mexico, and Nevada. Though the group was allegedly nonpartisan, the project was a joint venture between George Washington University and the Nader-created State Public Interest Research Groups, a nonprofit entity hostile to Republicans.

"Voting is an acquired habit," Rimel told the *Philadelphia Inquirer*. "Some people say that young people are distracted. Once they get a house and kids, they'll vote. So, in 10 or 15 years, you've got less than half of the people participating in what is arguably our most important civic responsibility."[71]

- Pew also spent millions pursuing campaign-finance reform. In 2005, *New York Post* columnist Ryan Sager discovered a 2004 videotape made by Sean Treglia, a Pew vice president for many years, at a conference at the University of Southern California. In the tape, Treglia said that Pew had created fake grassroots organizations designed to persuade Congress that there was a national call for campaign-finance reform. According to Political Money Line, Pew spent $40.1 million between 1994 and 2004 on campaign finance reform grants.

"The target audience for all this activity was 535 people in Washington," said Treglia, who was Pew's leader on campaign-finance reform. "The idea was to create an impression that a mass movement was afoot—that everywhere they spoke, to academic institutions, in the business community, in religious groups, everywhere, people were talking about reform."[72] This was especially dishonest because according to Pew Research Center's own polls, the public ranked the issue dead last among 22 issues they were asked about in January 2002, two months before the McCain-Feingold campaign-finance law passed.

In a letter to the *New York Post*, Rebecca Rimel said that Treglia had repudiated his charge that Pew was trying to hide its role in campaign-finance reform and "from the beginning, the Trusts' grants on campaign-finance reform were transparent and were intended to be."[73]

- Since the third edition of this book, Pew has continued its evolution into a center-left think tank combining valuable nonpartisan parts (such as its polling unit) with highly partisan parts that vigorously advance a statist agenda which would be anathema to the Pews who founded the philanthropy. The key move marking this evolution was in 2009, when Pew transferred most of its staff from Philadelphia to Washington, after the nonprofit spent $155 million buying and renovating the former headquarters of the Securities and Exchange Commission. Pew moved 300 staff members from Philadelphia to Washington while retaining 190 staff members in Philadelphia. The Pew Research Center for the People and the Press, the polling unit that remained the most nonpartisan part of the Pew complex, was deliberately not relocated to the new building as a way of symbolizing the center's independence.

Rimel told *Politico* in 2009 that her organization's partial move to Washington was done because "this (i.e., Washington) is where the talent is. We're not here because we want to be Washington insiders or a Washington player. We made a business decision, not a philosophical or policy decision. And I have to admit, I resisted it for a long time."[74]

- Pew continues to be an active force in environmental policy. In 2007, the National Environmental Trust, a nonprofit created in 1994, merged with Pew's environmental section to form the Pew Environmental Group, with a $70 million budget and offices on four continents.[75] In a 2009 *Politico* interview, Joshua Richert, who remained the head of Pew's environmental efforts, said that Pew's efforts were primarily focused on climate change and on ocean policy. On the issue of climate change, "We've been working on that for 20 years and never expected it to take this long" to alter U.S. climate policy.[76]

- Another environmental issue in which Pew has been heavily involved is retarding oil production in Canada. Brian Seasholes, drawing on the work of Canadian blogger and *National Post* columnist Vivian Krause, calculates that Pew spent $57.2 million between 1999 and 2011 on anti-oil sands activities, of which the bulk ($48.7 million) went to Ducks Unlimited, which then passed some of its grants back to Pew. Seasholes showed that most of the groups opposed to development of Canada's boreal forest (where the oil sands are located) were either divisions of Pew or largely controlled by them.[77] Pew's interference in Canadian politics and public policy led to a Parliamentary inquiry.

- Pew also led the effort to successfully persuade the Federal Communications Commission in 2010 to pass "net neutrality" regulations. While supposedly designed to prohibit different users of the Internet from receiving data at different speeds, the result of net neutrality rules was to tighten government control of the Internet. The regulations were imposed despite over 300 members of Congress stating their opposition to them, and a federal court's ruling that the FCC lacked authority to regulate the Internet.

Wall Street Journal columnist John Fund noted that the primary backers of net neutrality were the Pew Charitable Trusts and most of the same foundations that supported the campaign-finance reform efforts of Sean Treglia, including the Joyce, Ford, and MacArthur Foundations, the Open Society Institute, and the Schumann Center for Media and Democracy, controlled by liberal pundit Bill Moyers. Among the organizations supported by Pew and its allies was Free Press, whose founder, Robert McChesney, a Marxist, told the website Socialist Project that his "ultimate goal is to get rid of the media capitalists in the phone and cable companies."

The FCC's primary evidence for its net neutrality decision was a report it commissioned from Harvard's Berkman Center for Internet and Society, which was paid for by the Ford and MacArthur Foundations. The vast majority of the citations from the FCC's National Broadband Plan come from Free Press, the Berkman Center—and directly from the Pew Charitable Trusts.

"The 'media reform' movement," concluded Fund, "paid for research that backed its views, paid activists to promote the research, saw its allies installed in the FCC and other key agencies, and paid for the FCC research that evaluated the research they had already paid for. Now they have their policy. That's quite a coup."[78]

"Give the Pew Charitable Trusts and its foundation friends credit," commented Scott Walter of the Capital Research Center. "Pew is indefatigable in its efforts to shape—even circumscribe—Americans' political speech.... Today Pew leads the way in developing and funding proposals to reeducate citizens and voters to understand the benefits of democracy guided by elites."

Pew's work, Walter concluded, "aims to help the public understand that freedom does not consist in letting people think and say and buy what they want. Freedom is instead the product of dialogue and conversation—led by those who are properly informed about the dangers of commercial speech and corporate organization."[79]

Rimel has continued to advocate for her views on donor intent. Her most lengthy discussion on this subject came in 2012, in response to an article at PhilanthropyDaily.com by Hudson Institute fellow William Schambra on the lessons philanthropists could learn from the work of political scientist James Q. Wilson. In his article, Schambra cited Rimel's 1999 statement that "we have to do more than offer Band-Aids, and, ideally, work on more than symptoms. We aim to identify underlying causes, because attacking them is the only way that finite resources can make a difference." Schambra charged that "the Rimels of the world, intoxicated by the utopian notion that the root causes are within our reach and control," now ignore small-scale grants, such as repairing broken windows, creating gardens, and cleaning up litter in low-income communities, which the research of Wilson has shown helped to make communities better and tell criminals they are unwelcome.[80]

Although Schambra's article did not mention donor intent, Rebecca Rimel, in her response, claimed that a "largely family board, with a third generation of donor descendants serving now, provides the organization of the intent of our founders." According to Rimel, Joseph N. Pew III (who died in 2011) stated that "70 or 80 percent of the problems we work on today did not exist when the donors were alive" and that the Pews "gave us the stewardship responsibility to lead this institution as the needs of society change." Rimel did not address the issue of who these Pew family members were, if they ever disagreed with Rimel, and why vague memories of long-dead grandparents were a better guide to donor intent than the forceful and precise words of the J. Howard Pew Freedom Trust indenture, which thunders that the Trust's mission is to "acquaint the American people with the evils of bureaucracy and the values of a free market and to inform our people of the struggle, persecution, hardship, sacrifice and death by which freedom of the individual was won."[81]

In 2015, the *Washington Post* reported that Rebecca Rimel had an internal sale within the Pew offices of record albums from her collection, with bids beginning at $3. *Nonprofit Quarterly* national correspondent Rick Cohen thought this was curious, considering that her compensation from the Pew Charitable Trusts in the trusts' 2013 Form 990 was $4.1 million, which included in that year $3.2 million from a retirement plan that the IRS required to be listed as income. (Rimel's compensation in the 2014 Form 990, the most recent available, was $1.1 million.) Cohen also reported that Rimel received a six-figure salary and stock compensation for being on the boards of Becton-Dickinson, BioTelemetry, and Deutsche Fund and Asset Management.

"Selling her album collection is her business—that's fine," Cohen wrote. "But the idea of a foundation official making the kind of money Rimel is taking home strikes many people in the foundation world as absurd, inconceivable, unwarranted, and unjustifiable.... Some philanthropic compensation levels are just plain wrong."[82]

In 2017, *Town and Country* asked Rimel to write about the Pew Charitable Trusts, 26 years after the 1991 profile where Rimel said her goal was "to infuse the spirit of the Sixties into our work." In a piece co-written with R. Anderson Pew, they declared that the Pew Charitable Trusts were "a global nonprofit dedicated to making long-lasting, positive change, based on high-quality research... at our core we remain unflinchingly committed to high-quality research that can be deployed to guide positive and memorable change."[83]

Readers might compare this statement with J. Howard Pew's forceful commitment to limited government and traditional virtues. And then consider whether establishing a perpetual foundation is worth the risk.

6

The Barnes Foundation

The problems of donor intent also exist in the art world. In many cases, donors create art collections and will them to museums with very specific instructions regarding how they should be maintained and expanded. Later, the donors' wishes are partly or totally violated.

Charles Lang Freer (1854-1919), a Detroit industrialist who made a fortune building railroad cars, retired at the age of 45 to collect Asian art. When he died, his collection went to the Smithsonian Institution along with an endowment and very detailed instructions on how the new Freer Gallery of Art was to operate. But as Benjamin Forgey reported in the *Washington Post,* the Smithsonian has in many cases ignored Freer's intentions. Although Freer insisted that the collection be seen in natural light, the Smithsonian installed artificial lighting during a 1980s renovation. Freer also insisted that only a small number of close friends be allowed to donate additional art to the gallery. The Smithsonian, however, spent years exploring ways to technically comply with this clause, such as buying objects for a dollar that were actually worth millions. In the 1970s, Freer officers "simply reinterpreted the will in a way that allowed gifts."[1]

In other ways, however, the Smithsonian has upheld Freer's will. As requested, it has obeyed the clause saying, "nothing else shall ever be exhibited with the collection," and has honored Freer's request to always keep his art in the building. In a codicil to Freer's will, Freer stated that the purpose of the Freer Gallery was to support "the study of civilization of the Far East, as the Regents of the Smithsonian Institution shall determine."[2] For years, some Smithsonian executives tried to broadly interpret this so that the Freer endowment could be spent on research projects only loosely connected to Asia. Eventually, however, Freer Gallery officials won the dispute, and the endowment is now used to maintain the Freer Gallery and to buy new pieces for the collection.

While the Freer case is relatively straightforward, a far more controversial case is the Barnes Foundation. This example shows that courts have, in fact, taken very specific instructions and declared them null and void, thus destroying donor intent.

☙ Albert C. Barnes: Entrepreneur and Art Collector

For many people, the creator of the Barnes Foundation, Albert Coombs Barnes (1872-1951), was an unpleasant man. Carl W. McCardle, whose four-part *Saturday Evening Post* profile was the longest article written about Barnes during the donor's lifetime, observed that Barnes "in his dealings with the public is a combination of Peck's Bad Boy and Donald Duck."[3]

"A love of fighting," A.H. Shaw noted in a 1928 *New Yorker* profile, "seems to have been the dominant characteristic of his entire career."[4]

"If Barnes had peacefully assembled his paintings, written his books, and directed the educational work of his Foundation," notes biographer Howard Greenfeld, "he would have been unqualifiedly respected and universally mourned at this death. Yet such was not the case, and he left behind him far more enemies than he did friends. The former despised and feared him; the latter worshipped him and remain, even today, stubbornly loyal to his memory."[5]

An essay Barnes wrote in 1945, "Sabotage of Public Education," indicates his general temperament. He condemned the Philadelphia public schools for

> poisoning the wells of public enlightenment by maintaining pseudo-modern educational projects that nullify everything which the leaders of modern scientific education have striven for and accomplished; in doing lip-service to spontaneity and liberty they condemn their deluded followers to frustration and futility.... Exposed as mountebanks and educational illiterates, they refuse the public the explanations to which it is entitled and take refuge in silence, with their political barricades assuring them continued access to the public funds.... The Board of Education's sponsorship of the

puerile and pretentious chatter of Invitation to the Arts puts a fitting climax upon a long career of educational sabotage.[6]

In short, Barnes had strong views that made him many enemies. "He was an outsider fighting to get inside, an unpleasant man in a society that valued good manners, a self-made millionaire of little breeding in a city ruled by men of superior upbringing," Greenfeld writes. "Yet his personality and his outrageous behavior should not be allowed to overshadow his very real achievement: his collection."[7] Further, those who have violated Barnes's wishes seem to have had reasonable and sensible goals. Barnes did not want his paintings to be shown at other museums. He did not want his collection reproduced in color. Even conservative Supreme Court Justice Antonin Scalia described the lawsuit that voided large parts of Barnes's will as "one of the few productive lawsuits in modern times."[8]

Albert C. Barnes was a Philadelphia chemist and entrepreneur. In 1900, he formed a venture with Hermann Hille to create new pharmaceutical products. In 1902, Hille perfected Argyrol, a type of silver nitrate. Doctors knew that silver nitrate was a powerful and effective antiseptic, but also an extremely caustic compound that could easily cause burns, particularly when treating small children and infants. Hille's achievement was to create a variant of silver nitrate that was therapeutic and far less dangerous than existing forms of the compound.

Argyrol became very popular. "In America," Greenfeld notes, "its acceptance was so complete that many states passed laws requiring that a few drops of the solution be placed in the eyes of newborn infants to prevent infant blindness."[9] By 1910, Barnes was so wealthy that his only business concern was hunting down competitors who sold bogus versions of Argyrol. He began to immerse himself in three passions that would engage him for the rest of his life: philanthropy, radical politics, and art.

Politically, Barnes was a leftist—somewhat more radical than the typical New Deal Democrat. He was one of the early backers of the *New Republic* and supported the National Urban League. He also funded *The Masses* (a radical weekly) and aided Leon Trotsky in his years of exile from the Soviet Union. He was a friend and supporter of John Dewey and gave him the title of director of education at the Barnes Foundation. In 1941, when Bertrand Russell was fired by the City College of New York, Barnes hired him to lecture at the foundation. (He fired Russell a year later for reasons that seem to have been largely personal.)

Barnes's political outlook is important because it underscores what the Barnes case is *not* about. Unlike the cases of the Pew, MacArthur, and Ford foundations, the Barnes Foundation did not involve liberals violating the beliefs and wishes of pro-capitalist donors. Henry Hart, a former Barnes Foundation employee who in 1963 wrote an appreciative memoir, best summarized Barnes's political views. Barnes, he said, "never wittingly contributed to a Communist cause, though he did contribute to things in which Communists had injected themselves, as, for example, the Sacco-Vanzetti case." According to Hart, Barnes was anti-Stalinist but not anti-Communist. He believed "a certain amount of government control was necessary, and he thought Roosevelt and his New Deal had prevented totalitarianism here [in the United States]. He believed in a mixed economy—some socialism, democratically arrived at, and some private enterprise."[10]

By 1910, Barnes had become a full-time art collector. He later explained that his passion for collecting was largely due to his own inability to master painting. Barnes completed over 200 canvases before realizing that his talents lay elsewhere. "I collected my own pictures when I didn't have money," he later said, "and when I had money I collected better ones."[11] Barnes was one of the first Americans to recognize the importance of French modernist art. He bought over 100 paintings by Cezanne, over 30 Picassos, 60 canvasses by Matisse, as well as others by Daumier, Manet, Monet, and Modigliani and fine examples of ancient art from Egypt, Africa, Persia, and China. By 1922, he had acquired so much that he felt it was time to formally organize his collection.

ℰ Creation of the Barnes Foundation

The Barnes Foundation, created in 1922, was intended to be different from other museums. It was not to be a place where the idle could derive some amusement by breezing through a collection. The paintings of the Barnes Foundation were to be *tools*. The museum was to be a giant textbook to teach Barnes's views of art appreciation.

One reason Barnes felt the need to explain his views was the reaction he experienced after some of the paintings he bought were displayed at a small show at the Pennsylvania Academy of the Fine Arts in 1923. Barnes's paintings were savagely attacked. "Dr. Barnes has long been one of the most enthusiastic admirers of the extreme tendencies of modern art and a staunch admirer of the men and women who follow them," a report in the *Philadelphia Inquirer* noted. "In fact, the museum (the Barnes Foundation) is to be an enduring protest against the charges made some time ago by a group of famous alienists [i.e., psychiatrists] to the effect that most of the cubist and futurist artists are the unhappy victims of mental disease."

The critics were equally nasty. Dr. William H. Wadsworth told the *Inquirer* "the drawings of insane patients are far superior to the alleged works of art I saw at the exhibition." "It is hard to see why the Academy should sponsor this sort of trash," opined *Philadelphia Record* art critic Francis J. Ziegler. *Philadelphia Public Ledger* critic Edith Powell declared that the 19 paintings of Chaim Soutine displayed in the show "were the creations of a disintegrating mind."[12]

The fury over the Pennsylvania Academy show hardened Barnes's views. He vowed that in the future his paintings would only be seen at his foundation and according to his rules. Barnes explained his views in a 1923 *New Republic*: "We believe that paintings, trees, or any objects representing genuine human values can be made more vital, more valuable if they are studied according to methods which it has been the great achievement of a few educators to put into such shape that they can be used by teaching organizations," Barnes wrote. "We hope to effect some working plan with colleges and universities in which the scientific approach to the study of our resources shall be made a part of the curriculum."[13]

Violetta de Mazia, Barnes's closest associate, explained the foundation's teaching methods in an article published in 1942. "We do not teach students how to paint, because that would be like teaching a duck how to swim," de Mazia wrote. "We teach them how to learn to see; that is, to *perceive* the *meanings* in the events of everyday life, as well as in paintings, sculpture, music, furniture, objects in wrought-iron, trees and flowers.... We endeavor to create new habits of perception by means of objective analysis of pictures; that is, by observation of the component parts, the interrelationships of which determine the form of a painting."[14]

Barnes discussed his ideas in five books. Two points are noteworthy. First, he believed that to understand a painting, one had to spend considerable time observing the original. Barnes fervently opposed studying art by means of reproductions. Second, he believed that only those seriously interested in art should see his collection. Among his many dislikes was using a collection to create a trendy gathering place. As clause 34 of the Barnes Foundation bylaws says,

> It is ... expressly stipulated by the Donor that at no time after the death of said Donor, shall there be held in any building or buildings any society functions commonly designated receptions, tea parties, dinners, banquets, dances, musicales or similar affairs, whether such functions be given by officials, Trustees, or employees of The Barnes Foundation or any other person or persons whatsoever, or whether such functions be private or public. It is further stipulated that any citizen of the Commonwealth of Pennsylvania who shall present to the courts a petition for injunction based on what reputable legal counsel consider is sufficient evidence that the above mentioned stipulation has been violated, shall have his total legal expenses paid by The Barnes Foundation.[15]

To view the Barnes Foundation collection during Barnes's lifetime, one had to obtain a card of admission. Without a self-addressed stamped envelope, one's letter was automatically rejected. Cynthia Flannery Stine, who was Barnes's secretary in the 1930s, said that the rules for admission were simple:

> If you wrote on fine stationery engraved with your estate, if your name lurked in the social register, if you belonged to outstanding clubs and schools, you were out. But if you lived in South Philadelphia, the scene of Dr. Barnes's emergence, if you wrote on cheap paper, misspelling words, and your name was Italian or Jewish, you had a nine-to-one chance of being accepted. At least you were given an interview in our office.[16]

James Michener, a student at Swarthmore College, learned about these rules in 1928 when he tried to visit the foundation. After being turned down three times, he acquired a Pittsburgh mailing address and wrote Barnes pretending to be an unemployed steelworker. Barnes enthusiastically accepted, and spent two hours showing him around. Then Barnes found out about the deception, and began a feud with Michener that lasted the rest of Barnes's life.

ℰ Critic of the Art Establishment

In 1947, after Michener published *Tales from the South Pacific* and began a career as a novelist, Barnes routinely sent a chauffeur 50 miles to his house to deliver what Michener called "letters that were pure venom." Michener also told *Art News's* Milton Esterow about the time Barnes showed up at a lecture he was giving and spent the evening excoriating him, calling him "a damn fool" and "a lousy writer" who didn't know what he was talking about. "He challenged me to a series of public debates—on anything," Michener said. "I must say I chickened out. He was too tough."[17]

Barnes's behavior towards Michener was typical of his behavior toward those he disliked. For the last 30 years of his life, when not acquiring more art, writing books, or running the foundation, Barnes engaged in vitriolic feuds with the Pennsylvania Academy of the Fine Arts, the Philadelphia Museum of Art, the art faculties of Haverford, Swarthmore, and Bryn Mawr colleges, Temple University, the University of Pennsylvania, numerous art critics and historians, and nearly all the newspapers and magazines that wrote about him. Cynthia Stine recalled that Barnes spent twenty minutes of each working day instructing her how to forge his signature so that he could deny writing a vituperative letter if he was ever challenged in court. She also routinely signed letters with the name "Peter Kelly," an imaginary secretary who "would fill his letters with stinging insults, usually at people who wanted to visit the collection."[18] Even Barnes's dog, Fidele-de-Port-Manech, conducted an extensive ghostwritten correspondence.

Carl W. McCardle gives illustrative examples of Barnes's temper. "The Barnes gallery," McCardle wrote, "is practically hermetically sealed to socialites." "Take your guest to the movies," he would thunder to a member of the upper class who wanted to see his paintings. "You can probably understand the movies." In addition, any rich collectors were also rejected. When art collector Walter F. Chrysler Jr. asked to see the collection, a note sent by "Peter Kelly" said that Barnes "gave strict orders not to be disturbed during his present strenuous efforts to break the world's record for goldfish swallowing."[19]

Here, in its entirety, is a 1951 letter Barnes wrote to Sir Kenneth Clark, the eminent British art historian, who asked to see Barnes's paintings.

> Dear Clark:
> Your recent letter telling me of your proposed visit here prompts me to inform you that all participants in the current ballyhoos of the institution known as "The House of Prostitution of Art and Education on the Parkway," are barred from admission to the foundation's gallery.
>
> Yours truly,
> Albert C. Barnes[20]

Barnes also engaged in a feud with the Lower Merion Township Commission. In 1927, the commissioners approved the construction of houses for low-income families in areas that Barnes thought were too close to his building. He loudly announced that he was going to convert his foundation to a "national negro education center" and donate all the paintings to the Metropolitan Museum. "I shall be an humble and unworthy follower of great people" like Leopold Stokowski and Mary Cassatt, Barnes said, "who leave Philadelphia to get a breath of fresh air and never come back."

After a heated meeting, the commissioners reminded Barnes that the owner of the adjacent property bought the land with no restrictions on its use. Barnes calmed down and agreed to stay.[21]

But by the late 1940s, this protracted warfare left Barnes unsure how his collection would be maintained after his death. In his original will, he declared that the University of Pennsylvania, upon the death of himself, his wife Laura, and the trustees he had appointed, would have the power to appoint more trustees who would take control. But according to Howard Greenfeld, in the late 1940s Barnes became distressed after the University of Pennsylvania appointed Harold Stassen as president. Barnes had been dissatisfied with the university's earlier presidents and had a low opinion of the university's School of Fine Arts. Stassen initially promised to make changes in the arts school, but he did not make them fast enough to satisfy Barnes. By the summer of 1950, Barnes declared that Stassen still wore "the dunce cap that Tom Dewey had placed on him" and was "what psychologists term a 'mental delinquent,' variously known to laymen as 'dumb bunny, false alarm, phony.'"[22]

☙ The Barnes Foundation Bylaws

On August 18, 1950, Barnes received a letter from Horace Mann Bond, president of Lincoln University, an African-American school located 30 miles from the Barnes Foundation. Bond offered Barnes a position as lecturer in art for the 1950-51 school year. The job would pay only $9.25 an hour for four to six lectures a year, Bond wrote, but would be "endowed with complete prerogatives of giving the President and his fellow faculty members Hell with no restrictions.... The African people, from whom I have the honor of claiming descent, are people generally endowed with a loving, affectionate and grateful soul. I believe that you could help increase that fund of love and affection and arm it with greater intelligence and appreciation."[23]

Barnes quickly wrote back, saying he was "so overwhelmed with joy and admiration at the ease with which you disposed of the work and worry that face me in the future, that I danced the cancan." He offered to place his collection under Lincoln University's control, saying this would ensure that "when given the proper opportunity, the Negro demonstrates that his intellectual capacity is at least equal to that of the white man" and that "his endowment for aesthetic appreciation is even greater than that of the average white man."[24]

On October 17, 1950, Barnes amended paragraph 17 of the Barnes Foundation bylaws for the second and last time. After the death of Barnes and his wife, the Girard Trust bank was to fill the first vacancy on the five-person board. (After a merger, Mellon Bank assumed the Girard Trust's role.) The next four positions would be chosen "by election of persons nominated by Lincoln University, Chester County, Pennsylvania." Thereafter, new vacancies would be filled by the Girard Trust and Lincoln University acting jointly—"provided, however, anything to the contrary herein notwithstanding, that no Trustee shall be a member of the faculty or Board of Trustees or Directors of the University of Pennsylvania, Temple University, Bryn Mawr, Haverford or Swarthmore Colleges, or Pennsylvania Academy of the Fine Arts."[25]

Barnes had no further chance to change the bylaws, because on July 24, 1951, he died after a car crash. The terms of the bylaws then came into force. These are quoted at length to indicate why they were later disputed. After eight articles setting forth the structure of the Barnes Foundation, including its size, structure, and board membership, a ninth article described the "management of the corporation," and included the following paragraphs:

> 9. At the death of Donor, the collection shall be closed, and thereafter no change therein shall be made by the purchase, bequest, or otherwise obtaining of additional pictures, or other works of art, or other objects of whatsoever description. Furthermore, after the death of Donor and his wife, no buildings, for any purpose whatsoever, shall be built or erected on any part of the property of Donor.

> 10. After Donor's death no picture belonging to the collection shall ever be loaned, sold, or otherwise disposed of except that if any picture passes into a state of actual decay so that it no longer is of any value it may be removed for that reason only from the collection.

> 13. All the paintings shall remain in exactly the places they are at the time of the death of Donor and his said wife.... No individual, institution, academy, college or university shall use or employ the said administration building or its contents for any purpose other than the promotion of the advancement of education and the appreciation of the fine arts, and only in connection with the purposes of the Barnes Foundation as stated and implied in the covenants and agreements as set forth in various aspects in this Indenture and Agreement.[26]

27. During Donor's lifetime moneys available for investment or reinvestment, whether principal or income, may be invested in any good securities whether legal investments for Trustees or not; but after Donor's death, such moneys may only be invested by Donee in such obligations of the United States of America, obligations of the several States of the United States and obligations of municipal corporations and districts in the several states of the United States which are legal investments for savings banks under the laws of the state of New York."[27] [Barnes believed in investing in government securities as part of his political beliefs.][28]

30. After the death of Donor and his said wife, the gallery and the arboretum shall be open five days of each week, except during the months of July and August of each year—and solely and exclusively for educational purposes—to students and instructors of institutions which conduct courses in art and art appreciation, which are approved by the Trustees of Donee. On Saturday of each week, except during the months of July and August of each year, the gallery and the arboretum shall be open to the public between the hours of ten o'clock in the morning and four o'clock in the afternoon, under such rules and regulations as the Board of Trustees or Donee may make. It will be incumbent upon the Board of Trustees to make such rules and regulations as will ensure that the plain people, that is, men and women who gain their livelihood by daily toil in shops, factories, schools, stores and similar places, shall have free access to the art gallery and arboretum upon these days when the gallery and arboretum are to be open to the public, as hereintofore provided. On Sunday of each week during the entire year the gallery and the arboretum shall be closed to students and public alike.

34. At no times after the death of the Donor shall the art gallery be used for exhibitions of paintings or other works of art, or of any work whatsoever, that are not the property of The Barnes Foundation. At no time after the death of the Donor shall the art gallery

be used for painting, drawing, or sculpturing by any person or persons, whether said persons be students or instructors of The Barnes Foundation, or from any other institution where students are instructed how to paint, draw, or sculpture. This means specifically that The Barnes Foundation is to be maintained perpetually for education in the appreciation of the fine arts and not as a school for instruction in painting, drawing, sculpturing or any other branch of art or craftsmanship. This restriction also prohibits the copying of any of the works of art of The Barnes Foundation by any person whatsoever.[29]

To ensure that his intent would be respected, Barnes inserted a tenth article in the bylaws on amendments, saying that five of the previous articles, including Article IX, "are unamendable and shall never be amended in any manner whatsoever."[30]

❧ Early Lawsuits

In February 1952, six months after Barnes's death, the *Philadelphia Inquirer* began an assault on the Barnes will. Editorialist Harold J. Wiegand filed a suit in the Court of Common Pleas of Montgomery County, Pennsylvania, asking that the Barnes Foundation be open to the public more than one day a week. The *Inquirer* urged the court to overturn *Barnes Foundation v. Keely,* a 1934 Pennsylvania Supreme Court ruling that declared that the Barnes Foundation, because it had received a tax exemption—not as an art gallery, but as an educational institution—was entitled as a privately owned college or university to determine who could use its facilities.

In June 1952, the Court of Common Pleas dismissed the *Inquirer's* case, saying that it had no jurisdiction and that only the state of Pennsylvania could set rules for how nonprofits should function.

Laura Barnes, in an August 1952 interview with the *Washington Post*, said she hoped the Barnes Foundation's admission restrictions would continue indefinitely. "The Barnes Foundation is an educational institution," Laura Barnes said. "The pictures are a part of the art school. Not a museum. It will remain that way. There is no reason to change our policy."[31] In 1958, the state of Pennsylvania finally decided it had jurisdiction. It sued the Barnes Foundation, saying it had to show why it could restrict entrance to its collections.

The case moved through the Pennsylvania state courts. The Court of Common Pleas ruled in favor of the Barnes Foundation. On appeal, the Pennsylvania Supreme Court overturned the decision. But in ruling against the foundation, Justice Michael A. Musmanno, who wrote the decision, declared that the foundation had to be more open to the public because of clauses in its bylaws that stated the foundation would open its doors one additional day upon the death of Laura Barnes. The Commonwealth of Pennsylvania's petition, Justice Musmanno declared, called "upon the Barnes Foundation and its Trustees to show cause why they should not unsheathe the canvases to the public in accordance with the terms of the indenture and agreement entered into by Albert C. Barnes, the donor, and the Barnes Foundation, the donee."[32] In short, the court said it based its decision on its interpretation of clauses 29 and 30 of the bylaws. (But as Gilbert M. Cantor notes, the clauses could also be read as saying that the foundation could not be open to the public until after the death of Laura Barnes.)

In 1961, the Barnes Foundation agreed to open its galleries to 200 people two days a week, and would add a third afternoon after the death of Laura Barnes (which occurred in 1966). The foundation then announced that it would charge two dollars to pay for additional security. The state of Pennsylvania sued, and the Pennsylvania Supreme Court ruled that the Barnes Foundation could only charge a dollar.

Lois G. Forer, a Pennsylvania Deputy Attorney General who helped successfully prosecute the 1961 cases, said in a 1964 article in *Horizon* that the state had considered trying to remove four of the five Barnes trustees at this time for incompetence, but decided against it. She added that "certain friends of the Foundation, including lawyers who should know better," proposed that the Barnes abandon its tax-exempt status and begin to pay property taxes in return for being left alone. She says that these Barnes supporters changed their mind after being told that the foundation might have to sell its art to pay 40 years' worth of property taxes.[33]

Aside from these suits, the affairs of the Barnes Foundation were at this point exactly as Barnes would have wanted them. This is because the trustees—chiefly Violetta de Mazia, a close friend of Barnes—were very long-lived. When Howard Greenfeld surveyed the Barnes Foundation in 1986, he found that three of five members of the board were associates of Barnes; the fourth was a representative of Mellon Bank, and the fifth a Lincoln University representative. "Clearly, time had stood still behind the Foundation's walls," Greenfeld concluded. "Yet change seems inevitable.... When each of the next four trustees resigns, becomes incapacitated, or dies, he or she is to be replaced by persons nominated by Lincoln University. The Foundation's future is in their hands.... When the time comes for them to exercise their responsibility, it can only be hoped that they will act in the best interests of art, education, and the public."[34]

The only change to the Barnes Foundation indenture during de Mazia's lifetime came in 1969. The indenture stated that instructors would only be paid $5,000 per year, while gardeners would receive $2,000 and museum attendants $3,000. The foundation successfully petitioned the Montgomery County, Pa. Orphans' Court to adjust these salaries for inflation.[35]

☙ Continuing Controversies

In 1988, Violetta de Mazia died at age 89. Her $9 million estate went into a trust to support the Barnes Foundation. To replace her, under the terms of the Barnes will, Lincoln nominated its first trustee. Lincoln University chairman of the board Franklin Williams told the *Philadelphia Inquirer* that he rejected "the notion that because Lincoln University designates the trustees to be elected that it follows that Lincoln University 'controls' the foundation. It does not. The board does."[36]

In addition to the Barnes Foundation's loss of de Mazia, by 1990, two of the original trustees—Barnes Foundation president Sidney W. Frick and landscape architect Joe Langran—had also retired. Under the terms of Barnes's will, Lincoln University appointed replacements, ensuring that it had four seats on the Barnes board. The new board began to relax some of the rules Albert C. Barnes imposed. Reservations were no longer required for groups of fewer than 10, and the restrictions on the number of visitors allowed per day ended.[37] For the first time in its history, people who did not know Barnes controlled the Barnes Foundation.

The most vocal of these was Richard Glanton, Lincoln University's general counsel. A Republican, Glanton served as a fundraiser for George H.W. Bush in the 1988 presidential campaign and also worked as an assistant to Pennsylvania Governor Richard Thornburgh. Glanton was appointed president of the Barnes Foundation in 1990 for a five-year term. What he saw was a foundation with assets (art) worth between $300 million and $3 billion, but with an endowment of only $10 million that provided $1 million annually for operating costs. (The $9 million De Mazia Trust was an independent charity not under Barnes Foundation control.) The Barnes Foundation building had also deteriorated over the years. In 1985, a steam explosion damaged nine paintings. The building's electrical system had not been changed since 1923.

The amount needed to renovate the Barnes Foundation was in dispute. Glanton claimed that up to $15 million was needed to renovate the building. Glanton's foes believed the damage was far less severe. "I just laughed when Glanton got in there and started screaming about how the Barnes was sinking," former Barnes trustee David Rawson told author John Anderson. "Not only was the Barnes solvent financially when Glanton 'inherited' it, the physical plant was in good shape. We'd replaced the roof. The place was watertight."[38]

Also disputed was whether Glanton's estimate was only for the foundation's galleries or included administration buildings not used for displaying art. No independent estimates existed. Glanton's goal, according to a 1993 interview by Carol Vogel, was to turn the Barnes Foundation into "a high-visibility institution with state-of-the-art facilities and the cachet of the Frick collection." Glanton told Vogel "the problems of the Barnes were so obvious Ray Charles could see them in a swamp at midnight."[39]

Glanton also wanted to have the Barnes Foundation affiliated with a major museum, such as the Philadelphia Museum of Art. Classes could be taught, but not according to Barnes's principles. (Glanton described Barnes's theories of art as "not art history" but "hokum.")[40] A few scholarships might be available to the needy, but the classes would be as expensive as tuition at major art schools. Paintings would be freely bought and sold. In short, the Barnes Foundation would be systematically purged of everything that Albert C. Barnes believed.

To achieve these goals, Glanton faced two major obstacles. The first was the foundation bylaws. The second was opposition from the De Mazia Trust and former students of Barnes. In February 1991, Glanton petitioned the Orphans' Court of Montgomery County, Pennsylvania (which specializes in trusts and estates) to sell (or, as museums describe it, "de-accession") as many as fifteen paintings from the Barnes Foundation collection.[41]

The art world was in an uproar. "De-accessioning" is seen as a last resort, taken only when all other methods of fundraising have failed. Glanton's request also came when the global art market was in a recession. Further, it was unclear whether the Orphans' Court would grant Glanton's request without calling for a full investigation of the Barnes Foundation's books.

ℰ Breaking the Barnes Will

In June 1991, Glanton announced that the de-accessioning plan would not proceed. (According to a *Philadelphia Inquirer* article, the plan had failed because four of the five Barnes Foundation trustees were opposed to it, thinking that other measures to raise money needed to be tried before any paintings were sold.)[42] That same month, the foundation announced an agreement with Alfred A. Knopf to publish two books of art that would reproduce the foundation's collections in color in return for an advance of $700,000. (In April 1991, the Samuel I. Newhouse Jr. Foundation, whose wealth derives from publishing enterprises, including Alfred A. Knopf, donated $2 million to Lincoln University.) Glanton also allowed the Barnes Foundation building to hold parties for a private school and for the Union League Club of Philadelphia.

The Newhouse donation prompted the De Mazia Trust to petition the Orphans' Court for standing in the Barnes Foundation controversies. Standing was granted, and in 1991 the trust sued, stating that Lincoln University had improperly diverted funds that should have been used for the Barnes Foundation, and that higher bids from other publishers were not considered. The Barnes Foundation filed a counter-suit, claiming that most of the assets of the De Mazia Trust, including all of the art Violetta de Mazia collected, were stolen from the Barnes Foundation, and that all the assets of the De Mazia Trust should be transferred to the Barnes Foundation.

Richard Glanton told the *Washington Post* in May 1993 that attorneys for the De Mazia Trust were charging excessive legal fees in an effort to "loot" the trust's assets. "Mr. Glanton says whatever comes to his head," De Mazia Trust attorney Gordon Elkins told the *Post*. "It's not true, but that doesn't stop him. It's a kind of Joseph Goebbels approach."[43]

In 1992, the Barnes Foundation petitioned the Orphans' Court to allow some of the foundation's paintings to be sent on tour. Judge Louis Stefan granted the request, but imposed severe restrictions on how the exhibition could be handled. The paintings were to be removed from the foundation walls only once, and only those in good condition could be removed. Before a single painting was removed, the foundation had to submit a new program of education, which the court had to approve. When the paintings returned to the foundation, they had to be put back in the exact spots where they had been. In making these restrictions, Stefan said that he had little tolerance for the efforts of the trustees to violate Barnes's intentions. The trustees' actions "give rise to the suspicion that [their] intentions ... might be somewhat more ambitious than what their present request has indicated."[44]

In January 1995, the Barnes Foundation and the De Mazia Trust reached an out-of-court settlement in which the Foundation agreed to permanently offer art courses based on Barnes's views. It further agreed that the Trust is an independent organization over which it has no legal authority. In return, the Trust agreed to donate $2,750,000 over seven years to pay for the art courses. Montgomery County Orphans' Court Judge Stanley Ott rejected this settlement in July 1995, and litigation between the Trust and the Foundation continued.[45]

In November 1995, the Barnes Foundation reopened its galleries after being shut for 32 months. The around-the-world tour netted the foundation between $16 and $17.5 million (accounts differ on the precise amount raised), and $12 million was spent on the renovation. At first glance, nothing had changed. The renovators, employees of renowned architect Robert Venturi, restored the paintings to the positions they occupied before the tour began. Even the old thermostats were restored. The long-closed French quarry, which had cut the rock for the Barnes's steps, was reopened so that new rock could be cut.

But if the Barnes Foundation at the beginning of Richard Glanton's tenure was an educational institution with a gallery, the foundation had now become a museum. Included in the renovation was a museum shop, which sold a CD-ROM of the paintings. "The Barnes is no longer an intimate place," wrote *Philadelphia Inquirer* art critic Edward J. Sozanski. "It's more of a popular experience—that is to say, a tourist experience—and it will become more so."[46]

But even if the Barnes Foundation was a museum, it had never been zoned as one. This led Richard Glanton to yet another battle, this time with the Lower Merion Township Zoning Hearing Board—a battle that ultimately led to his downfall. Glanton announced at the time of the Barnes Foundation opening that he had grand ambitions. In an interview with the *Wall Street Journal*, he listed some of them: opening the foundation for six days a week (instead of the court-mandated three-and-a-half days), increasing the admission price from $5 to $10, building a new exhibition space on the Barnes Foundation grounds, and increasing museum attendance from 30,000 to 120,000. Without these measures, he threatened, either the Barnes paintings would go on a second world tour or the foundation would be forced to close.[47]

The courts, however, were reluctant to further violate the wishes of Albert Barnes. Only one further deviation from Barnes's wishes was permitted—the termination of the clause restricting fundraisers and parties on the Barnes grounds. In October 1995, after invitations had been sent out, the Barnes Foundation asked the Orphans' Court to allow the foundation to hold a fundraiser to celebrate the paintings' return to Merion.[48]

Judge Ott said the fundraiser could only be held if guests were barred from touring the galleries. In November 1995, the Pennsylvania Superior Court overturned the judge, allowing the fundraiser to be held as long as there was adequate security at the event."[49]

The Pennsylvania Superior Court upheld its ruling in 1996, stating that fundraising events did not violate Barnes's seemingly explicit ban on them, so long as they were not "trivial." Superior Court Justice John T. J. Kelly, writing for the majority, stated that Barnes did not explicitly prohibit "on-site fund-raising functions" at the Barnes Foundation, but that Barnes's intentions were that he did not want his "gallery trivialized by the use of it as a mere rental hall for socialites.... There is a decided difference," Justice Kelly wrote, "between fundraising functions which have as their purpose the preservation and enrichment of the assets which the Foundation is charged with protecting and a social affair which has as its purpose the inclusion of some and the exclusion of many."[50]

At the time of this victory, Glanton was in the middle of a battle with the zoning board. The battle began as the Barnes Foundation was re-opened in November 1995. The night before the re-opening, the Lower Merion Board of Commissioners passed a resolution calling on the foundation to stay closed until the parking problems were solved. The action was symbolic, since the board had no power to control museum hours.[51]

In December 1995, the board, citing overcrowding of township streets, ordered the Barnes Foundation to cut its hours to two and a half days a week and allow no more than 500 visitors a week. Glanton called the zoning board's decision a "frivolous action."[52] The board's order was not enforced, and in July 1996, the Pennsylvania Superior Court allowed the Barnes Foundation to open in July and August for the first time, once again violating an explicit instruction of Albert Barnes. However, the court upheld Judge Ott's decision to limit admission to three and a half days a week.[53]

In response to the zoning board's actions, in January 1996, Glanton launched a counter-suit against the township commissioners and 17 nearby residents. He claimed that his civil rights were violated because the zoning board's request for a limit on the Barnes's hours was prompted by racism, in as much as a majority of the Barnes board was made up of African-Americans. Glanton also charged that the township had required the Barnes Foundation to implement parking restrictions that it did not impose on nearby universities, high schools, or religious institutions; in addition, the township's insistence that the Barnes Foundation spend $10,000 on off-duty police officers for its November 1995 re-opening was unreasonable.[54]

According to court documents, Glanton denounced Barnes Watch, an organization dedicated to supporting Albert Barnes's ideals, as "sort of like a vigilante Klan organization ... a bunch of weird racists masquerading as being concerned about the Barnes." The township commissioners then counter-sued, claiming that Glanton had defamed them.[55]

Glanton's playing of the race card poisoned relations between the Barnes Foundation and the Merion community. The board responded to the Barnes Foundation's lawsuit by launching a countersuit in March 1996, charging Glanton with defamation. The countersuit charged that Glanton was a "power-hungry, politically connected" person who was determined to use the courts to crush his opponents.[56] (Niara Sudarkasa, who voted with Glanton to sue the zoning board, later recalled to John Anderson that the dispute "didn't have anything to do with race. It had to do with Richard wanting a parking lot. That's all it was about. A parking lot that would generate money.")[57]

In April 1996, Glanton held a meeting with Merion residents where he said that the foundation would drop its lawsuit against the zoning board if the board would agree to the creation of a parking lot. Robert Marmon, who was one of the residents named in the lawsuit, said that Glanton's insistence that people who opposed the foundation were racists made negotiations impossible. "Oh, so if I agree to the parking lot, I'm only a little bit racist?" Marmon told the *Philadelphia Inquirer*.[58]

Next, the board of commissioners launched a second suit against the Barnes Foundation, stating that Richard Glanton was trying to abuse the legal process by suing over phony racist charges. The suit charged that Glanton's actions against the board "were and are knowingly intentional, willful, wanton, outrageous, and were performed with evil intent."

The board filed a deposition from Charles A. Frank, who was about to resign from the Barnes board. Frank stated that Glanton never charged the board of commissioners or the zoning board with racism until two days before he launched his lawsuit against them.

Glanton told the *Philadelphia Inquirer* that the charges against him were "legal gobbledygook" and that "most racists don't like being called racists."[59] (The defamation suit was settled in 1999, when Glanton agreed to conditionally retract his charge that the Lower Merion commissioners and zoning board were racist and to pay $400,000 in damages.)[60]

The Barnes Foundation's next move came in November 1996, when Richard Glanton was added as a plaintiff. Glanton stated that this was necessary because Lower Merion commissioners and the zoning board treated the Barnes Foundation's parking problems differently from those of comparable white-run institutions and that this difference was "damaging to my reputation." The commissioners' lawyer, Paul Rosen, told the *Philadelphia Inquirer* that he believed Glanton wanted to be a plaintiff to win damages from the commissioners.[61]

In August 1997, the zoning board won a victory. Montgomery County Court Judge Bernard Moore said the Barnes Foundation had illegally transformed itself from an educational institution into a museum, and he ordered the foundation to limit its hours to two and a half days a week, with attendance at no more than 200 per day. Neighbors of the Barnes stood watch outside the museum with cameras and counters ensuring that the court's decision was enforced. Richard Glanton denounced the decision, and then flew to China in an unsuccessful attempt to negotiate a tour of Barnes paintings in Shanghai.[62]

One month later, the Barnes Foundation's allegations of racism against the Lower Merion Township commissioners were thrown out of court. District Court Judge Anita B. Brody declared that there was "no evidence whatsoever" that the commissioners made the decision against Barnes because of race, and that "the vast majority of the Barnes's evidence has nothing to do with race, but merely details various stages of a run-of-the-mill land dispute." Earlier, Judge Brody dismissed the complaint against the neighbors, stating that they had a First Amendment right to voice their opinions.[63]

Still, the controversy would not die. Lower Merion Township commissioners sued to recover court costs, which they estimated at $1.5 million. The Barnes Foundation hired former Judge A. Leon Higginbotham Jr., a veteran civil rights activist, to defend it. In November 1997, the Montgomery County Court upheld the zoning board and ordered the board and foundation to negotiate an attendance figure acceptable to both sides. (This figure would be less than the 97,000 people who visited the Barnes Foundation in 1995-1996, but more than the average 1990-1992 attendance of 42,000.)[64]

Then, in February 1998, Richard Glanton abruptly resigned. Not surprisingly, tensions between Glanton and his board had been increasing. One trustee, Lincoln University president Niara Sudarkasa, fumed that she learned about a Barnes hiring decision from press reports, not from Glanton. Glanton claimed that another trustee, Mellon Bank executive Sherman White, was secretly working with township commissioners "to prove the township's point that I was out of control."[65]

Glanton's departure was hastened by the cost of the Barnes's lawsuits. According to *Philadelphia Inquirer* reporter Anne Barnard, tax records showed that the Barnes Foundation spent $1.6 million on legal fees between 1993 and 1996. Reports at the time stated that if the zoning board won its suit to recover court costs, the

Barnes Foundation could be faced with a bill of $1.8 million. (The zoning board case dragged on for another eight years, until it was finally settled in 2006, with the zoning board being awarded $153,000.)[66] Meanwhile, the city of Rome, Italy, filed a suit against the Foundation, charging that it had agreed to make the city's Museo Capitolino a stop on the Barnes's world tour, and that Richard Glanton had breached the contract. (The city of Rome also entered documents into the court record charging that Glanton, while courting the Italians, also tried to solicit business for his law firm from Fiat and other potential clients.)[67]

While the Barnes Foundation eventually won the lawsuit against the city of Rome, the costs incurred by those who ignored Albert Barnes's wishes were considerable. In 1998, two people were named to replace Glanton. Kenneth A. Sadler, a North Carolina dentist and chairman of the Lincoln University board of trustees, was appointed president. Like Glanton, he had no professional training in arts administration. Another member of the Lincoln University board, former Arco Chemical executive Earle L. Bradford Jr., was named acting chief administrative officer. Both promised to be less confrontational and litigious, and Sadler promised to mend relationships with "those who have traditionally been friends with the Barnes," including the De Mazia Trust and Barnes Watch. He added that it was his goal to "honor the wishes of the donor to the extent that it is possible in the modern world."[68]

The day after Glanton left the Barnes Foundation presidency, foundation spokesman A. Bruce Crawley said that an immediate goal of the foundation was calming the "very litigious relationship" between the Barnes Foundation and the Lower Merion commissioners and zoning board. The lawsuits, Crawley said, were "bad for our image and bad for expenses, too."[69] After the legal fury died down, the Lower Merion commissioners tightened restrictions on how schools and other institutions in the township could expand to make the regulations more compatible with those imposed on the Barnes Foundation.[70]

Following Glanton's departure, some analysts observed that Albert Barnes's ideas were not all bad ones. *Philadelphia Inquirer* art critic Edward J. Sozanski, for example, noted in a commentary that "it always seems to me that Barnes's achievement was underplayed. The media doted on his 'eccentricities,' which included refusing admittance to people he didn't like, but the boldness of his connoisseurship—and the passion for art that inspired it—wasn't sufficiently appreciated.... One can only hope that Glanton's successors will pay closer attention to their moral obligation to the founder and be more sensitive to the need to preserve and protect this unique collection. The Barnes experience isn't just the paintings on the walls but the sense of the whole."[71]

It may be that Barnes's method of intensely looking at great art has merits that the trustees overlooked. "Are we going to provide a rich, lasting experience for a small group of people," barber Danni Melitsky told the *Washington Post,* "or are we going to trek these paintings around the world and allow a lot of people to look at them for three seconds? If you want to see the Sistine Chapel, you get on a plane and go to Italy. If scholars really are interested in the fantastic Cézannes, they can get their butts to Merion."[72]

"What the Barnes controversy is very much about," notes *Washington Times* art critic Eric Gibson, "is trusteeship. How responsibly are the officers of the Barnes living up to their obligations to perpetuate Albert Barnes's manifold legacy, a gift that is now a public trust? Are they really rescuing it for the future, or does 'saving' the Barnes now mean altering it beyond recognition?"[73]

"The Barnes affair is one of the great scandals in American art museums," noted Smithsonian Institution assistant secretary Tom Freudenheim in a 1995 interview with *National Law Journal,* "and it sets a dangerous precedent. If a will isn't sacrosanct under the law, what is? The Fricks, Barnes, and Carnegies of the future are going to think very carefully before donating their masterpieces to our institutions and to our future generations. And that is a more dangerous situation than the public understands it to be."[74]

Nevertheless, the Barnes Foundation continued to chip away at Barnes's intentions. In August 1998, the foundation received permission from Judge Ott to remain open during the months of July and August. Acting Chief Officer Earle Bradford said that Barnes's fear that summer humidity would damage the paintings was now, with better air conditioning, unfounded.[75]

As usual, the rationale the foundation gave for its efforts to escape from Barnes's provisions was that its financial condition was perilous. By 2000, the foundation had spent out its $10 million endowment and was surviving on $760,000 from the Violetta de Mazia estate. The legal expenses for all of Richard

Glanton's lawsuits had cost the foundation $5.9 million. A new climate control system had increased the foundation's expenses for electricity by $100,000 annually. A small parking lot had cost $1.7 million.

Philadelphia Inquirer reporter Patrick Kerkstra interviewed Barnes Foundation director Kimberly Camp, who said that the Barnes's situation was "critical." "Without donations, the Barnes would be unable to meet payroll and other basic expenses in six months to a year," Kerkstra reported. The foundation was making plans about what would happen if it had to dissolve. It was also starting to fundraise, and hired its first development director, Anthony Ng, away from the Pew Charitable Trusts.[76]

A 2000 Deloitte and Touche report stated that the foundation needed $85 million in the long term and $15 million in the short term to become a stable organization. The foundation began to receive $500,000 grants from the J. Paul Getty Trust, the Pew Charitable Trusts, the Wilmington Trust, and the Henry Luce Foundation.[77]

A further financial drain arose from the Third Circuit Court of Appeals ruling in 2001 that the Barnes Foundation had to pay $125,000 in legal fees to five neighbors of Barnes whom Glanton accused of being racists. The court said there was no evidence that the neighbors were racists and ordered a lower court to determine if the Barnes lawsuit was made in bad faith.

Lincoln president and Barnes trustee Niara Sudarkasa then filed a $7 million lawsuit against Richard Glanton, claiming "Mr. Glanton was corrupted by his power—he used his power to reward his friends and punish his enemies." She accused him of conducting a smear campaign against her, saying he leaked evidence to two Pennsylvania state senators alleging corruption on her part. In August 2001, Common Pleas Judge Howland W. Abramson dismissed the suit after a four-week trial, saying that Sudarkasa, a public figure, offered no evidence that Glanton acted maliciously.[78]

As a fundraising tool, the Foundation in April 2001 petitioned the Orphans' Court for permission to lend art it had in storage to other institutions, a move that the foundation calculated would bring in $500,000 in revenue. The petition stated "extending the indenture's 'no movement' and 'no loan' provisions to reach all the way to these non-gallery paintings is at odds with Dr. Barnes's treatment of them during his lifetime." The court quietly granted this petition.

☙ Bombshell

Then in September 2002, the Barnes Foundation dropped a bombshell. In order to preserve the foundation, they argued, Barnes's intentions had to be completely destroyed. They announced that they would file a suit in Montgomery County Orphans' Court to allow the foundation to move to downtown Philadelphia. They stated that if the move took place, the Pew Charitable Trusts and the Lenfest Foundation would raise $150 million to ensure the Barnes Foundation's survival. The pact between Barnes, Pew, and Lenfest was formalized in an agreement signed on September 13, 2002, by Barnes board chairman Bernard Watson, Rebecca Rimel, and H.F. "Gerry" Lenfest, with an additional third party (which turned out to be the Annenberg Foundation) to be named later. In the agreement, the Barnes Foundation agreed to expand its board from 5 to 15 members, 4 of whom Lincoln University would have the power to appoint.[79] The Pew Charitable Trusts and the Lenfest Foundation would have veto power over the next 7 nominees to the board, but not over any future nominations after the board's expansion. The Barnes Foundation would also agree to move the collections to downtown Philadelphia and support the construction of a new building on the site of the Youth Study Center at 2020 Pennsylvania Avenue. In return Pew and Lenfest agreed to donate $3.1 million between 2002-2004 to the Barnes Foundation and help to raise an additional $150 million.[80] All of the pact's terms were subsequently carried out, except that Lincoln University received five seats on the Barnes board instead of four.

Lenfest, Rimel, and Watson had previously met in December 2001, where Rimel recalled Watson saying that he wanted a "long-term solution," one that was "not a band-aid and not something that was going to work for three years and then, yet again, another crisis at the Barnes. We told him that that was the only type of, in essence, effort that we could justify because we really didn't feel that short-term fixes were in anyone's best interests"[81]

Over the next eight months, all other options for saving the Barnes Foundation were ruled out, including de-accessioning artwork or selling Ker-Feal. Barnes's intentions were apparently ruled out as well. Twice on cross-examination Rimel stated that

"I'm not familiar" with the Barnes Foundation Indenture of 1922.[82]

As soon as the Barnes, Pew, and Lenfest pact was announced, three Barnes Foundation students sued to block the move. Lincoln University also filed suit to preserve its control of the foundation. The Barnes Foundation countered by saying that the students did not have standing and that the additional trustees were necessary to aid the foundation's fundraising efforts.[83]

The foundation's next move was to answer Lincoln University's charges. It argued that the foundation would not be able to function with Lincoln controlling 80 percent of the trustees. In addition, foundation lawyers claimed that Barnes had planned to sever ties with Lincoln. In June 1951, Barnes refused to attend the Lincoln University commencement. He also did not establish formal academic ties between the foundation and the university before his death. These actions, Barnes Foundation lawyers argued, were evidence that Barnes was planning to alter his will—an action they said he was unable to take because of his sudden death in a car crash a month later.[84]

At the same time, the De Mazia Trust asked to have standing in the case. The trust's lawyers said that they were not opposed to moving the foundation or expanding the board, but insisted that the foundation's educational programs be preserved.[85]

In January 2003, newly elected Pennsylvania Governor Ed Rendell offered to act as a broker to settle the Barnes Foundation lawsuit before it came to trial. Both sides declined Rendell's offer.

Judge Ott made his first rulings in February 2003. He granted Lincoln University standing in the case, but refused to grant standing to the Barnes Foundation students and the De Mazia Trust, whom he said would be represented by Pennsylvania Attorney General Mike Fisher.[86]

A month later, Judge Ott ruled that the Barnes Foundation had to make public a "forensic audit" of the foundation's finances between 1992 and 1997 that was conducted by Deloitte and Touche. (Lincoln University lawyers requested the audit.) Barnes Watch spokesman Nick Tinari said that the audit would show that the foundation was not in dire shape. "It has always been my contention," Tinari told the *Philadelphia Inquirer*, "that the financial problems at the foundation, including the most recent ones, are its own doings, are correctable, and should not cause the intent of Dr. Barnes to be thwarted."[87]

Judge Ott gave the Barnes Foundation a month to produce the audit. After the deadline, the foundation refused, saying that the report "contains candid discussions about former personnel…that might be embarrassing to those individuals if publicly disclosed."[88]

Attorney General Fisher then stated which parts of Barnes's intentions he wished to preserve—that the art could not be moved from its original positions and could not be sold, that the foundation continue to provide educational programs, that the Barnes Foundation not merge into another institution, and that no Barnes Foundation trustee be a professor or trustee of the University of Pennsylvania; Temple University; Bryn Mawr, Haverford, or Swarthmore Colleges; or the Pennsylvania Academy of the Fine Arts.

Attorney General Fisher expressed ambivalence about whether or not art in storage could be sold. As for Lincoln University's role, he told the *Philadelphia Inquirer,* "We have said to the attorney for the Barnes Foundation, 'Look, you need to reach out and figure out a way to preserve Lincoln's role in the operations of the Barnes.'"[89]

In June 2003, Bernard Watson said that the Pew, Lenfest, and Annenberg Foundations were threatening to withdraw their support because they feared they would be accused of a "white takeover" of the foundation if they were successful. He said that Rebecca Rimel was "more concerned" about the issue of racism than the heads of the other two foundations.[90]

The next move came with the release of the Deloitte and Touche audit in July 2003. Among the audit's findings:

- The Barnes Foundation board secretly voted to fire Richard Glanton in 1993, but reversed their decision.

- The Foundation received $16 million from the world tour of the Barnes paintings and $3.2 million from sales of associated merchandise. But despite this cash flow, the foundation posted a deficit every year from 1993 to 1998.

- In 1994, Glanton allegedly told Charles Frank (Mellon Bank's trustee on the foundation board) that if he would "stop the fighting" among board trustees,

Glanton would give Frank certain financial information and allow the bank to control $2.6 million in revenues from the world tour. (Glanton told the *Philadelphia Inquirer* that this allegation was false and that Mellon would have controlled the money anyway.)

- Glanton hired a partner at his law firm, Thomas Massaro, to oversee reconstruction of the Barnes gallery, without telling the board that Massaro was a partner. Massaro billed the foundation $391,644 between 1995-98 for his services.

- Glanton hired another partner at his law firm, Eugene Cliett, to provide printing, computer, and telephone services to the Barnes Foundation without telling the board that Cliett was his law partner. Cliett billed the foundation $292,455 between 1996-97.

- In 1997, at a time the audit reported that "Glanton had reason to believe he might be replaced as president," Glanton spent $22,000 of foundation money redoing the foundation's introductory brochure, largely to replace a Barnes quotation on the brochure's front cover with one by Glanton.[91]

The Barnes Foundation argued that the audit's findings showed that Lincoln University was an incompetent steward of the foundation's assets. "We don't understand," said foundation lawyer Carl Solano, "how Lincoln can claim that it had no responsibility for what happened in the 1990s when the people who ran the foundation were the same people who simultaneously were running Lincoln as its trustees, president, and legal counsel."

Lincoln University president Ivory Nelson responded that Lincoln's control of the foundation was indirect. "Remember, Lincoln's role is simply to nominate," he told the *Philadelphia Inquirer*. "Its role is not for management and oversight." He added that when the university discovered the abuses, it took action to make sure they didn't happen again.[92]

In September 2003, some of the outside donors stated they would withdraw their support if Lincoln retained control of the

Barnes. However, Rebecca Rimel said that Pew had made no decision to withdraw funding. Lenfest said, "We felt it was fruitless to continue if Lincoln was not going to give up their control of the Barnes board.[93]

Bernard Watson warned that if the outside charities withdrew their offer, the Barnes Foundation could go bankrupt. "Given our financial situation, given the unlikely situation where we're going to get the kind of support that we need, we're going into bankruptcy, and it's that simple," Watson told the *Philadelphia Inquirer.* "We go into bankruptcy, at which point the attorney general of the Commonwealth of Pennsylvania takes over, and it's up to him what happens to the Barnes after that."[94]

Two weeks after these gloomy pronouncements, Lincoln University and the Barnes Foundation reached a compromise that allowed expansion of the foundation board to fifteen members, five of whom would be appointed by Lincoln (one more than it appointed at the time).

This concession by Lincoln University coincided with Gov. Ed Rendell's statement that he would ask the Pennsylvania state legislature to give the university $50 million for a science and technology center and for one more building; in addition, the state would help the university in a $100 million capital campaign. Both Gov. Rendell and university officials denied any *quid pro quo* between Lincoln University's decision to settle the lawsuit and the financial aid. (Lincoln, although a private university, was "state-related," meaning it was under partial state control. Gov. Rendell nominated two members of the Lincoln board.) [95]

In another move, *Los Angeles Times* art critic Christopher Knight wrote that the J. Paul Getty Trust should buy the Barnes Foundation and leave it in Merion. The Getty refused. "Unequivocally we support the plan" to move the collection, Getty president Barry Munitz told the *Philadelphia Inquirer.* "We have no interest in breaking up the collection. We have no interest in disturbing the educational philosophy" of the foundation.[96]

The three Barnes Foundation students—Sue S. Hood, William Phillips, and Harvey A. Wanik—then asked Judge Ott to grant them standing, arguing that since Attorney General Fisher supported the move, no one now represented the students' interest. In November 2003, Judge Ott allowed the students to be "friends of the court," meaning they had a limited power to seek information from the foundation, but couldn't participate in the discovery process or appeal Judge Ott's rulings. Their lawyer was also limited to asking questions about the foundation's educational program.[97]

Meanwhile, the Pew Charitable Trusts was completing its conversion into a public charity. As one condition of such a conversion, the IRS requires public charities to raise funds from outside organizations. In filings with the IRS, Pew lawyers said that the Barnes Foundation capital campaign was the "best example" of Pew's "ability to attract outside funding" and was "a prime example of the valuable role" that Pew would play as a public charity.

John Anderson, author of *Art Held Hostage*, an investigative history of the Barnes Foundation battles, noted that if Pew controlled the $150 million endowment, it could control the foundation, making its effort more like a hostile takeover of the Barnes Foundation than a bailout. "In controlling the money," Anderson charged, "Pew would have de facto control over the Barnes Foundation itself, with a powerful role in determining the future character and direction of the Barnes. In such circumstances, would the interests of Pew coincide with those of Dr. Barnes?"

Rebecca Rimel, in an interview with the *Philadelphia Inquirer*, responded that Pew would "administer" the $150 million, but Pew program officers would examine Barnes Foundation invoices and pay what was needed. This, she argued, was short of Pew actively controlling the Barnes Foundation.[98]

In December 2003, Judge Ott convened a hearing on the case. Bernard Watson testified that he had tried to get other donors interested in funding the Barnes, but only the offer from Pew, Lenfest, and Annenberg allowed the Barnes to keep its independence. Under questioning from the students' lawyer, Watson admitted that the foundation had never considered other options for raising money, such as selling Ker-Feal, selling art that wasn't on display, or raising the admission fee. Barnes Foundation director Kimberly Camp, questioned by Judge Ott, said that the foundation had never considered another tour because such a move would ensure that some of the artwork would "not be part of the collection." She said that such a tour would be a graver violation of donor intent than moving the museum.[99]

The hearing concluded with testimony from Rebecca Rimel. She stated that should Judge Ott rule that the Barnes Foundation could not move, the Pew Charitable Trusts would cut off support to the foundation. Pew had paid the Barnes Foundation's legal bills and operating expenses since 2002. Rimel said that Pew's funding of the Barnes Foundation was highly unusual for Pew, but maintained it was done because "the need was so great and the opportunity was so compelling."[100]

Judge Ott made the first of his two major rulings in *In Re Barnes Foundation* in January 2004. He allowed the expansion of the Barnes Foundation board to 15 members. But he deferred a decision on moving the museum until the Barnes Foundation presented more evidence that such a move was necessary. "The fact-finding in this case has been seriously hamstrung by the total absence of hard numbers in evaluating these proposals," Judge Ott said.

"Other than the offers for the land surrounding Ker-Feal," Judge Ott ruled, "we have not heard even a wild estimate of the value of the items owned by the foundation but not on display in the gallery in Merion. Nevertheless, the possibility of selling some or all of these holdings has been floated as the only lifeboat in the entire sea. Since the outside charities are footing the foundation's legal bills in these hearings, we accept their single-option theory as the product of zealous advocacy."

The judge noted that the Barnes Foundation indenture "does not specifically state that the gallery must be maintained in Merion or cease to exist. Nevertheless, it is difficult to dismiss Dr. Barnes's choice of venue as a minor detail."

Judge Ott also denounced Attorney General Fisher for declaring that he supported the foundation's move before the hearing was held. "The course of action chosen by the Office of the Attorney General prevented the court from seeing a balanced, objective presentation of the situation, and constituted an abdication of that office's responsibility," Judge Ott declared.[101]

While the Barnes Foundation gathered the evidence for the move's necessity requested by Judge Ott, its neighbors on Latches Lane in Merion quietly started a campaign to let it be known that they in fact wanted the foundation to stay. Judge Ott, as part of his ruling, had stated, "Lower Merion Township certainly bears some of the responsibility for the financial crisis. The foundation's attempt to raise revenues by increased public access to the gallery was met with hostility, bordering on hysteria, from some of the owners of the adjacent houses." Moreover, some of the neighbors were still suing the foundation for payment of legal fees for the civil rights lawsuit.

In September 2004, Judge Ott convened a second hearing. The Barnes Foundation presented as witnesses real estate appraisers Glen Perry and William Wood II, who testified that the 4,532 pieces of art not on display plus the Ker-Feal property were worth $24.7 million—$5 million for the real estate, $19 million for the art. The students presented an appraisal by art dealer Richard Feigen stating that the art was worth $32.8 million and the property $10 million.[102]

The next day, Barnes Foundation finance committee chair Stephen J. Harmelin described the foundation's annual deficit as "$1 million, plus, or minus," and admitted that this deficit would be covered by a $25 million endowment, which the students contended could be met without moving the foundation. Barnes Foundation attorney Ralph Wellington countered that if the foundation stayed in Merion, "donors would drop away" if the foundation lost the court case or had to sell art.[103]

The court then heard from Marie C. Malaro, former Smithsonian associate general counsel, who was called as a witness by the students. Malaro said that because the Barnes Foundation was still legally an educational institution and not a museum, the prohibitions against museums selling their art did not apply to it. "I believe that…what Dr. Barnes wanted was for his foundation to perpetuate his particular unique method of teaching art appreciation in a school format. That was made very clear in the indenture." She added that the proposed new downtown museum "will overwhelm, or at least put in the background, Dr. Barnes's purpose."

Barnes Foundation archivist Barbara Beaucar pointed to a 1923 letter Barnes wrote to his lawyer saying that "I want the gallery to be a public one after my death." Judge Ott, however, quoted from a 1941 letter from Barnes to Winterthur Museum director Henry du Pont, saying that many people wanted to come to the foundation because they were "curiosity seekers." "It is because of this that we have formulated strict regulations concerning admission to our gallery," Barnes wrote.[104]

Lower Merion Township Commissioner Joseph Manko then announced he was going to try to allow the Barnes Foundation to build an access road, which would allow visitors to come to the foundation without tying up traffic on Latches Lane. Manko and another commissioner, James Ettelson, said they would work with the Barnes Foundation to solve their parking problems if they stayed.[105]

Paul Kelly Jr., director of the Paul E. Kelly Foundation, announced that his foundation would give $100,000 to the Barnes Foundation over a two-year period if they didn't move. According to Kelly, he made the offer in the hopes that other donors would oppose the move. "Barnes was obviously an unusual man," Kelly told the *Philadelphia Inquirer*. "But I don't think it is required that the trust indenture be totally thrown out, and that is the effect of it moving downtown."[106]

The hearing then concluded. In December 2004, Judge Ott made his second, and decisive, ruling in *In Re Barnes Foundation*. The Barnes Foundation had triumphed. Barnes's indenture was destroyed. Judge Ott ruled that because the students couldn't show that the foundation could raise enough money from selling the non-displayed art and the Ker-Feal property, "we find that the foundation showed clearly and convincingly the need to deviate from the terms of Dr. Barnes's indenture."

"By many interested observers, permitting the gallery to move to Philadelphia will be viewed as an outrageous violation of the donor's intent," Judge Ott wrote. He said the foundation introduced letters by Barnes suggesting that he thought that, after his death, the foundation should become important. "To the court's thinking, these clues make the decision—that there is no viable alternative—easily reconcilable with the law of charitable trusts. When we add this revelation to the foundation's absolute guarantee that Dr. Barnes's primary mission—the formal education programs—will be preserved and, indeed, enhanced as a result of these changes, we can sanction this bold new venture with a clear conscience."

He warned, however, that if the foundation failed to meet the revenue projections it forecast, the foundation could be in court again. "If the admissions do not meet expectations, or any of the other components of the Deloitte model do not reach their targets, something will have to give."[107]

It remained unclear, however, if the restrictions in the Barnes Foundation indenture limiting hours, barring fundraising events, selling art that it wasn't exhibiting, or hosting exhibitions of art that it didn't own were still in place. Judge Ott amended his original decision to state that all those restrictions were gone as well.[108]

Because students Sue Hood, William Phillips, and Harvey Wanik were not granted standing, they couldn't appeal Judge Ott's decision. But another student, Jay Raymond, asked to appeal the decision. In March 2005, the Pennsylvania Superior Court said that it would allow Raymond to appeal Judge Ott's decision. Raymond argued that the proposed move was "such a huge change" to Barnes's intentions "that it just should not be allowed, and certainly it should not go unchallenged."[109]

The Pew, Lenfest, and Annenberg Foundations then stated they would suspend their payments until the appeal was settled. The Barnes Foundation announced it was once again in a precarious financial condition, and doubled the admission fee to $10. It persuaded the Supreme Court to hear the case on an expedited schedule (known as a "King's Bench petition").

In April 2005, the Pennsylvania Superior Court declined to hear the appeal on the grounds that Judge Ott had denied Raymond standing in February 2003, and Raymond had not appealed Judge Ott's decision within 30 days, as required by Pennsylvania Rule of Appellate Procedure 903. "We find that Mr. Raymond's failure to attain intervenor status before the orphans' court foreclosed his ability to file a cognizable appeal relative to the court's final decree," declared Pennsylvania Justice Thomas G. Saylor.[110]

Los Angeles Times reporter Christopher Knight discovered in October 2006 the Pennsylvania legislature secretly earmarked $107 million to aid the Barnes. This was after the Pew, Annenberg, and Lenfest foundations offered their bailout plan but before the start of the legal battles between the Barnes Foundation and Lincoln University. The earmarks were part of the 2001-02 Pennsylvania state budget, and included $7 million for "restoration, stabilization, and site enhancements of the Barnes Foundation and $100 million for "design and construction of a museum facility" for the foundation.

The earmarks were never mentioned during the trial or in any news stories about the Barnes Foundation. Judge Ott, responding to a letter "written by a Barnes Foundation neighbor who had discovered" the hidden appropriation, said the letter was "to my knowledge, the first time I've seen or heard" about the $107 million. Representatives from the Barnes Foundation or the

Pew, Lenfest, and Annenberg foundations did not comment on Knight's revelation.

The foundation continued to raise money. In May 2006, the foundation announced that its $150 million fundraising drive had been met. Donors of over $10 million included $30 million from the Annenberg Foundation, $25 million from the Commonwealth of Pennsylvania, $20 million from the Pew Charitable Trusts, $15 million from the Lenfest Foundation, and $10 million from the Neubauer Family and William Penn Foundations.[111]

Kimberly Camp resigned and was replaced by Derek Gilman, director of the Pennsylvania Academy of the Fine Arts.

The Barnes Foundation case was a severe blow to the cause of donor intent. Albert C. Barnes could not have been more explicit about what he wanted. But the foundation was now under the control of people he likely would have despised—the Pew Charitable Trusts, well known for their cavalier disregard of donor intent, the Lenfest Foundation, whose founder was a major patron of the Philadelphia Museum of Art, and the Annenberg Foundation, whose founder was one of Barnes's principal foes.

"Doesn't this decision," Julian Bond told the *Chronicle of Philanthropy,* "say to every donor that no matter how strong your intentions are someone with more money and better lawyers can come along some years later and change the gift?"[112]

Leslie Lenkowsky, an Indiana University public affairs professor, wrote that Judge Ott's ruling was a dangerous precedent. The decision, he noted, "cannot help but encourage courts to act more assertively to alter donations that trustees or political officials, such as state attorneys general, regard as antiquated or problematic. Since clear standards of when such intervention might be justified or what remedies might be warranted are often difficult to determine (such as in the Barnes case), the potential for overdoing it is great. The result will be not just a great deal of second-guessing about how money set aside for particular charitable purposes ought to be spent, but also greater caution on the part of donors about making unusual or politically controversial bequests."[113]

Thomas Freudenheim added that the Barnes decision should provide a warning for donors seeking to build their own museums that the likelihood that these museums would honor posthumous donor requests was nil. "I'm all for supporting our museums—so go ahead, be generous," Freudenheim wrote. "But if you really love what you've collected and want to find a good home for it, you should probably face reality: there is no good home. And you might find that, when you're ready, selling what you own while you're around (along with the joy of playing cat-and-mouse with competing auction houses, getting your name on a sales catalog and having a front-row seat at the auction) can be just as exciting as collecting was. And, in any case, you won't be fooling yourself."[114]

Drexel University historian Robert Zaller hoped that the destruction of the Barnes Foundation could be stopped before the museum was forced to move. "No deed, no trust, no donor is ever completely proof against changing circumstances," he writes. "That is why the law of trust provides for prudent adjustment to such changes. The Barnes Foundation wasn't perfectly provided against all contingencies, more than any other child of time, and it was certainly not immune to the abuse of fools. But the trust need not have been betrayed. And we, the community, need not accept that betrayal in our name."[115]

Although the obstacle to the Barnes Foundation move posed by the Barnes's bylaws had been removed by Judge Ott's decision, the move stalled in 2007, due to a battle between Philadelphia Mayor John Street and Philadelphia City Council Majority Leader Jannie Blackwell about where to put the Youth Study Center.

Meanwhile, the next legal move came from Montgomery County, Pennsylvania. In June 2007, the county proposed that the Barnes Foundation sell its Merion properties to it for $50 million, which the foundation could use for an endowment. The foundation would then pay rent to the county. The county proposed selling tax-exempt bonds to pay for the purchase. In a separate move, the county formally petitioned Judge Ott to reconsider his December 2004 decision, claiming that it had new information not considered three years earlier.[116]

Bernard Watson rejected the county's offer, stating that the foundation had made "binding commitments to carry out the move" to Philadelphia.[117]

In August 2007, the Friends of the Barnes Foundation held a fundraiser across the street from the Barnes Foundation. Signs facing the Barnes now read "The Barnes Belongs in Merion" and "Join The Fight to Save The Barnes." According to retired physician Walter Herman, the Friends of the Barnes had spent

$75,000 in legal fees, but "we're optimistic" that their group would ultimately prevail.[118]

In March 2008, Councilwoman Janine Blackwell removed the block on the transfer of the Youth Study Center, in return for the city constructing a new community center in her district and a new high school.[119] (The replacement Youth Study Center was opened in December 2012, costing taxpayers $112 million.)[120]

In March 2008, Judge Ott considered the cases of Montgomery County and the Friends of the Barnes Foundation. Joining the Barnes Foundation was the Pennsylvania Attorney General's office, in its role as regulator of charities in the state.

Montgomery County stated that the "new information" it had to present was its offer to buy the Barnes Foundation property and recoup the costs of the purchase through the rent the foundation would pay. It also noted that Lower Merion Township had changed its zoning codes to allow the foundation to create a bigger parking lot that would enable 140,000 people to visit the Barnes Foundation each year.

The Barnes Foundation countered that Judge Ott had denied the Friends of the Barnes Foundation standing in the past, so he should deny the organization standing again. It argued that the only organization with standing to challenge the foundation's decision was the Pennsylvania Attorney General, as charitable regulator. Montgomery County's statement that it had standing "to nurture the economic welfare of its citizens," the foundation contended, was a dangerous precedent that if allowed by the court could mean that the county could intervene at any time for any reason in cases involving county residents or businesses.[121]

In May 2008, Judge Ott ruled in favor of the Barnes Foundation. He agreed that neither Montgomery County nor the Friends of the Barnes Foundation had standing to sue. The Pennsylvania Supreme Court had ruled that a private school's alumni association could not challenge school administrators. Because of that precedent, "we conclude that, as many who have gone before, the Friends lack standing because they have no interest beyond that of the general public." Judge Ott disqualified Montgomery County because of a Commonwealth Court decision that the state attorney general's power to represent the public interest outranked any powers Montgomery County had in this case.[122]

The Montgomery County Commissioners held a contentious public hearing about what they should do, and then decided, by a 2-1 margin, not to appeal Judge Ott's decision.[123]

The Friends of the Barnes Foundation also announced they were ending their suit. Walter Herman, a member of the group who lived across the street from the Barnes Foundation building in Merion, told the *Philadelphia Inquirer*, "we recognized very well that the issue of standing, narrow as they were, did not favor us at all."[124]

The second Barnes Foundation was still two years away from construction, but improvements on the Benjamin Franklin Parkway, home of the new Barnes Foundation as well as other Philadelphia art museums, began in July 2008. The improvements in landscaping and highway design cost $17.1 million, which was paid for by $6.4 million from the city of Philadelphia, $6.4 million from the state of Pennsylvania, and $4.8 million from foundations, including $2 million from Pew, $1.3 million from the Knight Foundation, and $1 million from the William Penn Foundation.[125]

Ground was broken for the new Barnes building in November 2009 and construction proceeded steadily through 2010. The Friends of the Barnes Foundation continued to protest. In January 2011, on Albert Barnes's 139th birthday, the group stretched crime-scene tape across the street from the Barnes Foundation in Merion, with signs reading, "A Man's Will Should be Honored."[126]

The Friends of the Barnes Foundation returned to court, this time inspired by *The Art of the Steal*, a 2009 documentary highly critical of the Barnes Foundation's move. Most of the people involved in the Barnes Foundation case refused to be interviewed, but one of the few involved in the case who was willing to go on the record was former Pennsylvania Attorney General Mike Fisher.

At issue was the question of whether Lincoln University had received any sort of payback from the state in return for surrendering control of the Barnes Foundation in 2003. It was true that between 2005 and 2010 the state of Pennsylvania had opened up its checkbook to pay for many new buildings at Lincoln, including $22 million for a residence hall, $40 million for a science and technology center, as well as tens of millions more for a cultural center, new computer labs, and a new student union.

State officials and the university vigorously denied that all this funding had anything to do with the Barnes Foundation.

Philadelphia Inquirer reporter Kristin E. Holmes reported in 2011 that university officials "called the influx of funding an effort to make up for the years that the school lagged behind other state-related schools in the funding allotted."[127]

Mike Fisher, however, stated in *The Art of the Steal* that he told Lincoln University in 2002 and 2003, "It was pretty clear to me that they [Pew, Lenfest, and Annenberg] weren't going to give 50, 70, 100 million dollars without getting control of the Barnes board. I had to explain to them [Lincoln's trustees] that maybe the Attorney General's office would have to take some action involving them that might have to change the complexion of the board. Whether I said that directly or I implied it, I think that they finally got the message."[128]

It was this comment that led the Friends of the Barnes Foundation in February 2011 to ask Judge Ott to re-open the case, arguing Fisher had, as attorney general, "absolutely violated his fiduciary duties by taking an improper role and without advising the honorable court of this role."[129]

A month later, Judge Ott asked the Barnes Foundation and the Pennsylvania Attorney General's office why he should not re-open the case. Pennsylvania's Senior Deputy Attorney General, Lawrence Barth, told the *Philadelphia Inquirer* that his office's role as charitable regulator was to be "an advocate. In this case, we advocated along with the Barnes Foundation" to support the move "because we thought it was the best way…to maintain the Barnes."[130]

The Barnes Foundation closed in Merion in July 2011. At this time, the foundation announced that its $150 million capital campaign had succeeded, with over $200 million in pledges. The major donors included $47 million from the state of Pennsylvania, $30 million from Annenberg, $20 million from Pew, $15 million from Lenfest, $10 million from the Neubauer Family Foundation, and $10 million from the William Penn Foundation. Donors of between $1.5 million and $10 million included the Comcast, Horace W. Goldsmith, Dorrance, Mellon, and Wells Fargo Foundations, Comcast and PNC Corporations, and Aileen and Brian Roberts. (Brian Roberts was the president of Comcast.)[131]

Richard Ralph Feudale, a lawyer and author of *Barnes Rune 2012: Decoding the Mysteries of Pennsylvania's Barnes Foundation*, joined the Friends of the Barnes Foundation in court: In October 2011, Judge Ott once again declared that neither the Friends of the Barnes nor Feudale had standing and rejected reopening the case. He also stated that at no point did General Fisher "hide his position from me" about Lincoln University or anything else.[132]

The Barnes Foundation then asked Judge Ott to allow it to recover $65,000 in court costs. In March 2012, the judge demanded that the Friends of the Barnes pay $25,000 to the Barnes Foundation and that Feudale pay $15,000, stating that both parties were guilty of "vexatious, arbitrary, and bad-faith conduct." He also declared the only reason Feudale entered the case was to promote his book and that Feudale's "brief and argument were devoid of any legal substance, relying instead on historical anecdotes, snippets of art history, and his own brand of philosophical musings."[133]

May 2012 marked the Barnes Foundation's opening in downtown Philadelphia. The event was a triumph, and everyone involved in the move covered themselves in glory. The architects of the new Barnes building, Tod Williams and Billie Tsien, won major architectural prizes. The Philadelphia Award, the city's highest civic honor, went in 2012 to Aileen Roberts and Joseph Neubauer for their role in raising money for the move. By the end of 2012, over 216,000 patrons had paid $18 to visit the Barnes—eight percent more than the museum projected.

Even the Barnes Foundation's lawyers got to bask in victory. In January 2013, Ralph Wellington of Schander Harrison Segal & Lewis told members of the International Association of Trial Lawyers how he spent a decade destroying the Barnes Foundation indenture. The conference was held in the auditorium of the new Barnes Foundation building.

Wellington's destruction of donor intent, reported the *Philadelphia Inquirer*'s Chris Mondics, "is now grist for law schools and a staple in the lore of U.S. litigation."[134]

Foes of the Barnes move were comforted by the statements of former Barnes director Kimberly Camp, who blogged about the opening of the new Barnes Foundation. Camp stated that the reason for the Barnes move had nothing to do with the foundation's alleged near-bankruptcy in 2002. "Bankruptcy was not the reason we filed the petition to move the Foundation to the city," Camp wrote. "At the time the petition was filed, the Barnes Foundation had a cash surplus and we had no debt—none." She said the reason for the Barnes moving was the statement in the Barnes Foundation Indenture that "if the foundation was no longer viable in Merion, the collection should go to a Philadelphia institution."[135]

Philadelphia Inquirer columnist Joseph DiStefano noted that, while Camp may never have said the Barnes Foundation was headed towards bankruptcy, many other people at the time warned of the foundation's financial peril. Bernard Watson, for example, told the *Philadelphia Inquirer* in 2003 that "given our financial situation, given the unlikely situation where we're going to get this kind of support that we need, we're going into bankruptcy, and it's that simple."[136]

The Barnes Foundation case remains a troubling one, leaving unanswered the fundamental question: *Why* was the solution agreed upon by Bernard Watson, Rebecca Rimel, and H.F. "Gerry" Lenfest in 2002 the one best way, the only answer to the Barnes's problems? *Why* did the Barnes have to move—particularly since the building in Merion was renovated in 1995? Wouldn't it have made more sense to raise money for the Barnes endowment and work things out with the residents of Latches Lane? Was the Barnes move a titanic achievement—or a major philanthropic mistake?

"The Barnes Foundation, that grand old curmudgeonly lion of a museum, has been turned into what may be the world's most elegant petting zoo," observed *New Republic* art critic Jed Perl. "The new building, in a tastefully glamorous late-modern minimalist style familiar from the shelter magazines, suggests a posh spa, with the building's comfortable seating, casual coffee bar, reflecting pool, and courtyard gardens."[137]

Philadelphia Inquirer critic Peter Dobrin warned that the event most comparable to replacing the real Barnes building in Merion with a fake replica in Philadelphia was what happened to the Philadelphia Orchestra when it left its old, small home at the Academy of Music for the acoustically excellent, aesthetically sterile Verizon Hall. "The move did nothing to arrest the decline in attendance," Dobrin wrote, "or the public's love for the Academy as the only authentic setting for the orchestra...All that planning, and that stumping, all those marketing studies—and no one heeded the fact that for many, a night at the orchestra wasn't simply a transaction of bringing the orchestra's sound faithfully to the listener."[138]

Could it be that in a decade, art lovers might wonder what had been lost when the Barnes moved?

New Criterion managing editor James Panero, while considering the Barnes Foundation indenture of 1923 an example of "over-precision" that "rendered the foundation brittle," nonetheless concludes that "breaking the independence of the Barnes Foundation—and moving the collection into a museum that, however extraordinary, would horrify Barnes himself—nevertheless comes with a serious cost. These actions undermine the general principle of donor intent. They set a precedent that could discourage future donors from believing that their intent will be honored. All philanthropy involves an act of trust between giver and recipient. These actions erode that sense of trust, to the detriment of future philanthropy."[139]

In 2014, Bernard Watson retired as chairman of the Barnes board. Joseph Neubauer, long-time chairman of Aramark and head of the Neubauer Family Foundation, succeeded him.[140]

The Barnes Foundation in 2015 then selected Thomas Collins, head of the Pérez Art Museum in Miami, to be its director.[141]

The arboretum of the original Barnes Foundation building in Merion was reorganized in 2014 to be an autonomous nonprofit with an admission fee of $5, reduced from the $15 when the Barnes Foundation was at Merion. Reservations were also ended and parking was made free. The *Philadelphia Inquirer*'s Virginia A. Smith said that the arboretum was "an understated, old-school affair" and that its management hoped that visitors would learn about the horticultural ideas of Laura Barnes.[142]

In 2015, the Montgomery County Orphans' Court and the Pennsylvania Attorney General's Office approved a merger between the Violetta De Mazia Trust and the Barnes Foundation. The court ruled that the "Barnes-De Mazia Education Program," as the merged organization was called, would be used to support programs related to Albert C. Barnes's ideas about seeing art, including scholarships, an annual De Mazia lecture, and a research fellowship. The De Mazia Trust's programs of art education for public schools and prisoners would also be continued. The merger added $8 million to the Barnes Foundation endowment.[143]

While the De Mazia Trust merger strengthened Albert Barnes's ideas, in many other ways the Barnes Foundation belittled its founder. The foundation funded *Barnes and Beyond: In The End, Truth Prevails,* a documentary done in response to the 2009 film *The Art of the Steal* and including interviews with many of the people who refused to be interviewed in 2009. The film was put on

YouTube in 2016, but as of July 2017 only had 188 hits compared to *The Art of the Steal's* 164,000.[144]

A 2015 exhibition, "The Order of Things," had installation artists Mark Dion, Judy Pfaff, and Fred Wilson mock Albert C. Barnes's ideas about how his paintings and other objects were arranged. "Even though we can't take them [the paintings] apart because of Barnes's mandate," curator Martha Lucy told the *New York Times*, "we can still have artists engage in what's great and what's problematic about them.... Once Barnes collected his works and froze them in a very particular context, the art is not allowed any other kinds of discussions."[145]

Thomas Collins announced in 2016 that the Barnes Foundation, having completed "Phase 1" with the move to downtown Philadelphia, would launch "Phase 2," in which Barnes's paintings would be deemphasized further in favor of special exhibitions which had little or nothing to do with Barnes's ideas. Martha Lucy, who was promoted to deputy director, said that the adult education courses would be re-organized to emphasize "a broader interpretive paradigm" that had nothing to do with Barnes's views.[146]

In January 2017, the foundation spent $5.8 million to add an additional 6,000 square feet of space, including an expanded area for classes and a new restaurant.[147] The foundation also announced that beginning in the 2017-18 school year, Lincoln University would have a museum studies major, with many courses offered at the Barnes Foundation.[14]

In March 2017, nearly five years after the Barnes Foundation re-opened in downtown Philadelphia, the *Philadelphia Business Journal* surveyed the museum's economic impact in Philadelphia. Attendance at the Barnes Foundation, capped at 60,000 a year in Merion, rose to 265,396 in 2016, with an admission price of $25. The foundation's 2015 Form 990 reported income of $28.4 million, expenses of $22.7 million, and an endowment of $62 million. Over 18,000 people had become members of the foundation, and fundraising for 2016 brought in $9.6 million.

The piece did not address the issue of donor intent, and Rebecca Rimel, H.G. "Gerry" Lenfest, and Bernard Watson were not interviewed. Ralph Wellington said that seeing busloads of children visiting the Barnes Foundation "just made me so happy." He was not asked why it was necessary to spend $150 million just to have children visit the museum.[149]

Drexel University historian Robert Zaller offered a contrary view. "The experience of the collection, and its educational function, has been transmogrified by the so-called museum in which it is now housed and the 'cultural' carnival that now surrounds and tarts it up," he wrote. "What Henri Matisse called the only sane place in the world to view art has now become just another stop on the bus tour."[150]

All in all, a very sobering story of how endangered donor intent has become in the nonprofit world.

7

The Buck Trust and
Marin Community Foundation

The Buck Trust case is the most obscure of the nine philanthropies discussed in this section.[1] It is the only one that involves a regional foundation rather than a national one. On the surface, it was concluded in a way that upheld donor intent. After a lengthy battle described by newspapers as "the Super Bowl of Probate," the courts ruled that the fortune of Beryl Buck, a long-time resident of Marin County, California, should be used in the way she intended—to help the people of that county.

But the Buck Trust case is not that simple. Two lessons can be learned from it. First, it clearly shows the doctrines that opponents of donor intent use. Second, the case was a Pyrrhic victory for supporters of donor intent. The trust's money is now largely used in ways favored by those who wanted to break the will. The only restriction is that those funds are limited to charities and nonprofits in Marin County.

☙ The Estate of Beryl Buck

Aaron Wildavsky, a political scientist at the University of California at Berkeley, noted that the Buck case has deep implications for nonprofits: "Does inconvenience satisfy the general rule that bequests may be set aside if they cannot be fulfilled?"

> What mattered more, however, was the ideological-cum-philosophical question: Did foundation policy include a commitment to carry out public policy defined as achieving greater equality of condition or should foundation policy respect the will of the benefactor and the social and economic systems that made this largesse possible...? At stake was the

143

legitimacy of using money derived from the private sector of society to oppose capitalism.[2]

The wealth of the Buck estate came from oil. In 1870, the Buck family settled in California to begin farming. In 1911, Frank Buck, Beryl Buck's father-in-law, bought 30,000 acres of land in Kern County, California, which had some oil wells. He founded the Belridge Oil Company, a private corporation, to handle the family's oil business. His son, Leonard Buck II, who died in 1953, held a large portion of Belridge Oil shares, but his primary interest was medicine. He spent his career at the University of California at San Francisco, where he organized the university's museum of pathology. When he died, his entire estate, including the Belridge Oil shares, was willed to his widow, Beryl. This gave her a 7 percent interest in Belridge Oil.

By all accounts, Beryl Buck (1896-1975) was a private woman who preferred to do charitable work quietly. "Mrs. Buck was a generous person," Judge Homer Thompson concluded in his decision on the Buck Trust case. "She made many charitable gifts during her lifetime. For example, she gave gifts of money, food and/or clothing to people who had worked for her and people she knew who suffered from catastrophic illness. Mrs. Buck preferred to make her charitable gifts anonymously. She especially wanted to help persons who had done what they could to help themselves, but because of illness or accident, needed assistance."[3]

Beryl Buck's nephew, Lee Hamilton, told the *Los Angeles Times* that his aunt was particularly worried about middle-class people who had few resources to fall back on when misfortune struck. "One thing that she always stressed with me was charity for the middle-class people that had catastrophic diseases and disorders and accidents. A man would be making good money, but for some reason someone in the family had high medical bills, and they would have to slowly sell off his assets, and then he'd end up on welfare."[4] Likewise, in a memorandum to her attorney, John E. Cook, Beryl Buck responded to one of the drafts of her will that Cook had prepared, stating that the language restricting donations to Marin County "isn't as specific as I think it should be for Marin County only, and for middle-class people for illnesses, rehabilitation so they won't lose their homes, automobiles, et cetera, which they have saved for all their lives."[5]

Beryl Buck lived in Marin County from 1938 until her death. The county changed considerably during that time. When she settled there, it was largely farmland; when she died, it was one of America's wealthiest counties. But her interest in improving the county remained constant.

In 1961, John E. Cook went to the San Francisco Foundation (SFF), a community foundation, to see if it was willing to manage what was then called the Leonard W. Buck Trust. Beryl Buck asked that the trust's distributions be limited to Marin County, and the foundation agreed to the restriction. On July 11, 1961, foundation president John May wrote to Beryl Buck, saying, "I can assure you that the Foundation will do its best to administer the Leonard W. Buck Foundation in accordance with your wishes."[6]

Five versions of Beryl Buck's will were drafted between 1961 and 1973. Each contained a clause limiting donations to Marin County. No one from the foundation informed Mrs. Buck or her attorney of any intention to change or challenge this clause. On June 25, 1973, Beryl Buck executed her fifth and final will. The second clause of the tenth article contained this provision:

> The trustees shall have investment, management, and custody of the assets to be known as THE LEONARD AND BERYL BUCK FOUNDATION, to be held by a separate fund subject to distribution through the SAN FRANCISCO FOUNDATION. They shall be governed by the rules, regulations, resolutions, and declarations governing THE SAN FRANCISCO FOUNDATION as now or here after existing: provided always that such rules, regulations, resolutions, and declarations are not inconsistent with the provisions of decedent's will and any decree of final distribution directing that the distribution from THE LEONARD AND BERYL BUCK FOUNDATION shall always be held and used for exclusively nonprofit, charitable, religious, or educational purposes in providing care for the needy in Marin County, California, and for other nonprofit charitable, religious or educational purposes in Marin County, California.[7]

By accepting these terms, the foundation agreed that the Buck Trust would be limited to Marin County, and that this limitation would have precedence over any of the foundation's own rules and regulations.

In Beryl Buck's last years, the worth of her estate grew as the Belridge Oil shares became more valuable in the wake of the 1973 oil embargo. Descendants of its two founders largely owned Belridge Oil. Since its stock was rarely traded, the exact value of the company was not known. The courts concluded, however, that Beryl Buck knew the worth of her shares was increasing. In a conversation with Rev. John Evans, a long-time friend, she said that Belridge Oil's Kern County properties were "the largest untapped oil reserves in the United States." She told another friend that the stock should not be sold because "it was a gold mine and it would be for future generations."[8]

Beryl Buck died on May 30, 1975. The worth of her estate was finally determined in December 1979, when Belridge Oil was bought by Shell Oil for $3.65 billion. This made Beryl Buck's seven percent worth $253 million. The San Francisco Foundation became the third largest community foundation in the country, with total assets of over $280 million. In the same month, the foundation signed a preliminary decree, stating that it would honor Beryl Buck's restrictions on the distribution of funds. It also agreed to Buck's stipulations in March 1980, when the courts published a final decree awarding the administration of the Buck Trust to the San Francisco Foundation.

As late as 1983, the San Francisco Foundation still publicly stated that it would honor Beryl Buck's wishes. "We feel a deep responsibility for spending Mrs. Buck's money the way she wanted it spent," board member Robert C. Harris told *The Nation's* Peg Brickley and Fred Powledge. Harris added that the trust would be honored until "the day ... comes that we fill every rut in the roads in Marin County."[9] Privately, however, the foundation was plotting to break the will.

ℰ The Foundation Moves to Break the Will

In determining donor intent, courts use a rule known as *cy pres,* taken from the French term *cy pres comme possible*—"as close as possible." When it is no longer possible to honor a donor's wishes exactly, courts try to honor them as closely as possible. In deciding whether a donor's original intent can be fulfilled, courts first seek to determine if the donor's wishes are illegal, impracticable, or impossible. If they are, the will is modified.

Some employees of the San Francisco Foundation apparently knew about *cy pres*. In an internal memo dated July 26, 1979, and addressed to foundation counsel Robert C. Harris, Wayne Lamprey, the foundation's legal counsel, argued that "the San Francisco Foundation will in all [likelihood] never be able to establish that expenditures for charitable purposes in Marin County are impossible,"[10] since even an area as wealthy as Marin County has many people in need of charity. But it might be shown that the Buck Trust was inexpedient, or that Beryl Buck did not know how large her estate would be, and that therefore she would have wanted the funds to be used elsewhere.

Lamprey cited as evidence *Hoyt v. Bliss,* a 1919 Connecticut case in which a trust was established for a single student. The court ruled that if the trust's income was large enough to support a second student, then this change in the trust should occur, since the donor did not know how large the trust would be. To support a single student in "extravagance or wastefulness" was not what the donor intended.[11] "Like the trustor in *Hoyt,* it could be argued," Lamprey wrote, "Mrs. Buck did not anticipate that trust income would exceed the amount reasonably required to accomplish the trust purpose." Since Marin County was wealthy, the funds needed to help the poor there were far less than the amount of the Buck Trust, so the best way to honor Beryl Buck's wishes was to have a court overturn the Marin County restriction.

On November 10, 1979, while the Buck will was still being probated, the San Francisco Foundation distribution committee met to discuss changing the will. In June and July 1980, three months after the probate court's final decree, the committee again discussed breaking the will. That July, it "agreed to follow the letter of the will until [the foundation had] enough experience to determine that this is not feasible." As foundation president Martin Paley later testified, the agreement to honor the Buck Trust was "not a forever commitment."[12]

The Buck Trust increased the San Francisco Foundation's endowment tenfold. This entirely changed the nature of the foundation. One distribution committee member said at an April 1983 meeting, "we must figure out more creative ways for the SFF to retain its integrity in the presence of a 'thousand pound gorilla' sitting in our midst. Buck has been a great opportunity and a great dilemma."

In May 1983, the San Francisco Foundation launched a formal effort to break the will. On May 24, Martin Paley wrote a memorandum saying that

> it is my judgment that the present method of organization and management of The San Francisco Foundation does not easily accommodate the long-term pursuit of full expenditure of Buck monies in Marin County. I believe this because I see an increasing strain placed on policies, procedures and personnel of the organization by maintaining two rather disparate standards of operation between Marin and the rest of the Bay Area. The Foundation therefore is faced with one of two choices—either redesign the structure and program of the San Francisco Foundation in order to accommodate the Marin responsibility with less strain to the institution or modify the nature of the Buck Trust to conform to and become compatible with the values and procedures of the Foundation as a whole.[13]

The foundation chose the latter course and spent the last half of 1983 preparing its lawsuit. On December 13, the distribution committee voted 4-2 to file suit to break Beryl Buck's will. The two votes opposing the suit were from Marin County residents.

The San Francisco Foundation seems to have consulted few people before deciding to break the will. Recipients of Buck Trust grants were only told of the lawsuit on January 28, 1984—one day before it was filed. Even Judy Edgar, the foundation's grants officer for Marin County, was told only a week before. The foundation also had few allies. One group that did offer support was Public Advocates, a San Francisco public-interest law firm that believed the Buck Trust funds would be better spent on low-cost housing and social services. (As early as 1980, Public Advocates employees were exploring ways to break the Buck Trust.) [14]

❧ 'Effective' Philanthropy

In a December 22, 1983 memorandum to California Attorney General John Van de Kamp, the San Francisco Foundation

148

outlined its plan. It had "consulted with a number of nationally recognized experts in various aspects of philanthropy" who were "substantially unanimous" in their view that the Buck Trust should be broken. But the foundation cited only two experts: John Gardner, former president of the Carnegie Corporation, and John Simon, a Yale Law School professor who also directed Yale's Program on Non-Profit Organizations. In a brief filed with the court, the San Francisco Foundation said it had also met with Ford Foundation president Susan Berresford, former Ford program officer Paul Ylvisaker, the Gerbode Foundation's Tom Layton, and the Minneapolis Foundation's Tom Berresford.[15]

Simon was an advocate of "strategic" or "effective" philanthropy. In a petition filed with the Marin County Superior Court in February 1984, he argued that historically, all foundations begin with local concerns; as their endowments grow, however, they expand—or should expand—to include national issues. "In its infancy, a foundation's charitable program may be narrowly constructed, with severe limits on the size and shape of the beneficiary community. But as the resources grow, the giving program reaches out beyond its parochial origins to address a more populous and diverse slice of humanity." The Ford Foundation, he said, began with Henry Ford's efforts to help Detroit, but later expanded to improve the country. "Charity may begin at home, but large-scale charity does not stay there."[16] Restricting the Buck Trust to Marin County "seems to violate principles of fairness and distributive justice," given that federal and state tax exemptions enabled the trust's endowment to grow.[17]

But as Robert B. Buck, Beryl Buck's grandnephew, noted, using "distributive justice" as a standard for judging donor intent would have two harmful consequences. First, it would create "reluctance on the part of persons wishing to make a charitable bequest, simply because few if any individuals wish to have their wishes second-guessed by those who presume to know better how to spend the donor's charitable dollars." Second, "breaking Beryl Buck's Will could only result in an avalanche of litigation, since the result would be ample precedent for an attack on any charitable institution and its trustees wherever and whenever it is perceived by some that the use of the charitable funds is not the 'best use' of these funds."[18]

For two years, the parties in the suit argued in pre-trial negotiations. At least twenty settlements were proposed, and all were rejected, including one by Public Advocates lawyer Sid Wolinsky. This would have divided the Buck Trust into two funds: one for Marin County and the remainder for the San Francisco Bay area. Martin Paley became extremely unpopular in Marin County; billboards were erected to denounce him. One dry cleaner collected 30,000 signatures for a petition demanding that the Buck Trust be upheld, and also distributed 6,000 bumper stickers that said, "The Buck Stops Here."[19]

Paley publicly argued that if Beryl Buck knew how much she was worth, she would have altered her will. He told the *Chronicle of Higher Education* in 1985 that his goal was not to destroy Buck's intentions "but rather to enforce her primary goals of making a meaningful, productive contribution to charity and creating a significant memorial to her husband. We believe that had Mrs. Buck known of the true value of her trust, she would not have limited the use of its income so narrowly."[20]

On January 2, 1986, California Attorney General John Van de Kamp announced that he would oppose the San Francisco Foundation. In a memorandum, he said that the lawsuit was "premature" in that the foundation had arbitrarily restricted the Buck Trust funds by barring "religious grants, grants for medical research and other scientific research, endowments, literary publications, government funded programs and funding of deficits for ongoing charitable projects." Further, the foundation was using "new and untested concepts of 'relative need' or 'inefficient philanthropy,'" seeking to replace time-honored means of modifying trusts (that is, determining whether the donor's wishes were illegal, impossible, or impracticable). He also suggested that the foundation might be removed as administrator of the trust, and contended that it should be "surcharged" for the lawsuit's growing legal bills.[21]

If "distributive justice" was to be the new standard of donor intent, California Deputy Attorney General Carole Kornblum noted, "there would be no reason that the trustees and directors of other charities could not sit back and say, 'There are starving people in Africa, why don't we change things?'" Should the San Francisco Foundation prevail, "you destroy the certainty that exists under trust law now, and that law is designed to encourage people to leave money to charities."[22]

❧ The Trial

On February 3, 1986, the case of *Estate of Beryl H. Buck, Deceased* began in Marin County Probate Court. Marin County, the California Attorney General, the Buck Trust's lawyer and bank, and a group of Marin County charities opposed the San Francisco Foundation, Public Advocates, and 46 San Francisco-area charities. From the beginning, the foundation was forced to retreat. Two days into the trial, Judge Homer Thompson ordered the release of 60 documents. These showed that the foundation had begun considering ways to break the trust ten days after it signed an initial decree to receive the funds, and that it had spent $230,000 in trust assets publicizing its efforts. A 1983 memorandum by Martin Paley noted that the foundation "presently has little difficulty in responding to an abundance of qualified grant proposals" from Marin County charities.[23]

A month into the trial, Judge Thompson ruled that the foundation could not compare the "efficiency" of grants in Marin County with grants outside the county. In other words, the charitable needs of the San Francisco area were not pertinent to the case; only Marin County's needs would be considered. Thompson also ruled that if the foundation were to argue that the Buck Trust restrictions were impracticable because of the foundation's own policy for distributing funds, the foundation's opponents could use this to argue that the foundation had done a poor job and should be removed as the trust's administrator. The foundation's attorney, Stephen Bomse, pleaded with the judge, arguing that evidence of the needs of people outside Marin County was necessary to show why the foundation acted as it did. "If we are wrong," Bomse said, "we really do not have a case to offer the court.[24]

Judge Thompson denied Bomse's request, but agreed to allow a one-week recess. Out of court negotiations began, and the foundation agreed to allow 80 percent of the Buck Trust funds to remain in Marin County. This offer was accepted by Marin County, but rejected by the Buck Trust and the California Attorney General. In late April, Thompson made two more rulings. He refused to set a standard for applying *cy pres,* and he declared that much of the testimony by expert witnesses about the "relative need" of various counties, including all the testimony of John Simon, was irrelevant to the question of whether Buck Trust funds were being spent wisely.

The foundation appealed these rulings, asking that the case be split in half, one part setting the *cy pres* standard for the case, the other addressing whether the foundation was qualified to manage the Buck Trust. Both a district court and the California Supreme Court upheld Thompson's ruling. The foundation and its allies were devastated. "This is Vietnam for us," Public Advocates's Sid Wolinsky told the *San Francisco Chronicle* in early May. "[W]e spent months brainstorming this case, and never in our wildest imagination did we dream that testimony comparing Marin County to other counties would be ruled inadmissible."[25]

The foundation also pursued a risky strategy that backfired. In order to prove that the Marin County restriction was impracticable, San Francisco Foundation program officers repeatedly testified that they weren't able to find useful ways to spend the Buck Trust money in Marin County, and therefore made bad grants to county organizations. "Marin's lawyers delighted in the tactic," wrote *Foundation News*'s Roger M. Williams, "which made the foundation look like a bunch of bumblers; foundation staff, on the other hand, loathed it."

"For all of us, this was the single most offensive aspect of the whole case," a former San Francisco Foundation staff member told Williams. "We knew it would backfire, and anyway, we didn't believe it. 'Go out and tell the world what a lousy grantmaker you are.'"[26]

As the trial continued, the foundation further retreated. Beryl Buck's attorney, John Cook, testified that "I am responsible for having brought the foundation into the picture, and I am very ashamed." He added that if he had known that the foundation would try to break the trust, "I would never ever have used the foundation, and I don't think anybody else would, either. I think that's a shocking thing, to destroy the intention of the [donor]."[27]

By mid-June, it was clear that the San Francisco Foundation would lose. In a speech before the Commonwealth Club, Martin Paley told the audience,

> To borrow a phrase from a popular movie, "I'm mad as hell, and I'm not going to take it any more." ... I'm mad because, for trying to do the right and proper thing, we

have been besmirched as "grave robbers" and accused of trying to break the will of an elderly widow.... We thought it proper to exercise restraint in what we expected to be a dignified legal procedure.... Our reward for this has been continued demagogic attacks, most recently as a Dickensian villain who "takes his little ward and kicks him down and throws him in the snow."[28]

Two weeks later, the foundation announced that it would end the case and cease to be the administrator of the Buck Trust.

ℰ A Mixed Victory for Donor Intent

After a month's negotiations (chiefly over who would pay the case's legal bills), Judge Thompson made his ruling. Initially, it seemed that *Estate of Buck* would be a major victory for supporters of donor intent. Thompson ruled that the San Francisco Foundation had shown an inability to fairly administer the Buck Trust and ordered that a new foundation, to be known as the Marin Community Foundation (MCF), be created to spend the Buck Trust funds. He also ruled that "the Petitioners failed to prove that it was impracticable, permanently or otherwise, to spend all of the annual income from the Buck Trust in accordance with the terms of the [Trust]. Neither 'inefficiency' nor 'ineffective philanthropy' constitute impracticability, nor does either constitute an appropriate standard for the application of *cy pres*."[29] Martin Paley resigned as president of the San Francisco Foundation. As of 1993, the foundation's endowment was $265 million—about a third of what it would have been with the Buck Trust.

But Judge Thompson did not give a clear-cut victory for supporters of donor intent. He required that the Marin Community Foundation spend part of its funds (an amount that would decrease from 25 percent of total grantmaking in 1987 to 20 percent in 1993) on "major projects" that "shall be of national and international importance and significance, the benefits from which will inure not only to Marin County but all mankind."[30] By ordering the creation of three new nonprofit organizations—the Buck Center for Research on Aging, the Beryl Buck Institute for Education, and the Marin Institute for the Prevention of Alcohol and Other Drug Abuse Problems—Thompson technically adhered to Beryl

Buck's wishes, since the organizations would be headquartered in Marin County. But their creation was also a response to the San Francisco Foundation's argument that the Buck Trust could be better used to address national rather than local problems. There is little evidence that Beryl Buck was interested in using her estate to study drug abuse, gerontology, or any other national problem.

In a 1987 *University of San Francisco Law Review* article, Yale law professor John Simon expressed dissatisfaction with the verdict. While continuing to support the San Francisco Foundation's position, he believed the court's decision to create national organizations headquartered in Marin County was misguided, since there was no evidence that Beryl Buck favored such organizations. The language of the Buck Trust will, he said, "is not the language a testator would use if she wished to support a national or international grant program merely headquartered in Marin County.... Under the terms of Mrs. Buck's will, therefore, it is, to put it mildly, very difficult to justify a national-international 'major projects' scheme."[31]

Moreover, the three court-mandated nonprofits were to receive some $8 million in Buck Trust funds a year, some of which has arguably been used lavishly. Many Marin County residents criticized plans of the Buck Center for Research on Aging to build a 500-acre headquarters designed by renowned architect I.M. Pei. "They're spending far too much money," retired judge Harold Brown told the *San Jose Mercury News*. Brown, brother of former California Governor Pat Brown and uncle of current (in 2017) California Governor Jerry Brown, charged that the Buck Center was "building over 100 condominiums and a swimming pool and tennis courts and recreation areas, all for the researchers. That will run into many millions. With people going homeless and hungry and the jail overcrowded, there are hundreds of other needs here for this money."[32] (The center nonetheless went ahead with the I.M. Pei buildings, two of which were completed in 1999 and a third in 2011.[33])

The Marin Community Foundation spent its first few years organizing meetings to decide what to do with the Buck funds. But it often chose to continue grants that were made by the San Francisco Foundation. Environmental groups have received funds, even though Beryl Buck was evidently unconcerned with environmental issues. Though the Marin Community Foundation (unlike the San Francisco Foundation) has given money to religious organizations, many of these groups have used the funds for esoteric purposes. The National Conference of Christians and Jews used a grant "to support the Green Circle program which helps young children (grades Kindergarten through 6th) to build their self-esteem, understand and appreciate cultural and racial differences, and develop peaceful conflict resolution skills."[34]

In June 1990, the Marin Community Foundation's first president, Douglas X. Patino, resigned over disputes about whether the Marin County Board of Supervisors could intervene in the affairs of the foundation. Stephen Dobbs, former head of the Koret Foundation, succeeded Patino. He left the Marin Community Foundation at the end of 1997. Tom Peters, who remains president of the Marin Community Foundation today, succeeded him.

The Marin Community Foundation does fulfill Beryl Buck's wishes by spending money in Marin County. But there is little evidence that it supports causes she would have favored. Supporters of donor intent won the battle over the Buck Trust, but lost the war over how the trust's funds should be spent.

Over the years, the Buck Trust assets rose. By 1996, they had risen to $748 million, and the Marin Community Foundation (which has a staff of 35) had distributed $22.3 million from the trust's assets to various Marin County programs. Among these, the three court-mandated nonprofits created by the Buck Trust settlement—the Buck Center for Research on Aging, the Beryl Buck Institute for Education, and the Marin Institute—received 20 percent of the income generated by the trust's assets, or $6.3 million. Among recipients of Buck Trust funds were the cities of San Rafael and Novato, the United Nations Association ("for support of storytelling programs in Marin public schools based on the 50th anniversary of UNICEF"), the National Conference of Christians and Jews, the Spectrum Center for Lesbian, Gay, and Bisexual Concerns ("for a one-time technical assistance to develop an evaluation tool"), the Earth Island Institute, the Marin Audubon Society, the National Audubon Society, the Natural Resources Defense Council, the World Without War Council, and the POINT Foundation, publishers of the *Whole Earth Review*.[35]

In 2002, the controversy about Beryl Buck's rule made a brief reappearance. A Latino group called the Greenlining Institute demanded that the Marin County Foundation redistribute $150 million of Buck Trust money to poor Latinos in the city of San Francisco. Greenlining's efforts appealed to the San Francisco Board of Supervisors, who unanimously passed a resolution demanding that the Marin Community Foundation create "a regional plan to effectively address the needs of the poor in the Bay Area." At issue was the clause of Beryl Buck's will that said the Buck Trust should be used for "providing care for the needy in Marin County." The Greenlining Institute claimed the clause meant that the trust should be used exclusively for the poor, and that the Marin Community Foundation was improperly diverting money to grants for the "environmental elite."

Marin Community Foundation president Tom Peters told the *San Francisco Chronicle* that Judge Thompson's interpretation of the will was that "needy" meant all people in Marin County with needs, not just the poor. "Easily 75 percent of the money we granted over the past year could be classified as pointed towards families where economic, social, and linguistic needs were paramount."[36] The San Francisco Board of Supervisors never pursued its resolution, and the issue quietly died.

In 2004, the Marin Community Foundation moved into fancy new offices. It continued to spend money on poor people and arts organizations, but also began to put much of its resources into land trusts to preserve the remaining farmland in Marin County.

The Buck Center for Research on Aging renamed itself the Buck Institute for Age Research. In 2006, the institute started its first capital campaign, and announced that it was eager to receive grants from other foundations.

In June 2006, the foundation announced that it would radically change its grantmaking: Instead of 70 percent of its Buck Trust funds being used for sustaining grants, the foundation would use half its grants each year for new projects. The reason, foundation president Tom Peters told the *Marin Independent Journal*, was that the foundation now wanted to make grants that had "clearly identified goals and some measurable impacts."[37]

"We don't want to be just a United Way, spreading around little grants," said Marin Community Foundation trustee Gary Giacomini. "We're going to do big, big stuff."[38]

By 2007, the Marin Community Foundation's assets had risen to $923 million, with an additional $223 million in donor-advised funds under its control. In 2012, assets had risen to $1.3 billion, and other donors had contributed $193 million to donor-advised funds supervised by the foundation.

In 2009, the Marin Community Foundation announced four five-year grant programs: a $15 million one to help to create individual development accounts to enable poor people to save, a $35 million one to improve early-childhood education for low-income families, a $10 million one to increase affordable housing by renovating old apartment buildings and helping families with foreclosed homes, and a $10 million one to deal with climate change by encouraging farmers to come up with ways to capture more carbon dioxide in their farms and by coming up with ways to encourage Marin residents to bicycle and walk more. The foundation in 2010 announced a partnership with Sutter Health, with each organization providing $10 million over five years to improve health care for low-income families in Marin County.

In the end, the story of Beryl Buck's philanthropy remains a murky one that should give future donors pause. Clearly courts are uncertain allies for donors, prey to their own preferences and to popular demands for change.

8

The Robertson Foundation

Had the battle between the children of Charles and Marie Robertson (heirs to the A&P grocery fortune) and Princeton University over control of the Robertson Foundation ever come to trial, it would have been a promising contender for the most important donor intent case of the twenty-first century. The Robertson family agreed to a settlement in December 2008, after six years of pre-trial motions but no firm trial date. In hopes of defeating the Robertson family in *Robertson v. Princeton*, the university spent more on this case than on any other in its venerable history. Spending millions of dollars was understandable, because the Robertson Foundation's wealth amounted to as much as six percent of Princeton's endowment.

The case and its settlement were complicated, but on balance Princeton could claim victory in the case, which means it was another severe blow to donor intent.

At stake were these questions: Should the Robertson Foundation be independent of Princeton, or should the foundation's funds be absorbed into Princeton's endowment? Should the foundation's grants be used exclusively to benefit the Woodrow Wilson School to train students for careers in public service? Or may the foundation's fortune be used for anything that Princeton feels would benefit itself?

Charles Robertson (1905-81), a Princeton alumnus of the class of 1926, wanted to use his wealth to help his alma mater. In 1934, he married Marie Hartford Hoffman Reed, whose grandfather, George Huntington Hartford, founded the A&P supermarket chain.[1]

In 1961, Charles and Marie Robertson created the Robertson Foundation and endowed it with 700,000 shares of A&P stock, worth $35 million. Clause three of the foundation's certificate of incorporation states the following purposes for the philanthropy:

(a) To establish or maintain and support, at Princeton University, and as part of the Woodrow Wilson School, a Graduate School, where men and women dedicated to public service may prepare themselves for careers in government service, with particular emphasis on the education of such persons for careers in those areas of the Federal Government that are concerned with international relations and affairs;

(b) To establish and maintain scholarships or fellowships, which will provide full, or partial support to students to each Graduate School, whether such students are candidates for degrees, special students, or part-time students;

(c) To provide collateral and auxiliary services, plans and programs in furtherance of the object and purpose above set forth, including but without limitation, internship programs, plans for public service assignments of faculty or administrative personnel, mid-career study help, and programs for foreign students or officials training.[2]

After stating that "no substantial part of the corporation's activities shall be carrying on propaganda, or otherwise attempting, to influence legislation," the incorporation certificate concludes by stating that the Robertson Foundation could only be dissolved during the lifetime of Charles or Marie Robertson by their written permission, and then, within fourteen years after the death of either founder, by the consent of three of the Robertson children. Thereafter, unanimous consent of the trustees was needed. In the event of dissolution, the foundation's endowment would "for investment purposes, be made a part of the general endowment fund but which otherwise shall be considered and administered as a separate and distinct endowment fund to be known as the 'Robertson Fund' and to be used by Princeton University to further the object and purpose above set forth."[3]

Gen. Andrew Goodpaster, a former NATO commander who served as a Robertson Foundation trustee from 1961-2002, recalled in a 2002 deposition that the Robertson Foundation was set up as a nonprofit controlled by Princeton but legally independent of Princeton because it was Charles Robertson's "observation, and

I might say mine as well, that on occasion gifts were made to universities, and they were not applied in the way intended by the giver, and he and his wife really wanted to be sure that this gift, which is of magnificent size, would be applied in the ways that they envisaged, so rather than make it outright because of that concern of giving assurance that the intent would be fulfilled, he wanted to stay in considerable degree of contact with just what was done with the money."[4]

In a 1979 letter to his son William, Charles Robertson explained that "the reason for the creation of the Robertson Foundation, as a separate entity from Princeton University, was the need for family and independent guidance as to the management and expenditure of Foundation income and assets. The founders felt that for the Foundation to achieve its stated objectives, family and outside, independent elements must be closely meshed with all phases of the management and spending policies of the Foundation. Moreover, they must enforce the official documents."[5]

Princeton University president Robert F. Goheen, on accepting the gift, said the money would be used for an "objective to develop, in the Woodrow Wilson School, post-graduate programs of instruction that will augment the flow of well-prepared people into positions of public responsibility and set new patterns of excellence throughout the nation for the training of men for the public service, with particular attention to international and foreign affairs."[6]

One of the grounds of dispute between the Robertson family and Princeton was whether or not the "public service" President Goheen referred to is the same as "government service." Princeton's position was that if Woodrow Wilson School graduates pursue careers in nonprofits, they are pursuing careers in "public service" and are therefore fulfilling Charles Robertson's intent. The Robertson family disagreed, maintaining that only Woodrow Wilson alumni who pursue careers in the federal government are doing what the Robertson Foundation wanted.

The $35 million gift was the largest donation Princeton had received at the time, and remained the biggest Princeton donation until 1995. But the Robertsons refused to claim any credit for the gift. They insisted on anonymity, to the extent of keeping the Robertson Foundation out of any reference works on foundations. Princeton announced only that the donor was "Foundation X."

"The gift," the *New York Times* reported, "is the largest in Princeton's 215-year history and is believed to be the largest anonymous donation to American higher education…. Princeton is expected to set new patterns in the approach by American universities to the professional training of the policy-making echelons of government."[7]

But the anonymous nature of the gift led to rampant speculation on campus on who the Woodrow Wilson School's mysterious benefactor was; according to the *New York Times,* some even thought the CIA was behind it all.

In 1973, after the death of Marie Robertson, the Robertson family publicly acknowledged their generosity. One of the Robertson children (who would not give his first name) told the *New York Times* that the reason for initial anonymity was "entirely the family's idea, and the children abided by the desire for no publicity. They [Charles and Marie Robertson] are very, very quiet people, very reticent. Publicity is anathema to both of them."

He added that "the pressure on the school to reveal the source of the donation income grew" and that after the death of Marie Robertson, Charles Robertson finally decided to go public. "The family wanted to emphasize the importance of the school and not the family," the son added, "But the public demanded to know who the hell's money it was, even though it was none of their damned business."[8]

Because of the Robertson family's desire to avoid the limelight, the evidence for Charles and Marie Robertson's intentions rests on letters of Charles Robertson introduced into the trial as evidence. The earliest is a letter from Charles Robertson to his son William, dated July 3, 1962.

"Possessed of a large fortune, in the making of which we had no part whatsoever, the proud and devoted parents of a wonderful young family and ever mindful of our countless blessings we for years had searched for a cause, a project, so that we might serve to strengthen the Government of the United States and, in so doing, to assist people everywhere who sought freedom with justice," Charles Robertson wrote. "In due course and after a diligent search we, solely through our own initiative, decided to finance through a foundation a school in which outstanding college graduates truly dedicated to the service of the public would be educated to assume the responsibilities of important positions in those areas of the Federal Government concerned with international affairs."

"The Robertson Foundation was created in 1961 as a vehicle for underwriting the initial costs of establishing and operating, through the Trustees of Princeton University, the new Woodrow Wilson School of Public and International Affairs," Charles Robertson continued. After explaining that he expected his children to actively participate in the foundation, he added that "we are all prone to take for granted the gifts of freedom and of justice we as Americans enjoy forgetting that these great privileges simply do not just happen and flourish—bestowed to us by a benign and generous Providence. Men by the millions have fought for freedom and men by the uncounted thousands have died that you and Mother and I, along with our fellow countrymen might live securely and happily in this free country."

"It may well be that your life and the lives of those who follow you will be enriched by reason of your and of their identity with this project which was conceived with the express and clearly defined purpose of strengthening our government and our country," Robertson concluded. "As many times as you travel abroad you, like Mother and I, will return with the firm and lasting motivation that 'this is my own my native land'— cherish it and protect it."[9]

Charles and Marie Robertson expanded on this idea in a 1962 letter to the directors of the Banbury Fund, the Robertson family's personal foundation. "If substantial numbers of persons trained in the School do not go into government service, or do not remain in government service, or, if by reasons of politics, or bureaucracy, or any other reason, the recipients of the training provided by the school are unable to achieve positions of major responsibility in the government, then no matter how excellent their training may have been, the basic purpose of the School is not being achieved."[10]

"Success to Charlie," Gen. Goodpaster said in his deposition, "would be providing a large group of graduates to the government…to support the conduct of foreign policy and international policy, security policy and the like. That to him would have been the real measure of success."[11]

As the years went by, the unusual form of the Robertson Foundation was legally clarified. In forms submitted to the IRS in 1970, Charles Robertson stated that "the Foundation was organized exclusively for the benefit of, to perform the functions of, and to carry out the purposes of Princeton University…the

Robertson Foundation is controlled by Princeton University. The university made it clear from the outset that it would not undertake the long-term commitment involved in the project (e.g., faculty contracts, student fellowships) unless it had effective control of the foundation." The way in which the university would control the foundation, Robertson continued, would be to have four of the seven seats on the foundation's board (with the Robertson family having the remaining three).[12]

In November 1970, the IRS responded that the Robertson Foundation was not a private foundation, but was a 509(a)(3) nonprofit organization. Princeton claimed that this ruling showed that the Robertson Foundation is a supporting organization of Princeton; the Robertson family disagreed.

There is substantial evidence that during the 1970s Charles Robertson was dissatisfied with the number of Woodrow Wilson School graduates who were being hired by the federal government. In 1971, a memorandum from Woodrow Wilson School dean John Lewis to Princeton President William Bowen stated that "with 45 million in the till to work with it should be possible to guide annually into the main stream of the Federal Government three or four dozen highly motivated…young Americans (if not one hundred)." [13]

This lofty goal was never met. A letter from Charles Robertson to Princeton University president William Bowen on November 18, 1972, shows that the benefactor was dissatisfied with how Princeton was spending the Robertson money. By then the Robertson Foundation endowment had grown to $50 million, ensuring $1.5 million for support of the Woodrow Wilson School. Robertson noted that in 1972, the school had 47 students who were graduated with masters in public affairs (MPA) degrees. Of these, the federal government hired 10, and 4 became Foreign Service officers. Similar graduation rates had taken place in 1971.

> In 1971 and again in 1972 the School conferred MPA degrees on ten candidates each year who were able to secure jobs in the Federal Government—irrespective of careers concerned with international relations. Would I be very far off target remarking that the amount spent by the University to educate each MPA candidate exceeds by a very wide margin the cost of educating any M.D.,

L.L. B., Ph.D. in this or any other country? And would I be guilty of gross exaggeration were I to remark that the cost (total annual income divided by the number of MPA's entering the Federal Government service) is, to express it with true British understatement, truly astronomical?

"And what are my suggestions?" Robertson added. "Simply to turn this School around and start over again with the avowed purpose of living up to the terms and conditions of the donor's gift and the acceptance of the University of this gift with these terms and conditions in good faith. The time has come to face up to the obvious fact that the School has never come within shouting distance of achieving the goal and I personally doubt that it ever will as long as it continues on its present course."[14] Robertson requested that the university place someone in Washington to convince mid-level civil servants that it would be in their best interest to advance their careers by obtaining Woodrow Wilson School MPAs.

In a memoir published in 2011, William Bowen claimed that the reason more Woodrow Wilson School students didn't join the State or the Defense Department in the 1970s was "because of the dramatic reversal of attitudes toward government that resulted from the Vietnam War."[15] Bowen didn't explain why students hostile to government would join a graduate school designed to prepare students for government service.

The Robertson family charges that for the next thirty years, Princeton gradually drifted away from Charles and Marie Robertson's intentions. In 1972, for example, Dean Lewis wrote to President Bowen in a confidential memo that "what bothers me" about the Robertson Foundation 'is the unspoken premise that, with respect to any American institution dealing in public affairs, the highest per se loyalty automatically must be to the U.S. Government.... [That] is not a philosophical premise to which the Woodrow Wilson School, as an agent of general public-affairs enlightenment, really can be bound. I guess I hope the issue does not explicitly surface.... But if it were to do so, the University should resist a blind commitment to nation-state parochialism."[16]

A 1973 memo from Princeton's provost, Sheldon Hackney, to President Bowen said that the Robertson Foundation funds violated academic freedom. "Eventually, in the very long run, it would be a good thing if the Foundation itself were to be dissolved and the funds given to the University earmarked for the same purposes for which they are currently being used.... We must make it clear that the School's autonomy and its independence of judgment are not impaired by the existence of the Foundation board...I assume you share the sense of discomfort that John [Lewis] and I have about the existence of the Robertson Foundation as a separate entity with control over its own investment decisions...and with an ill-defined degree of oversight of the school's decisions."[17]

The dispute between the Robertson family and Princeton continued quietly behind the scenes for the next thirty years. On the surface, all was serene. A profile of the Woodrow Wilson School published in the *New York Times* late in 2001 found that the school had, in the 2001-2002 school year, 65 students in its MPA program, an additional 30 in a Ph.D. program, and 20 mid-career civil students studying at Princeton for one year. The school had 2,463 alumni in the labor force, of whom 19 percent worked for nongovernmental organizations, 18 percent worked for the federal government, and 8 percent worked for foreign governments. The school's most famous federal government alumnus was Anthony Lake, who served as one of President Clinton's national security advisors.

As of 2001, the Robertson Foundation endowment was $550 million. The foundation's funds paid for scholarships that provided up to half the cost of Princeton's annual tuition of $26,000. And many Woodrow Wilson School classes met in Robertson Hall.

"My parents wanted to make a significant gesture of philanthropy," William Robertson told the *Times*, "and I think they wanted to address the current state of world affairs, which included the Cold War and the threat from the Soviet Union."[18]

Seven months later, in July 2002, four of William Robertson's children and a cousin launched their lawsuit against Princeton.[19] The initial charge in the complaint was that the university was illicitly commingling Robertson Foundation money with the university's endowment and using foundation funds for activities that had nothing to do with training students for careers in civil service. One charge was that in 1991 the school had taken $13 million from the foundation's endowment and used the funds for various construction projects, including Wallace Hall, used in part by the sociology department.

The Robertson family particularly objected to a university plan to have PRINCO, the entity that managed Princeton investments, also manage the Robertson Foundation endowment. They noted that Charles Robertson, in a 1979 letter, stated that he was opposed to "either commingling or University control over the portfolio" of the Robertson Foundation. They charged that Princeton had shifted $54 million of the endowment away from the foundation's endowment manager, Essex Street Investments, and placed it in the control of a PRINCO subsidiary—even though Essex Street had achieved greater returns on its investments than PRINCO had.

Princeton University president Shirley A. Tilghman told the *New York Times* that the Robertson Foundation's "funds are in fact only allowed to be used for the benefit of Princeton University. They [the Robertson family] cannot take it out of university control without the vote of the foundation board, and the university appoints four of its trustees."[20]

In November 2002, Princeton requested that the lawsuit be dismissed. They said that only Robertson Foundation trustees had the standing to sue. Thus, according to Princeton, of the five Robertson family members who were plaintiffs, only William Robertson and his cousin, Robert Halligan, had standing to sue. But Princeton's view was that since both these trustees had been on the Robertson Foundation board for over 20 years, "they actively participated in and either approved or acquiesced in many of the actions challenged by the lawsuit and on repeated occasions expressed their support and admiration for the Woodrow Wilson School and its leadership."[21]

Princeton's lawyer, Douglas Eakeley, told the *Daily Princetonian* "there has been one board meeting since the complaint was filed and there was consensus reached on a number of issues." President Tilghman said that it was "time to let the legal action run its course" and that he hoped the appointment of a new Wilson School dean would result in "an opportunity for an entirely new beginning with the Robertsons."[22]

In February 2003, the Robertsons responded by adding new charges. They said that Princeton University internal memos obtained during discovery showed that the foundation board was not given current financial information, ensuring that "the Foundation was accorded no real-time oversight of the spending decisions made by Princeton." They added that they had obtained evidence that Woodrow Wilson School officials complained to the university that the foundation was charged excessive overhead by Princeton. Finally, they produced internal memos to claim that Princeton officials were "quietly contemptuous" of Robertson family complaints about the foundation's funds being used to build Wallace Hall.[23]

Princeton responded in a filing of March 2003 that they and the trustees they appointed to the Robertson Foundation did not misuse the foundation's endowment. "The University Trustees have done their utmost to respond to the family trustees' requests for information, suggestions for changes in operating procedures and expressions of concern about the Foundation's mission," the university said.[24]

In June 2003, Princeton asked Judge Neil Shuster to dismiss the lawsuit, saying the matter was an internal conflict between the Robertson Foundation's university-appointed trustees and the family trustees. They also claimed that the Robertson family had no right to sue in the Robertson Foundation's name.[25]

On September 8, 2003, Judge Shuster dismissed Princeton's filing and set a tentative trial date of October 2005. By this time, the Robertson Foundation case had become national news, with major pieces about the case in *National Review* and the *Washington Post*. John J. Miller, writing in *National Review*, unearthed new details. He reported that the Robertson family now claimed that thanks to Essex Street management, the Robertson Foundation's endowment was $150 million larger than it would have been if PRINCO had administered the funds. Miller also wrote about an internal 1997 email from Michael Rothschild, dean of the Woodrow Wilson School, to Princeton president Harold Shapiro, about the Wallace Hall construction project and Princeton's request that the Robertson Foundation cover any gaps in the construction cost if Princeton failed to raise $25 million. William Robertson, according to the email, "is unhappy" about the Wallace Hall project "and if we use large amounts of Robertson money to pay for the building he will be more so."[26]

For the *Washington Post*, Robertson said for the first time that the ultimate goal of the lawsuit would be to sever all ties between

Princeton and the Robertson Foundation. "Princeton has known for decades that the goal of our foundation is to send students into federal government, and they've ignored us. Princeton has abused the largest charitable gift in the history of American higher education and that's embarrassing. They will lose the money."[27]

Faced with this upping of the stakes by the Robertsons, the four university-appointed trustees outvoted the three Robertson family members at a Robertson Foundation board of trustees meeting and declared PRINCO would now manage the Robertson Foundation endowment. The Robertson family issued a statement saying that "the University's intentions are perfectly clear: grab the money." Princeton lawyer Douglas Eakeley told the *Daily Princetonian* "the university-designated trustees acted as they did because they felt it was in their fiduciary interest to do so." He claimed that PRINCO had won in a competition over nine other investment management companies.[28]

William Robertson then wrote an op-ed for the *Christian Science Monitor* stating that his family's lawsuit against Princeton was not unusual, in that other donors had sued the recipients of their generosity for the return of misused gifts. He noted that the New York Attorney General had ordered New York City's St. Luke's-Roosevelt Hospital to return $5 million of a $10 million bequest after finding that the hospital had not used the money for alcoholism-treatment programs. Another lawsuit was by the heirs of patron Sybil Harrington, charging that the Metropolitan Opera had failed to spend Harrington's $5 million bequest on traditional opera, as she had instructed.

"Nonprofit organizations need to be governed by the highest ethical standards," Robertson wrote. "When they accept donations for a specific purpose, that's how the money should be used."[29]

The Robertson family's next action, in July 2004, was to amend their suit to request punitive damages from Princeton on the grounds that the university had defrauded not only the Robertson Foundation, but also other donors. "Princeton has a pattern and practice of violating donors' intentions and improperly spending restricted gifts in ways that benefit the university's own general fund," the Robertson family lawyers wrote in a brief that charged that the university had misspent at least $100 million of Robertson Foundation money. They said that the university should alter the charter of the Robertson

Foundation so that the Robertson family would appoint all trustees and restore with interest any misused money.

As evidence, they cited an audit done by former Princeton development official Jessie Washington of Princeton's School of Religious Life, in which the employee wrote that "funding allocations are not in alignment with their intended purpose; i.e., the donors' wishes have been ignored; money for religious life has been knowingly withheld."

Princeton responded in a statement that the Robertson family claims were "unsubstantiated and misleading" and that the allegation that donors interested in supporting religion at Princeton were defrauded "was thoroughly investigated and determined to involve no wrongdoing."[30]

The *Daily Princetonian* subsequently found out that Washington was asked to audit restricted funds to the Office of Religious Life by Princeton vice-president for campus life Janet Dickerson. Washington found "inadequate information systems, poor business processes and questionable actions" by Princeton in the use of these restricted funds.

"I started to see problems by just standing at the photocopying machine and putting documents in order," Washington said. "It was like a psychological double-take. Am I seeing what I'm seeing?"

University officials refused to discuss Washington's audit because it had become part of the Robertson Foundation lawsuit. But Robertson family attorney Seth Lapidow admitted that no one else had come forward to support Washington's allegations that Princeton routinely abused donor intent.[31]

The Robertson family lawyers also charged that the foundation's money was being used to pay for graduate school fellowships in sociology, political science, and economics, and that the foundation was billed for faculty salaries in Princeton's Office of Population Research and the Center for International Studies.

"We feel the money should be used to pay teachers to teach and encourage students to go into government service," Robertson family lawyer Seth Lapidow told the *Daily Princetonian*. "Princeton has lost sight of that vision."

Princeton lawyer Douglas Eakeley said the foundation money being used for departments outside the Wilson School was necessary to strengthen interdisciplinary studies between these departments and the Wilson School. "There are various elements that go into having a vibrant program in public and international affairs," Eakeley said, including interdisciplinary programs.[32]

In October 2004, Judge Shuster accepted the amendments. If Princeton was found guilty of fraud, the university could be held for punitive damages should the Robertson family win. Douglas Eakeley told the *New Jersey Law Journal* that the new charges "only add to the decibel level. They just make it harder for Shirley Tilghman to assist the foundation and make it harder to effect a reconciliation."[33]

By November 2004, the Robertson suit had become the most expensive legal case. Princeton said that it had spent $2 million defending itself, while the Banbury Fund had committed $5 million. The Robertson family had four lawyers working on the case; Princeton had two partners and two senior associates. Over 40 depositions were recorded, with 25 left to go. Three former Princeton presidents had been deposed; President Goheen's deposition had taken six days due to his age.

The Robertson Foundation board still regularly met while the lawsuit was taking place. "The closed-door meetings" of the Robertson Foundation trustees, reported the Newark *Star-Ledger*'s Kelly Heyboer, "according to both sides, are tense and swarming with lawyers."[34]

Princeton filed the next salvo in February 2005. They asked Judge Shuster to declare that the Robertson Foundation funds could not be transferred to another university, that it was all right to have PRINCO manage the Princeton endowment, and that the university could spend capital gains from the Robertson Foundation endowment as well as interest. They also declared that the Robertson family trustees were "attempting to hold the foundation and the Woodrow Wilson School hostage" and that the Robertson family was engaging in a "gratuitous, baseless public relations campaign" which would harm both "the potential pool of student applicants [and] the receptiveness of funding agencies to Woodrow Wilson School grant applications."

Princeton general counsel Peter McDonough told the *Daily Princetonian* that these rulings were necessary in order to make sure the board did its job of supervising routine matters at the Woodrow Wilson School. "Board members have had to continue to be responsive to the needs of the foundation," he said, "and it's very difficult to do that in real time while these very fundamental issues are in dispute and are affecting the ability of the foundation to be managed."

Princeton also introduced a letter by Robert Goheen written early in the 1960s when the Robertson Foundation was applying for tax-exempt status. "From the very inception of the proposal," the letter stated, "the prospective donor has understood and agreed that the University must have the responsibility for the direction, maintenance, and operation of the School in all its aspects…. Thus, there is no question that the gift is for the sole use of Princeton University."

Robertson family lawyer Frank Cialone said that Goheen's declaration did not in any way inhibit the Robertson family from suing to sever the bond between Princeton and the foundation. "Nothing that Dr. Goheen says here supports the notion that the University's actions are beyond judicial review."[35]

In June, the Robertson family again sought to amend their complaint, stating that they had obtained evidence during discovery that the university had diverted $100 million from the Robertson Foundation endowment to programs that shouldn't have been funded with foundation money. The amendment charged that "the pattern and practice of diverting donations from their intended purpose" was "systemic" at the university.[36]

The 2005-2006 school year began with the resignation of the Robertson Foundation's auditor, Grant Thornton LLP. The Robertson family wanted an independent audit of the Robertson Foundation books, and did not want to use the university's accountants, Deloitte Touche Tomatsu.

"We are aware of a sharp division of opinion among the parties relating to the Foundation's accounting for certain transactions, investment management, internal controls, and allegations of fraud," Grant Thornton said in its resignation letter. "Based on these matters and the substantial uncertainty surrounding their ultimate resolution, we have made the professional judgment to resign as auditors of the Foundation for the year ended June 30, 2004."

William Robertson told the *Daily Princetonian* that for an "auditor to resign suggests that the client was just not cooperating or was concealing considerable information from them."

"Mr. Robertson should know better than to suggest that we were not complying with the auditor," Douglas Eakeley responded. "There's no basis for that statement."

Alyesha Day, an accounting expert at the University of Chicago business school, speculated "especially in the post Sarbanes-Oxley regime, the liability of auditors has gone up." She thought that Grant Thornton would not want to involve itself in an enterprise where members of the board were suing each other.[37]

The Robertson family's next move was in December 2005, when they released a Zogby poll about donor intent. The poll reported the following:

- Fifty-three percent of Americans surveyed said they would "definitely stop giving" if a charity "used your donation for a specific purpose and you know they ignored your request." An additional 36 percent said that they would "probably stop giving" if a charity misused their donations.

- When asked if a charity should return a donation "if they used your money for a purpose other than the one for which it was given," 36 percent surveyed said that the charity should definitely return the money and an additional 23 percent said that the charity should probably return the money.

- The survey asked if charities who misuse donations "should be held legally or criminally liable for acting in a fraudulent matter." Forty-seven percent said that the charity should be held legally and criminally liable, while 24 percent said that the nonprofit should just be held legally liable and 3 percent said the organization should be criminally liable. Only 18 percent said that the charity should not be held legally or criminally liable.

- When asked, "how important do you think showing respect for a donor's wishes is to the ethical governance of nonprofit charitable organizations," 83 percent of those surveyed said it was very important and 15 percent said it was somewhat important.[38]

In January 2006, Princeton resubmitted its request to Judge Shuster that he rule that Princeton "is and will continue to be the sole beneficiary of the Robertson Foundation," that the university can continue to choose four of the foundation's seven trustees, that the foundation can spend capital gains from its endowment, and that the foundation's decision to retain PRINCO as investment advisers "represented a good faith exercise of its independent business judgment."

"It seems clear that these three issues can and should be resolved as a matter of law on the basis of the undisputed facts," Douglas Eakeley said.[39]

"Princeton's motion for summary judgment," Robertson family attorney Ronald Malone said in a statement, "like its position throughout this controversy, betrays an attitude of arrogance and profound disrespect for commitments made to long-deceased donors."[40]

A front-page investigative piece in the *Wall Street Journal* in February 2006 substantially enhanced the Robertson family cause. "*Robertson v. Princeton*," noted reporters John Hechinger and Daniel Golden, "may be the most important case higher education has faced over the question of honoring the wishes of a donor."

According to Hechinger and Golden, the Robertson family had spent $10 million on the suit, resulting in over 170,000 pages of depositions, including from four former Princeton presidents. Princeton, they estimated, had spent $12 million defending itself.

The *Wall Street Journal* reporters charged that Jessie Washington's audit had unearthed one major and one minor violation of donor intent. Washington unearthed a 1988 donation of $5,000 from alumna Lois Thompson, stating that the funds should be used to "maintain and preserve" the organ in the university chapel. Washington found writing on the sheet that was used to record the donation which stated that the money should be used "to relieve general funds" and "Dept. is not to know." She also said that when she told Steven Gill, now the Princeton budget director, about Thompson's misused donation, Gill said, "don't tell the *New York Times*." (Douglas Eakeley said that the notation meant that Princeton was going to reallocate general funds that had been used to maintain the organ and that Gill was joking.)

Princeton, Washington contended, also misused a $1 million donation made by the Danforth Foundation in 1959 to strengthen "religious work" on campus. Over the years, the donation had grown to $18.5 million. She reported that in fiscal year 2003, only $6,000 of the Danforth grant was used to support religion and $650,000 that was supposed to be used to support scholarships for students studying religion was instead used for general funds.

The *Journal* article also made public a 1993 investigation of the Woodrow Wilson School by a team led by former Federal Reserve Chairman Paul Volcker, who was teaching at Princeton at the time. The Volcker report found that the faculty was engaged "more and more in theoretical abstractions further and further removed from public policy" and that Robertson Foundation funds were being used in ways "hard to relate to the mission" of the Woodrow Wilson School.

Hechinger and Golden also reported that in 2002, in the early stages of *Robertson v. Princeton*, Princeton university secretary Thomas M. Wright sent an email to President Tilghman stating that the foundation was spending $750,000 for student tuition for courses that weren't part of the Wilson School curriculum and for general purposes and that this spending would "greatly upset" the Robertson family and the university should act "fast" to disclose it. Princeton failed to disclose this diversion of funds but told the *Journal* that this failure to disclose was "inappropriate" and wouldn't happen again.

Finally, the *Journal* was the first to report the analysis of the Robertson Foundation's books by Michael McGuire, a PricewaterhouseCoopers accountant who formerly was the Harvard Medical School's finance director. McGuire, hired by the Robertson family, issued a report in which he declared that $207 million of the $330 million the Robertson Foundation spent between 1996-2003 was "diverted" improperly, and that only $26 million of the $330 million was used for classroom instruction. He found that Princeton double-billed the foundation for building and equipment expenses by first charging the foundation for construction of a building, then charging the foundation a second time when the building or the equipment depreciated. "In effect," said Hechinger and Golden, "the foundation was like a consumer who pays for a car once with cash upfront and then again on the installment plan."[41]

Princeton responded to the *Wall Street Journal* article in several ways. It said that Hechinger and Golden's reporting on the hundreds of thousands of pages of documents obtained during discovery was "selective," although it did not say how anyone could write about such a huge amount of material without being selective. The university also stated that the Danforth Foundation gift was, despite Washington's allegations, properly used for "academic and non-academic programs of a religious nature."[42]

As for the misused $750,000, Princeton responded to an article about this that appeared in the *Times of Trenton*. "These funds," said Princeton vice-president Robert K. Durkee, "were not diverted to outside uses and she had no role in how they were reported."[43]

In February, Princeton announced that it would create a new Woodrow Wilson School fellowship called "Charles and Marie Robertson Scholars in the Nation's Service," which would be funded with $10 million of Robertson Foundation money. The fellowship would give five students grants for summer internships in their junior and senior years, and then place these students in $50,000 a year jobs for two-year tours of duty in the federal government, to be followed by a return to Princeton for a master's degree program. The nonprofit group Partnership for Public Service would be hired to help place scholars in federal agencies, and if no openings were available, Princeton would pay the scholars' salaries.

At a press conference flanked by famous Woodrow Wilson School alumni, including New York Attorney General Eliot Spitzer, New Jersey state senate minority leader Leonard Lance, and Mike McCurry, President Clinton's press secretary, Woodrow Wilson School dean Anne-Marie Slaughter said that the Robertson Scholarship program "is a direct response to the critical need in this country to attract students to careers in the federal government."[44]

Robert K. Durkee told the *Wall Street Journal* that the Robertson Scholars program had been in development before the Robertson family launched their lawsuit and that the creation of the scholarship program was "not at all" related to the lawsuit.[45]

In March 2006 Princeton filed a brief with the New Jersey Superior Court stating that it had "undercharged" the Robertson Foundation by $235 million over the years by not charging the foundation for programs that existed at the Woodrow Wilson School before 1961. Princeton now said that it had erred for only charging the Robertson Foundation for programs created with the foundation's money.

Princeton also said that William Robertson should be thrown off the Robertson Foundation board, and that "by his actions and words Mr. Robertson has demonstrated that he is no longer qualified to serve as a Trustee of the Robertson Foundation." They also said that William Robertson had approved all Robertson Foundation grants prior to the beginning of the lawsuit in 2002.

Robertson told the *Daily Princetonian* that part of the reason for the family's lawsuit was that Princeton had covered up the misallocation of Robertson Foundation funds during many of his years as a trustee. "I had been in the dark as to what we know now. Princeton has been keeping secrets from us. A main part of our allegation is that they've been covering up information for a long time."[46]

The case stalled for the rest of 2006. Both sides testified before Judge Shuster in November 2006, but the judge did not issue a ruling at that time. The Robertson family set up a website, robertsonvprinceton.org, to present its point of view. Wilson School dean Anne-Marie Slaughter held a "town meeting" with students, where she said she would encourage students to pursue government careers even if the Robertson Foundation never existed. She added that in her view, since the 1960s "all the public policy schools are sending less grads to government. The government doesn't have the jobs graduates are being hired for…. This is not a rational lawsuit at this time."[47]

The next move in the case came in May 2007, when Princeton returned $782,000 to the Robertson Foundation that the university said was used on graduate student fellowships in the economics, politics, and sociology departments between 2000-2002. Princeton said the money (which was known as the "Graduate Funding Agreement") needed to be returned because the university spent the money without informing the Robertson Foundation board. Princeton claimed the fellowships were "closely related" to the work of the Robertson Foundation, although it had previously argued that the fellowships were not paid for with Robertson money.

Princeton spokeswoman Cass Cliatt stated the decision was part of Princeton's "commitment to good governance." Robertson family lawyer Seth Lapidow told the *Chronicle of Higher Education* that Princeton paid the money because "they have been caught with a story that didn't measure up."[48]

In October 2007, Judge Shuster issued his ruling in response to the hearing held 11 months before. In a 335-page ruling, the judge gave both sides some victories. He rejected Princeton's claim that the university was the "sole beneficiary" of the Robertson gift.

Had he not made this decision, Princeton would have retained control of the Robertson funds even if the Robertson Foundation had been allowed to secede.

But several of his rulings supported Princeton's case. Judge Shuster rejected the Robertson family's request for a jury trial. While he ordered Princeton to refund $62,000 in overcharges to the Robertson Foundation, he also declared that the Robertsons' claims that Princeton misused $17.6 million of foundation money would have to be determined at the trial. He ruled that the Robertson Foundation could spend capital gains from its portfolio, instead of having them reinvested in its endowment. Finally, he ruled that the Robertsons had to show "egregious and nefarious" behavior by Princeton if they were to win their case.[49]

Princeton appeared to be wearying of the case. In the December 2007 issue of *University Business*, Princeton spokeswoman Cass Cliatt denounced the Robertson family for having "a very aggressive PR machine" that resulted in reports "casting doubt on the university and its donors." She said that Princeton's public relations effort was "necessary to correct the record."[50]

Robertson v. Princeton was further delayed when Judge Shuster announced his retirement in March 2008; Robertson family attorney Seth Lapidow told the *Daily Princetonian* that he looked forward to working with Judge Shuster's successor, Judge Maria Sypek. Lapidow estimated that with a "normal, four-day-a-week, full-day trial schedule," it would take four months for both sides to present their cases.[51]

Judge Sypek announced a trial date of October 2008.[52] In June she announced a further delay of the case to January 2009, and asked Princeton to compile a list of items that had not been turned over to the Robertson family. Princeton told the *Times of Trenton* it was compiling a list of witnesses, including Gen. David Petraeus, who was graduated from the Woodrow Wilson School in 1985.[53]

While *Robertson v. Princeton* was delayed, Princeton got more funds to pay for the lawsuit by winning a case against one of its insurers. In June 2008, a New York State appeals court upheld a $9.6 million judgment for Princeton against National Union Fire Insurance, a subsidiary of the giant American International Group (AIG). In 1998, Princeton purchased a $15 million "directors and officers" liability policy protecting its officials from lawsuits like those from the Robertson family. Princeton sued the insurer, which was only willing to pay the university $5 million. The insurer argued that because the Robertson Foundation was an entity controlled by Princeton, it should not have to compensate the university for suing itself. The New York State court disagreed and ordered AIG to pay Princeton the rest of the $15 million, giving the university additional resources to drag out the very costly case.[54]

Judge Sypek then withdrew from *Robertson v. Princeton*, citing an increasingly heavy caseload, including a rising number of foreclosure cases. She agreed to remain in charge of the case until the trial started, while John A. Fratto was called out of retirement to preside over the case. Assignment Judge Linda R. Feinberg told the *Times of Trenton* that "it would be difficult if not impossible" for Judge Sypek to preside over the Robertson case "and do her other work. That's the bottom line."[55]

Judge Fratto issued his first rulings. He decided to maintain the trial date of January 2009. He ruled that the trial would be divided into two parts. The first part of the trial would determine if Princeton was liable for violating the donor intent of the Robertson family, and the second part would determine what damages Princeton would have to pay. The judge rejected Princeton's request that the charges against the individuals named in the lawsuit—Princeton president Shirley Tilghman and two trustees appointed to the Robertson Foundation board by Princeton, Stephen Oxman and Peter Wendell—be considered before charges against Princeton University.[56] Princeton bought a building near the Mercer County courthouse, and planned to staff a "war room" with 30 lawyers.[57]

Then in December 2008, a month before the trial was scheduled to begin, the Robertson family and Princeton settled out of court. The Robertson Foundation was transformed into the Robertson Fund, which was completely controlled by Princeton. The Robertson family would have its court costs, estimated at $40 million, paid for by Princeton between 2009-2011. The Robertson Fund would pay for Princeton's court costs not previously covered by insurance. Between 2014-2018 Princeton will pay $50 million to a new foundation, the Robertson Foundation for Government.[58]

Princeton president Shirley Tilghman issued a statement saying, "It is tragic that this lawsuit required the expenditure of tens of millions of dollars in legal fees that could have and should have been spent on educational and charitable purposes." Maureen

O'Connor, commenting on the IvyGate blog, observed, "Lady, 'tragic' is when someone dies. Spending a few million dollars to safeguard your hoard of billions of dollars is by its definition the passionless pursuit of institutional self-interest."[59]

President Tilghman, in an interview with the *Princeton Alumni Weekly*, claimed that 10 percent of her time was taken up with the Robertson Foundation case. She said that from 2002 onwards, "the foundation board was almost completely dysfunctional. Our meetings were held with a mass of lawyers around the table; every word taken down by a court stenographer, almost every vote taken during the 2 ½ years of this litigation were 4-3 votes with the University trustees voting in favor and the Robertson trustees voting against."

She added that, freed of the restrictions of donor intent, Princeton was planning to use the Robertson funds in ways the donors would never have considered. Among them was global warming, in which Woodrow Wilson professors would collaborate with professors in other branches of Princeton. "Those collaborations would have been very difficult to get through the Robertson Foundation, because the argument would have been that it has nothing to do with training foreign-service officers."[60]

Outside of Princeton, there was substantial support for the Robertsons' position. Indiana University philanthropy professor Leslie Lenkowsky told the *Chronicle of Higher Education* that Princeton's $90 million payout was "certainly a victory for donor intent.... It does send a message this wasn't an entirely frivolous complaint. Donors are emboldened to challenge university discretion."[61]

"I give kudos to the Robertsons for fighting the battle as long as they did," said William E. Simon Foundation president William E. Simon Jr. "It took a lot of guts and a lot of courage."[62]

New York University law professor Harvey Dale told InsideHigherEd.com that he would have testified as an expert witness on Princeton's side had the case gone to trial. "I have said for a long time that I did not think Princeton could win this case," Dale said, "because even if it won in court, it would lose in the court of public opinion."[63]

Foundation Management Institute chairman Neal B. Freeman, who provided counsel to the Robertsons, explained in a Hudson Institute paper that "the Robertsons reclaimed funds sufficient to the family task and secured at least for this generation the principle of donor rights. Princeton, for its part, was publicly embarrassed and financially penalized, but it managed to avoid the death penalty. Even before the legal contest was settled, Princeton set up a new Office of Stewardship, whose responsibility it is to conform campus spending to donor intention. At this moment in time, the safest place on the planet for donor intent may well be Princeton, New Jersey."[64]

The Robertson Foundation for Government began operations in 2010 with grant programs at four schools. As of 2015, it had assets of $20.4 million and made grants of $1.8 million. It provided scholarships to students at five schools: the University of California (San Diego), Syracuse, the University of Maryland, Tufts, and Texas A&M.

The Robertson case shows just how little respect for donor intent many universities have, and how terribly difficult it is for donors and their families to receive justice in our legal system.

9

The David and Lucile
Packard Foundation

Name this donor: He co-founded Silicon Valley's first great corporation. He worked for, funded, and was a friend of every Republican president between Richard Nixon and George H.W. Bush. His decisive actions helped save the Hoover Institution in the 1950s and the American Enterprise Institute in the 1980s. In 1992, he declared that "the Democratic Party has been the party of socialism since President Roosevelt's term" and that "the Democratic Party is indentured to union labor." Today, the foundation that donates money in his name, one of America's largest, is a pillar of the liberal philanthropic establishment.

The answer is David Packard, co-founder of Hewlett-Packard. This chapter will document how the David and Lucile Packard Foundation has largely betrayed Packard's commitment to free-market principles, even though he was one of the most important donors in the twentieth century, where building the nation's conservative infrastructure is concerned.

David Packard was born in Pueblo, Colorado, in 1912. In 1930 he entered Stanford. Packard was 6' 5" and lettered in basketball, football, and track. But he swiftly established his brilliance as an electrical engineer and attracted the attention of Frederick Terman, a Stanford electrical engineering professor who recalled after his retirement that he was proud of helping bright students who were "electronic nuts, these young men who show as much interest in vacuum tubes, transistors, and computers as in girls."[1]

In 1933 Packard took Terman's radio-engineering course, where he met William Hewlett, who shared Packard's love of ham radio. Hewlett and Packard became close friends. Packard was such a bright student that he wrote the publishers of one electrical engineering textbook he used, correcting the textbook's errors.

After Packard's graduation in 1934, he spent a few years working for General Electric. But he and Hewlett both wanted to be entrepreneurs, and in 1939 they decided to start their own company. They flipped a coin to see whose name would come first; Hewlett won, so the company became Hewlett-Packard.[2]

The garage that was Hewlett-Packard's first home is now a national historic landmark, but thanks to Fred Terman, the company eventually found a more permanent home. Terman, who had loaned Hewlett and Packard $538 to get the company started, convinced Stanford to convert some of its open land to an area that would give growing companies new homes. Hewlett-Packard moved to the new Stanford Industrial Park in 1951, where its corporate headquarters has been ever since. (Among the other famous tenants of the Stanford Industrial Park is Xerox, which has its PARC research lab there.)[3]

At Hewlett-Packard, William Hewlett, who was executive vice president, was more of the chief technology officer and idea man, while David Packard, the company president, ran day-to-day operations. "Bill's a much better design engineer and I liked the management and production side," Packard said in a 1974 interview with *Nation's Business.*[4]

Packard became famous for his practice of wandering around the shop floor every day and talking with his engineers about their projects, a practice that since has been taught in business schools as "management by walking around."

"David Packard, 50, and William R. Hewlett, 49, are shirtsleeved electrical engineers whose idea of a satisfying day's work is just puttering around in a laboratory," *Time* noted in 1963. "Somewhat to their bemusement, Packard and Hewlett now find themselves running a $100 million corporation." *Time* added that only the top six HP executives had offices; "the rest work in a giant, noisy bullpen together with clerks and secretaries."[5]

One critical element of Hewlett-Packard's success was that the company remained union-free when the founders were in charge. "The most important element in our personnel policy is the degree to which we are able to get over to our people that we have faith in them and are more interested in them than someone else is," Packard told *Nation's Business.*

"My philosophy on unions is very simple," Packard added. "If our people think a union can do a better job for them than we can, then they ought to have a union. If they have faith in us, they don't need a union."[6] Hewlett-Packard stayed union-free.

As a boss, Packard delighted in old-fashioned paternalism. He enjoyed grilling meaty steaks at the annual company picnic, wearing an apron that said, 'I AM THE BOSS!" Until the rise of feminism in the 1970s ended such single-sex gatherings, Packard and the other male managers of HP held an annual weekend in the woods, where they would hunt, fish, drink, camp, and do a little business.

Although Hewlett-Packard offered its employees generous benefits (it was one of the first corporations to offer employees catastrophic health insurance), Packard personally could be quite brutal towards subordinates who failed to meet his exacting standards.

George Anders reports that Packard told the finance department that one proposal was "manifestly absurd and evidence of total stupidity." Another blast from Packard was so vicious that, while the text has disappeared, generations of engineers talked about the "Wow! Ouch!" memo.[7]

Anders interviewed Eric Hammerquist, an engineer who was hired by Hewlett-Packard in 1957 to work on a new version of an oscilloscope. The oscilloscope was meant to withstand heavy industrial use, but Hammerquist had used thinner 16-gauge aluminum for the outer casing instead of the traditional 14-gauge. One morning Hammerquist came to the office to find the oscilloscope smashed into bits. Attached to the wreckage was this note: "You can do better than this—Dave Packard."

"Within minutes, a new legend was born," Anders writes. "Engineers crowded around Hammerquist's workbench to marvel at the damage. Some roared with laughter. Others wanted to touch the twisted sheet metal so that they could feel the raw power of a boss who would destroy bad work rather than let it leave the shop. They talked about nothing else for hours. By lunchtime, Hewlett-Packard's lab engineers agreed that Dave Packard was surely the toughest, most brilliant boss in America and that they were damn lucky to be working for him. They also agreed it would be better to use stronger sheet metal from now on."[8]

Even as he became a billionaire, Packard retained his decency and humility. "David Packard was extraordinarily talented and extraordinarily nice," said Peter Flanigan, a special assistant to

President Richard Nixon who lived next door to Packard when he was deputy secretary of defense.[9]

Christopher DeMuth, who worked closely with Packard after DeMuth became president of the American Enterprise Institute in 1986, said in an interview that Packard was "completely unaffected by his great wealth." As an example, DeMuth recalled one trip to Packard's Los Altos, California, home when DeMuth needed to get to the San Jose airport. DeMuth asked for a phone to call a cab. Packard told him not to bother and personally drove DeMuth to the airport himself. "He was very proud of knowing the best routes" to the airport, DeMuth recalled.[10]

Tom Perkins worked for Hewlett-Packard twice in the 1960s and 1970s before becoming a partner in the venture capital firm Kleiner Perkins Caufield and Byers. He saw both Packard's anger and his kindness.

"Dave's anger was legendary, and pretty frightening," Perkins recalled in his memoir, *Valley Boy*. "As his temper frayed during the course of a day, he would gradually roll up his shirt sleeves, and by the time they were above his elbows it was smart to steer clear. Also, his pace of cigarette smoking so increased that he seemed nearly to chew them."[11]

"Dave Packard was my mentor, an inspiration, and, I am sure, the father I so desperately needed," Perkins recalled. "He taught me everything I know about entrepreneurship, and was the most important influence in my life. Dave was a giant, and the proof is, probably, that there are many dozens of others who feel just as strongly about him as I do."[12]

Under Packard and Hewlett's leadership, HP turned out scores of innovative products, including one of the first handheld calculators in 1972 and the first inkjet printer in 1984. As the company grew, Packard could turn more of his time and attention to philanthropy.

ℰ A Mixed Victory for Donor Intent

Stanford University was the earliest recipient of David Packard's philanthropy and received more money than any other recipient. Packard was a major donor to Stanford for over 40 years. He served as a trustee from 1954 to 1969 and was president of the board from 1958 to 1960. Stanford refuses to say how much

Packard gave, citing donor confidentiality, but *USA Today* stated in 1994 that Packard and Hewlett together donated more than $300 million during Packard's lifetime.[13]

Much of the money Packard gave Stanford was given anonymously. In a 1996 obituary for Packard, *Business Week* reporter Joan O'C. Hamilton recalled covering Stanford board of trustee meetings as a *Stanford Daily* reporter in the early 1980s. "Each month, I was reminded that I must keep confidential the section of the agenda in which anonymous gifts to the university were noted," Hamilton recalled. "Often, such contributions had come from Packard, Hewlett, or their personal foundations. I always wanted to write about it. I would invariably be told, 'No, thank you. The donors did not wish any publicity.'"[14]

In 1964, Packard served as head of Stanford's major gifts committee, which successfully completed a $100 million capital campaign (known as PACE) in three years. Because Stanford had completed this campaign two years ahead of schedule, the Ford Foundation provided a 1-4 match and donated an additional $25 million.[15]

But as a donor and trustee, Packard served as Stanford's loyal opposition. While his giving was fairly steady, Packard was primarily concerned with enhancing Stanford's excellence as an engineering school. For example, in 1959 Packard gave a speech to the local chapter of the American Association of University Professors where he called on Stanford to primarily produce engineers, scientists, and linguists who could help the U.S. fight the Cold War.

Packard's next active involvement at Stanford came in 1968. Stanford, like many universities, was in the throes of campus unrest. Radicals demanded that Stanford cut its ties to the Defense Department and end all research that involved the Vietnam War,

In May 1968, students held a "sit-in" at the student union. David Packard decided to take action and went into the building alone, without informing anyone at Stanford that he was planning to do this. This took considerable courage: *Fortune* that month had identified Packard as being worth $250 million, making him a tempting target for militants.

"If you get into these confrontations, you may lose everything you may have gained," Packard told the students, adding that his goal was to avoid the violent confrontations that had recently rocked Columbia University. "Keep working with us, and you will find a good solution to this.... We are willing in principle to allow you to have a larger voice, but not at this point to decide everything."[16]

Two days later, the sit-in ended without violence. In 1969 Packard left California for a three-year stint as Deputy Secretary of Defense. He remained a target for the militant Left. "The corporate liberals who run Stanford, like former trustee David Packard, see the university as a bastion of imperialism, while the dynamic of the Stanford environment is negating their purpose," noted a 1969 article in the Students for a Democratic Society publication *New Left Notes*.[17]

Packard had one more confrontation with the militant Left. According to former Hoover Institution president W. Glenn Campbell, in the fall of 1970 a group of militants announced they were going to visit Hewlett-Packard headquarters to confront David Packard and charge him with being a "war criminal." When they learned that Packard was in the Hoover Institution's main tower, they decided to seize Hoover instead. Stanford announced they would do nothing to help Hoover out, so one of Campbell's assistants "lined up a large number of volunteers, including several librarians,"[18] and at least five Hoover fellows to protect the building.

Two hours after the Hoover staff decided to protect their building, about twenty Santa Clara County cops showed up in full riot gear. The militants attempted to charge into the building several times, but were pushed back by the police. Eventually the militants dispersed, having gotten nowhere near Packard.

But Packard never forgot his encounters with the radical Left. In 1971, he left the Defense Department and resumed his duties as Hewlett-Packard president. He also resumed his gifts to Stanford, but tightened the strings. In October 1973, he expressed his concerns in a speech to the Committee for Corporate Support of American Universities.

Packard listed several problems on campuses of the day, ranging from "kicking R.O.T.C. programs off the campus" to "prohibiting businesses from recruiting on the campus." He said that someone (whom he didn't name) had done a study showing that as many as 90 percent of students were taught "that American corporations are evil and deserve to be brought under government control."[19]

Packard added that he thought the radical Left now dominated campuses. "I happen to believe," Packard said, "that such hostile groups of scholars are, to a large degree, responsible for the antibusiness bias of many of our young people today. And I do not believe it is in the corporate interest to support them—which is what we do to a greater or lesser degree with unrestricted funds."[20]

The solution, in Packard's view, was for businesses to tighten the strings on their gifts to universities, only giving money to programs and departments that "contribute in some specific way to our individual companies, or to the general welfare of the free enterprise system."[21]

Packard's speech was, in hindsight, the first blow in a battle that has taken place since then on what strings donors should place on their gifts to universities.[22] His speech provoked a great deal of reaction. Some CEOs, such as Sears, Roebuck president Arthur M. Wood, announced they would never place any strings on their corporate gifts to higher education.[23] Other corporate leaders sided with Packard. At a panel at the 1974 convention of the Association of American Colleges, Olin Corporation vice president William F. Leonard said his company was considering a six-figure contribution to one large university's capital campaign until the corporation read about a sociologist at the school who was advocating massive nationalization of businesses. The corporation decided to give a $250,000 grant to the school's engineering department instead.

"This was still an unrestricted grant with broad benefit," Leonard explained, "but we did not run the risk of money going into an area without specification that could militate against the competitive enterprise system."[24]

Many commentators excoriated Packard. "In urging corporations to put a stop to the practice of making unrestricted gifts to colleges and universities," the *New York Times* editorialized, "David Packard is attempting to turn back the clock of educational and social progress."[25] Ford Foundation president McGeorge Bundy (who was seven years younger than Packard) said that Packard was part of "the elderly right" who were peeved about giving to "free institutions of learning...where the prevailing values are seldom those of the ordinary corporate boardroom."[26]

Change, the magazine of the American Association of University Professors, even compared Packard's speech to the excesses of

Watergate. "Mr. Packard's underlying conviction," the magazine said, was "that money ought to buy influence or it ought not to be given at all. It is a view of life not far removed from that of the Committee to Re-Elect the President...it is perhaps not all that surprising that intelligent men, be they Patrick Buchanan or David Packard, attempt to yoke the still freest of American institutions to their own ideology." [27]

For several years, according to Packard biographer Michael S. Malone, Packard restricted his gifts to Stanford to the Hoover Institution and the athletic department. William Hewlett, however, had never reduced his giving, even though radicals once firebombed his home. Malone quotes former Stanford president Richard Lyman as saying that "Bill never stopped [giving], and I think Bill was instrumental in bringing Dave back into the fold."[28]

Ironically, the project that restored Packard to the rank of Stanford's major givers was the Terman Engineering Building, which, as we've seen, was torn down by Stanford in 2011. Afterwards, Packard gave many major gifts to Stanford, including some that remain anonymous.[29]

It should be noted, however, that Packard's gifts to Stanford were for buildings and for scholarships. A 1994 gift of $77.4 million, made by Hewlett and Packard jointly, was for new buildings for the engineering department. An additional $25 million gift in 1994, also made jointly with Hewlett, was for fellowships for junior science and engineering professors. As we'll see later, in 1986 Packard began donations for the Lucile Salter Packard Children's Hospital at Stanford with a $70 million grant. There is no evidence that Packard publicly gave any unrestricted gifts to Stanford at any point in his career (although he could have done so anonymously).

Packard had one final confrontation with Stanford. In 1990, Stanford was caught in a scandal when it became known that it billed as part of its overhead on government research contracts, among other things, $45,250 for a trustees retreat at Lake Tahoe, $4,000 spent on President Donald Kennedy's wedding reception, and $184,000 in depreciation on a yacht donated to Stanford. The revelations led to congressional hearings, as well as to Stanford's returning $1.35 million to the government, cuts in the federal grants to Stanford of at least $26 million, and the eventual resignation of Kennedy.[30]

In 1991 Packard gave an extensive interview about Stanford's excesses to the *San Francisco Chronicle*. On the one hand, he said that Stanford president Kennedy had been "a whipping boy" for congressional investigators and that the dubious expenses Stanford was caught billing the government for were "charged by all the universities" as part of their overhead charges. But on the other hand, he called on the government to tighten accounting rules to prevent future fraud, in order to "take away the temptations" for abuse from "all the trustees, presidents, and administrators of our great research schools."

Packard added that the congressional hearing investigating Stanford's overhead charges was "a sad day for Stanford" and that "the country club atmosphere at Stanford makes not one iota of contribution to the great research at the university."[31]

In an interview with the *Chronicle of Higher Education*, Packard said that the Stanford overhead scandal might affect his future gifts to Stanford. "I'm considering what I might have to do," he said. "I can't go into any details on it."[32]

What changes Packard made in his giving to Stanford—if he made them—remain unknown.

℮ Packard as a Republican

David Packard served several decades on the boards of two of the nation's most prominent conservative think tanks, the Hoover Institution and the American Enterprise Institute. In addition, he was a founder of the Committee on the Present Danger, a national-security nonprofit that warned about the threats the Soviet Union posed to the world. In 1977 Packard endorsed a report the committee produced stating that the Soviet Union would be likely to pursue "an expansionist policy" of global domination and evade any restrictions imposed by arms control treaties.[33]

Before we discuss his activities at these two institutions, it's important to discuss his role in the Republican Party. Packard was a Republican all his life and a major donor to the campaigns of Richard Nixon, Gerald Ford, Ronald Reagan, and George H.W. Bush, as well as numerous California campaigns for senator and governor.

Former AEI president Christopher DeMuth had many discussions about politics with Packard. DeMuth said that while "it's a little hard to characterize David politically, one should think of him as conservative in a California Goldwater way—libertarian rather than social conservative. He was not a highly political person, but was an engineer and a businessman first."[34]

In 1969, Packard took a leave of absence from Hewlett-Packard to serve as Deputy Secretary of Defense. Packard's two years in the Pentagon were spent trying to simplify the ways the military procured weapons. His efforts quickly made him a great many enemies, most of them career civil servants.

"Let there be no doubt about it. Deputy Defense Secretary Packard is the majordomo of Pentagon procurement policy in this administration," Claude Witze wrote in a 1971 article in *Air Force Magazine*. "A highly competent businessman, he is outspoken and has not hesitated to scold industry audiences. He is equally rough with the military brass, charging that too many of them 'want to get in on the act,' even when they can make no contribution to the effort."[35]

Even while in the government, Packard did not abandon his commitment to free-market capitalism. At Packard's memorial service in 1996, George Shultz, who served as director of the Bureau of the Budget in the Nixon Administration, recalled a meeting he had in the White House with President Richard Nixon and Secretary of the Treasury John Connally about providing a massive loan to Lockheed, a defense contractor teetering on the edge of bankruptcy. Nixon and Connally supported the loan, and Packard and Shultz were opposed.

According to Shultz, the meeting began with Shultz "expressing skepticism" about the Lockheed loan. Connally then said, "Lockheed is a very big defense contractor, so there are major national security concerns here. Isn't that right, Dave?"

"Well, the defense business in Lockheed is a sound, profitable, solid business," Packard said. "Lockheed's problem is entirely because of their effort to get into the commercial airplane business through the L-1011, and the easiest way is to slough that off and let it go bankrupt, and then the solid defense business will emerge. There won't be any national security problem."

"That was obviously unwelcome," Shultz said. "But it was dead honest. Neither Dave nor I was ever invited back to the White House to discuss that issue."[36]

In a 1995 interview with the National Museum of American History, Packard said that the Defense Department:

was a very large organization, and difficult to get what you want done. I always said it was like pushing on one end of a forty-foot boat and getting the other end to go where you wanted it to go. It was also a little tough on my wife because the first six weeks she lost sixteen pounds. She said it happened because she would get up in the morning and hear someone say something nasty about my husband [sic], and that would spoil her breakfast. Then she would hear some[thing] further and that would spoil her lunch. Then I would come home and tell her [what] a terrible time I had and that would spoil her dinner. She finally got over that when she stopped listening to the radio.[37]

Packard vented his frustrations on his resignation speech on December 1971, when he stated that he could cut the Defense Department budget by a billion dollars a year if the department had more freedom to close military bases that were no longer necessary. "There's no question that we could make savings if we were able to take actions without any constraints," he told the *New York Times*, adding, "We have a great many constraints, as everyone knows, on what you can do about a particular base in a particular area."[38]

Tom Perkins recalled that shortly before Packard left the Defense Department in 1971, he invited Perkins and John Young (a future president of Hewlett-Packard) for drinks in his hotel room while he was in New York attending "some political/social event."

Packard, Perkins recalled, "was in a tux, and I had never seen him looking so fancy, but he also looked exhausted, really devastated. This was during the height of the Vietnam War, and John and I were amazed as Dave told us in detail how he had to become directly involved in managing that horror. Like civilians before, he found the military bureaucracy intractable—we were astonished at his stories of deploying troops and planning battles. He was officially upbeat, but we both concluded that his heart wasn't in it."

After Packard's return to HP, Perkins noted, "Dave would never talk about his Washington years, but I believe they had a profound and depressing effect upon him at the deepest level."[39]

In 1971, Packard returned to HP. He was an elector for Richard Nixon in 1972, and grew close to Gerald Ford. A 1975 *U.S. News and World Report* article identified Packard as part of Ford's "kitchen cabinet," informal advisers who met with President Ford at least once a month.[40]

In August 1975, Packard went half time at Hewlett-Packard to serve as finance chairman for President Ford's 1976 re-election campaign. Three months later he resigned: He had relied on the traditional method of trying to get large donations from rich people instead of relying on direct mail. But rules implemented in 1974 gave larger amounts of federal matching funds to contributions of less than $250. Because Packard didn't get enough of these small contributions, the Ford campaign felt it was lagging in its effort to get federal subsidies and sacked Packard to bring in someone who understood the new rules of campaign finance.[41]

Packard played a smaller role in the 1980 presidential election. He contributed to Americans for an Effective Presidency, a political action committee headed by Dillon, Read managing partner Peter Flanigan that expected to raise between three and eight million dollars to support the Reagan campaign.[42] In addition, Packard was a major donor to the Ronald Reagan Presidential Foundation and was part of a failed effort to bring the Reagan presidential library to the Stanford campus.[43]

Packard's last political activity came in 1992. By this time he had retired as Hewlett-Packard CEO, but remained HP's chairman of the board. Packard was disturbed that his handpicked successor to head HP, John Young, had endorsed Bill Clinton. So Packard sent a letter to the editor to the *San Jose Mercury News*.

Packard said he "shared the concern" of Young and Apple Computer CEO John Sculley "about the platform of the Republican Party and the influence of the right-wing deviates in Orange County. My friends have overlooked the fact that the Democratic Party has been the party of socialism" since the Roosevelt Administration. "Roosevelt's disastrous agreement with Stalin at Yalta was a clear signal that he fundamentally supported socialism rather than freedom," Packard added.

"The Democratic Party is indentured to union labor and has expressed opposition to the North American Free Trade Agreement, which will generate millions of jobs in Canada, the United States, and Mexico in the years ahead," Packard wrote. "The Democratic Party is also indentured to the teachers' union.

As long as the teachers' union places survival ahead of the need to have knowledge about the subject being taught, there is no hope of improving America's educational system."

Packard added that if Democrats such as Rep. Pat Schroeder and Sen. Barbara Boxer had their way, "the United States, under President Bush's leadership, could not have undertaken Desert Storm, which was the greatest military victory in the history of the world." By contrast, "Gov. Clinton's military expertise is limited to calling up the National Guard in one of our smaller, less important states."[44]

❧ Packard and Hoover

David Packard's longest relationship with a conservative organization occurred with the Hoover Institution, on whose board he served from 1972 to 1996. He donated $4.5 million to Hoover during his lifetime, or $8.5 million in constant 2012 dollars, with $1 million of this coming in a 1993 grant to support Hoover's Russian programs.[45] His most important service, however, came in the late 1950s, when his actions helped save Hoover from total collapse.

The Hoover Institution is generally regarded as the oldest conservative think tank, but a better way to see it is as the oldest conservative center on a campus. Hoover is not an independent nonprofit but legally a division of Stanford with limited but not complete independence. In a 1967 oral history interview, David Packard said that Herbert Hoover intended the organization he created be a semi-autonomous part of Stanford. Hoover, Packard said, "was very anxious that it (the Hoover Institution) be part of the University. He thought, and rightly so, that it would prosper better as being part of the University than as an independent research institution and library."[46]

The reason for this can be found in Herbert Hoover's motivations as a donor. Hoover loved his alma mater, Stanford University, passionately. When it came time to settle down in 1920, Hoover built a home on the Stanford campus, in which he lived briefly before moving to Washington to join the Harding Administration in 1921. He returned to the Stanford campus in 1933 and lived there until 1944, when his wife, Lou Henry Hoover, died. Hoover willed the house to Stanford, moving to a suite in New York City's Waldorf-Astoria Hotel, where he lived until his death in 1964. The Lou Henry Hoover House remains the official home of the Stanford University president.[47]

The Hoover Institution has experienced a certain historical cycle: about once a decade someone at Stanford, suspicious of Hoover's robust conservatism, envious of Hoover's endowment, or both, strives to take control of Hoover. Such a moment came in the late 1950s.

In 1950 Herbert Hoover was Stanford's most generous benefactor and most prominent alumnus. But as George H. Nash shows in his book *Herbert Hoover and Stanford University*, "Hoover's relationship to the university became increasingly tense and discordant."[48]

In the 1950s, C. Easton Rothwell, who came to Hoover from Brookings and before that was a protégé of Alger Hiss at the State Department, headed Hoover. Rothwell, using grants from the Carnegie Endowment for International Peace, the Carnegie Corporation, the Rockefeller Foundation, and the Ford Foundation, produced a series of books on the U.S.S.R. and mainland China that seemed to Herbert Hoover to be apologies for Soviet and Chinese Communism. In addition, Rothwell hired left-wing staff, so that by the mid-1950s, except for Polish émigré Witold Sworakowski and Herbert Hoover's personal archivist, Thomas Thalken, "every member of the administrative staff of the Hoover Institution was politically left-of-center."[49]

Stanford also began siphoning off money meant to support the Hoover Institution. In the early 1950s, Herbert Hoover persuaded William Robertson Coe to donate eight percent of his estate to Stanford "to establish and maintain a Program of American Studies designed as a positive and affirmative method of meeting the threat of Communism, Socialism, Collectivism, Totalitarianism, and other ideologies opposed to the preservation of our system of Free Enterprise."[50] Stanford president Wallace Sterling[51] personally told Coe that he did not have to specify that the Hoover Institution had to be named in his will. Coe instead left his money to Stanford, which took it and made sure the Hoover Institution received none of it. "Sterling's move infuriated Hoover; the wedge between the two men grew greater," Nash writes.[52]

Grants from Herbert Hoover and his allies to the Hoover Institution gradually dried up and a $4 million endowment-building campaign in 1956 fizzled. Herbert Hoover refused to speak to

Easton Rothwell, and grants from Stanford became increasingly difficult to obtain.

So in April 1958, Easton Rothwell made his move. He called for all Hoover Institution fellowships in the future to be jointly made with Stanford and subject to Stanford tenure review, which would have amounted to a left-wing veto of Hoover appointees. In addition, Rothwell called for the Hoover Institution's budget to be controlled by Stanford.

Herbert Hoover retaliated in two ways. In 1955 Congress had passed a law subsidizing presidential libraries. Hoover's presidential papers (which he owned) were part of the Hoover Institution at the time, and Stanford relished the government subsidies that would come with operating a Hoover presidential library. The newly created Herbert Hoover Presidential Foundation invited Hoover to create a presidential library in his birthplace of West Branch, Iowa. Hoover decided to strip his personal office on the Stanford campus and send all the awards and honors on the walls to Iowa. Hoover also held several meetings with Wallace Sterling, and reminded him that the Hoover Institution was founded on the basis that it would have the freedom to hire and fire its staff.

Hoover had several complaints about Stanford, including that Stanford encouraged publication of "interpretative" histories (under the Hoover Institution imprint) that Hoover felt were apologies for Communism. Hoover wanted Hoover Institution books limited to reprinted and annotated documents.

But the fundamental difference between Herbert Hoover and Wallace Sterling was this: Hoover believed the Hoover Institution was an *independent* organization under Stanford's aegis. That independence included having a budget that was independent of Stanford control. Sterling believed that the Hoover Institution was a *department* of Stanford, and subject to as much control by the university as the political science department or departments of foreign languages.

In November 1958, Sterling presented his proposal to the Stanford trustees. On November 25, 1958, the trustees appointed a special committee to deal with the Hoover Institution. The Stanford trustees, according to a report of the meeting, "registered consensus on two points": that "the relation between the Hoover Institution to the University should revert to the relationship that was obtained in the early Twenties," and that the Hoover

Institution be made part of a new Center for International Studies, which would be a department of Stanford.[53] Had these motions prevailed, the Hoover Institution would have had very limited independence and Herbert Hoover would have lost.

During these negotiations, Easton Rothwell resigned to become president of Mills College. But where would the new president of Hoover come from—and what would the Hoover Institution's relationship to Stanford be?

Here David Packard played a role as negotiator between Herbert Hoover and a skeptical Stanford faculty. In his 1967 oral history, Packard said that Hoover "told me on several occasions that the founding of the Hoover Institution was probably the most important thing he had done in his life. And that, of course, is why he was so very much concerned that it be set up and established properly and continued to be run on the plane that he would hope it would reach."[54]

Files in the Herbert Hoover Presidential Library show that the first known contact between David Packard and Herbert Hoover took place on November 18, 1958. According to a summary of the phone call, "BEM (Hoover's assistant, Bernice Miller) mentions to Mr. Packard that HH (Herbert Hoover) has had nothing in writing from Dr. Sterling, that HH knows nothing of what he may be presenting: that often what Dr. Sterling presents as HH's views are not HH's understanding or views.... It looks to me as if all this (decisions about the Hoover Institution) was going to be a fait accompli." Packard's ambiguous response was "that he understood Mr. Hoover's views and everything was being worked out that way."[55]

On January 23, 1959, Packard wrote to Hoover to reassure him that Stanford would not cut its $125,000 contribution to the Hoover Institution (which was 30 percent of the think tank's budget) and that Wallace Sterling "will consult with you carefully" about who the next head of the Hoover Institution would be. "I want to reaffirm that the trustees share with you great pride in, and enthusiasm for, the Hoover Institution," Packard added.[56]

Three months later, Hoover submitted to the Stanford trustees a resolution (formally known as the Nth +1 Resolution) that stated, among its 10 points, that the Hoover Institution be independent of Stanford with an independent endowment and that Herbert Hoover have some say over who the next director would be.

Wallace Sterling countered on two fronts. He named Philip Rhinelander as acting director of the Hoover Institution. On April 4, 1959, Hoover replied to a letter from Sterling about Rhinelander's appointment, on which he had not been consulted. "I need not mention the half dozen assurances I have had that no one be appointed Director of the Institution without my approval," Hoover wrote.[57]

Sterling responded to Hoover on April 11, 1959. He said that Rhinelander "was acting as my designate," was not appointed or under the control of any faculty committees, and frequently met with all members of the Hoover Institution, including Herbert Hoover's few remaining allies.

Sterling claimed that Hoover's veto power over the appointment of a new Hoover Institution director was ambiguous. "This is a matter in which precision of language and understanding is important," Sterling wrote on April 11, 1959. He claimed that on October 30, 1958, Hoover had said that he "wanted a voice" in the appointment of a new director. "I am not disposed to quarrel about semantics, but there would appear to be a difference between 'having a voice' and 'approval.' Certainly, as far as the Trustees are concerned, it is unthinkable that you should not 'have a voice.' Whether or not this amounts to your privilege to approve or disapprove is something which should be clarified, because, as I understand my office, it is the Trustees and not the President who have the right to grant or withhold such a privilege."

"I am extremely anxious," Sterling concluded, "to have the earliest possible resolution of all matters concerning the Hoover Institution. I dislike having you upset about it, and I dislike being upset about it."[58]

David Packard noted Rhinelander's appointment in a letter to Hoover dated April 17, 1959. Packard wrote that he understood Hoover's concerns about Rhinelander's appointment. "I agree that this misunderstanding points to the need for a clarification of procedures and policies and for these to be reduced to writing at the earliest possible date," Packard wrote. "I regret very much that we have caused you additional worry about the Institution. I sincerely believe we have made great progress in the last year on this problem and I am confident we will be able to do this job for you the way you would like to have it done."[59]

Packard then proposed meeting in New York with Hoover in May. This would be the second of three meetings Packard and

Hoover would have in New York in 1959; they also met once at Stanford, as part of a celebration of Hoover's 85th birthday.

A second charge concerned the financial relationship between Herbert Hoover and Stanford. Herbert Hoover's presidential papers, like those of all former presidents before Richard Nixon, were his personal property. They were stored at Stanford and maintained by archivists whose salaries were paid for by Stanford. Wallace Sterling charged that this arrangement made Hoover a tax cheat, since Stanford was maintaining Hoover's property for free.

Hoover hired the accounting firm of Blumenthal and Sharp, who noted that Hoover personally paid Stanford a fee each year to pay for part of the costs of maintaining his archive, and paid part of the salaries of the archivists. Accountant Morton Blumenthal stated that Hoover was careful to make sure the fees he paid to Stanford for archivists' salaries were not part of the charitable contributions he made to Stanford and deducted from his taxes. The idea of Hoover as a tax cheat quietly disappeared.[60]

Wallace Sterling responded to Herbert Hoover's proposals. The major difference between Sterling and Hoover concerned how the next director of the Hoover Institution would be chosen. Sterling suggested this arrangement:

"There shall be a Director of the Hoover Institution whose appointment shall be recommended to the Committee of the Trustees (Chapter III, Section 13) and thence to the Trustees by the President of the University after his previous consultation with the Founder. Such recommendation of the President shall not require approval of the Advisory Board of the Faculty of Stanford University."

Hoover erupted. "I cannot accept the idea of mere consultation in a matter which reaches to the whole fundamental of my relation to the Institution. The Institution is obviously my creation. Its major financial support for forty-four years has come from my friends and myself. The largest parts of its collections were acquired either directly by myself or the staffs which I have headed. I have hoped it would be my major contribution to American life. The pledge to confidence of restricted collections is my personal pledge and the Director must need be a man in whom I can have confidence."[61]

On May 25, 1959, the committee of the Stanford trustees devoted to the Hoover Institution issued its report about the

Hoover Institution, under the signature of David Packard as acting chairman of the Stanford board. Herbert Hoover, aided by David Packard as negotiator and peacemaker, had achieved a decisive victory.

The agreement opened with a long preamble about the purpose of the Hoover Institution and included the following clauses:

> Paragraph 3. That the Hoover Institution on War, Revolution, and Peace is an independent Institution within the frame of Stanford University. The relation to the University is that the President of the University will propose all appointments, promotions, and the budget of the Institution directly to the Board of Trustees. There shall be no reference to any faculty committees between the President and the Board of Trustees.

> Paragraph 7. The Director of the Institution shall be recommended to the Board of Trustees by the President of the University for appointment by the Trustees. He shall have been previously approved by Mr. Hoover. Such recommendation of the President shall not require approval of the Advisory Board of the Academic Council of Stanford University.

> Paragraph 9. That gifts made to Stanford University and designated for support of the Hoover Institution shall be used for that designated purpose and no other. The funds available to the Hoover Institution from such gifts, be they income from endowment or gifts from annual expenditure or gifts for special purposes on a special schedule, shall be made part of and shown in the annual budget of the Institution.

Other clauses of the agreement stated that the director and staff of the Hoover Institution would be subject to administrative tenure, not the academic tenure that required approval of a fellow by faculty committees.[62] Another clause stated that Stanford would never cut its contribution to the Hoover budget below $125,000.

The debate now turned to who would be the next Hoover Institution director. Hoover's preferred candidate was Arthur

Kemp, an economist at Claremont Men's College (now Claremont McKenna College). Kemp had been Hoover's research assistant in the 1940s and remained a close friend.[63]

Kemp, however, was an outspoken conservative who frequently contributed to *The Freeman* and other right-wing journals. On August 21, 1959, Packard wrote to Hoover, "Dr. Sterling is strongly opposed to the appointment. It would create a serious problem with the faculty. The staff of the Institution would look on Mr. Kemp's appointment with no favor."

"I have made a brief investigation of my own in order to decide whether to recommend his appointment under these circumstances," Packard continued. "I find he is not well known even in his own field of Economics. Those who know him say he is an able and a careful worker but has done nothing of great distinction. His background in library work, history, and languages does not seem to be very impressive for such an important assignment."

"I think he would be a good choice if he came with the enthusiastic support of the people here," Packard concluded, "but he does not appeal to me as the right man for the directorship under present conditions. I therefore cannot recommend the appointment of Mr. Kemp to you at this time."[64]

Hoover responded on August 26, 1959, in a letter to Packard that was "only for your information." Hoover said that Kemp had received unsolicited endorsements from many people including Russell Kirk and Felix Morley, an economics commentator who had once been president of Haverford College. He said that Kemp, in 1956, had, with Wallace Sterling's approval, reviewed "the publications of the Hoover Institution. He deleted from them many slanted and leftish statements, as he is an intrepid soldier for free enterprise. As a result, Rothwell, the Wrights, and others in the Institution started a smear campaign to get him removed, which even reached to Wally" (Sterling).[65]

Kemp might have withstood Sterling's veto, but with both Sterling and Packard opposed, Kemp's nomination was quietly dropped. Kemp remained at Claremont until his retirement in 1981.

Hoover, however, had an alternative candidate. In "Mr. Hoover's Twelve-Year Fight," Bernice Miller states that Hoover "for nearly a year, searched the highways and byways to find an acceptable director."[66] On June 29, 1959, Raymond Moley, a one-time Brains

Truster for Franklin D. Roosevelt who had abandoned the Left and become a prominent free-market advocate, recommended W. Glenn Campbell, director of research at the American Enterprise Association (now the American Enterprise Institute).

Campbell's references were formidable. In addition to Raymond Moley, Campbell was endorsed by Felix Morley, former General Foods chairman of the board Colby Chester, and Lewis Strauss, a former Atomic Energy Commission chairman who had worked as an assistant to Hoover in his efforts to feed Europe after World War I.[67]

Most importantly, Campbell had the endorsement of Wallace Sterling. "I very much like the cut of his jib," Sterling wrote to Hoover on October 13, 1959. "I also like the questions he asked me about the University, the Institution, you, and myself."[68]

Campbell received the endorsement of the Hoover Institution subcommittee of the Stanford trustees in October 1959. Following endorsements from Sterling and Hoover, he was named director of the Hoover Institution in November 1959.[69]

With matters being settled, Herbert Hoover resumed his quiet fundraising. In a letter to David Packard in December 1959, he summed up the gifts he had received for the Hoover Institution: $25,000 from the Pew Memorial Trust, two grants from Jeremiah Milbank of $200,000, and two grants from the Fleischmann Foundation of $275,000.[70]

The controversy over the Hoover Institution, however, was not over. Remember that the statement of the Stanford board of trustees endorsing the independence of the Hoover Institution included a lengthy statement by Herbert Hoover about the institution's purposes. The crucial paragraph was this: "The purpose of this Institution must be, by its research and publications, to demonstrate the evils of the doctrines of Karl Marx—whether Communism, Socialism, economic materialism, or atheism—thus to protect the American way of life from such ideologies, their conspiracies, and to reaffirm the validity of the American system."[71]

In March 1960, the *Stanford Daily* published an interview with W. Glenn Campbell and decided to publish the entire trustees statement as part of its story. When asked about the paragraph about "the doctrines of Karl Marx," W. Glenn Campbell said, "I see nothing wrong with it, do you?" and added that "there are evils in Marxism, and I hope to expose them."[72]

In an editorial accompanying the article, the *Stanford Daily* declared, "the Hoover Institution has no right to predetermine the goals of scholarship."[73] The next day Wallace Sterling told the *Stanford Daily* that the statement "had been issued unilaterally by Mr. Hoover" and that the board had only found out about the statement in January 1960. Neither statement was true; Hoover's statement had been edited by the board before its approval.[74]

The campus newspaper also issued many statements by professors (including Philip Rhinelander) denouncing Herbert Hoover's statement. *Oakland Tribune* columnist Raymond Lawrence defended Herbert Hoover, declaring, "There may be some misguided liberals who feel they do not want to work in the Hoover library because of the statement by the founder, but if they feel that way then their labors probably would be no loss to scholarship, anyway."[75]

The Stanford trustees debated about what to do about Herbert Hoover's statement for some months. On May 27, 1960, David Packard wrote to Hoover, stating "We are, I think, making some progress on the faculty problem" and adding in a hand-written note, "No action was taken by the Trustees. I will keep you advised on any possible action in advance."[76]

On June 2, 1960, Hoover replied, stating that "I had originally prepared a letter of great violence on these matters," which he decided not to send in favor of a factual reiteration of his position. He added, "so far as the campus is concerned, the Hoover Institution seems to be the Frankenstein of my old age."[77]

In the fall of 1960, the Stanford trustees engineered a compromise. Hoover's statement was allowed to remain unedited, but the trustees declared it to be "a preface" expressing the donor's personal opinion and not a formal statement of Hoover Institution policy.[78]

The academic freedom debate was not quite over. In December 1960, the *Saturday Evening Post* ran a fawning profile of Wallace Sterling, mostly celebrating his success as a master fundraiser who had doubled Stanford's endowment from $46 million to $92 million and who had snagged a $25 million grant from the Ford Foundation. The article mentioned the debate over academic freedom at the Hoover Institution and paraphrased but did not quote directly Hoover's statement that the Hoover Institution should fight "the evils of Karl Marx."[79]

Hoover wanted the entire paragraph quoted, and enlisted John Stewart, a financial adviser in San Francisco and a member of the Hoover Institution board, to write a letter to the *Post* demanding a correction. An exchange of about 20 letters followed between Stewart, Hoover, several Stanford officials, and *Saturday Evening Post* editor Ben Hibbs and managing editor Robert Sherrod.

In January 1961, David Packard wrote to Hoover informing him that he had become an emeritus trustee of Stanford. The rest of the letter concerned the *Saturday Evening Post* debate. Packard wrote that Wallace Sterling "reported on the status of the Hoover Institution and concluded by saying that in his opinion the recent discussions should be terminated and the matter closed."

Packard said that when he read Taylor's article "it caused me some concern, but I concluded that it will mean little or nothing to people who are not familiar with the detail background. I have discussed this with Jim Black and a number of other Trustees and we believe it would be very advisable to ask Mr. Stewart to withdraw his request to the *Saturday Evening Post* to publish his letter.... While Mr. Stewart's letter would, no doubt, help to correct the record it might trigger further public discussions and could upset the situation out here, which in my opinion is going very well."[80]

Stewart and Hoover obeyed. On February 8, 1961, Stewart wrote to Packard, informing Packard that he had formally withdrawn his letter and had an acknowledgement from the *Post* of the withdrawal. "I will make no move without first consulting you," Stewart concluded.[81]

With this letter, the controversy about the Hoover Institution formally ended. Packard and Hoover remained friends, and soon after admonishing Hoover, Packard and his wife spent a week fishing in Florida with the former President. Hoover even felt compelled to share news of his aches and pains with Packard. His doctors, Hoover wrote, had banned him from eating "all good food except cranshaw melons."[82]

The one substantial change in the relations between Herbert Hoover and Stanford clarified how Herbert Hoover's intentions would be upheld after his death. In 1962, the Stanford trustees agreed that any future director of the Hoover Institution had to receive the approval of the Hoover Foundation, which Nash described as "a New York corporation comprising various Hoover family members and friends."[83] Once this was done, Hoover formally transferred control of his non-presidential papers to Stanford. (His presidential papers had been moved to his Iowa birthplace.)

Hoover repaid the support David Packard had given him by supporting the PACE capital campaign Packard headed. Occasionally some of the PACE funds were diverted to the Hoover Institution, such as an unrestricted $100,000 grant in 1962 from the Irvine Foundation, of which $25,000 went to the Hoover Institution.

In April 1964, Hoover wrote to Packard, congratulating him on securing the largest grant to the Hoover Institution so far: $750,000 from Richard Mellon Scaife. "I want you to know of my appreciation for the part you played in securing this contribution," Hoover wrote, adding that "it is the most substantial gift the Institution has received" and "Glenn Campbell has proved to be everything I believed him to be when I urged him upon the trustees."[84] Hoover persuaded donors to contribute substantial sums, including Alfred P. Sloan Jr., who contributed a million dollars to the Stanford business school, and William P. Keck, who donated $5.6 million, the largest unrestricted gift Stanford had received up to that time. In addition, Hoover personally addressed one fundraising dinner and sent a filmed message to another dinner. "Hoover had a love for Stanford University that defied logic," archivist Thomas Thalken observed.[85]

The Scaife grant was used to aid in the construction of a second building for the Hoover Institution. According to Glenn Campbell, this grant came about after a meeting of Scaife, Campbell, and Packard in the spring of 1964 at the Pacific Union Club in San Francisco, in which "Mr. Packard eloquently seconded my appeal for a second building."[86]

Packard responded to Hoover on April 28, 1964, with more good news: The Stanford trustees had decided to allot $500,000 of PACE funds to the Hoover Institution. "It is our plan that these funds will be made available either for endowment or buildings," Packard wrote. "This will give us assurance that we will be in a position to go ahead with the proposed new building, whether or not we have additional gifts forthcoming."[87]

On May 6, 1964, Herbert Hoover sent one final telegram to David Packard. "Mr. Milbank will put up $250,000 towards completion of the building," Hoover wrote.[88] Three months later, Herbert Hoover died at age 90.

Other donors who contributed to the construction of the new building included the Joseph N. Pew Jr. Trust, which provided $100,000, and David Packard, who personally contributed $50,000. In fact, donors were so generous that the $500,000 in PACE money was unused and was added to the Hoover endowment when the Lou Henry Hoover Building opened in 1967.

Packard's next major contribution to the Hoover Institution came in 1969. When Packard joined the Nixon Administration, he had to place his Hewlett-Packard stock in a blind trust. Packard proposed donating the income from the trust to Hoover. Stanford's development office objected, wanting to claim all the money for Stanford. After a furious debate, the blind trust income was split, with both Hoover and Stanford receiving $340,000. Once again, the Scaife Family Foundation matched Packard's grant, providing an additional $500,000.

The Hoover Institution at this time was a foreign-policy think tank, but they had thought about expanding into domestic policy, and Packard's gift went to the fledgling "national affairs" program. His money was used to hire the first National Affairs Fellow, Dennis Bark. It is possible that Packard coined the term "National Affairs Fellow"[89] to describe the Hoover domestic policy program.

❧ David Packard and AEI

David Packard was also instrumental in saving the American Enterprise Institute from a grave financial crisis. The troubles began when William Baroody Sr. retired from AEI in 1978 and was succeeded by his son, William Baroody Jr.

In a 1987 article, Alvin P. Sanoff showed that the younger Baroody was spectacularly inept in financial matters, "Baroody, for all practical purposes, ran a one-man show, and a loosely run one at that," Sanoff reported. "His budgeting system was informal; some of the bookkeeping was done by hand." This led one former AEI scholar to tell Sanoff that AEI's financial department was so antiquated "that it was like something out of a Dickens novel."[90]

According to Sanoff, William Baroody Jr.'s policy was to create programs he liked and come up with the money to pay for them later. AEI began to borrow in June 1981, and by the end of

Baroody's tenure, a $3 million line of credit was nearly exhausted. "An organization like AEI should never have to borrow," James Hicks, who became vice president for finance for AEI after Baroody was fired, told Sanoff. "It should only spend money after it gets the grant in hand."[91]

In mid-1985, AEI aborted a plan to move their offices to a newer office building; $500,000 was wasted on the failed move. In Christmas 1985, 50 support staff were fired, with another 20 scholars and staff let go a month later. At a staff retreat in January 1986, staff were told that AEI had skipped pension payments for the past three months.

Baroody was fired in June 1986 and his successor, Christopher DeMuth, became president six months later. When DeMuth became president in December 1986, AEI was $9 million in debt and on the verge of closing. The organization had spent not only its endowment, but also all of the funds used to endow chairs. The rent had not been paid in months, and AEI was also far behind in paying Social Security taxes for its employees. The organization was so strapped for cash that it faced possible bankruptcy if a million dollars wasn't raised immediately.

DeMuth's first task, he recalled, was to ask for emergency aid from the AEI board of trustees. He turned to Packard, who was a trustee at the time. "David committed immediately to pay several hundred thousand dollars if all the other trustees agreed to put in $25,000 each," DeMuth recalled. The trustees agreed, and AEI's immediate financial crisis was averted thanks to Packard's matching gift.[92]

"David was the market-maker, the *sine qua non*," DeMuth said. The plan that saved AEI "wouldn't have happened" if Packard hadn't proposed it.

DeMuth met Packard many times before his death. He found that Packard was keenly interested in AEI's finances, particularly in recovering the money used to fund endowed chairs. DeMuth recalls that he and Packard had only one major disagreement.

When AEI was in its financial crisis, all members of the think tank's foreign policy staff were laid off except for Jeane Kirkpatrick. After AEI received a million-dollar grant from the Lynde and Harry Bradley Foundation in early 1987, DeMuth appointed a new staff of foreign and defense policy specialists, including Mark Falloff, Constantine Menges, Joshua Muravchik, and Richard Perle. When

Perle had previously served as an assistant secretary of defense in the Reagan Administration, he had persuaded the Administration to impose tough export controls on American companies that wanted to sell goods that could be used by a Communist country's military. This blocked Hewlett-Packard from exporting computers to China.

DeMuth is convinced that Packard, who was Hewlett-Packard chairman at the time, had read internal company reports warning about Perle, who was known as "the Prince of Darkness" because of his love for behind-the-scenes machinations.

"David probably got a memo from HP's man in China, saying, 'The Defense Department, thanks to the Prince of Darkness, is preventing us from trying to sell'" to the Chinese. When Packard called to complain about Perle's appointment, DeMuth said, "I was caught completely by surprise."

The conversation, DeMuth recalled, was civil. DeMuth explained why he thought Perle would be a good addition to the AEI staff. Packard patiently listened. "David never asked me to rescind the appointment, or suggested that there would be a black spot in the future" affecting Packard's donations to AEI. Packard's objections were duly noted, and both Packard and DeMuth moved forward. However, in future meetings, Packard "would always ask, 'How's Richard Perle doing?'"[93]

ℰ The Packard Foundation Gets Started

Although the David and Lucile Packard Foundation was founded in 1964, it did not begin significant giving until the early 1980s and was not fully funded until Packard donated $2 billion in Hewlett-Packard stock to the foundation in 1988. Before we discuss how the Packard Foundation largely abandoned David Packard's conservative principles, it's important to discuss David Packard's views on population control and the environment, since these are two causes the Packard Foundation continues to support.

David Packard was an advocate of population control. In a 1986 interview with the *Christian Science Monitor*, he stated that "the most important question we have to deal with is a combination of population control and the control of our environment—how to utilize the world in as effective a way as we can for the future of mankind. Anytime you look at the long-range situation, you come to the conclusion that, unless we can limit the population, the other problems are eventually going to become unmanageable." He added that the solution to global population problems was to be "more rational about birth control and abortion," topics he said at times "get very emotional." Finally, "the United States should be a leader in helping with this problem" of population control.[94]

According to George Anders in his history of HP, David Packard expressed his intentions as a donor in a document, written sometime in the late 1980s, called "Some Random Thoughts About the Packard Foundation." While this document has never been made public, according to Anders, Packard wrote that the foundation's first concern should be population control. Packard stated that an annual global population increase of two percent per year would mean "utter chaos for humanity.... The highest priority of our foundation must be to do what can be done to get the worldwide population growth" back to lower levels. "We must support abortion and any other policy that will help," Packard wrote.[95]

Indeed, while the Packard Foundation has always funded population programs, his daughters, who ended up in control of it after his death, have tried to make global population control less of a priority than their father had wanted: "The Packard Foundation wouldn't be turned upside down to be a tool of the most severe Malthusians," Anders writes. "Times had changed. The specter of a world ruined by too many hungry mouths seemed a lot less worrisome a decade after Dave Packard wrote his letter, thanks largely to an abrupt drop in China's birth rate."[96]

After the Packard Foundation received its $2 billion in 1988 from David Packard, one of its first reactions was to increase its population control program from $1 million in annual grantmaking to $10 million. *New York Times* philanthropy reporter Kathleen Teltsch interviewed Packard Foundation consultant Anne Firth Murray. Teltsch reported that the additional funds would "emphasize Third World assistance and cover adolescent pregnancy and assured access to abortion."[97] Packard was actively involved in the foundation when this decision was made.

The best expression of Packard's views on the environment also appears in his 1986 *Christian Science Monitor* interview. There, he stated that environmental degradation was a problem because "the environment is going to determine, in the final analysis, what population can be supported." He said "a lot can be done" in the area of environmental policy, including "trying to preserve some attractive examples of ecology—so that you can keep some of the original character of our country and [countries] around the world—on down to [questions of] food production and the preservation of farmland."

Summarizing Packard's thoughts, Kidder wrote that Packard felt that "the greatest danger to the environment...arises from intensive farming: loss of topsoil through erosion, the disappearance of forests through land-clearing and harvesting firewood, and toxic pollution through the use of insecticides and fertilizers."

Another one of Packard's concerns was climate change. "We're changing the character of our atmosphere, which might change the character of our (planet)." The result could be "some very drastic changes in our climate."[98]

In his lifetime, David Packard was an active conservationist. In 1981, the *New York Times* reported that Packard chaired the Nature Conservancy's Critical Areas Program Committee, which was raising $15 million by the end of 1982 to buy 22,000 acres of habitat.[99] Four years later, Packard was one of the initial board members of the National Fish and Wildlife Foundation, set up by former Interior Secretary William P. Clark to buy and preserve habitats.[100]

In the 1980s, Packard launched three major philanthropic projects the Packard Foundation continues today: the Monterey Bay Aquarium, the Lucile S. Packard Children's Hospital at Stanford, and the Packard Fellowships in Science and Engineering.

The Monterey Bay Aquarium was the largest philanthropic project David Packard funded in his lifetime. Two of Packard's daughters, Julie Packard and Nancy Packard Burnett, are marine biologists, and as Julie Packard told the *New York Times* when the aquarium opened in Monterey, California, in 1984, "my father sort of challenged us to come up with a project that was all our own."[101] Julie Packard has been the Monterey Bay Aquarium's first—and so far, only—executive director.

In his 1995 Smithsonian oral history interview, David Packard explained why his foundation became interested in funding an aquarium. He said that when the Packard Foundation began operations in 1964, "we spent the first ten years or so just responding to all the requests, just like any other foundation. About the middle 1970s I decided we should be developing some programs of our own, instead of just doing whatever people requested. I have two daughters and a son-in-law and some friends who are active in the Hopkins Marine Station down on the Monterey Peninsula. They had been interested in an old cannery" on the Monterey waterfront as the site for an aquarium.

"So we did a feasibility study and were told, yes, it is a viable program, and we could build an aquarium there which would cost about ten million dollars, and it would be successful and would pay its own way. So with that information we hired architects and engineers and proceeded to design the aquarium. Well, I didn't know a damned thing about aquariums, but my wife and I visited every aquarium in the country, and my children visited some of the aquariums overseas."

"What we learned was that most aquariums are built on a fixed budget, and they made short cuts." So Packard bought equipment that made fiberglass-reinforced cement and plastics, and hired experts in building fiberglass boats to handle the construction.

"The result was that the aquarium cost us forty million dollars instead of ten million dollars. My children thought we shouldn't charge admission so that poor people could come. I said we weren't going to do it that way. If what we did was right, people would pay for it. If it wasn't right, we shouldn't have done it."[102]

The Monterey Bay Aquarium has since become a major tourist attraction, with a 2016 budget of $136.6 million. According to the aquarium, Packard Foundation donations in 2016 were between $1 million and $10 million. The aquarium gives the David Packard Award to its most generous donor. In 2016, this was Intel co-founder Gordon Moore, who received his prize at a ceremony at Hewlett-Packard Enterprise.

Former American Enterprise Institute president Christopher DeMuth recalled that Packard, in his late 70s, became intent on spending down more of his fortune during his lifetime, on projects he personally approved of. At one meeting, Packard told of his latest major venture—mapping the ocean floor around Monterey Bay with an undersea robot. Among other things, Packard explained, the project would yield important military applications in improved underwater data transmission.

DeMuth told Packard, "Congratulations, but you're still moving negatively on your goal"—by which DeMuth meant that during the months Packard devoted to the ocean-mapping project, his wealth had grown by more than the amount he'd invested in it.[103]

George Anders says that the children's hospital "was Lucile Packard's project. She cared deeply about children, dating back to the 1930s, when she was an active volunteer in a children's convalescent home."[104] Planning for the hospital began around 1983, and Lucile Packard saw some of the plans for the hospital before her death in 1987. As she was dying, David Packard decided to name the hospital for his wife. It was the first building on the Stanford campus to bear the Packard name. When asked why the hospital wasn't named for the entire Packard family, Packard said, "This is her project. I'm not going to agree to anything less than that."[105]

The Lucile Salter Packard Children's Hospital opened in 1991. David Packard was present at the opening, as was California Gov. Pete Wilson and (on Packard's request) First Lady Barbara Bush. "Mrs. Packard's idea was to make this as friendly a place as possible and not have it look like a hospital," Packard told the *San Francisco Chronicle*. "All I was really interested in was having it come out the way she wanted it to."

As for the Packard Fellowships in Science and Engineering, they have been awarded since 1988, and are currently five-year, $875,000 grants. The foundation works with 50 leading universities. Each of the universities nominates two professors, and panelists winnow the field down to a smaller number; in 2016, 18 fellowships were awarded to professors at Princeton, Yale, and Stanford, among other places. The foundation says that it has awarded $378 million in fellowships since 1988 and that its fellows have gone on to win MacArthur fellowships, the Nobel Prize in Physics, and the Fields Medal, the highest honor in mathematics.[106]

❧ The Packard Foundation Betrays Donor Intent

When David Packard died in 1996, additional Hewlett-Packard shares were willed to the foundation, and these shares, combined with high share prices for Hewlett-Packard common, led the value of the Packard Foundation endowment to rise from $2.4 billion in 1995 to $13.5 billion in 1999.[107]

After Packard's death, control of the Packard Foundation passed to Packard's three liberal daughters, Nancy Packard Burnett, Susan Packard Orr, and Julie Packard, and to his conservative son, David W. Packard. The foundation decided to betray David Packard's commitment to conservative causes by defining donor intent in a way that ignored Packard's conservatism.

The evidence suggests that David Packard, in his "Random Thoughts" paper that set forth his intentions, imposed no restrictions on how the Packard Foundation should spend its money. His successors took that freedom to define donor intent and proceeded to do whatever they felt like.

In a 1999 interview with *Foundation News and Commentary*, Colburn S. Wilbur, who served as Packard Foundation president from 1976-99 and who remains on the Packard board, explained the family's thinking. "The Packard family takes donor intent and our donor's values [integrity, respect for the individual, effectiveness, building leadership and thinking big] very seriously," Wilbur said, adding, "David Packard always intended to leave discretion and flexibility to future boards. He trusted them and realized that organizations need to change over time."[108]

"Mother and Father knew they wouldn't be here forever to know what the issues of the day would be," Susan Packard Orr told the *Chronicle of Philanthropy* in 1998. "I wouldn't say we make a lot of decisions based on exactly what they might have done. We feel their presence, but not a heavy hand."[109]

Of course, as we've already seen in other chapters, donors who decide to create perpetual foundations and leave "discretion and flexibility to future boards" nearly always have their wishes betrayed, as has largely happened with the Packard Foundation. When a donor defines his or her intent in such a vague way, it allows boards to do whatever they want to in their dead creator's name.

As for David W. Packard, David Packard's only son and only non-liberal heir, the foundation in 1999 allowed him to secede with 11 percent (or $1.6 billion) of the Packard endowment, which it paid to the Packard Humanities Institute, a foundation created in 1987. The institute's endowment has since shrunk to $723.9 million in 2015.

The younger David Packard has a doctorate in classics. His first love was film preservation, and his first philanthropic activity was restoring the Stanford Theatre, a classic old movie house in Palo Alto that had fallen on hard times.[110] The institute has continued to fund film preservation and restoration; the Library of Congress's film preservation laboratory in Culpeper, Virginia, is named the Packard Campus because of the institute's long-term support. (The building had previously been used by the Federal Reserve to store currency in case of atomic attack by the Russians.) Other emphases of the institute include placing the works of great composers online and supporting archeological research.

An article in *Philanthropy* magazine in 2000 suggested that the Packard Humanities Institute was exploring entering public policy through grants supporting research in school choice and aiding such noted education scholars as economist Eric Hanushek of the Hoover Institution.[111]These grants have since been stopped. According to the institute's most recent Form 990, the institute provided $20.8 million in grants in 2010. Its three largest grants were $4.6 million to the Instituto Packard, an organization devoted to preserving the archeology of the ancient Roman town of Herculaneum,[112] $1.8 million to the International Mozarteum Foundation to put the complete works of Wolfgang Amadeus Mozart online, and $1.1 million to Founding Fathers Papers, a nonprofit which works to publish the papers of George Washington, Thomas Jefferson, and other Founders.

After Packard's death, the Packard Foundation provided one grant to AEI and a three-year, $600,000 grant to Hoover.[113] It has occasionally given money to Hoover since then for special projects.

Christopher DeMuth says that he went to the Packard Foundation many times after David Packard's death, including meeting several times with then-president Colburn Wilbur. The foundation's officers, he said, were very nice, telling him everything he needed to do—and then rejected every proposal. "As a fundraiser, I know when donors are saying 'no,'" DeMuth said, eventually giving up raising any money from them.[114]

The Packard Foundation, however, did not entirely abandon its founders' principles. Grants to the Monterey Bay Aquarium, the Packard Fellowships, and the Lucile Packard Children's Hospital continued. And Susan Packard Orr, who became Packard Foundation chairman after her father's death, shares her father's enthusiasm for population control. "If you're really concerned about the future of the human race, what it comes down to is that there are too many people," she told *Stanford Business* magazine in 1997. "We're not shy about stepping up to the plate and talking about the importance of family planning."[115]

The foundation's leading effort in population control came in 2000, when the Food and Drug Administration authorized use of mifepristone, an abortion pill more commonly known as "RU-486." Roussel Uclaf in France developed the drug, but the French company donated the American rights to the drug to the Population Council, which conducted clinical trials and hired Danco Laboratories to manufacture the pill. Danco, a start-up company, had trouble attracting investors, and couldn't manufacture RU-486 until the Packard Foundation provided a $10 million loan, which enabled Danco to begin production.

Sarah Clark, head of the Packard population control program, told *Time* that Danco Laboratories was "not able to raise the money through regular channels. It didn't surprise me. It made me sad."[116]

❧ The Packard Foundation's Crisis

In 1999, the Packard Foundation's future seemed limitless. With a gain of $4 billion in its endowment, it appeared that the Packard Foundation would grow exponentially, with the wealth created by steadily rising Hewlett-Packard shares enabling the foundation to create scores of new programs.

But within a few years the Packard Foundation was headed for a near-collapse.

Part of the decline was due to the general slump in tech stocks, particularly during the recession of 2001. But the Packard Foundation's receding fortunes can be traced to one woman: Carleton "Carly" Fiorina, who became Hewlett-Packard CEO in 1999. Fiorina was convinced that Hewlett-Packard had to expand or stagnate, and in 2000 launched a $23.8 billion takeover bid for Compaq Computer.

As we've seen, David Packard's "Random Thoughts" document of 1988 imposed no restrictions on the Packard Foundation's grantmaking. But Packard *did* tell his heirs to make sure that most of the foundation's endowment remained in stock of Hewlett-Packard and Agilent, an HP spin-off company. According to George Anders, Packard said that his heirs should "disregard entirely" any advice that the Packard Foundation endowment portfolio should be diversified. Endowment portfolio managers, he wrote, should think about "the impact on the company, the employees, and in the communities in which H-P operates" if the foundation unloaded its HP stock.[117]

As a result, when Fiorina launched her takeover bid, the Packard Foundation and the Packard Humanities Institute controlled just fewer than ten percent of the Hewlett-Packard shares, making them the largest shareholders in the company, while the heirs of William Hewlett controlled an additional eight percent. The Packards and the Hewletts strongly resisted the takeover of Compaq, but Fiorina was able to rally institutional investors and the merger went through in 2002.[118]

As the battle over the HP-Compaq merger raged, the value of the Packard Foundation endowment plunged from $13 billion to under $5 billion, including one day in 2002 when the value of Hewlett-Packard stock fell by $5 a share in a single day, which wiped out a billion dollars of endowment.

The foundation responded by massive cuts, including reducing grants from $500 million annually to $250 million. They slashed the number of staff from 100 to 60, including firing 39 program officers. (The sacked employees, however, received 7½ months of severance pay.) They eliminated programs they considered tangential, including gun control and restricting children's access to guns and all programs that aided American Indians. Also hard hit was the Center for Budget and Policy Priorities, a liberal think tank. The Packard Foundation had given them $3.5 million between 1991-2003, but had cut them off. The center's director, Robert Greenstein, estimated that the center's budget would be cut by 15 percent.[119]

Even in its budget crisis, the Packard Foundation continued its grants to the Monterey Bay Aquarium and the Lucille Packard Children's Hospital, which received a seven-year, $270 million grant in 2001.

The Packard Foundation also continued its program of land acquisition. In a 2004 op-ed in the *Los Angeles Times*, Kevin Starr, a historian at the University of Southern California, said that by the end of 2003, the Packard Foundation had, in the previous five years, spent $175 million buying and preserving 342,000 acres of California land, or the equivalent of Sequoia National Park. Packard's grants had resulted in an additional $700 million in private and state grants to preserve land.

"Never before in California history has a nongovernmental agency acted with such sweeping and bold effect on public value, policy, and action," Starr noted. Packard's land acquisition program,

Starr said, showed that "foundation-based philanthropy… may come to rival tax-supported government as a mode of governance."[120] But one of Packard's land-use grants had long-term consequences.

The University of California had not opened any new branches since 1965. Debates over the tenth campus took several decades, but planners and politicians finally settled on Merced, a dusty country town located in California's central valley. One advantage Merced had over other sites was that a single landowner, the Virginia Smith Trust, controlled the land the new university needed. The trust was willing to offer the land to the state—but much of the property had "vernal pools" brimming with fairy shrimp, an endangered species.

In 2001, the Packard Foundation spent $11 million to buy land near that of the Virginia Smith Trust, including a former golf course that had no endangered species on it. The Packard grant enabled the university to begin construction and allow the land with vernal pools to remain as a wildlife preserve. When the University of California Merced opened in 2005, at a cost to the state of $500 million, the *Chronicle of Higher Education* interviewed the school's associate vice chancellor for university advancement, Michael I. Campbell, who "credits the Packard Foundation with saving the Merced campus."[121]

In April 2012, journalist Charlotte Allen visited Merced and found that there's still considerable debate whether UC Merced is a good idea. The school is the only one in the University of California system that remains in the "referral pool," which means it has to accept any student who applies, including those rejected by other University of California branches. The majority of students live in desolate housing projects left vacant because of the city's housing collapse (according to *Forbes*, Merced had the third-highest number of housing foreclosures of any city in America). There's little parking because the state can no longer afford to build parking lots. Only 27 percent of UC Merced students graduate, a rate far lower than any other University of California branch.

"UC Merced may turn out to be the Little Campus That Could," Allen writes, "Or it may be an unfortunate object lesson in the triumph of regional and ideological politics over realistic planning."[122]

Whatever the campus's fate, it would not have been created without the Packard Foundation.

❧The Packard Foundation Today

In its most recent publicly available Form 990, for 2014, the Packard Foundation stated that it gave $291.7 million from an endowment of $7.1 billion.

Susan Packard Orr remains Packard Foundation chair, while Julie E. Packard and Nancy Packard Burnett are vice chairmen. Susan Packard Orr personally continues her funding of the liberal agenda. She contributed at least $2,500 to Obama's 2012 re-election[123] and $100,000 to Planned Parenthood Votes, a Super PAC. The *New York Times* noted that the principal activity of this Super PAC was to broadcast "advertisements seeking to undermine Mitt Romney's support among women."[124]

The Packard Foundation is also heavily involved in state politics. In 2007 the foundation, collaborating with the California Endowment, the Walter Haas Fund, the William and Flora Hewlett Foundation, and the Irvine Foundation, created California Forward (cafwd.org), which calls for shifting congressional redistricting to an independent commission, not allowing any secret donors to California state campaigns, and possibly replacing the California state legislature either with a unicameral legislature or with regional legislatures.[125] The organization's greatest victory came in 2010, when it persuaded voters to pass Proposition 14, which changed the law so that the top two winners of a congressional primary faced each other in the general election, instead of having a Republican and Democrat square off. In the 2012 election, this meant that two of California's 53 Congressional races were all Republican and three were entirely Democratic.

In 2012, California Forward backed Proposition 31, which would have required California to produce a budget every two years instead of annually. The proposition would have allowed a city and county to join together and implement their own versions of state programs such as foster care or medical assistance for the poor while continuing to receive state funding, unless both branches of the California legislature vetoed the decision within 60 days.

The liberal *Sacramento Bee* editorialized that Proposition 31 was a bad idea. "Do we really need a patchwork of county-by-county rules when it comes to provision of basic services? No."[126] Voters agreed, and Proposition 31 was defeated by a 60-40 margin.[127]

As for its grantees, Packard continues to be heavily invested in population control activities. Its website says the goal of Packard population programs in the U.S. is to "expand the availability of abortion technologies and providers, support advocacy and litigation, and research to inform positive reproductive health policies, especially at the state level, build support for abortion funding for low-income women by positioning abortion as part of the broad spectrum of women's health care, and demonstrate innovative models and build evidence to expand comprehensive sexuality education for young people."[128]

Among the "success stories" Packard claims is the Abortion Access Project, which provides training for doctors willing to perform abortions at the one abortion clinic currently operating in West Virginia.[129] Packard, in collaboration with the Grove, Ford, and Hewlett foundations, has also worked with school districts in seven states "to incorporate comprehensive sex education into their curricula."[130]

Packard remains active in international population control activities. In 2011 the *Times of India* reported that a Packard grant to Population Services International would be used to distribute condoms at gas stations and convenience stores in the state of Bihar. The Packard grant also included funds for "four trained street theatre teams" who would conduct 800 performances on the importance of condom use.[131]

Packard's spending on population control, however, is dwarfed by the massive amount it spends on the environment. In 2014, for example, Packard awarded $1.3 million to the Environmental Defense Fund, and $600,000 to the Environmental Working Group—and those are just for organizations with "environmental" in the title. Also receiving grants in 2014 was Greenpeace, including affiliates in Australia, Japan, and southeast Asia, which received four grants totaling $225,000, and the Tides Foundation, which received ten grants totaling $2.9 million.

But Packard's statist environmental mission shows up in all sorts of grants. The second-largest single grantee in 2014 was the Monterey Bay Aquarium, which received $38.7 million from Packard. Julie Packard has used her role as the aquarium's executive director to promote large increases in government funding to save the oceans. As the Democratic Women of Monterey County, California noted in 2011 when they gave Julie Packard and Nancy Packard Burnett their Visionary Leadership Award, "Through her leadership of the Monterey Bay Aquarium, Julie Packard has redefined aquariums as a force for education, conservation, and environmental protection."[132]

Visitors to the aquarium don't just look at fish. They also view what the *Monterey County Herald* called "dramatic and, perhaps, controversial exhibits" about global warming. One of them, "Hot Pink Flamingos, Stories of Hope in a Changing Sea," featured a cow with a gas mask, designed to demonstrate the alleged effects of bovine flatulence on the environment. Under protests from dairy farmers, the aquarium took away the gas mask.

Julie Packard defended the use of propaganda as part of her exhibits. "Opinion polling shows that our knowledge and concern about climate change ends at the shore," Packard said. "I've seen the power of ocean animals to motivate and inspire the public. And I've seen the capacity of the public to move from caring about fish to caring for our oceans."

Affiliated with the Monterey Bay Aquarium is the Center for the Future of the Oceans, which tries to manipulate people into lobbying for ever-increasing government funds to save the oceans. "The creation of an aquarium-based conservation advocacy center was not without risk," Packard said. "We realized that people might not welcome our increased focus on conservation messages. Our visitors might not want to get involved with conservation action.... [Some] might disagree with our points of view or feel we should not be taking positions on issues. As our work unfolded, none of these issues turned out to be barriers; instead, the public response was overwhelmingly positive."[133]

Two other Packard grantees should be mentioned. The largest grantee of the Packard Foundation is the ClimateWorks Foundation, which received $66.1 million from Packard in 2014. ClimateWorks was founded in 2008 as a joint venture of the Packard, Hewlett, and McKnight foundations, with additional grants from the Ford, Kresge, Moore, and Rockefeller foundations, among others.

ClimateWorks was created as a result of *Design to Win*, a 2007 study that stated, "Transitioning to a low-carbon economy will demand the use of a diverse set of tools. Foundations must invest in every stage of this progression—from policy development and advocacy to public and media education, to the implementation of international best practices."[134] The foundation funds several nonprofits around the world that lobby relentlessly for restricting coal use, implementing national carbon taxes, tightening international treaties that limit carbon dioxide production, and discouraging the use of cars in as many ways as possible.

Another major beneficiary of Packard environmental money is the Resources Legacy Fund and an affiliated supporting organization, the Resources Legacy Fund Foundation, which received a combined $8.8 million from Packard in 2014. The fund both networks with land trusts in particular areas and acts as a pass-through organization for nonprofits interested in buying and preserving land. In particular, the fund has worked with the Packard Foundation in the San Francisco Bay area and in the northern Sierra Nevadas. One branch of the Resources Legacy Fund specializes in lobbying for tougher global warming regulations, including providing "public opinion research and administrative advocacy experts" to promote draconian climate change policies.[135]

In 2016, Packard, collaborating with the Hewlett, Wilburforce, and Wyss foundations and the Grand Canyon Trust, donated $1.5 million to try to preserve the Bears Ears National Monument, created late in the Obama administration. *Salt Lake Tribune* reporter Brian Maffly said the grants were meant for "collaborative management of the new monument and [to] ensure inclusion of a diversity of local voices."

Janet Wilcox, an active member of the anti-monument group Stewards of San Juan, said that "these outside groups" making the grants "used their money to manipulate this designation" of the area as a national monument.[136]

Packard's massive environmental grantmaking has attracted little attention in the United States but has proven quite controversial in Canada, thanks largely to the reporting of blogger and *National Post* contributor Vivian Krause. As Brian Seasholes noted in *Green Watch*, Krause calculated that the Packard Foundation has contributed at least $28.7 million to environmental groups opposed to increased production in the oil sands of Alberta.[137]

Krause's reporting attracted the attention of Patrick Daniel, president of Enbridge, the company constructing a pipeline from the Alberta oil sands to Kitimat, British Columbia, that would increase Canadian oil exports to China. "I guess one's mind runs to why do U.S. foundations feel they need to come here to fund a project that is obviously not in the U.S. national best interest," Daniel told the *Edmonton Journal*.[138]

Krause discovered that the Packard Foundation was particularly strenuous in attempting to restrict or eliminate production of salmon from farms in British Columbia. In a 2011 *Financial Post* article, she calculated that between 2000-2010 at least $85 million in Packard grants went to at least 56 organizations that worked to reduce or eliminate the consumption of farmed Canadian salmon in favor of either explicitly Alaskan salmon or "wild" salmon, 90 percent of which comes from Alaska. These groups included the Marine Stewardship Council, which received $68 million to certify what salmon was environmentally friendly. In 2006, Wal-Mart announced that it would buy salmon only from fisheries certified by the Stewardship Council, which barred Canadian salmon from the world's largest retailer. Part of the reason Wal-Mart made this decision was the $3.5 million grant to the World Wide Fund for Nature specifically so that it could lobby Wal-Mart to eliminate their purchases of farmed salmon.

Among other Packard-funded groups using their grants to promote American over Canadian salmon were the Georgia Strait Alliance and Tides Canada, an offshoot of the highly controversial Tides Foundation of San Francisco. Even the Monterey Bay Aquarium did their part, with a display that warned visitors "farming seafood isn't the answer to saving salmon."[139]

The Packard-funded anti-farmed salmon campaign may have unforeseen consequences. In April 2012, Canadian Finance Minister Jim Flaherty announced that Canada planned to introduce restrictions on Canadian nonprofits that would reduce the share of their budgets they could spend on political activity from ten percent to five percent. Canadian Senator Nicole Eaton, who led a Senate investigation into the political activities of Canadian nonprofits, said one reason for the investigation was the effort by Packard-funded grantees to restrict the sales and consumption of farmed British Columbia salmon. "The Packard Foundation was very responsible for demarketing Canadian B.C. salmon," Sen. Eaton said. "It in effect destroyed B.C. salmon, and it increased the value of Alaskan salmon."[140] In other words, the foundation's highly politicized philanthropy led it to have high economic impacts: hurting British Columbian fishermen and helping their competitors.

☙ Conclusion

David Packard's legacy is complicated. As we have seen, he was a population controller, and, to some degree, a conservationist, although much about his views on the environment remains unknown. The Packard Foundation, to its credit, has continued and expanded the three largest philanthropic projects implemented during the donor's lifetime: the Monterey Bay Aquarium, the Lucile Packard Children's Hospital, and the Packard Fellowships.

But David Packard was also a conservative. By cutting off grants to the American Enterprise Institute and the Hoover Institution, the Packard Foundation has abandoned a large part of what motivated Packard as a philanthropist. In 2014, the Packard Foundation gave hundreds of millions to the Left and a single grant to the Right: a $25,000 donation to the Philanthropy Roundtable. This imbalance ensures that the Packard Foundation severely distorts the ideals of its founder, which may well explain why the foundation refuses to make public its founder's "Random Thoughts About the Packard Foundation" memo that may offer evidence of his intent.

The lessons David Packard provides future donors are timeless: Don't assume that future generations will respect your wishes. Make your intentions as clear as possible, impose as many restrictions as possible—and, if possible, spend your fortunes within your lifetime.

PART II

PRESERVING
DONOR INTENT

10

The JM Foundation

The debate over donor intent is largely ideological. Usually, the entrepreneurs who create great fortunes tend to be conservative or libertarian. Those who inherit their wealth, including most foundation executives and heirs to estates, tend to be liberal or socialist. The transformation of philanthropy from an avocation to a profession has also increased the likelihood that donor intent will be violated. Quite simply, many people in the nonprofit world look down on donors who want some say in how their money is used.

Some foundations, however, continue to spend money in ways their founders intended. This chapter examines five such foundations, which provide important lessons in how donor intent can best be preserved.

❧ The JM Foundation

The JM Foundation, created in 1924 and based in New York City, is a family foundation with assets of $25.7 million, whose president at this writing is the grandson of its founder. Biographer John Briggs shows in his recent book, *The Face of a Family,* how the foundation has managed to uphold the intent of its founder.

In 1857, inventor Gail Borden perfected the process of canning condensed milk, allowing this product for the first time to be transported long distances without spoiling. (In the days before pasteurization, most milk was locally produced and quickly consumed.) Borden had opened a milk-condensation plant in Connecticut, but capital for operating the facility was hard to acquire because the country was in the midst of the Panic of 1857. Creditors often sued Borden, and the scarcity of funds forced several closures of his plant.

One day, Borden left his plant "not knowing where to go or what to do," notes his biographer, Clarence R. Wharton; "he took the train for New York on a vain hunt for something or somebody and crowded his tall, wistful figure into a railway seat. It was one of those accidents which determine great issues in life."[1] Borden met Jeremiah Milbank (1818-1884), a New York banker looking for new investments. Milbank became convinced that Borden's factory could be profitable and invested $50,000 in return for a 50 percent interest in the venture; a year later, he invested another $50,000. (As Briggs notes, this would be equivalent to $2 million today.)

During the Civil War, both Borden and Milbank made huge fortunes selling canned milk to the victorious Union forces. Milbank used his share to start an investment banking firm and the Chicago, Milwaukee & St. Paul Railroad, one of the nation's first cross-country routes.[2] When he died in 1884, he left an enormous estate. This was equally divided between his two children, Joseph Milbank (1838-1914) and Elizabeth Milbank Anderson (1850-1921), each of whom also received 25 percent of the stock in Borden's company, known then as the New York Condensed Milk Company.

❧ The Milbanks: Pioneers in Philanthropy

Both Joseph Milbank and Elizabeth Milbank Anderson were philanthropists. Joseph Milbank continued to run the family's investment banking firm, which grew substantially after he sold his share of the Borden stock. Elizabeth Milbank Anderson used much of her fortune, as did many late Victorian philanthropists, to directly help the poor. Her millions provided free lunches to public school children (a project later assumed by government), public baths for tenement dwellers, and the like. With Joseph Milbank she created a "People's Palace" in Jersey City, New Jersey, where the poor could enjoy sports and entertainment at minimal cost.[3] Her most lasting philanthropic achievement, however, was the creation of the Milbank Memorial Fund in 1905. Started with an endowment of $3 million, it has become one of the nation's leading philanthropies devoted to medical and scientific research.

By the time the second Jeremiah Milbank was born in 1887, the family had a firm tradition of philanthropy. The younger Jeremiah was educated at private schools, and later went to Yale University, where he was graduated in 1909. He married and began working in his father's investment banking firm. After Joseph Milbank's sudden death in 1914, Jeremiah Milbank became president of J. Milbank & Company, and continued a long career until his death in 1972.[4]

In 1917, Jeremiah Milbank became concerned about the problems of those with disabilities. John Briggs says that the roots of this interest are unclear, but Milbank began to worry about the many men with disabilities he saw begging on New York streets. A survey he commissioned found that most of these men were ready and eager to work if some way could be found to accommodate their handicaps.[5]

In 1917, Milbank gave the Red Cross $50,000, as well as a building, to establish an institute to provide training for men with disabilities. When the Red Cross Institute for Crippled and Disabled Men opened later that year, Milbank ensured that his name was nowhere on the building. Milbank made sure he was only the vice chairman of the new institute, even though he was the principal funder.[6]

For the rest of his life, Milbank's main philanthropic concern was helping those with disabilities. In 1924, he created The JM Foundation. The largest recipient of JM Foundation grants has been the International Center for the Disabled (ICD), originally called the Institute for the Crippled and Disabled. During his life, Milbank gave the organization $36 million.

Milbank didn't just write checks. He delighted in an annual excursion from New York up the Hudson to Indian Point, where disabled people could have some summer fun. In 1929, for example, 600 disabled people had lunch and competed in contests, including rowing, running, a potato race, and baseball. "Orchestral selections" were played for people not strong enough to compete.[7]

Milbank's interest in helping those with disabilities changed as needs changed. In the late 1920s, he began a campaign to eradicate diphtheria, a scourge of the young. Due in part to his efforts, this debilitating disease was largely eradicated by 1930. In 1928, he joined other prominent Americans to form the International Committee for the Study of Infantile Paralysis, a clearinghouse for information on ways to treat and prevent polio. He gave $1.6 million that year to help establish the committee, and added millions more until Jonas Salk's polio vaccine became widely available in the mid-1950s. "The war against disease in all its forms," Milbank wrote in 1928, "presents a stirring challenge and maintains a keen and never-failing interest. One of its satisfactions is that the battle line never retreats and, while progress may prove slow, each gain is held and forms the base for further advance."[8]

꩜ Conservation Efforts

In the late 1930s, Milbank developed an interest in conservation. In 1939, he purchased 28,000 acres of land in Jasper County, South Carolina for a farm and vacation home. Although the farm, called Turkey Hill Plantation, was run as a profit-making venture, Milbank wished to preserve part of the land for future generations. In his only book, *Turkey Hill Plantation* (1966), he wrote that 10,000 acres were set aside as a recreation reserve for shooting, hunting, and other sports. To ensure high-quality hunting, Milbank protected the entire farm. The plantation, he wrote, "provides not only protection for game, but cover and feed as well, to sustain and perpetuate types of wildlife that range many, many miles beyond our property. Therefore I think that, in essence, it represents a 28,000 acre refuge for South Carolina's whole coastal plain."[9]

But Milbank's interest in conservation went further. Three thousand acres of the plantation were set aside as a game sanctuary, and leased without charge to the South Carolina Wildlife Resources Department. All Turkey Hill employees were designated unpaid South Carolina game wardens, and given full powers to arrest poachers. Milbank was thus an innovator in using private funds to preserve and protect natural resources.

In the mid-1920s Milbank made what we would call a program-related investment. Milbank became acquainted with filmmaker Cecil B. DeMille and became the principal investor in DeMille's biographical life of Jesus, *King of Kings* (1927). Milbank invested in the film as a way of promoting Christianity and used the profits he made to increase distribution of the film.

DeMille biographer Scott Eyman writes that DeMille found Milbank a pleasure to deal with, particularly when compared to penny-pinching Hollywood tycoons. In Jeremiah Milbank, Eyman writes, DeMille was "partnering with a man of idealism and religious conviction, who was fully prepared to put his money where his mouth was."[10] That was Milbank's only Hollywood venture; he never made a similar investment.

❧ Milbank's Political Career

Milbank was also active in the Republican Party. In the 1928 presidential campaign, he served as a fundraiser for Republican candidate Herbert Hoover. Trying to broaden the party's financial base, Milbank announced that the Republican Party would accept no contributions over $25,000, and received thousands of small contributions from first-time donors. He was so successful in this effort that the Republican Party emerged from the race with a surplus in its bank accounts.

Time, profiling Milbank as part of an article on Hoover's fundraisers, described Milbank as a "mild-mannered Yale graduate ('09), careful investor of a multi-million patrimony, clubman, generous donor for philanthropies (especially for cripples).... Mr. Milbank is new to politics but widely acquainted, keen to learn."[11]

After winning the election, Hoover asked Milbank to work for him. As Briggs notes, "there were many who assumed that the office of secretary of the treasury could be his for the asking." But Milbank declined all government posts, saying, "The one thing I want to do is to keep out of Washington."[12] After serving again as a fundraiser in the 1932 presidential contest, he abandoned active involvement in politics.

Because Milbank rarely commented on public policy, his political beliefs cannot be precisely known. But he was a loyal Republican throughout his life and retained his friendship with Herbert Hoover. In 1964, he gave $250,000 to the Hoover Institution on War, Revolution and Peace, a pioneering conservative think tank. In 1968, Richard Nixon wrote him to seek advice on a vice presidential running mate. Milbank responded that his pick would be Ronald Reagan. "I believe that Governor Reagan of California would add the greatest strength to your ticket as a campaigner for the election. His position on the issues is consistent with yours and therefore would be enunciated with great clarity. His recognition factor is undoubtedly the greatest among the various possibilities, and his television appeal I believe is very strong."[13]

❧ Principles of Giving

Milbank had strong views on how foundations should be run. In the 1960s, he formulated five principles of grantmaking that forcefully show how he wanted his money used:

- Grants should be made to organizations working to prevent illness. According to John Briggs, Milbank "drew no distinction between illness in the physical sense, which could cripple or kill, and illness in the social sense, which deprived children from poor backgrounds of a fair chance in life."[14]

  Before beginning a new project, experts should be consulted and the best advice gathered. The goals of the project should be determined, and grant recipients should not be allowed to deviate from them. As Briggs notes, this principle later became known as "management by objectives."

- Innovation in the social sciences should be the responsibility of the private sector. Although Milbank believed that government had some responsibilities in meeting human needs and alleviating suffering, he devoted his life to private initiatives as the preferred alternative to government programs.[15]

- Since intentions of the creators of great foundations are often diluted over time, the "long, strong thread of family involvement [is] the only way of ensuring consistency of purpose."[16] Milbank sought to ensure that his children and grandchildren understood his views and were motivated to continue the JM Foundation in a way he would approve.

- Gifts should be made as anonymously as possible. Milbank never sought publicity or fame for his philanthropy, nor saw it as a way to acquire power. He believed giving was simply the right way to live. He never asked that any buildings or institutions be named after him, and always requested to be treasurer of the organizations he founded or favored, as this was a fairly inconspicuous position.

Milbank's reticence extended to his personal life. Few journalists knew that Milbank was one of the wealthiest Americans of his time. When *Fortune* profiled the Milbanks in a 1959 article (the only one to appear in Milbank's lifetime), the anonymous author noted that the family was so quiet about its wealth that the magazine missed counting them in another survey. "The Milbank family of New York controls what is probably the least publicized of the 'mature' great fortunes of America," it observed. "It is a tribute to the Milbanks' dislike of publicity, and their skill in avoiding it, that so little is known about them."[17] Jeremiah Milbank's collaborator in the Turkey Hill Plantation book, Grace Fox Perry, summed up the Milbanks' reticence: "Avoidance of publicity is an inherent tradition in the Milbank family."[18]

℮ Continuing a Tradition

Milbank's clearly articulated principles were largely followed by his successor as president of the JM Foundation, Jeremiah Milbank Jr. The younger Jeremiah's views were best expressed in a 1984 article he wrote for *Leaders* magazine. He said he believed that corporations should not give in order to redistribute wealth, nor to provide social services, but to provide themselves with "an opportunity to invest in a program or an enterprise offering a long-range benefit that will strengthen and enhance the overall growth and development of that corporation within a free society."[19] For example, he believed that corporate grants to organizations that seek to motivate troubled urban youth to work hard help ensure that businesses will have committed future employees.

Jeremiah Milbank Jr. urged philanthropists to keep their staffs small and to limit grantmaking to groups that fit corporate objectives. The leader of a corporate foundation, he believed, should be someone with both an extensive business background and experience in local community service organizations. While such people are admittedly rare, finding them is necessary if businesses are to avoid giving to groups that oppose free enterprise as well as to groups that are ineffective in aiding the distressed.

Jeremiah Milbank Jr. died in 2007. In a tribute, John J. Miller noted that one of the younger Milbank's philanthropic achievements was founding the Institute for Educational Affairs (IEA), one of the leading conservative nonprofits of the 1970s and 1980s, and an organization that helped to create the Federalist Society, the Collegiate Network, and the Philanthropy Roundtable. "The JM Foundation was a key financial backer of the IEA,"

Miller wrote, "and Milbank was a steady presence at its board meetings."[20]

William F. Buckley Jr. recalled in an appreciation that "if memory serves, the very first person I called upon to give a little corporate substance to National Review Inc. was Jeremiah Milbank Jr." Buckley wrote that Milbank was "an unabashedly forthright conservative but a conventional citizen who cultivated his longtime attachment to the Republican party.... He was a steadfast friend of this journal, on which he never made or even intimated demands of his own for institutional conformism."[21]

Many of the JM Foundation's recent grants have gone to organizations that have long been favored. One major change in the JM Foundation's giving has been a rising number of grants to market-oriented public policy organizations, including the Heritage Foundation, Madison Center for Educational Affairs, National Center for Neighborhood Enterprise, and Manhattan Institute for Policy Research. While such grants are not known to have been made in Jeremiah Milbank Sr.'s day—indeed, few conservative or libertarian organizations existed during his lifetime—such gifts seem clearly consistent with the elder Milbank's beliefs and intentions.

In 1995, the JM Foundation reorganized and spun off much of its grantmaking for the disabled to the newly created Milbank Foundation for Rehabilitation, now headed by Jeremiah Milbank III's cousin, Jeremiah Milbank Bogert. In 2012, the Milbank Foundation made grants of $1.3 million, including a $250,000 grant to the Yale Cancer Center as the first installment of a four-year, million-dollar grant. Carl Helstrom, who has served as executive director of both the JM Foundation and the Milbank Foundation for Rehabilitation, told the *Yale Daily News* that "we're not a huge foundation, so we like to get into situations that are highly leveraged."[22] He hoped that other donors would match or exceed the Milbank Foundation's gift.

One result of the spinoff was that by 2012, the JM Foundation's grants had shrunk to $1.1 million. The foundation made two six-figure grants, $100,000 each to the State Policy Network and the Boys and Girls Clubs of America. In 2015, the foundation's two largest grants were $50,000 each to the American Enterprise Institute and the Fund for American Studies.

The JM Foundation is a successful example of donor intent for two reasons: Jeremiah Milbank Sr. made his charitable intentions explicit, and his family has honored those intentions. "Everyone in the family believes in limited government, economic freedom, and personal responsibility," Jeremiah Milbank III said in 2007. "This is a family foundation, but the next generation must accept the foundation's mission. We've never used the foundation for pet projects."[23]

Such fidelity is rare in the history of foundations. If the creators of foundations routinely made their wishes clear, and if the children of philanthropists honored those wishes, many of the problems of donor intent could be avoided.

11

The Lynde and Harry Bradley Foundation

The Lynde and Harry Bradley Foundation, founded in 1946 and reorganized in 1985, is a large Milwaukee-based foundation that has traditionally had few family members on its board. Nonetheless, as historian John Gurda shows in his book, *The Bradley Legacy: Lynde and Harry Bradley, Their Company, and Their Foundation,* the Bradley Foundation, like the JM Foundation, has managed to uphold donor intent.[1]

Lynde Bradley (1878-1942) came from a family interested in invention. Bradley's mother and father both held patents, and Bradley himself acquired his first patent at age 16. While growing up in Milwaukee, Bradley experimented with electricity, built Milwaukee's first X-ray machine, and made headsets that allowed people to listen to live concerts over the telephone.

Because of the family's financial problems, Lynde Bradley was forced to begin a career before finishing high school. While working on his X-ray device, he met Stanton Allen, a physician interested in using X-rays in medicine. When an effort to start an X-ray business failed, Bradley decided to create a company to build rheostats—devices that ensure a steady flow of electric current to electromechanical products.

The Allen-Bradley Company

In 1901, Allen and Bradley formed a partnership, creating what would become the Allen-Bradley Company. Allen provided $1,000 in capital as well as workspace and moral support, while Bradley supplied inventive know-how. The business expanded steadily, and employees were hired. Among the first was Lynde Bradley's brother, Harry Bradley (1880-1965), and Fred Loock, an engineer who was to work for the Allen-Bradley Company for 57 years.

In 1916, the Bradleys acquired Allen's share of the business, thus making the Allen-Bradley Company a privately held firm with most shares owned by the Bradley brothers. With the boom in radio sales in the 1920s, millions of hobbyists bought Bradley stat capacitors and resistors to make their home-built radios work better. When mass-produced radios became common in the late 1920s, Bradley units "became standard components in factory-built radios, and manufacturers bought tons of them."[2] Thousands more were used in Singer sewing machines.

The Allen-Bradley Company limped through the Great Depression and survived a major strike in 1939. During World War II, however, the firm prospered, as Allen-Bradley resistors were needed in walkie-talkies, radar, and aircraft. Allen-Bradley electromechanical controls were also used to improve machine tools in defense plants. In 1940, Allen-Bradley Company sales were $4.2 million; by 1945, they had increased to $15.4 million.

℮ Creation of the Foundation

By the mid-1940s, ownership of the Allen-Bradley Company had become complex. Lynde Bradley died in 1942, leaving a will that appeared to transfer his shares in the company to Harry Bradley, thus making him sole owner of the firm. Lynde Bradley also wanted to use his estate to create a foundation, but it took three years for his will to be probated. The settlement occurred largely through the efforts of Harvey Peters, a Milwaukee tax lawyer who had the Bradleys as "practically his only client."[3]

In December 1945, an agreement was reached. Under the probate of Bradley's will, Lynde Bradley's wife, Caroline, claimed the traditional "widow's third" of the Allen-Bradley shares (17 percent of the total Allen-Bradley stock). The rest of the shares went to Harry Bradley, who transferred most of this to five trusts whose beneficiaries included his wife, three children, and Margaret Loock, wife of Fred Loock. (Peters established the fifth trust in Margaret Loock's name for fear that its income might be taxable if Fred Loock were the beneficiary.) In 1951, Caroline Bradley created three additional trusts from her share of the company, the beneficiaries of which were herself, her nephew, and her niece. Together, these eight trusts controlled nearly all the Allen-Bradley stock.

Lynde Bradley began to consider the idea of creating a foundation in 1941, when his lawyers persuaded him that this would allow inheritance taxes to be substantially cut. But he died before definite plans could be made. Further, the creation of the Bradley Trusts nullified an original plan to endow a foundation with Bradley's portion of the Allen-Bradley shares. Instead, the Allen-Bradley Company regularly gave part of its profits to what would become the Lynde Bradley Foundation. The foundation's endowment climbed from $500,000 in 1946 to $1 million in 1951, and reached almost $4 million in 1960. In 1958, the Lynde Bradley Foundation was renamed the Allen-Bradley Foundation to signify its role as the philanthropic arm of the Allen-Bradley Company.

ℰ Champions of Free Enterprise

John Gurda notes that Lynde Bradley was so uninterested in politics that only one relevant remark by him is known to exist—a cryptic quotation in a 1935 Allen-Bradley Company newsletter: "the blight of politics will rest upon us, as upon all others."[3] However, both Harry Bradley and Fred Loock, who succeeded Harry Bradley as company president in 1945, were vocal champions of free enterprise. Their views, says Gurda, were simple: "any force that sought to restrict the free market or the free individual was anathema. The pair directed their fire, accordingly, at what they considered the two major threats to freedom: the federal government and world Communism."[5]

Fred Loock wrote in a memorandum to employees in 1952,

> At the rate our government is spending and we are paying—it won't be long before all money in excess of bare living will be taken away from us in Taxes ... except for the bureaucrats, you and I and everyone else will become "slaves of the state"—a title no one should be proud of. It will be the end of "Free Americans." Fact is that we in this country are much farther along on the road to complete socialism than most of us are aware...[6]

Both Harry Bradley and Fred Loock used their wealth to advance conservative causes. Bradley was an early backer of William F. Buckley's magazine *National Review* and sought unsuccessfully to buy both *Newsweek* and the *Milwaukee Sentinel*. He and Loock also gave to such conservative presidential candidates as Robert Taft and Barry Goldwater. In 1964, Loock bought thousands of copies of the popular conservative books *A Texan Looks at Lyndon; A Choice, Not an Echo;* and *None Dare Call It Treason* for the Allen-Bradley sales force, telling them that these books "ought to be required reading at the present time."[7]

Bradley was also a major supporter of the Christian Anti-Communist Crusade, whose founder, Frederick Schwarz, was a regular visitor to the Allen-Bradley plant, where he would often receive hefty donations. In 1957, the Allen-Bradley Company bought two pages in dozens of major dailies to reprint Schwarz's testimony on Communism before the House Un-American Activities Committee. At the end of the ads, the company announced that it "was trying to sell you nothing except the importance of holding fast to your American freedoms, including the freedom to live, the freedom to worship your God, and the freedom to work as you choose, which freedoms are still here in America, but have disappeared in much of the world."[8]

Bradley and Loock also withheld Allen-Bradley funds from causes they opposed. In 1964, Loock withdrew $100,000 worth of advertising from the *Saturday Evening Post* after it criticized Barry Goldwater in an editorial. When Allen-Bradley's New York bank hosted a luncheon in 1959 for Soviet diplomat Anastas Mikoyan, Bradley promptly withdrew company funds from the bank and blasted Mikoyan as a "Soviet murderer." According to Gurda, a Russian visitor to the Allen-Bradley plant in the 1950s reportedly "turned white" when he saw Harry Bradley's library, which included such works as *The Black Deeds of the Kremlin; Communist-Socialist Propaganda in the American Schools;* and *McCarthyism: The Fight for America.*[9]

An appreciative obituary in the August 24, 1965 issue of *National Review* described Harry Bradley as

> a phenomenon. He was professionally shy, and soft-spoken, and among the most adamant of men, who, if he believed in anything, was absolutely immovable.... But his extraordinary generosity, much of it anonymous, to schools and hospitals and art galleries, made him a civic institution, and his death, even at his advanced age, deprived Milwaukee of one of its freshest and

most resourceful sources of commercial and spiritual energy.[10]

Bradley drew a firm line between what he gave personally through the Allen-Bradley Company and what he gave through the Allen-Bradley Foundation. The foundation, while occasionally giving to conservative causes, was not primarily an outlet for supporting activists. "Conservative groups like the Christian Anti-Communist Crusade, the Manion Forum, and the Committee for Constitutional Government could generally count on a friendly response" from the foundation, Gurda writes. "Support for the right wing, however, constituted only a fractional percentage of the Foundation's total contributions. Harry Bradley and his colleagues had a strong interest in public policy but, from a philanthropic viewpoint, they considered public service more important."[11]

The Allen-Bradley Foundation's primary aim was simple: to support worthy projects in Milwaukee and Wisconsin. Harry Bradley wished to give some of the Allen-Bradley Company profits to the city that helped make him wealthy. In a 1977 interview, Harry Bradley's wife, Reg, told Gurda that her husband's "love was Milwaukee, you know, and Allen-Bradley. That's all he cared about. He never cared about going anywhere, doing anything, meeting anyone else. It was just centered right there, with all the people he cared so much about."[12]

The Allen-Bradley Foundation made grants in three areas: education, youth work, and health care. Each year a $5,000 check went to all the private colleges in Wisconsin, even though Bradley worried that they might be supporting "communistic and socialistic ideas." In the1960s, the schools received $10,000 checks. St. Luke's Hospital and the Milwaukee Boys Club also received major contributions.

An additional insight into Allen-Bradley's giving comes from Harvey Peters, the lawyer who created the Bradley Trusts in 1945. According to Gurda, Peters was not a natural philanthropist: "his reluctance to part with money was legendary, and his fears of a 'financial catastrophe' were so acute that he once persuaded the [Allen-Bradley] company to start a corporate gold reserve."[13] Nonetheless, Peters was active in the Allen-Bradley Foundation from 1954 until the 1970s. A book he wrote, *America's Coming Bankruptcy: How the Government Is Wrecking Your Dollar* (1973), includes a chapter critical of nonprofits.

Peters worried that the growth of nonprofits would, in the long run, damage the American economy in two ways. First, since nonprofits were unrestrained by the profit motive, they had little incentive to keep costs low and could spend more for labor than their for-profit competitors. "If the employer that produces goods and services wants to survive," Peters warned, "he must meet the competition of the nonprofit sector in striving to get, and keep capable employees. This can only mean that the employer producing goods and services has had to incur higher costs and, of course, this has increased the prices for goods and services that the consumer has had to pay."[14]

Second, Peters believed that nonprofits were spending too much on administration and unnecessary frills. The charity that once was happy to receive used furniture for its low-rent offices in a bad neighborhood now had a fancy office in a new high-rise:

> As uncontrolled monopolies, supported by tax-deductible dollars, nonprofit organizations have reflected the general American prosperity philosophy in that they have become quite materialistic. They have acquired costly real estate, they have built rather elaborate structures for office facilities, and they have considerably expanded their staffs of employees and administrators. There are even instances where a particular organization has actually accomplished the purpose for which it had been organized, and the organization promptly undertook new ventures rather than dismiss its staff and discontinue accepting contributions.[15]

Thus, the intent of Harry Bradley and his associates in their giving was as follows: benefit Milwaukee and the state of Wisconsin. Aid people who champion free enterprise. And ensure that administrative costs are as low as possible.

ℰ Reorganization of the Foundation

In 1985, the eight Bradley Trusts sold the Allen-Bradley Company to Rockwell International for $1.65 billion. Six of the trusts benefited either their original recipients or those recipients' legatees. The largest beneficiary was Harry Bradley's daughter, Jane Bradley Pettit, who received $600 million.[16]

When Caroline Bradley and Margaret Loock died, they willed that the Allen-Bradley Foundation inherit their trusts. These two trusts, however, controlled 22 percent of the Allen-Bradley stock, and Harvey Peters worried that this amount could violate tax laws restricting the amount of stock a foundation can hold in one company.

In 1977, the Allen-Bradley Company bought Caroline Bradley's stock for $5.8 million, but decided it could not afford to pay $23 million for the shares held by the Margaret Loock Trust. The Allen-Bradley Foundation's assets rose from $14 million that year to over $290 million in 1985. The foundation promptly reorganized, renaming itself the Lynde and Harry Bradley Foundation and moving out of the Allen-Bradley plant to larger space in downtown Milwaukee.

The Bradley Foundation's executives, led by Milwaukee industrialist W.H. Brady and I. Andrew "Tiny" Rader, a long-time Allen-Bradley Company president, began a nationwide search for a president for the foundation. They selected Michael Joyce, who at the time was executive director of the John M. Olin Foundation. In 1985, he became executive director of the Bradley Foundation; in 1988, he became president, with "Tiny" Rader assuming the post of chairman. Rader stayed on as chairman until 2000, when he retired and was succeeded by Allen M. Taylor.[17] The most recent chairman, chosen in 2017, is Art Pope, chairman of Variety Wholesalers and founder and chairman of the John William Pope Foundation.[18]

℮ Honoring Tradition

In 2015, assets of the Lynde and Harry Bradley Foundation totaled $845.1 million. This included $200 million willed to it in 2014 from Sarah Doll Barder, a niece of Caroline Bradley. Of this $200 million, $53 million was restricted for scholarships to a limited number of prep schools, while the remaining $147 million was unrestricted.[19]

In its grantmaking, the Bradley Foundation continues to emphasize Harvey Peters's business-like practices. It has fewer than 20 full-time employees, and administrative costs are kept to a minimum. "Applicants with bloated budgets for staff and office," Gurda writes, "generally go away empty-handed."[20]

The foundation is best known for its concern with public policy. It has supported scholars at such conservative thinks tanks as the Heritage Foundation and the American Enterprise Institute, as well as at a host of academic institutions, including the City University of New York, the Duke University Marine Laboratory, Claremont McKenna College, the universities of Chicago, Notre Dame, Rochester, Toronto, Virginia, and California at Berkeley and Los Angeles, as well as Boston, Carnegie-Mellon, George Mason, Johns Hopkins, New York, Princeton, Stanford, Texas A & M, Washington (in St. Louis), and Yale universities. Harvard University has had Bradley Fellows in its economics department, Graduate School of Education, Russian Research Center, and Kennedy School of Government.

The Bradley Foundation has long been particularly interested in education reforms that promote parental choice. For example, in 2004 it made major grants to the Alliance for School Choice ($45,000), Black Alliance for Educational Options ($300,000), the Boston group Building Excellent Schools ($190,000), Marquette University's Institute for the Transformation of Learning ($250,000), School Choice Wisconsin ($150,000), the Heartland Institute in Chicago ($125,000), and the Thomas B. Fordham Foundation ($95,000). It gave $2.9 million to PAVE, Partners Advancing Values in Education, which provides private scholarships to poor families in Bradley's home town of Milwaukee, and it made grants to the Marva Collins School in Wisconsin and the Big Shoulders fund in Chicago.

In Steven Schindler's 2007 book *Casebook for The Foundation*, he notes that the Bradley Foundation's support for school choice in Milwaukee had at that point extended for at least 15 years, including at least half of PAVE's support for the first five years of its existence. When Wisconsin's attorney general said he would not support the state's effort to create publicly funded vouchers, the foundation donated $350,000 to the state so that then-Gov. Tommy Thompson could hire renowned litigator Kenneth Starr to represent the state before the Wisconsin Supreme Court. When the state supreme court approved publicly funded vouchers, the foundation gave a $246,000 grant to the Public Policy Forum of Wisconsin to analyze the voucher program and see what other states could learn from Milwaukee's successes and failures. Most significantly, when Milwaukee's private schools had taken as many voucher recipients as they could, the foundation in 2001-2002 donated $20 million to these schools so that they could expand and enroll more students. Bradley's steady funding of school choice, Schindler writes, ensured "victories for the voucher movement" across America.[21]

Milwaukee's ballet, art museum, historical society, library, orchestra, and local theaters also receive large gifts. Even the city of Milwaukee received a grant to improve its police force.[22]

In 1993, the Bradley Foundation announced that it would move away from scholarly research towards more support of "new citizenship" programs to encourage citizens to help make their communities better places to live. As an example, foundation president Michael Joyce told *National Journal* that he might fund programs that would provide toll-free numbers for parents who wanted to protest the sexual content of classroom materials.[23]

The Lynde and Harry Bradley Foundation is a successful example of donor intent in that it spends its funds in ways that Harry Bradley and Fred Loock would have approved and refrains from supporting causes they would have opposed. Longtime foundation president Michael Joyce, who stepped down in 2001, called donor intent the "North Star of Philanthropy." "You don't stand for elections, so there is no political check," he told the Philanthropy Roundtable, a national association of individual, corporate, and foundation donors. "There's no market, [so philanthropy] has to have some North Star, and that North Star is donor intent."[24]

The Bradley Foundation continues to be a leading patron of conservative causes. Eric Alterman, a columnist for the far-left *Nation* magazine, nonetheless paid tribute to the foundation's support of such noted authors as Charles Murray and Marvin Olasky. He cited Michael Joyce's estimate that the Bradley Foundation had supported the publication of over 400 books between 1985-1999 and had also provided support for Encounter Books, a conservative book publisher.

While calling these books "ideologically revanchist," Alterman noted that "while many of the most promising intellectual talents of the left have eschewed the 'real' world of public discourse for the cloistered confines of narrow academic concerns, the right has been taking its message to 'the people' in the form of bestselling book after bestselling book." Unlike liberals, Alterman admitted, conservatives "wrote books directed at a mass audience and received funding and support from conservative sources that understood the fundamental importance of the battle of ideas."[25]

"Where the traditional, well-established and more liberal lions of the foundation world such as the Ford Foundation and the Carnegie Corporation of New York were once seen as the trendsetters," *National Journal*'s Shawn Zeller reported in 2003, "today it is the conservative grantmakers—the Bradley Foundation, the David H. Koch Charitable Foundation, the John M. Olin Foundation, the Sarah Scaife Foundation, and others— that are creating a buzz."[26]

The Bradley Foundation also has been active in supporting inner-city groups in Milwaukee that encourage poor people to become self-reliant. In 2002, President Bush, in a visit to Milwaukee, praised the Bradley Foundation for promoting compassionate conservatism. "The Bradley Foundation has always been willing to seek different solutions," President Bush said. "They've been willing to challenge the status quo."[27]

The foundation has continued to introduce new programs. In 2003, it launched the Bradley Center for Philanthropy and Civic Renewal at the Hudson Institute. The center, which operated until 2015 under the guidance of former Bradley program officer William Schambra, funded and published books and monographs (including my book *Great Philanthropic Mistakes*) and held conferences on philanthropic issues.[28] In 2003, the foundation established the Bradley Prizes, four annual awards that could be considered the conservative counterpart to the MacArthur Fellows Program.[29]

Michael Joyce resigned as Bradley Foundation president in 2001 to head a new nonprofit designed to support funding of faith-based nonprofits. Joyce died in 2006; his death was marked by numerous tributes recognizing his importance as a grantmaker.[30]

Joyce's successor, Michael S. Grebe, was previously chairman of Foley & Lardner, a large law firm in Milwaukee. He is also a Vietnam War veteran who earned two Bronze Stars for his service. In a 2003 interview in *Philanthropy*, Grebe stressed the importance of donor intent. "We are guided by donor intent," Grebe said. "We are fortunate to have a well-documented historical record of the philanthropy of the Bradley brothers, who created the wealth that funded this foundation. So even though they have not been with us for several decades, we have a good understanding of their philanthropic principles."[31]

A 2011 article in the *Milwaukee Journal Sentinel* summarized the Bradley Foundation's importance both to the conservative movement and to Milwaukee.[32] As of 2011, the foundation had a $600 million endowment. In the previous decade, the foundation had awarded $350 million in grants. The foundation had contributed as much money to conservative causes as did the foundations connected to Charles and David Koch and the Scaife family. Every well-known conservative nonprofit has received Bradley grants, as have some lesser-known ones (for instance, Bradley granted $1.5 million to *Inside the Vatican*).

While 62 percent of the Bradley Foundation's grants during this period were to national organizations, the remaining 38 percent were to groups located in Milwaukee. Among these organizations receiving grants between 2001-2011 were the Milwaukee Art Museum, which received $8.5 million, while the Milwaukee Symphony Orchestra received $6 million, and the Milwaukee Public Museum received $5.1 million. Local homeless shelters and rehab centers also received grants, as did the Wisconsin Policy Research Institute, a state think tank in Milwaukee that received $3.8 million.

Michael S. Grebe told the *Journal Sentinel* that the Bradley Foundation was like the great Green Bay Packers teams of the 1960s that overpowered the opposition with a simple but forceful running game. "We're going to run off tackle, right over there, and we're telling you we're going to run there and we're going to knock you on your butt and carry the ball down the field," Grebe said. "There are no surprises."[33]

In May 2017, the *Milwaukee Journal Sentinel* obtained internal foundation documents from hackers that showed that from 2009 onwards, the Bradley Foundation made a significant shift away from national organizations towards state-based think tanks and state-based policy organizations. In an interview, Grebe said the effort began in 2009 when the Bradley Foundation commissioned a report from former Wisconsin Assembly Speaker Scott Jensen and his former chief of staff, Brett Healy, about the comparative strength of liberal and conservative organizations in Wisconsin. "We wanted to see the relative array of resources from the left and right," Grebe said. "What we took away from that was that conservatives (in Wisconsin) were being outresourced, outspent by people on the left."

Since then, the *Journal Sentinel* reported, the foundation has increased its grantmaking to groups in eight states, including Minnesota, North Carolina, Colorado, Oregon, and Washington. According to the *Journal Sentinel*, between 2011-2015, the five groups receiving the largest grants from the Bradley Foundation were the Institute for Educational Advancement, which provides scholarships for gifted children ($13.3 million); Charter Growth Fund, a charter school operator ($12.2 million); Encounter for Culture and Education, the nonprofit which runs Encounter Books ($5.3 million); the Hudson Institute, which ran the Bradley Center for Philanthropy and Civic Renewal ($3.8 million); and the Wisconsin Institute for Law and Liberty, a state think tank ($2.9 million).[34]

Michael S. Grebe retired in 2016. He told *National Review* that "I always tried to approach the job as a steward, upholding the legacy of the Bradley brothers." Grebe added that he was proud not only of the Bradley Foundation's national grants in "democratic capitalism, competent and limited government, and a rigorous defense of American interests at home and abroad," but also the third of Bradley's grantmaking devoted to Milwaukee-based grants, which he called "small local institutions doing good things for people in neighborhoods."[35]

Grebe's successor as president of the Bradley Foundation is Richard Graber. Graber, a vice president of Honeywell International, had earlier been a Bradley Foundation board member and served as Ambassador to the Czech Republic between 2006-2009. He was a former partner in the Milwaukee-based firm of Reinhart Boerner Van Dueren and headed the Wisconsin Republican Party for several years, beginning in 1999.[36]

Like his predecessors, Graber stresses devotion to donor intent: "The biggest challenge that any foundation has is trying to stay true to the founders' intent," he told the *Milwaukee Journal Sentinel*. He added that "Historically, our grants have been anywhere from 25 to 35% that have stayed locally," and that will continue. "The Bradley brothers would want it that way. They loved this community."[37]

And so, half a century after the death of its founders, the Bradley Foundation proves that it is possible for a philanthropy to honor the intentions of its framers, including their devotion to the system of government and to the community which made their wealth possible.

12

The Duke Endowment

The Duke Endowment is a major counter-example to the stories of foundations created by the heroic entrepreneurs of the late nineteenth century. James Buchanan "Buck" Duke (1856-1925), like John D. Rockefeller and Andrew Carnegie, was considered a "robber baron" in his day. Like Rockefeller, he created a huge corporation that was declared illegal by the Supreme Court. His creation of the Duke Endowment in 1924 with a gift of $40 million was surpassed at the time only by the gifts of Carnegie and Rockefeller.

Yet while the Carnegie Corporation and the Rockefeller Foundation have long since abandoned the philosophies of their founders, the Duke Endowment still gives grants according to the wishes of James B. Duke. Though it is currently the twentieth-largest foundation in America, it makes little news. But in its quiet way, it continues to do what Duke wanted—help the people of North and South Carolina by providing good hospitals, prosperous universities, and strong churches.

Like the foundation he created, James Duke did not court publicity, and most of his papers were destroyed after his death. He is known to have written only one article, and he gave few interviews. "I don't talk," he once said. "I work."[1] But from the interviews he gave, the recollections of his associates, and the indenture creating the Duke Endowment, his beliefs and intentions are clear and well defined.

The Duke Fortune

The Duke fortune began to be created by James Duke's father, Washington Duke, after the Civil War. Washington Duke returned to his farm near Durham, North Carolina, with little more than a fifty-cent piece in his pocket and a dream of starting a tobacco company. In 1866, he formed W. Duke, Sons & Company to sell chewing tobacco. In 1878, the business became a partnership when James Duke and his brother Benjamin Duke (1854-1929) entered the company.

James Duke built the family enterprise into a big business. His success had two main causes. First, he shifted resources from chewing tobacco to cigarettes. He was the first to realize the potential of the cigarette-rolling machine, patented by James Bonsack in 1881. Before then, cigarettes were rolled individually by hand. Duke's competitors tried the Bonsack machine but rejected it, believing that consumers preferred hand-rolled to machine-made cigarettes. But Duke realized that Bonsack's invention could transform cigarettes from a handcrafted to a mass-produced item. By supporting Bonsack and using his machines extensively, Duke was able to cut the cost of cigarette production from 80 cents to 30 cents per thousand. Like most great capitalists of the nineteenth century, Duke increased his profits by offering a wider range of goods at steadily falling prices.

Second, Duke was one of the first American manufacturers to realize the importance of national advertising. In 1883, he shipped 380,000 chairs with Cameo cigarette labels emblazoned on their backs to cigar stores—a highly unusual move at the time. He also invented the cigarette box, ensuring that his company's cigarettes were less likely to be damaged during shipping than competitors' products, which were simply wrapped in paper. "James Duke was the leading innovator in the American cigarette industry during the 1880's," notes historian Patrick G. Porter. "He made entrepreneurial contributions in marketing, in purchasing, and in production which were the driving force for change."[2]

By 1890, these innovations allowed Duke to buy out many of his competitors and form the American Tobacco Company, which came to dominate the steadily expanding U.S. cigarette market and also held a major position in the more competitive cigar industry. The trustbusters in the Theodore Roosevelt Administration began attacking American Tobacco's near-monopoly. In 1908, a circuit court ruled that American Tobacco was an illegal trust under the terms of the Sherman Antitrust Act. In making its ruling, however, the court admitted that despite the company's dominant position, it did not arbitrarily raise prices or suppress competition. "There is an absence of persuasive evidence that by unfair competition or improper practices independent dealers have been dragooned into giving up their individual enterprises and selling out to the principal defendant," the court's majority declared.[3]

In 1911, shortly after ordering the dissolution of John D. Rockefeller's Standard Oil Company, the Supreme Court, ordered the American Tobacco Company divided into several parts, of which the most important were Liggett and Myers, P. Lorillard, R.J. Reynolds, and a vastly reduced American Tobacco. For a few years, Duke ran British-American Tobacco, one of the world's first multinational corporations.[4] But around 1915, he abandoned the tobacco trade and began a career as a utility executive.

Duke was one of the first Americans to realize that waterpower could be harnessed to produce large amounts of electricity. He created the Southern Power System to turn energy from the rivers flowing from the Appalachian Mountains into electricity.[5] Renamed the Duke Power Company after his death, and later Duke Energy, this firm is still the electric utility for the western part of North Carolina.[6]

❧ A Tradition of Philanthropy

From 1915 onwards, Duke increasingly turned his attention to philanthropy. The Duke family, as devout Methodists, thought it their Christian duty to help the less fortunate. But until the creation of the Duke Endowment, Benjamin Duke, not James Duke, was better known for his philanthropic endeavors. This was a deliberate division of labor in the Duke family; Ben Duke dealt with charities, while "Buck" Duke ran the family business.

Historian Robert F. Durden cites an 1893 letter that elucidates Benjamin Duke's charitable interests:

> "I want to talk to you about money matters," Ben Duke wrote to his brother, telling him that he contributed $7,500 to Trinity College and $4,016 to other charities and churches, which included "contributions to the poor fund of the town during the severe weather last winter, amounts given to the pastor of our church for the poor during the year which he used in doctoring the sick, burying the dead &c &c (all of which he rendered itemized statement of) Oxford Orphans Asylum, current expenses of our church of every kind. Colored

School at Kittrell N.C. $500. Worn out Preachers of the
N.C. Conference $500. To poor churches over the state
&c &c.... Of course, this does not count money that I
have given kin people."[7]

"The amounts of money mentioned were yet small," Durden
writes, "but there would be a striking continuity of purpose
between the small-scale gifts of the 1890's, the larger donations
of the 1900's, and the immense bequests of the 1920's."[8] In fact,
the Duke Endowment supports nearly every organization and
cause mentioned in Benjamin Duke's letter today. The only major
addition has been hospitals. In creating the foundation, James
Duke largely continued family traditions of philanthropy that
spanned two generations and thirty years.

One area not mentioned in Benjamin Duke's letter was politics.
Though named after Democratic President James Buchanan,
James Duke, like most members of his family, was a Republican.
As historian Robert Sobel notes, Duke's father, Washington Duke,
was a Republican "who voted for Abraham Lincoln in 1860, one
of the few North Carolinians to do so." Washington Duke was a
Confederate Army veteran drafted in 1863 at age 43. (He never
served in combat.)

"As unabashed Republicans," notes historian Earl W. Porter,
"the Dukes made good targets for those who disliked cigarettes,
trusts, Republicans, men of wealth, or the individuals and
institutions identified with them."[9]

James B. Duke's fiercest foes in the press were editorialists at
the *Raleigh News and Observer,* then (and now) a staunchly liberal
Democratic newspaper. Some of Duke's political views are
known. In a 1915 article in the *North American Review,* he attacked
anti-business policies such as high tariffs that severely hindered
export-oriented American firms in world markets. "Is it possible,"
he wrote, "that public men are more intent on the punishment
of successful business men [*sic*], and preventing the accumulation
of large personal fortunes, then on achieving a condition of
helpfulness to all?"[10]

In 1922, Clarence Barron, founder of *Barron's,* interviewed
Duke. Barron did not publish the interview, but preserved notes
for a book that was never completed. In the interview, Duke
supported a consumption tax, saying it would provide incentives

to increase capital, which would ensure that America "would dominate and make prices for the whole world."[11] He also supported Henry Ford's idea of using capital to build job-creating enterprises rather than saving capital in banks. "You don't get rich by loaning out money," he said, "a country gets rich by paying wages to labor, maintaining large outputs, large consumption, and large markets."[12] More evidence of Duke's political views comes from a 1924 interview with the *New York Times* on the occasion of the Duke Endowment's creation. Duke said he was "unalterably opposed" to the League of Nations, but beyond that, the reporter said, "Mr. Duke would not talk for publication on political matters."[13]

The clearest indication of Duke's attitude towards politics comes from his 1915 *North American Review* article. "Public office," Duke wrote, "requires talents that the business-builder has not time nor environment to cultivate."[14] This view was one Duke clearly expressed throughout his career. Unlike Andrew Carnegie, Duke did not use his fortune to affect the issues of the day. And unlike Henry Ford, he did not toy with the idea of running for president. He was not active in politics, and neither is the Duke Endowment.

The Duke family's giving grew as their businesses prospered. From 1890 onwards, the chief recipient of their charity was Trinity College. Like most Southern colleges of the time, Trinity had a small endowment and was struggling. In 1890, Duke gave Trinity College $85,000—enough money to enable the school to move 60 miles to Durham. Duke University archivist William E. King notes that "the items moved" from Trinity College "were meager indeed. A railroad car transported the college bell, clock, safe, and several thousand books."[15] The campus cows and horses walked to Durham.

Washington Duke followed his 1890 gift with three $100,000 gifts to Trinity, in 1896, 1898, and 1900. The 1896 gift was restricted; Trinity College had to "open its doors to women placing them on an equal footing with men," a clause Trinity accepted. This resulted in considerable controversy—and an offer by the National Suffrage Association to make Duke the organization's vice president, which Duke declined. (Duke subsequently removed the restrictions on this gift in 1903.) According to William King, the likely consequence of Washington Duke's gift was that Trinity

College built the first dormitory at Trinity College for women, allowing them to reside on campus instead of only being able to attend classes as day students, but King adds that much of the documentation of the history of women at Trinity College, including the reasons for Washington Duke's imposing restrictions in 1896, "does not exist."[16]

These gifts were quite substantial. King notes that the entire budget of the University of North Carolina in the 1899-1900 school year was $45,000, including $25,000 in state appropriations.[17]

By 1902, Benjamin Duke chaired the school's executive committee. He told a friend that Trinity "has reached that point of capacity and efficiency to warrant the claim that it is the best institution of learning in the South."[18] By 1909, Benjamin Duke's annual donation was $20,000.[19]

Duke University historian Earl W. Porter calculates that by the 1909-1910 school year, Benjamin and James B. Duke were supplying a third of Trinity College's budget, and that the Duke brothers had together donated $500,000 to Trinity College. Benjamin Duke stated in 1909 that "the burden of Trinity College" was a heavy one. "I am practically carrying that institution single handed," Duke wrote. "It needs more money than I am able to give it."[20]

In 1905, Washington Duke died at the age of 85. Much of his fortune had been dispersed before his death, with Trinity College receiving $500,000 during his lifetime. He left $20,000 to the North Carolina Methodist Church, half to support mission work and half for "worn-out preachers." The two North Carolina branches of the African Methodist Church each received $5,000. A hospital in Durham also received $5,000, and two local orphanages received $3,000 each. Washington Duke's benefactions are noteworthy because his charitable interests— Trinity College, black institutions, orphanages, hospitals, Methodist churches—were, and remain, ultimately the interests of the Duke Endowment. "The benefactions made in Washington Duke's will," historian Robert Durden notes, "not only recapitulated the dominant pattern of the family's philanthropy from the late 1880's on but also foreshadowed the pattern of the much larger giving that would be done by B.N. Duke and J.B. Duke in the twentieth century."[21]

❧ Trinity College

When William Preston Few became president of Trinity College in 1910, gifts by the Duke family substantially increased. Few was an empire-building president who would not rest until the school was first rate. From his first days at Trinity College, he believed James Duke would likely provide the money needed to bring national recognition to the school.

Historians disagree about when Few began courting Duke, but the most likely time is between 1914 and 1916. Until 1911, Duke was preoccupied with American Tobacco. After the Supreme Court divided the company, Duke was spending so much time in London overseeing British-American Tobacco that some speculated he was trying to become a British citizen. When World War I began, Duke returned to the United States. By 1916, he was usually in North Carolina developing Southern Power.

According to biographer Robert Woody, Few realized that Duke would not give to the school if Few appeared to have an insatiable appetite for money. "I do not want to feel that you have thrown us overboard," Few wrote to Duke in 1914. "But I do want you to feel that we will incur no added financial responsibilities without the approval before hand [*sic*] of your Brother and yourself; and that any further contributions are to be free will offerings made because you feel like making them and not because they are expected of you."[22]

Few picked the right moment to beseech Duke. By 1915, Duke had amassed a fortune, and even after the dissolution of American Tobacco, he was financially comfortable. At age 56, he finally had an heir in his first and only child, Doris Duke (1912-1993). But by becoming a father at such a late age, there was little chance he would have more heirs. His interest in the Southern Power System required him to spend far more time in the Carolinas. And there was the long-standing tradition of family charity to consider, begun by Washington Duke and largely continued by Benjamin Duke.

In an unpublished memoir, Few wrote that in 1916 James Duke "first spoke definitely to me concerning his purpose to give away during his lifetime a large part of his fortune."[23] Few knew that Duke would give much of this fortune to Trinity College, a gift that would fulfill Few's goal of transforming the school from a small liberal arts college into a major university. But until Few could cajole Duke into making the gift, he could only flatter his most important donor. When Duke gave a $100,000 gift around 1918, Few wrote that "I sincerely believe that the work planted here by the Duke family will stand out in the long years of the future as an unequalled contribution in Southern civilization to liberalism, to right thinking, and to the great moral causes of mankind."[24]

The economic burdens resulting from the end of World War I in 1918 increased pressure on Few to convince Duke to make up his mind. Postwar inflation reduced the value of salaries at Trinity College, and the flood of returning veterans strained the school's dormitories. Tuition income remained low, since the college during this period charged only $50 a year, and even waived the amount for children of preachers, anyone who planned to become a minister, and anyone pleading financial hardship. Moreover, around this time Benjamin Duke, the family philanthropist, had a near-fatal illness. While he recovered (and outlived his brother by four years), the episode reminded Few and his associates of the Duke family's advancing years.

In 1918, James Duke became a member of the Trinity College board of trustees. In February 1919, Few wrote to Duke proposing "that you create a separate corporation, perhaps to be called the James B. Duke Foundation or Fund, as you might prefer."[25] Few suggested that a seven-member Duke Foundation board of trustees also act as Trinity College's Executive Committee, responsible for the school's finances. But because the proposed foundation would be independent of Trinity College, "you could direct the business and manage the property of the new Foundation, and you could determine the allotments to be made each year. During your period of service you could determine all questions of policy, and then I am sure you could safely depend on the character of the men who survive and succeed you to carry on."[26]

Few then wrote to Clinton Toms, a former school superintendent who later became president of Liggett and Myers. As a close friend of both Few and the Duke family, Toms was to play a crucial role in negotiations that would create the Duke Endowment. Few urged Toms to nudge Duke toward creating a foundation. "I believe if you will give him an opportunity, he will talk to you on the subject," Few wrote. "We must do our level best now to impress upon him the needs of the College.... The time is upon us when we must go forward or take a second place."[27]

As Robert Durden notes, this pressure was not initially effective. "James B. Duke, for his part, probably felt annoyed that his brother, Few, Toms, and other friends of Trinity College would not leave him alone to proceed at his own pace in pursuit of his long-range goals."[28] According to Robert Woody, whenever Few's presence was announced, Duke would grumble, "here comes the hundred-million-dollar-man."[29] In December 1919, Duke agreed to give $100,000 to Trinity College provided that no more than $20,000 would be spent each year over a five-year period. Duke then returned to the Southern Power System, which was engaged in a battle with the North Carolina legislature over what rates the utility could charge.

❧ The Creation of Duke University

In the winter of 1920-1921, Few had a serious illness, and during a long period of recuperation, Durden reports, he conceived the idea of a "Duke University"—a school that would include Trinity College as well as a medical school, a vastly expanded law school, and an engineering program. It was Few, not Duke, who decided that the university would be named after its chief donor, since there were already three other colleges in the U.S. named Trinity College, as well as San Antonio's Trinity University. "There were both in North America and in Great Britain many colleges, some independent and some parts of universities, with the name Trinity," Few wrote, "and it seemed to me therefore to have too little individuality to be attached to a great university.... Mr. Duke has some times [*sic*] been blamed for insisting that the institution be named Duke University. It is for this reason that I am here going to some pains to make it plain that this was not his suggestion but mine."[30]

In spring 1921, Few sent Duke a draft document that outlined the transformation of Trinity College; it was written to be issued over Duke's signature:

> I wish to see Trinity College, the law school & other schools expanded into a fully developed university organization. It has been suggested to me that this

expanded institution be named Duke University as a memorial to my father whose gifts made possible the building of Trinity College in Durham, and I approve this suggestion. I desire this university to include Trinity College, a coordinate College for Women, a Law School, a School of Business Administration, a School of Engineering (emphasizing chemical & electrical engineering), a Graduate School of Arts & Sciences, and, when adequate funds are available, a Medical School. I desire this enlarged institution to be operated under the present charter with only such changes, if any changes at all, as the enlargement may require. To this university that is to be thus organized I will give _____ millions of dollars. I agree to pay in within _____ years _____ millions in cash or good securities.[31]

Duke did not fill in the blanks in this document. But Robert Durden notes evidence suggesting that Duke agreed to most of Few's plans at this time. Few told the Trinity College board of trustees in June 1921 that the school might well become a university soon, and also told close friends about "great plans which I think will in due course be completely realized."[32]

In 1923, Duke completed his legal battle with the North Carolina legislature. Southern Power was able to raise its rates enough to provide the dividends Duke felt necessary to ensure the company's stability. Duke then turned his attention to creating his foundation. He continued secret negotiations with Few and also began looking at the medical needs of the Carolinas. Duke asked his secretary, Alexander Sands, to conduct a survey of how much medical care was available to North and South Carolina residents. Sands concluded that more hospitals were needed in rural areas, and that a foundation would be very useful if it acted as a central clearinghouse for hospitals, providing information on hospital organization and structure, as well as expert nurses and technicians who could train local residents in health procedures.

While there is abundant evidence of Duke's intentions towards Trinity College, there is less about why he became interested in hospitals. Biographer John K. Winkler suggests that Duke was trying to imitate the philanthropy of John D. Rockefeller. But historian James F. Gifford Jr., whose account of Duke's interest in medicine is the most authoritative, argues that Duke's wish to build hospitals was consistent with other portions of the endowment, since his goal as an entrepreneur and philanthropist was the same: to help supply the needs of average residents in North and South Carolina. As a capitalist, he built a great power company to ensure that Carolinians would receive a constant supply of low-cost electricity. As a philanthropist, he wanted to ensure that his customers could easily see doctors. "Without good doctors," he once said, his customers "cannot live."[33]

Duke spent most of 1924 working on his foundation. According to Gifford, this included "consultation with officials of the Rockefeller foundations"[34] about the organization of the Duke Endowment, though it is unclear what advice was provided. Duke also authorized the architects who built his New York City mansion and part of his Somerville, New Jersey, estate to work with Few in deciding what style of architecture would be used for the university. Duke's estate was near Princeton University, and he admired the Tudor Gothic buildings erected there when Woodrow Wilson was president of the institution. After visiting about a dozen colleges and universities, Few decided that Duke University would be built in Tudor Gothic style. "It is but the sober truth," Few wrote to Benjamin Duke on September 9, 1924, "to say that when these buildings as now planned are put on the grounds we will have here the most harmonious, imposing, and altogether beautiful educational plant in America."[35]

❧ The Creation of the Duke Endowment

Duke's lawyer, William R. Perkins, completed work on the indenture for the Duke Endowment in late 1924. On December 1, Duke called a secret meeting of seven top business associates in Charlotte, North Carolina. They were presented with a draft of the indenture for the Duke Endowment, and spent four full days, from 8:30 in the morning until 10 at night, reviewing it. Apparently, very little was changed, according to Norman Cocke, a senior Southern Power executive who attended all the sessions. Duke, Cocke recalled decades later, "was a positive man, and when he made a positive assertion very few people controverted."[36]

This acquiescence, however, may have had other causes. In his memoir, Few, who attended some of the sessions, said the planning had to be cut short because someone had leaked the indenture to the press. [37]

On December 11, 1924, the Duke Endowment was formally created. After determining that the endowment was perpetual and was to be governed by up to fifteen trustees, mostly residents of North or South Carolina, the fourth clause of the indenture authorized spending $6 million

> in establishing at a location selected by them within the State of North Carolina an institution of learning to be known as Duke University.... However, should the name of Trinity College, located at Durham, North Carolina, a body politic and incorporate, within three months from the date hereof (or such further time as the trustees hereof may allow) be changed to Duke University, then, in lieu of the foregoing provisions of this division "FOURTH" of this Indenture, as a memorial to his father, Washington Duke, who spent his life in Durham and whose gifts, together with those of Benjamin N. Duke, the brother of the party of the first part, and of other members of the Duke family, have so largely contributed toward making Trinity College at that place, he directs that the trustees shall expend of the corpus of this trust as soon as may reasonably may be a sum not exceeding Six Million Dollars in expanding and extending said University....[38]

This clause is often misinterpreted to mean that Duke forced Trinity College to change its name as a monument to himself—or even, according to some rumors, that he tried to "buy" Yale or Princeton, and having failed, settled on "purchasing" Trinity College. But it was Few, not Duke, who wanted the institution to become Duke University, and as the clause clearly states, the school is named after James Duke's father.

Moreover, this was not the first time that Trinity College offered to rename itself for the Duke family. Duke University historian Earl W. Porter notes that in 1896, Trinity College's treasurer, A.P. Tyer, wrote to Benjamin Duke and stated that the financial situation was dire and asked Duke for a $500,000 donation, in return for which Trinity would rename itself "Duke

College." Benjamin Duke rejected the offer, although Washington Duke gave $100,000 that fall.[39]

While the university does feature a prominent statue of James Duke, there is no evidence that Duke wanted this to be erected.

℮ Recipients of the Duke Endowment

The fifth clause of the Duke Endowment indenture establishes where the funds are to go. Twenty percent of the disbursements were to be added to the foundation's capital until the total available reached $40 million. In addition,

- Thirty-two percent of the disbursements are to go to Duke University "to be utilized by its Board of Trustees in defraying its administration and operating expenses, increasing and improving its facilities and equipment, the erection and enlargement of buildings and the acquisition of additional acreage for it, adding to its endowment, or in such other manner for it as the Board of Trustees of said institution may from time to time deem to be to its best interests."[40] If Duke University was spending its funds in a way the endowment felt inappropriate, the endowment retained the power to deny a grant in any given year.

- Thirty-two percent of the disbursements are for nonprofit hospitals in North and South Carolina, either for construction or subsidization at a rate of one dollar per bed per day for patients too poor to pay for their care.

- Five percent is for Davidson College, a Presbyterian-affiliated institution in Davidson, North Carolina.

- Five percent is for Furman University, a Baptist-affiliated institution in Greenville, South Carolina.

- Four percent is for Johnson C. Smith University, an African-American institution in Charlotte, North Carolina.

- Ten percent is for nonprofit organizations "for the benefit of white or colored whole or half orphans within the states of North Carolina and/or South Carolina." The trustees are to have "uncontrolled discretion" in making grants as long as the funds go to "such organizations, institutions, agencies, and/or societies exclusively for the benefit of such orphans."[41]

- Two percent is for "the care and maintenance of needy and deserving superannuated preachers and needy and deserving widows and orphans of deceased preachers" who were Methodists who served in North Carolina.[42]

- Six percent is for building rural Methodist churches in North Carolina, provided that they are in towns that do not have populations over 1,500. Another four percent is for maintaining these churches.

The seventh section of the indenture establishes Duke's donor intent. Duke began by describing his waterpower projects in the Carolinas. Harnessing this power, he wrote, "which would otherwise run in waste to the sea and not remain and increase as a forest, both gives impetus to industrial life and provides a safe and enduring investment for capital. My ambition is that the revenues of such development shall administer to the social welfare, as the operation of such developments is administering to the economic welfare, of the communities which they serve."[43] Duke urged the endowment to retain a substantial investment in the Southern Power System, "and I advise the trustees that they do not change such investment except in response to the most urgent and extraordinary necessity."[44]

Duke University was to be the recipient of Duke funds because, Duke wrote, "I recognize that education, when conducted along sane and practical, as opposed to dogmatic and theoretical lines is, next to religion, the greatest civilizing influence." After requesting that students and teachers both possess "character, ability, and vision," he added that

I advise that the courses at this institution be arranged, first, with special reference to the training of preachers, teachers, lawyers, and physicians, because these are most in the public eye, and by precept and example can do most to uplift mankind, and, second, to instruction in chemistry, economics, and history, especially the lives of the great of earth, because I believe that such subjects will most help to develop our resources, increase our wisdom, and promote human happiness.[45]

Hospitals were worthy recipients, Duke explained, because they are crucial in "increasing the efficiency of mankind and prolonging human life…. So worthy do I deem the cause and so great do I deem the need that I very much hope that the people will see to it that adequate and convenient hospitals are assured in their respective communities, with especial reference to those who are unable to defray such expenses of their own."[46]

The funds for orphans, Duke said, were given "in an effort to help those who are most unable to help themselves." The monies for aiding retired preachers and building and maintaining rural churches were necessary to help men of God who were unable to accumulate retirement funds because of their devotion to religion. Duke said that giving to help build rural churches was part of a larger principle: "it is to these rural districts that we are to look in large measure for the bone and sinew of our country."[47]

In the last paragraph, Duke concluded that

> I have endeavored to make provisions in some measure for the needs of mankind along physical, mental, and spiritual lines, largely confining the benefactions to those sections served by these water power developments. I might have extended this aid to other charitable objects and to other sections, but my opinion is that so doing probably would be productive of less good by reason of attempting too much. I therefore urge the trustees to seek to administer well the trust hereby committed to them within the limits *set,* and to this end that at least one meeting each year this Indenture be read to the assembled trustees.[48]

This powerful conclusion is noteworthy for two reasons. First, Duke clearly and firmly established his wishes, and left the trustees an extraordinarily specific set of instructions. This was unusual for the time, when the conventional wisdom held that donors should leave vague instructions and trust professionals to do what was best. In an age when the "dead hand" was reviled, Duke created an endowment whose dead hand had sharp claws.

Second, by firmly stating that the endowment would be limited to residents of the two Carolinas and to the causes he favored, Duke ensured that it would be very difficult to break the will. No other philanthropist of his time, and few in ours, would have dared to fix the percentages to be given to causes. By doing this, Duke probably ensured the obscurity of the Duke Endowment, since the foundation has not—and cannot—engage in national crusades. But Duke's foresight ensured that the endowment still supports the causes he favored.

Additional evidence of Duke's intentions comes from an interview be gave to the *New York Times* shortly after the Duke Endowment was announced. In the interview, he explained that "I don't believe that men of wealth should leave their money to their sons unless it is to carry out some specific object. But I have no sons, so that particular problem does not trouble me." (As discussed below, Duke left ample provisions for his daughter, Doris.)[49] He said he wanted to leave funds to a private college rather than a state institution because "the State universities are supported by State funds. I selected private institutions because I believe they are run more efficiently than institutions controlled by the State." The *Times* reporter added, "to make sure that his ideas would be carried out, Mr. Duke explained that he had named as trustees of the endowment mostly men who had grown up in confidence with him, because they understood his ideas."[50]

❧ Early Criticisms

Many Carolinians celebrated Duke's beliefs, but the applause was not universal. Some Trinity College alumni were saddened to see their beloved college disappear, and others worried about the source of the university's new wealth. The Trinity College motto was *Eruditio et Religio,* and someone suggested that Duke University should add *et Tobacco.* (Given that the money for the Duke Endowment came from waterpower rather than tobacco, *et Aqua* might have been more appropriate.) Some Trinity College students proposed that the Duke University football team should have this fight song:

> Chesterfield! Bull Durham!
> [Lucky] Strikes and Plug!
> Duke University!
> Slug! Slug! Slug![51]

One disgruntled alumnus sent several letters to President Few, urging Duke to build his own university in Asheville, over a hundred miles away. "When you go out to get $40,000,000 from a man," Few responded, "you will find that he has some ideas of his own."

Prominent liberals also attacked the Duke Endowment. The *New Republic,* after complaining that Trinity College might well be defaced with billboards for "Duke's Mixture," said that the gift would be controlled by "conservators of established businesses and established educational types" who were "not competent to exercise anything other than a benevolent quietism over the educational institutions intrusted to their care." While not attacking donor intent ("it would be silly to kill the goose that lays the golden eggs because of a special taste for platinum"), the magazine longed for "the equally rare bird, the experimental millionaire," who would fund bold ventures in social change.[52]

The *Raleigh News and Observer,* while supporting Duke's gifts, said that Trinity College's name should not be changed, and attacked Duke as a ruthless monopolist whose fortune was partially built "by heartless destruction of his competitors and fixing a price on tobacco because of the monopoly control that denied proper prices to the grower of the weed." (That charge was untrue, according to the circuit court that declared the American Tobacco Company an illegal trust in 1908; the court noted that during the company's existence, prices paid to farmers for bright-leaf tobacco doubled.)[53]

Duke ignored these criticisms and forged ahead with building Duke University. After acquiring nearly 8,000 acres of land (much of which survives today as a forest preserve), he spent considerable time with landscape architects to determine what sort of stone should be used in constructing the new buildings. One trustee, Watson Rankin, was impressed with Duke's strength. "We walked all over those grounds" of the new campus, Rankin said, "jumping ditches and crossing wagon roads and going through shrubbery and all that kind of thing, with Mr. Duke always in the lead."[54] But it was a vigor that would soon end. In July 1925, Duke contracted a pernicious anemia from which he was to die. On October 10, 1925, Duke died in New York at the age of 68.

The year before his death, Duke gave $16 million to Duke University over and above the funds given to the Duke Endowment. He also pledged that, after all other bequests were made, the residue of his estate, which was worth around $40 million, would go to Duke University. On October 1, 1925, nine days before his death, he gave an additional $7 million to support building construction at the university. Thus, his total gifts to the school, not counting the Duke Endowment, were about $63 million.

❧ Initial Problems of the Duke Endowment

In order to establish the Duke Endowment, two steps had to be taken. The first was a legal matter. Duke's estate only partially went to charity; part of it also went to support his daughter, while some went to other relatives. The Revenue Act of 1924 declared that such mixed estates were subject to punitive taxes. This would transfer $8 million from the Duke Endowment to the federal government and reduce the endowment's income by $400,000. The Revenue Act of 1926 would remove these restrictions, but as historian James Gifford notes, "Few, Duke's executors, and apparently some congressmen feared that to apply for retroactive relief would seem to the public an appeal for special favors for big business."[55] Working behind the scenes, Few began an extensive lobbying campaign and persuaded North Carolina Senator Furnifold M. Simmons, an important member of the Senate Finance Committee, to make the relief offered by the 1926 Revenue Act retroactive. This was done, and the Duke Endowment's initial capital was preserved.

A second problem did not affect the Duke Endowment directly, but ensured that Duke's will would spend considerable time in probate. In the early 1920s, Benjamin Duke decided to give distant cousins a portion of his wealth. James Duke decided to follow his older brother's example, and set aside $2 million to be divided among any descendants of his parents or his parents' brothers and sisters. The executors found 167 people qualified to receive funds. In addition, a woman named Elizabeth Duke announced that she was a granddaughter of Thomas Duke, whose father Thomas Duke was allegedly a brother of Washington Duke. She produced a family Bible that allegedly proved Thomas Duke's connection to the Duke family, and demanded that she and her 106 relatives receive their share of the estate.

From January to May 1928, dozens of witnesses debated dusty volumes of Duke genealogy in the Somerset County, New Jersey Orphans Court. At one point in the trial, one Charles Thomas Duke of Pittsburgh, Texas, when not picking his teeth with a four-inch knife blade, provided what the *New York Times* called "a roistering savor of the Western plains" when asked about Elizabeth Duke's claim that the family Bible proved her connection to James Duke. He replied, "if there's any names in the book contrary to the names I gave they're false. If they've been written in there they were done forgily [*sic*]." He then recited what he knew of his family genealogy and also volunteered that he'd had an enjoyable fourteen months in prison for a murder charge, because lots of friends brought him good things to eat.[56]

In May 1928, Orphans Court Judge John A. Frech ruled against Elizabeth Duke, declaring that she and the other 106 claimants were spurious relatives. Judge Frech ordered the $2 million distributed to the 167 legitimate relations of James Duke, with each recipient getting just under $12,000. The Duke will was finally probated, and the Duke Endowment could proceed.[57]

☙ The Duke Endowment and the Doris Duke Charitable Foundation Contrasted

To assess the fidelity of the Duke Endowment to the wishes of James Duke, the history of the Duke Endowment can be compared to the portion of Duke's estate given to his daughter Doris. According to biographers Tom Valentine and Patrick Mahn, when Duke was on his deathbed, he summoned Doris to his side and told her to "promise to me that you will keep our fortune safe until I return in another life and lay claim to it once again." Valentine and Mahn allege that Duke told his daughter not to trust anyone, to "deny yourself nothing" and to never succumb to anyone else's will. Part of this message, they say, was delivered in Duke's last "glimmer of consciousness before coma cleaved it from his failing body."[58]

Valentine and Mahn provide no evidence for this episode, and the scene is inconsistent with other accounts of Duke's character. But whether it actually happened or was merely gossip from Duke's servants, it certainly fits Doris Duke's character: throughout her life she was extremely secretive. This secrecy is understandable; Doris Duke received most of her inheritance when she turned 21. But this was in 1933, when America's revulsion against inherited wealth was at a peak. Given Doris Duke's enormous fortune, she understandably would want to stay out of the public eye.

Doris Duke married James Cromwell, a major backer of the Democratic Party whom President Franklin Roosevelt rewarded with the ambassadorship to Canada. James B. Duke's biographer, John K. Winkler, notes that in 1936, in order to support her husband's political ambitions, Doris Duke donated $50,000 to the Democratic Party, "An act which probably caused her father, whose unyielding Republicanism was a fetish, to turn in his tomb."[59] The couple divorced in the early 1940s, and Duke had a series of brief marriages thereafter, most notably to Porfirio Rubirosa, the Latin adventurer.

She spent most of her career as a philanthropist. A 1938 profile of Doris Duke by Elsa Maxwell suggests that Doris Duke had decided to devote her life to charitable deeds before she was 25. "One thing can be taken for granted," Maxwell wrote, "someday she will transfer the bulk of her fortune to some charity in which she believes.... Both she and her husband believe—and they are in dead earnest about it—that she is but a trustee of an enormous estate which eventually should revert to the American people."[60]

During her lifetime, Doris Duke's most notable philanthropic achievement was funding the restoration of mansions in Newport, Rhode Island.

The Duke Endowment indenture states that Doris Duke was to become a trustee of the endowment on achieving her majority in 1933. She at first dutifully attended board meetings, but her attendance slackened as she began pursuing other interests. Although she remained a life-long trustee of the Duke Endowment, she stopped attending meetings in the late 1960s and refused to accept the fee the endowment paid to all trustees. In a 1988 statement, she explained that her refusal to take part in the Duke Endowment was "because I had disagreed with the policies the endowment was following. I was only one trustee, one voice, wanting to accomplish certain socially progressive objectives. The other trustees, however, disagreed with me."[61]

Duke Endowment trustee Marshall Pickens (who was one of James Duke's pallbearers at his 1925 funeral) told the *Charlotte Observer* in 1988 that Doris Duke had only attended two meetings of the Duke Endowment board since he had become a trustee in 1951. He explained that Doris Duke's estrangement was probably due to politics. She was "a pretty liberal lady in her thinking, socially and otherwise," Pickens said. "She probably thought we weren't doing what her father said when actually we were."[62] Similarly, Doris Duke at first regularly attended official functions of Duke University, but after the university's centennial in 1939, she drifted away. While historians debate why this happened, she did occasionally make donations to the university. More often, university fundraisers were rebuffed.

According to biographer Stephanie Mansfield, Doris Duke's last known visit to Duke University was in the early 1970s. The school's president was then Terry Sanford, a former North Carolina governor and future U.S. senator. Sanford told Mansfield that one day a woman walked into his office claiming she was a powerful psychic who had a vision in which James Duke was in the university chapel's crypt "dressed as Jesus. And Mr. Duke said, 'Go see Doris. Tell Doris that I want her to support financial efforts to find the truth about why I can be here.' In other words, psychic research."[63] The psychic said she wanted Sanford to arrange an introduction to Doris Duke. After Sanford declined, the psychic announced that she would use her paranormal powers to make contact with Doris Duke. Several weeks later, Duke and the psychic showed up on campus and were given a private luncheon with Sanford. Duke then left, and she is not known to have visited the university ever again.

According to Mansfield, Sanford told his fundraisers not to ask Doris Duke for any more money. "I was tired of everyone suggesting, 'Let's get Doris Duke to do this. We only need $6 million.' Her position was quite justifiably: My father's already done all of this, why should I? I think the university played it rather badly in the way they dealt with her. I think she had been mistreated. They hadn't paid attention to her and the students felt compelled to ridicule her."[64]

In the 1980s, Doris Duke began to worry about her estate. She had no children, and the terms of the Doris Duke Trust, created in 1924, stated that barring legitimate heirs, 21 years after her death the trust would dissolve and the assets would revert to the Duke Endowment. In 1986, Doris Duke sued to alter this provision, but lost.

For a time, Doris Duke had an heir. In the early 1980s, she met Charlene "Chandi" Heffner, a fellow student of her belly-dancing instructor. In 1985, Heffner moved into Doris Duke's Somerville, New Jersey, estate, and changed her name to "Chandi Duke Heffner." In 1988, Duke adopted Heffner. By 1991, however, the relationship had soured, and Duke disavowed the adoption. In her last will, written on March 8, 1993, she stated that "it is my intention that Chandi Heffner not be deemed my child for purposes of disposing of my property under this my Will (or any Codicil thereto). Further, it is not my intention, nor do I believe that it was ever my father's intention, that Chandi Heffner be deemed to be a child or lineal descendant of mine for purposes of disposing of the trust estate of May 2, 1917, which my father established for my benefit or the Doris Duke Trust, dated December 11, 1924, which my father established for the benefit of me, certain other members of the Duke family and ultimately for charity."[65]

In October 1993, Doris Duke died, leaving an estate worth about $1.2 billion, a considerable improvement on the $40 million she inherited upon her father's death in 1925. Heffner then sued for damages, charging that her relationship to Duke was so close that they had traveled together to Romania for "fountain of youth" treatments and shopped for a $25 million Boeing 737. The press quickly called Heffner's suit "galimony."[66] Duke Biographer Schwarz notes that it was unclear whether Duke could legally annul her adoption of Heffner, although it was clear that Heffner could be disinherited.[67]

❦ The Super Bowl of Probate

Duke's wishes led to a twisted and convoluted probate case. Part of the problem lay in her choice of executors. She wrote at least six wills between 1987 and 1993, and each had a different executor, including Chandi Heffner, Irwin Bloom (her accountant), Harry Demopoulos (one of her doctors), and Walker P. Inman Jr., son of Duke's half-brother and her closest living relative. By 1993, Duke had settled on her butler, Bernard Lafferty, to be sole executor. That choice, *Los Angeles Times* reporters Paul Lieberman and John J. Goldman observe, led to "the Super Bowl of probate battles" that consumed as much as $50 million in legal fees.[68] In August 1994, Lafferty selected trustees for the Doris Duke Charitable Foundation. They included himself, Duke University president Nan Keohane, actress Elizabeth Taylor, New Jersey governor Christine Todd Whitman, former National Gallery of Art director J. Carter Brown, and Marion Oates Charles, a long-time friend of Doris Duke. Chandi Heffner continued her suit against the Doris Duke estate. According to the *Raleigh News and Observer,* Heffner accused Lafferty of turning Doris Duke against her. She also said Duke was not of sound mind when she named Lafferty to execute her will.[69]

The Doris Duke probate case began to make national headlines in January 1995, when Tammy Payette, a nurse to Doris Duke, charged that Duke did not die of natural causes, but as a result of a "massive sedation regime" imposed by her doctors, including a fatal dose of morphine on the day of her death."[70] Duke's former chef, Colin Shanley, charged that on the day of her death, he had received a large package addressed to Lafferty containing Demerol, a powerful narcotic. Shanley charged that Lafferty "leapt across the kitchen, grabbed the parcel out of my hands, and stated that 'Miss Duke is going to die tonight.'"[71]

One month later, Shanley charged that Duke "did not understand what she was doing" when she signed her last will. Duke's housekeeper, Ann Bostich, charged that Duke was disoriented after a stroke in February 1993. When the day came to sign the will, she testified, Duke's lawyer, William Doyle, obtained Duke's signature by sliding "his own hand under her wrist. He propped her hand up with his hand. Doyle then pushed her hand along the page, guiding her hand" as she signed the final version of her will.[72] Subsequent medical records admitted into the Duke probate case revealed that during the hospital stay in question, Doris Duke was taking as many as 25 drugs a day, including such powerful mood-altering drugs as Valium, Zoloft, Darvocet, and Halcion.[73]

A week later, lawyers for Bernard Lafferty charged that Surrogate Court Judge Eve M. Preminger, a Manhattan judge overseeing the probate case, had appointed an investigator, Richard Kuh, who was trying to determine if Doris Duke's will was valid.[74] Nurse Payette, whose allegations ensured that the Duke case was front-page news, was arrested in April 1995 and subsequently charged with stealing $450,000 in jewelry, artwork, and other valuable objects from six of her clients, including Doris Duke and Max Factor, the cosmetics tycoon. In February 1996, Payette was sentenced to eight years for the thefts and ordered to pay $400,000 in restitution.[75]

In May 1995, Richard Kuh issued his report. Based on his recommendations, Surrogate Preminger removed Bernard Lafferty and U.S. Trust as executors. She contended that Bernard Lafferty had used estate credit cards to indulge in a massive spending spree and that he had smashed Doris Duke's Cadillac and billed the estate for a replacement, even though the Doris Duke estate was continuing to pay his $100,000-a-year butler's salary, a sum that would rise to $500,000 annually plus a one-time fee of $5 million if Lafferty survived as executor. She also questioned U.S. Trust's allowing Lafferty to use $260,000 of estate funds to renovate Duke's California home.

Surrogate Preminger also declared that U.S. Trust had created a conflict of interest by loaning Lafferty $825,000 at a time when he had no assets. It stood to gain substantially if it were subsequently to manage the Doris Duke Charitable Foundation endowment. Preminger ordered Morgan Guaranty Trust to replace U.S. Trust, and Alexander D. Forger, an attorney who was Jacqueline Kennedy Onassis's executor, to replace Lafferty.[76]

In June 1995, U.S. Trust won a temporary victory in the New York State Appeals Court. Judge Israel Rubin blocked Surrogate Preminger's ruling and reinstated U.S. Trust as joint manager of the Duke estate with Morgan Guaranty. He also restored Bernard Lafferty as executor on the condition that Lafferty leave Duke's Beverly Hills home. His decision was later overturned in October 1995, when the Court, by a 3-2 vote, overruled Rubin (who voted in the minority) and upheld Preminger.[77]

The case took several new turns. Three of Doris Duke's employees complained that U.S. Trust and Lafferty had mishandled several of Duke's pets, including her camels, Princess and Baby.

Their complaints were not motivated solely by the love of animals: a clause in Doris Duke's will awarded $100,000 to any dog "owned by me and residing at my death at my residence." Housekeeper Ann Bostich told the court that 10 dogs were qualified legatees and that she was entitled to a million-dollar bounty to care for them. Meanwhile, Chandi Heffner's case against the estate was settled at the end of 1995. In return for a payment of $65.8 million, Heffner agreed never to discuss her relationship with Duke.[78]

In January 1996, the New York State Appeals Court partially reversed itself. It ruled unanimously that Preminger had indeed acted improperly by ousting Lafferty and U.S. Trust without giving them a chance to appeal her decision. Judge Vito J. Titone ruled that Preminger acted largely on "untested hearsay," and he ordered Lafferty and U.S. Trust reinstated until they were able to properly appeal Preminger's ruling.[79]

U.S. Trust then proposed a deal. It would remain as co-executor, but Lafferty would resign in return for an unspecified payment while remaining one of five members on the Doris Duke Charitable Foundation board. When the deal collapsed, Lafferty sued to have Preminger removed from the case, claiming that her action removing him as executor occurred "without ever seeing Mr. Lafferty or hearing him speak."[80] More suits followed. Chemical Banking and Bank of New York charged that Doris Duke ended her relationship with them when she "was not of sound mind." (Chemical Banking had been named co-executor of Duke's 1987 and 1991 wills. Bank of New York was named a co-executor in a 1992 will.)[81]

By the spring of 1996, there were at least 100 motions in the Duke estate case accusing various people of various misdeeds. In March 1996, the New York State Appeals Court ruled in favor of U.S. Trust, and ordered the estate settlement postponed until a way could be found to continue the proceedings without Preminger. To break the logjam, U.S. Trust revised its settlement offer. It continued to suggest that Lafferty be removed as co-executor in return for a payment, but it proposed to keep him off the board of the Doris Duke Charitable Foundation as well. The board would consist of three trustees appointed by Lafferty— Nan Keohane, Marion Oates Charles, and J. Carter Brown—and three additional trustees: lawyer James Gill; Morgan Stanley president John Mack, a Duke University alumnus; and Harry

Demopoulos. Elizabeth Taylor and Christine Todd Whitman would not be trustees under this proposal.[82]

This settlement was agreed to in May 1996. U.S. Trust became sole executor of the estate. Surrogate Preminger ruled that the Doris Duke Charitable Foundation board had to appoint one additional member, a nationally recognized medical expert, and she retained the right to approve any new trustees to the board. But she approved the six proposed trustees. (Subsequently Anthony Fauci of the National Institutes of Health, an AIDS expert, was appointed to the board.) Bernard Lafferty was removed as executor and kept off the board, but he was paid $4.5 million and given an additional $500,000 annually.[83]

Two remaining questions about the Doris Duke estate also were settled in 1996. In July, the Los Angeles County District Attorney issued a report stating that Doris Duke died of natural causes and that there was "no credible evidence of criminal homicide." And in November, Bernard Lafferty died at age 51, leaving his $3.5 million estate to the Doris Duke Charitable Foundation instead of to his relatives.[84]

In 2000, Surrogate Preminger made one final ruling. She charged that Doris Duke's lawyers engaged in work that was "unnecessary, duplicative, or excessive," and ordered the compensation to these firms slashed from $21 million to $7 million. Hardest hit was the firm of Katten Muchin & Zavis, which requested $15.3 million from the court, a bill Surrogate Preminger cut to $3. 2 million.[85]

ᘓ The Doris Duke Charitable Foundation

Efforts were now made to have Doris Duke's philanthropy recognized by Duke University. In November 1996, two plaques (paid for by the Mary Duke Biddle Foundation) honoring Doris Duke were placed in the Duke family chapel on the Duke University campus in a service led by Duke's cousins, Anthony Drexel Duke and Mary D.B.T. Semans. Doris Duke was thus honored in the same area that honored Washington, Benjamin, and James B. Duke.[86]

The Doris Duke Charitable Foundation, now established, found a president: Undersecretary of State Joan Edelman Spero, who was given compensation of $400,000 a year.[87]

But what was the foundation to do? Doris Duke's instructions were not specific. She stated that she wanted to support "dancers, singers, musicians, and other artists of the entertainment world" as well as scientists fighting cancer, AIDS, and sickle-cell anemia, "provided no animals are used to conduct such research." She also had "a special interest in the preservation of wildlife, both flora and fauna, in the United States and elsewhere." She gave the trustees the option to spend out the foundation's endowment if they so chose.

Spero and her staff discovered that Doris Duke had given $97.7 million to various charities during her lifetime, including $22 million to restore Newport, Rhode Island homes and $4 million to Duke University. In 1998, *New York Times* writer Judith H. Dobryznski said that Spero had interviewed "dozens of people" close to Doris Duke to try to find out what her patron was like.

Doris Duke, Spero said, "was a hands-on person. And Oatsie Charles has said that she was a very take-charge person. When she led the restoration of Newport, she purchased the properties herself. These things were rundown, but she had a good eye and knew what had to be done with them."[88]

Based on these interviews, Spero decided that the Doris Duke Charitable Foundation's major efforts would be in the arts, medical research, and the environment. She told the *Chronicle* of *Philanthropy* that Doris Duke's will "doesn't say, 'You should do this, you should do that.' It says, 'Okay, Spero, you figure it out.'"[89]

One cause of Doris Duke that the Doris Duke Charitable Foundation does not support is animal rights. Humane Society of the United States senior policy adviser Bernard Unti told the *New York Times* in 2009 that he believed this was because Doris Duke's will said that her funds should be used for the prevention of cruelty to animals or children. "The trustees apparently said, 'Oh, well, she said animals or children, not animals and children, so let's just do children.'"[90]

In December 1997, the Doris Duke Charitable Foundation gave its first grants. It awarded $5 million to the Open Space Institute and the Trust for Public Land to buy Sterling Forest, a tract of land on the New York-New Jersey border. Other major awards went to the American Dance Festival ($1.9 million), the Nicholas School of the Environment ($1.7 million to endow a chair in ecology in Doris Duke's name), Jazz at Lincoln Center ($2 million), and $4.9 million to create the Doris Duke Clinical Scientist Award Program to provide fellowships for up to 10 promising young medical researchers.[91] Because the Doris Duke Charitable Foundation has an endowment of about $1.9 billion, it must disburse at least $90 million annually. It remains unclear whether the foundation can award its funds for medical research to credible scientists who don't use animals in research.[92]

The Doris Duke Charitable Trust has continued its emphasis on land preservation and arts funding. It has also helped open Doris Duke's homes in Hawaii and Newport as museums. Duke Farms has also been partially opened to visitors.

Since the third edition of this book, the Doris Duke Charitable Foundation has largely continued its philanthropic priorities. In 2007, the foundation announced a five-year, $100 million effort to combat global warming by, as the *Chronicle of Higher Education's* Jensen Brennen reported, exploring "ways that government policy can help spur the development and adoption of clean, climate-friendly energy sources, increase conservation, and lessen the demand for traditional fuels." As part of this program, the Doris Duke Charitable Foundation awarded a two-year, $750,000 grant to Harvard to come up with a replacement for the Kyoto Protocol global-warming pact.[93]

The Doris Duke Charitable Foundation also undertook a drastic transformation of Duke Farms, the Somerville, New Jersey, estate Duke inherited from her father. Although Doris Duke asked in her will that her homes in Newport, Rhode Island, and Honolulu be preserved as museums, she imposed no restrictions on Duke Farms, save that it be used for "horticultural research" and "to protect endangered species."

There is some evidence that Doris Duke at one point wanted Duke Farms preserved. In 1987 the state of New Jersey said it would widen U.S. Route 206 that bordered Duke Farms to the east, which would have torn down a wall surrounding Duke Farms. Duke Farms's response was to submit a 63-page, single-spaced application to the National Trust for Historic Preservation, saying Duke Farms was historically significant in eight categories, including "landscape architecture," "sculpture," and "philosophy."

Under the section of the historic preservation form for "significance," the anonymous writer of the form said the Duke estate "survives intact as a unique expression in New Jersey of the monumental scale of showplace estates built by Captains of Industry in the late 19th century as status symbols. The Duke Estate is also an expression of the genius of its creator.... [It] is a latter-day manifestation of the urge of the prominently wealthy for living in a style they could afford."

The writer stated that it was Doris Duke's "intention to maintain the entire estate in perpetuity."[94]

On June 12, 1987, New Jersey state historic preservation officer Gregory A. Marshall wrote to Andras Fekete, chief of the New Jersey Department of Transportation's Bureau of Economic Analysis about historic properties that might be affected by the U.S. 206 widening. "The Deputy SHPO (state historic preservation officer) is of the opinion that this property meets the National Register Criteria of Eligibility," Marshall wrote. "A formal nomination to the National Register is under way."[95]

But for reasons that remain unclear, the application to the National Trust stalled, and Doris Duke did not impose restrictions in her will protecting Duke Farms. This led the Doris Duke Charitable Foundation, in 2008, to close Duke Farms for four years, demolishing most of the gardens in an effort to turn the property into a nature preserve. "The future mission shouldn't be to make Duke Farms the poor man's Longwood Gardens, with smaller, less mature horticultural displays," Rutgers University ecologist Steven N. Handel told the *New York Times*. "Duke Farms is going to have an important, unique mission in land stewardship and research and education."[96]

Four years later, Duke Farms was re-opened in 2012, after $45 million was spent by the foundation. The land—four times larger than Disneyland—became an ecological preserve where, among other things, dogs and trashcans were banned. Admission was free, but only 400 cars were allowed at a given time. The only gardens allowed to remain were a 1,500-plant orchid range. The goal, said farm supervisor Thom Almendinger, was "to inspire visitors to be informed stewards of the land."[97]

In 2015, the Doris Duke Charitable Foundation began the process of getting permission to destroy Doris Duke's home. The home had been vacant since 1993 and had suffered some damage from Hurricane Floyd in 1999. The amount of damage remained unclear, because the foundation did not allow third-party assessments. (In 2009 the foundation received a $58 million low-interest loan from the New Jersey Economic Development Authority for infrastructure improvements at Duke Farms; none of the money went to preserving Doris Duke's home.)

A local historic preservation group, DORIS (Destruction of Residence is Senseless) was formed to fight the demolition. Their principal arguments in favor of preservation were the 1987 National Trust application and the testimony of Doris Duke's long-time secretary, Elizabeth McConville, who told the *Newark Star-Ledger* that Doris Duke "had five other houses, but this is the one she considered home. This was the place where she grew up and spent the most time with her father. It's where she kept her favorite dogs. It's where she could most be herself."

"On every tour I've ever been on of the estate," McConville added, "the first question people asked is, 'Where did she live?' And they were disappointed they couldn't see the house."[98]

DORIS's fight to preserve Doris Duke's home reached the New Jersey Supreme Court, but DORIS repeatedly lost because there was no restriction in Doris Duke's will that would have preserved the house. In March 2016, New Jersey Supreme Court Justice Lee Solomon refused to block the demolition, which was completed shortly after his ruling.[99]

The Doris Duke case shows the importance of finding the right executor. By choosing a man clearly unqualified to execute her wishes, Doris Duke allowed her estate to be tied up for years in unnecessary and protracted litigation. And by leaving vague instructions, it's probable that the Doris Duke Charitable Foundation will eventually spend money on causes she would have disfavored. It's also clear that Doris Duke's money will not go to causes that James B. Duke favored. Had James Duke willed that the portion of his wealth scheduled to go to Doris Duke be buried in a vault for 68 years, disinterred, and then given to the charities he admired, those nonprofits, even after seven decades of inflation, would have benefited more than they will from Doris Duke's estate.

☙ The Duke Endowment Today

The Duke Endowment more amply fulfilled Duke's wishes. The residents of North and South Carolina quickly became the beneficiaries of Duke Endowment funds. As early as 1931, journalist Louis Graves noted that all Carolinians, rich and poor alike, benefited from the programs that Duke supported. "The number of people who stand to benefit from the Duke benefactions is incalculable," Graves wrote, "for the stream of gold pours through the cities and trickles into the remotest corners of the two Carolinas."[100]

Duke Endowment funds also ensured that Duke University survived the worst years of the Great Depression. From 1927 to 1930, the endowment supplied half the university's budget. Between 1930 and 1932, it doubled its contributions, enabling the university to increase enrollment. Though donations fell after 1934, Duke University clearly would have encountered severe financial trouble—or like many other schools, temporarily closed—had the endowment not existed.[101] Other schools thanked the Duke Endowment for aid during hard economic times. In a special supplement to the April 26, 1937, *Charlotte Observer* commemorating the Duke Endowment, Davidson College president Walter L. Lingle said that "the income from the Duke Endowment has made it possible for the college to come through seven years of the severest depression on record without debt or deficit and without cutting and slashing salaries."[102]

The Duke Endowment has not changed much in the past 50 years. Only one change in the indenture has been made, and that was a major alteration of James B. Duke's intentions.

According to Robert Durden, James B. Duke "envisioned an ongoing, extremely close relationship between the Endowment and the Duke Power Company," as we noted earlier. Duke added that he hoped that the trustees of the Duke Endowment "see to it that at all times these [Duke Power] companies be managed and operated by the men best qualified for such a service."[103]

This "symmetrical and symbiotic relationship" between the Duke Endowment and Duke Power continued for decades. Every president of Duke Power between 1924 and 1971 was also a Duke Endowment trustee. As late as 1973 Duke Power chairman Thomas L. Perkins was also a Duke Endowment trustee.

But the Tax Reform Act of 1969 states that a foundation cannot own more than 25 percent of the shares of a corporation. When the act passed, the Duke Endowment had 56 percent of Duke Power stock. So the trustees convinced the North Carolina Supreme Court in 1972 to alter the indenture to allow the foundation to sell some of its Duke Power holdings.

The endowment's trustees, however, were blocked by another section of the indenture, in which Duke stated that they could only sell Duke Power shares "except in response to the most urgent and extraordinary necessity." Duke further said that the vote to sell the shares had to be unanimous, and Doris Duke insisted on blocking the sale.

Doris Duke was a trustee of the Duke Endowment her entire life, but ceased to play an active role after 1970. In a deposition in a 1979 court case involving the Doris Duke Trust, Doris Duke stated that "I thought there was little I as a single vote could contribute.... I was always the one asking all the questions and bringing up difficult points. It seemed like no one really wanted to hear me. So I said, what's the point of my going? So I stopped.[104]

In the same deposition, Doris Duke said she never sold any of her Duke Power shares (though she might have given some away). She said she opposed the Duke Power sale because it was "contrary to what my father wanted." Doris Duke said that her father told her that it was "the most stable stock he could give" for his foundation and "you couldn't have your money in anything safer."[105]

For most of the 1970s and 1980s, the Duke Endowment trustees tried to have a meeting with Doris Duke. In 1981, they voted to convene a special meeting at the Mayfair Regent Hotel in the hopes that Doris Duke would show up and change her mind about the Duke Power stock. Doris Duke refused to show up.

While the stock sale was delayed, Duke Power had issued massive numbers of new shares, ensuring that the percentage of stock held by the endowment fell from 56 percent to 11 percent between 1973 and 1994.

In March 1994, six months after Doris Duke's death, the Duke Endowment announced plans to sell 16 million of the 26 million Duke Power shares it still held, reducing the endowment's holdings to five percent of Duke Power's stock. Endowment spokesman Elizabeth Locke told the *Charlotte Observer* that the board tried to sell the shares earlier, but was blocked by Doris Duke. "I have heard that this was something she was opposed to," Locke said. "The board was never able to reach agreement because, perhaps, Miss Duke was against it."[106] Even after the proposed sale, however, Duke Power would remain the largest single holding in the endowment's investment portfolio, and it would still be the largest single shareholder in Duke Power.

While the recipients of Duke Endowment funds have not changed, some of the programs have. The endowment still contributes to orphanages, but they are now mostly called "children's homes." The funds to rural Methodist churches in North Carolina are still given only to churches that qualify under the terms of the 1924 indenture, though they are used for weatherization programs and not just construction. And while James Duke likely would be confused by some of the grants made to Duke University, Davidson College, Furman University, and Johnson C. Smith University ($800,000 in 1996 to buy computers at Duke University, $75,000 to Furman University for "a minority faculty recruitment initiative"), he never sought to control the curriculum either at Duke University or any institution mentioned in the Duke Endowment indenture.

Much of the money the Duke Endowment gives to education is used in ways that honor the Duke family. In 1996, for example, the endowment gave $4.5 million to Duke University for the Benjamin N. Duke Leadership Program, which provides scholarships and loans to North and South Carolina students, as well as $100,000 to endow the James B. Duke 100th Anniversary Fellowship Fund and $500,000 to endow the Angier B. Duke Memorial Scholarship Program. (Angier B. Duke was a grandson of Benjamin Duke.)

In the Duke Endowment's 1991 annual report, chairman Mary D.B.T. Semans, a granddaughter of Benjamin Duke who served as chairman of the Duke Endowment between 1982-2001, argues that because the endowment has given to a limited range of causes, it has been a more optimistic endeavor than many other foundations.[107] Because the Duke Endowment was limited to causes James Duke favored in North and South Carolina, it has often worked with the same grant recipients year after year, which has enabled it to see its work grow and progress. By giving local, long-term support, the endowment has been able to show, in a small but steady way, progress in solving the social problems of our time. Such a plan, Semans says, might make more sense than broad national efforts. It "is helpful to carve out a piece of the problem," she writes,

> so that we can manage to have an effect, so that we can recognize success when it occurs, so that we can rejoice with the individuals who achieved it. We cannot, alone, solve the problems of health care, or education, or children; but we can identify the issues in one community, we can find partners and work on those issues. We can see some successes.[108]

Semans also stresses the importance of donor intent:

> I suggest that we look back to our roots and gain strength and renewal from our founders' dreams ... in some cases, this is easy to do. The founders are still part of the foundation. In other cases, it involves going back into history, archives, and memories. But just as we now recognize the importance of children knowing their heritage, so, too, is it important for philanthropy to know from whence it came.[109]

The indenture that created the Duke Endowment provides one way for the trustees to understand James Duke's intentions. Once a year, following Duke's instructions, the Duke Endowment board of trustees reads aloud the entire indenture. "After the reading," Semans explains, "there is always a time of reflection and comment about Mr. Duke, his ideas, and our mission. This closeness to the founder renews us and gives us a sense of new energy."[110]

The Duke Endowment has, however, since made the news because of one clause of the endowment's indenture stating that trustee compensation was divided from three percent of the annual investment income made by the endowment. In 2001, this meant that trustees were paid $132,709.61. Trustee Juanita Kreps, a former commerce secretary, defended her pay to the *New York Times*. "We do a lot of work," Kreps said. "We meet two full days ten times a year in Charlotte, which isn't the easiest place to get to, and there's a great deal of correspondence to deal with in between."[111]

Since the third edition of this book, the Duke Endowment has drifted somewhat. Recall that while James B. Duke specified how the Duke Endowment should spend his money, he imposed no restrictions on the programs that the Duke Endowment should fund. While the endowment has made no attempts to alter its indenture, it has broadened the range of grants it has given in the categories which it funds. For example, the Duke Endowment has funded grants for energy conservation and power audits in the four schools it supports.[112]

The endowment has also chosen in recent years to give less frequent, larger gifts. In 2008 it pledged $50 million to Duke

University for construction of a new medical center. In 2011, the endowment awarded Duke University $80 million, the largest single grant in the endowment's history, for the renovation of Duke's student union and its two largest auditoriums, frequently used for concerts and performances. A 2011 grant of $35 million to Johnson C. Smith University for a new science center, scholarships, and renovation of a residence hall was one of the largest in that school's history. In October 2012, the endowment announced a ten-year, $45 million grant to Davidson College for a program that would build a new science center and renovate all of Davidson's science buildings.[113]

In January 2013, the Duke Endowment noted that it had now given away three billion dollars. While it took 68 years for the endowment to give away its first billion and 12 years more to reach the two billion dollar grantmaking mark, the endowment took only eight years to give away its third billion.[114]

Still, the Duke Endowment remains a large monument to the respect donor intent deserves. Its entrepreneurial owner deserves much of the credit for his careful structuring of the philanthropy, but credit is also due to generations of board members and staff who have honored his wishes. The grim comparison made by Doris Duke's philanthropy only heightens the Duke Endowment's achievement.

13

The Conrad N. Hilton Foundation

The story of the Conrad N. Hilton Foundation shows how donor intent can be preserved in our time. It is best contrasted with the story of Henry Ford, who created the Ford Foundation largely as a way of ensuring family control of the business he created.

Conrad Nicholson Hilton (1887-1979) faced the same problem. He wanted to be a philanthropist and also ensure that his son, Barron Hilton (born 1927), would control the Hilton Hotels Corporation. One obstacle was the Tax Reform Act of 1969, which forbids a foundation from controling more than 20 percent of the stock of any business. The resulting battle between Barron Hilton and the Conrad N. Hilton Foundation shows the difficulties this act has created for donor intent.

☙ Innovator in the Hotel Market

Conrad Hilton did not invent the modern hotel chain, nor was he the largest hotel proprietor. Throughout his life, he had to vie with hundreds of competitors. Though he was able to build an international corporation, he never dominated the highly decentralized hotel market. His two great innovations were in marketing and financial control.

Hilton ensured that every inch of space in his hotels was used to make money. When renovating the Waldorf-Astoria, for example, he discovered that two of the hotel's central pillars were hollow. He converted them into highly profitable "vitrines," or display cases, for merchandise. While not micromanaging his hotels, Hilton received daily financial reports from each property. This enabled him to quickly detect potential problems and also ensure that his company would make profits with relatively low occupancy rates.

One of Hilton's specialties was rewarding close associates for their hard work. During World War II, seven of his hotel managers served in the military. Hilton quietly set aside shares of a hotel in Longview, Texas, that he subsequently sold. When the men returned from the war, Hilton presented his veterans with checks for $21,000 from the hotel sale.

"I like to do things like that," Hilton told the *New York Times Magazine*. "I like to make people around me a little rich."[1]

During World War II, hotel room shortages caused Hilton to perfect his hotel chain's superior customer service. During the war, Hilton visited the Palmer House, one of his Chicago properties, and saw a sign at the front desk, "Sorry! No rooms today without reservations." Hilton ordered his managers to take the sign down. If the Palmer House was full, staff members were directed to help travelers find rooms at other hotels. In addition, Hilton said that guests who showed up before rooms were ready at 3 p.m. could shower, shave, and have messages left at the front desk while waiting for their rooms.

"What Hilton was virtually saying was this," says management consultant Jeffrey Gitomer, "Any man who comes to The Palmer House first is, by that act virtually making himself our guest and we will take care of him as an individual would take care of a guest at his house." Hilton also knew making friends during the war would pay off in new business once the war ended and hotel rooms became plentiful.[2]

Hilton also enjoyed the limelight. His hotels were often large, old, and prestigious, such as Chicago's Palmer House, New York's Plaza and Waldorf-Astoria, and Washington's Mayflower. They were also quite valuable. By 1990, the Palmer House, Waldorf-Astoria, and Hawaiian Village in Honolulu were worth an estimated $2 billion.[3] Because his hotels were a major employer of nightclub acts, Hilton knew many Hollywood stars. Zsa Zsa Gabor was his second wife. (His eldest son, Conrad "Nick" Hilton Jr., was married to Elizabeth Taylor for a time.) Whenever he opened a new hotel, Hilton ensured that plenty of stars were on hand, and the resulting publicity helped make "Hilton" a household word.

❧ Hilton's Spiritual Concerns

From about 1950 onwards, Hilton decided to speak his mind on nonpartisan public issues. He was not active in politics, except for the period between 1912 and 1913, when he served two terms in the New Mexico state legislature as a Republican. He also gave $250 to Ronald Reagan in his 1976 effort to defeat President Gerald Ford. But Hilton is not known to have made any other political contributions, or to have tried to change public policy in a partisan way.

Hilton was, however, very interested in spiritual matters. He was a devout Catholic. An anonymously written history of the Hilton Foundation published in 2009 reports that Hilton, while a student at St. Michael's College in New Mexico, met Fr. Jules Desraches, "who became his first confessor" and told him, "Connie, if three times daily you will say a Hail Mary and ask St. Joseph to 'Pray for Us,' He will always take care of you." "Conrad recited these prayers every day for the rest of his life, as well as other prayers suggested by Father Jules."[4]

In his autobiography *Be My Guest* (1957), Hilton credits the nuns of New Mexico for providing him with a strong faith in God that helped him endure the near-bankruptcy of his firm during the Great Depression. Prayer also helped him in the business world. Biographer Whitney Bolton notes that during negotiations to buy the Waldorf-Astoria, Hilton and his partners arose every morning at 6:15 to go to St. Patrick's Cathedral for a half-hour of prayer. After the sale of the hotel was complete, Hilton's partners thought they could finally sleep in; but the next day they received a 6:15 wake-up call. "But Connie," one pleaded, "you've got the Waldorf!" Hilton responded, "You can't pray for something you want and then not give thanks when you get it. Let's get started."[5]

Hilton saw prayer, in part, as a weapon to fight communism. In the early 1950s, he worked with noted author Fulton Oursler to compose an ecumenical prayer that would increase America's faith. "America on its knees," the prayer began, "not beaten there by the hammer and sickle. Freely, intelligently, responsibly, confidently, powerfully, America now knows it can destroy Communism and win the battle for peace. We need fear nothing or no one … except God." The Hilton Hotels Corporation donated more than 200,000 copies of the prayer to Americans. According to

Bolton, it was a favorite of President Eisenhower.[6] Later in the 1950s, Hilton placed public-service ads in international editions of *Time* and *Newsweek* that described what he called "the power of prayer in opposing imperialistic Communism." These received an enthusiastic response abroad.[7]

Though Hilton sought to increase America's spirituality, he was not an evangelical; nor was he a crusader for Catholicism. He was a founder of the National Prayer Breakfast and a major sponsor of the National Conference of Christians and Jews, an ecumenical organization devoted to combating anti-Semitism. In 1950, Hilton used an awards dinner held by the conference in his honor to warn of the perils of communism. The "spreading, deadly perils of communism," he said, "has seeped into the councils of our own nature, and, what is infinitely worse, has found defense and protection from irresolute officials in high office."[8]

In a 1957 address to the organization, he said that the world was divided into thirds—one-third Communist, one-third democratic, and one-third uncommitted. In order to help this uncommitted third toward freedom, he said, helpfulness rather than arrogance should be the order of the day. "The arrogance, bad manners, and tactlessness of our politicians, businessmen, and colonists in these countries have been so thoroughly resented. Exploitation of this resentment is one of the most effective features of Communist propaganda."[9]

Hilton also believed that "the military situation is at stalemate, so we have only the choice of living together as one family or destroying each other." To convince Third World nations that democracy and capitalism were better than communism, Hilton saw trade and God as the primary resources Americans could use in anti-communist efforts. Trade would improve a poor country's standard of living, and show the developing nations that American ideals were greater than armies and warheads. Religion would bind the peoples of the world in a way that was more permanent and important than any political effort. "The great question confronting us today is whether that religion will be strong enough to re-create its unity, and in consequence serve as the basis for a single civilization embracing all the spiritual riches of the world, all the cultures of the world, all the peoples of the world—including the uncommitted third."[10]

Hilton also discussed these themes in a 1961 address. In the frostiest period of the Cold War, he compared America to the

Western Roman Empire in the fifth century, shortly before it collapsed and was replaced by barbarian kingdoms. He predicted that in the struggle for world mastery, over half the world's 111 nations "are betting on Soviet Russia to win" because Communism could promise the gospel of revolution while America could "only hug itself in selfishness":

> For years America has been trying—and failing—in its efforts to convince the people of the world, that we are their friend, that we are willing to share with them the knowledge, the technology, the industrial know-how which we have accumulated over the centuries. We have got to recapture that image of America as the hope of all the little people in the world.[11]

Hilton did this in his business career by becoming America's first international hotel operator. In the 1950s and 1960s, he operated scores of hotels overseas. These were not only highly profitable, since Hilton persuaded other investors to put up most of the investment capital needed for construction, but provided a way for Hilton to show the rest of the world American manners and customs that they would otherwise never directly see.

In at least one case, Hilton personally fought communism. It took over ten years for him to persuade the Rome city government, one-third of which was communist, to allow construction of the Rome Hilton. "I guess they didn't want free enterprise in action there," Hilton said in a 1965 interview. "The Commies said the hotel was being built for billionaires. I guess they were talking about lira, not dollars."[12]

❧ Challenges to Hilton's Estate

Most of Hilton's efforts to advance international understanding were done personally or through Hilton businesses. Although the Conrad N. Hilton Foundation was created in 1944, it remained small throughout most of Hilton's business career. When in 1972 Hilton gave a ten-year, $10 million gift to the Mayo Foundation for a laboratory at the renowned Mayo Clinic (saying that the gift was made because he liked to see "what makes man tick"), he gave the money personally and not through the foundation.[13]

As the years passed, Hilton became less active in the enterprises he created. But he did not retire until 1978, at the age of 91. Even in his eighties, he still showed up at his office at eight every morning, six days a week, to put in a full day's work.[14] In his last years, he was increasingly preoccupied with the future of the Hilton Foundation. According to James Bates, Hilton's lawyer from the mid-1940s onwards, Hilton drafted 32 wills, and with each, the portion of the estate given to the foundation rose while the amount given to his children Barron, Eric, and Francesca fell. As Bates remarked in a 1985 interview with the *Los Angeles Times*, Hilton intended to "give back to the public all the wealth he had created."[15] In Hilton's last will, Barron Hilton received $750,000, Eric Hilton $300,000, and Francesca Hilton $100,000. (Conrad "Nick" Hilton Jr. died in 1969.)

After Hilton died in January 1979, his estate faced two major lawsuits. Francesca Hilton, who said that her father was suffering from "insane delusions" that influenced him to leave her only $100,000, filed the first. These delusions, she alleged, were due to the circumstances of her birth. When Hilton married her mother, Zsa Zsa Gabor, in 1942, he obtained a civil divorce from the marriage, but the Catholic Church refused to annul it, leaving Hilton allegedly guilt-ridden about having a daughter. This guilt, she charged, led to "the ravages of old age, illnesses, cerebral accidents, and his extreme obsession with his religious beliefs."[16]

Francesca Hilton demanded that her share be increased to $50 million. Her attorney, Robert D. Walker, told the *Los Angeles Times* that this sum was needed so that she would be "treated in the way that a daughter should be treated." Los Angeles County Superior Court Judge Jack D. Swink noted that there were doubts about Francesca Hilton's paternity, since Hilton and Gabor were separated in 1945 and Francesca Hilton was not born until 1947. Judge Swink dismissed the suit, but appeals kept the case alive until it was finally dismissed in 1983.[17]

The second effort to change Hilton's will came from Barron Hilton, who succeeded his father as president of Hilton Hotels on his father's death in 1979. When Conrad Hilton died, he owned 6.8 million shares in Hilton Hotels, making him the largest single owner with 27.4 percent. He could not transfer all of this to the Conrad N. Hilton Foundation, because of the Tax Reform Act of 1969, which prohibits a foundation from owning more than 20 percent of the stock of any corporation.

Hilton saw this problem, which he tried to address by declaring that all his shares would be willed to the foundation except those which, according to the Tax Reform Act, were an "excess business holding" that the foundation had to sell. He willed that Barron Hilton had an option to buy these shares at $24.20 each, the market price on the day of Hilton's death. (Barron Hilton already owned 3.6 percent of the Hilton Hotels stock, and Conrad Hilton had transferred 1.3 percent of the stock to the Hilton Foundation before his death.) The debate centered on how many shares qualified as "excess business holdings." The Hilton Foundation believed that only 7.4 percent of the Hilton Hotels stock qualified, while Barron Hilton argued that he was entitled to buy all the shares.

The dispute between the Conrad N. Hilton Foundation and Barron Hilton remained unsettled for six years. James Bates told the *Los Angeles Times* he believed Conrad Hilton wanted his foundation to receive most of his fortune as well as to control Hilton Hotels, which it could do even if it held only 20 percent of the stock. Bates said that Hilton tried to ensure that his wishes would be carried out by selecting trustees who were "members of his family, his longtime associates, those he had great confidence in carrying out the charitable purposes that he had eloquently provided for." Barron Hilton's attorney, Ronald Gother, responded, "we don't disagree with the basic thrust of Bates' feeling about Conrad's desire" that the foundation should own 20 percent of the Hilton Hotels stock. "It's just unfortunate that that's wrong. That's what we're struggling with here. The law is otherwise."[18]

A few months later, Bates allied himself with the California attorney general's office, asking that Conrad Hilton Foundation president Donald Hubbs disqualify himself from the dispute. Hubbs, who was Hilton's accountant and an attorney for over 30 years, admitted in a 1984 deposition that he had persuaded Hilton to insert the "excess business holdings" clause in the will in 1973, and that he had hired an attorney to persuade the Internal Revenue Service to declare the entire 27 percent an "excess business holding." The California attorney general charged that Hubbs was nominated for his position by Barron Hilton—an act, deputy attorney general James Cordi told the *Wall Street Journal,* that "may make anyone in Hubbs' position reluctant to bite a hand which has fed him over almost his entire career."[19] The state of California also asked Conrad Hilton's son Eric, a member of the foundation's board of trustees, to disqualify himself on the grounds that he was also a Hilton Hotels vice president, and thus had a conflict of interest. Eric Hilton declined to do this and remained on the Hilton Foundation board.[20]

In February 1986, the Internal Revenue Service, in three private letter rulings, declared that the Conrad N. Hilton Foundation could keep the entire block of Hilton Hotels stock if it created a "public supporting organization." This would have a fixed set of grantees that would receive funds and would give one-third of its funds to a single organization, most likely a group supporting Catholic Sisters, which Hilton said in his will should receive the largest share of support. The supporting foundation, the IRS declared, could have the same board of directors as the Hilton Foundation and operate out of the same offices, as long as it was a legally distinct organization.

Barron Hilton's attorney, Ronald Gother, responded that a supporting organization would contravene Hilton's will, since "the will didn't say leave it to a support organization, it said leave it to 'the Conrad N. Hilton Foundation, a private foundation.'" The Conrad N. Hilton Foundation board promptly voted to turn itself into a public supporting organization that could give funds only to 169 charities. (Foundation directors Eric Hilton and Barron Hilton voted in opposition.)[21]

The Trial Over Hilton's Will

In March 1986, the trial between Barron Hilton and the Conrad N. Hilton Foundation began in Los Angeles County Superior Court. In a last-minute effort to end the dispute, Roger Mahoney, the archbishop of Los Angeles, tried to act as a mediator. His attempt collapsed after an hour of negotiations, and he decided to side with the foundation against Barron Hilton.

The trial swiftly became a dispute over Conrad Hilton's intentions in drafting his will. Barron Hilton testified that his father's main concern was ensuring family control of the business he created. "My father was a philanthropist but also a businessman," Hilton testified. "He didn't want to see his company taken over by an unfriendly group. That's the primary consideration of his will." He added, "My father's first interest was his hotels. His second interest was charity." [22]

Conrad Hilton's executor James Bates testified that he believed Hilton created the foundation because "his desire was to have all of his relatives, his children, get out and go to work and earn their own living." He added that Hilton's desire "was not to leave unearned wealth to relatives and members of his family."[23]

Hilton Foundation president Donald Hubbs said that Conrad Hilton was not worried about family control of Hilton Hotels, and, at one point in the mid-1970s, he nearly sold his share of the company to RCA.

Los Angeles County Superior Court Judge Robert Weil ruled in favor of the Conrad N. Hilton Foundation. He declared that, by transforming itself into a public support organization, the foundation had come close "to mirroring what Conrad Hilton might have wanted and did in fact want for his private foundation." He ruled that when Conrad Hilton, a "very wise man," inserted the clause in his will allowing Barron Hilton to buy the shares that were declared to be excess business holdings, no one, including James Bates, "perceived or realized that by creating this option it was possible that Barron Hilton could receive 100 percent of the shares of the estate."[24]

Barron Hilton sued in district court to try to overturn the IRS' private letter rulings. In November 1987, he achieved a partial victory when U.S. District Court Judge Francis C. Whelan ruled that the IRS' decision to allow the Conrad N. Hilton Foundation to become a public support organization was invalid under existing tax law. In March 1988, the California Court of Appeals overturned the Superior Court's decision to award the entire block of Hilton Hotels stock to the Hilton Foundation, and ruled that Barron Hilton could buy the entire block of shares. The appeals court also ruled that the foundation had to become a private foundation, not a supporting organization, which it did.

In November 1988, an out-of-court compromise was finally reached. This divided the disputed shares into three parts. Barron Hilton received four million shares, worth about $212 million. The Conrad N. Hilton Foundation received 3.5 million shares, valued at about $184 million. The remaining six million shares, worth some $315 million, were placed in an irrevocable charitable remainder unitrust, known as the "1989 Barron Hilton Charitable Unitrust." Sixty percent of the income from this trust goes to Barron Hilton, while forty percent goes to the Hilton Foundation. Upon Barron Hilton's death, the shares in the trust will be transferred to the

Hilton Foundation. As of May 2017, the value of the shares in this unitrust was $812 million.[25]

The court also ruled that Barron Hilton should be trustee of these shares and be allowed to vote them in Hilton Hotels stockholder meetings. This means that Barron Hilton was left owning 25 percent of the shares and control over the votes of another nine percent, giving him voting control of 34 percent of the Hilton Hotels stock. [26]

With the end of the dispute, the litigants assumed the positions they had before the struggle began. Donald Hubbs remained the foundation's president until his retirement in 2005; Barron Hilton, Eric Hilton, and two other members of the Hilton family served as directors. In the fiscal year ending February 1993, the Conrad N. Hilton Foundation had assets of $494 million, while the charitable remainder trust had $276 million. (A third, much smaller trust had $15.6 million.)

In 1998, the 9.7 percent of the Hilton Hotels stock owned by the 1989 Barron Hilton Charitable Remainder Unitrust was sold, earning Barron Hilton a $700 million profit. By selling the stock, the Hilton Foundation and the Conrad Hilton Fund for Sisters reduced their holdings in Hilton Hotels to below five percent.[27]

❧ Fulfilling Hilton's Intent

In the 1992-93 Conrad N. Hilton Foundation annual report, president Donald Hubbs explains that the foundation operates primarily to fulfill the wishes of its founder. Arguments against donor intent, such as a fear of "dead hand" control or a donor's lack of professional philanthropic training, Hubbs writes,

> are nothing but excuses for those who would justify an arrogant conduct, avoiding moral and ethical responsibility by substituting their own judgment for that of a donor who had the wisdom, capability, and industry for creating the wealth in the first place.... Individuals during their lifetime can use their wealth— on which taxes have been paid—in any manner that is desired no matter how whimsical, idiosyncratic, or bizarre it may seem. Upon death, the funds suddenly become sacrosanct to the whims, fancies, and social causes of many strangers who may or may not consider

themselves to be morally or ethically responsible for honoring the philosophy of the donor.

The lack of training in philanthropy, Hubbs adds, "does not preclude a donor from having certain strongly held beliefs and philosophies [which are] usually soundly grounded in the life experience of the donor and, therefore, should be honored. Regrettably, we have no rule that makes it morally and ethically wrong to do otherwise."[28]

The Hilton Foundation's annual report includes excerpts from Hilton's will, which the foundation uses to show its support for donor intent. The foundation funds a limited number of programs with multi-year grants, enabling it to operate with a very small staff and thus fulfilling Conrad Hilton's wish to "beware of organized, professional charities with high-salaried executives and a heavy ratio of expense."[29]

The largest grants the foundation made were to the Conrad N. Hilton Fund for Sisters, a legally distinct organization controlled by the archdiocese of Los Angeles from 1986-2016, when it separated from the archdiocese and became an independent nonprofit. Under terms of a settlement reached with Catholic Sisters worldwide in 1986, it received 11.2 percent of the income produced by the foundation and its two allied trusts. Such Catholic charities receive the largest single part of the foundation's grants, because of a clause in Hilton's will specifying that the foundation provide support to Catholic Sisters "who devote their love and life's work for the good of mankind, for they appeal especially to me as being deserving of help from the Foundation."[30]

The 1986 settlement with Catholic Sisters also gave the Hilton Foundation the right to buy out its obligations under the settlement. In 2008, the foundation announced that it would exercise this right, which was completed in 2012. When the mandatory payments were completed, the Hilton Foundation decided to give most of its grants to Catholic Sisters through the foundation, instead of through the Fund for Sisters, although the foundation occasionally gives grants to the Fund for Sisters and allows the fund to rent space in foundation headquarters. As of 2017, the Conrad N. Hilton Fund for Sisters had assets of $170 million and makes annual grants of around $7.5 million.[31]

Conrad Hilton also stated in his will that the foundation's trustees should "be ever watchful for the opportunity to shelter little children with the umbrella of your charity; be generous to their schools, their hospitals and their places of worship."[32] One way the Hilton Foundation did this is through programs to combat drug use in schools. In the 1980s and 1990s, the foundation gave over $20 million to anti-drug programs. In the 1980s, it awarded grants to the RAND Corporation to prepare antidrug education materials; in 1992, it gave $3.6 million to the BEST Foundation For a Drug Free Tomorrow to distribute these materials in schools and to train teachers to detect and combat drug use.

The foundation also helped blind children through a continuing series of grants from 1989-2008 to the Perkins School for the Blind, the institution that Helen Keller attended. In *Be My Guest*, Hilton said that at age 15, he learned of Helen Keller's achievements in overcoming her disability after reading her memoir *Optimism*. "I regarded Helen Keller," Hilton wrote, "with an awed understanding which I have never lost."[33] To honor Helen Keller's memory, the Hilton/Perkins National and International Program (now known as Perkins International) uses foundation funds to train teachers, support families with blind children, publish scholarly research, and supply equipment to dozens of needy nations around the world, including five Central and Eastern European ones.

Grants and forgiven program-related investments to the Perkins School for the Blind from the Hilton Foundation between 1989-2008 totaled $50.4 million. In a 2015 interview, Steven Hilton said that Hilton Foundation grantmaking enabled the Perkins School to increase the number of countries where it aided people who were blind and had other disabilities from 9 to 60 and that the foundation's aid "moves the needle on a global scale" in helping to assist this group of disabled people.[34]

Other Hilton Foundation programs include a joint program with World Vision to provide clean water to rural villages in Ghana, a program to provide prenatal care to low-income women in Los Angeles County, a program that helps mentally ill homeless people in New York City, and several grants to groups addressing domestic violence.

The Conrad Hilton Foundation created the Hilton Humanitarian Prize, which awards a $2 million annual award to a deserving charity. In 2016, the prize went to the Task Force for Global Health, which coordinates efforts to fight diseases endemic to the Third World.

In 2005, when Donald Hubbs retired, he was succeeded as Hilton Foundation president by Steven Hilton, a son of Barron Hilton who had worked at the Conrad Hilton Foundation in various capacities since 1983. Steven Hilton served as president until 2015, when he retired and was succeeded by Peter Laugharn, formerly president of the Firelight Foundation.

In an interview with the *Chronicle of Philanthropy* conducted shortly after he became Hilton Foundation president, Steven Hilton said that the practices instituted by Donald Hubbs would not change. The foundation, Hilton said, would continue to pursue a "major project" approach. "Rather than taking the foundation's monies and spreading them over many organizations in one-year grants," Hilton said, "we thought we'd be more effective if we selected an area where there is a great need that might have been overlooked. Then we'd focus our attention and make one big grant."[35] As an example, Hilton said that the Hilton Foundation would give a multi-million, multiyear grant to provide clean water in Africa—and continue it if the program worked.

Hilton was interviewed in 2006 by the *Los Angeles Business Journal,* where he stated that the foundation would honor his grandfather's intentions in two ways: first, by having a majority of the trustees be Hilton family members, and second, by running the foundation with low overhead.

"Conrad Hilton's will advised future directors to be wary of charities with high salaried executives and a heavy ratio of expense," Steven Hilton said. "Although he was referring to the non-profit charities to which we give funds, we at the Hilton Foundation take that to heart regarding our own operations. One way we do that is by operating with a staff of only 14."[36]

In 2007, after selling Hilton Hotels to the Blackstone Group, and also selling $300 million of stock he held in Harrah's Entertainment, Barron Hilton announced that nearly all of the money from these transactions would ultimately go to the Hilton Foundation. "My father left nearly 97 percent of his wealth to the Conrad N. Hilton Foundation, and I want to follow his example," Barron Hilton stated.[37] The transaction caused the *Chronicle of Philanthropy* to name Hilton the most generous American for 2007.[38]

As with the settlement in 1989, the proceeds from Barron Hilton's 2007 sales were placed in an irrevocable charitable remainder unitrust. When Barron Hilton dies, the ownership of the trust will pass to the Hilton Foundation. As of May 2017, the value of this trust, known as the 2006 Barron Hilton Charitable Remainder Unitrust, is $2.23 billion.[39]

Beginning in 2007, the Hilton Foundation launched a major effort to fight poverty in Las Vegas after Eric Hilton, a Las Vegas resident, saw a news broadcast stating that a leading food distributor in that city was about to go out of business. "It didn't seem right that in Las Vegas, where people come to have a good time and money and food are plentiful, that people were going hungry," Hilton told the *Las Vegas Review-Journal*.[40]

Partnering with the Lincy and Donald W. Reynolds Foundations, the Hilton Foundation helped revive the Three Square Food Bank. By 2010 the food bank had a $43 million budget ($7.5 million of which came from the Hilton Foundation) and was supplying meals to 214,000 of the 250,000 hungry residents of southern Nevada. Ultimately, the Hilton Foundation stopped grants to Three Square after donating $12.9 million.[41]

Another Las Vegas initiative was the Hilton Foundation's $850,000 grant in 2009 to remodel and expand Las Vegas's largest medical clinic for poor people.[42] A year later, the foundation announced a $13 million multi-year grant to help build housing and provide support services for homeless people in Los Angeles. The grant continued an effort begun in 2004; the foundation spent $20 million between 2004-2010 helping to provide housing for homeless people in Los Angeles.[43]

In 2011, the Hilton Foundation launched the Chronic Homelessness Initiative, a five-year effort to fight homelessness in Los Angeles by supporting efforts to build housing for homeless people. In 2015, the foundation renewed the initiative for five years until 2020. A 2016 report from Abt Associates states that between 2011 and 2016, the Hilton Foundation spent $64.1 million on this initiative. According to Abt, the grants encouraged $18.9 million in additional grants, including seven-figure donations from United Way of Los Angeles and the Aileen Getty Foundation, and an additional $543.2 million in government spending.[44]

The Hilton Foundation continues to vigorously uphold Conrad Hilton's intentions. In 2005, the foundation's bylaws were changed so that Conrad Hilton's descendants would always be a majority of the board. Currently, the board includes six Hiltons, all grandchildren of Conrad N. Hilton. Steven Hilton is chairman of the board, and other board members include Conrad N. Hilton III, Hawley Hilton McAuliffe, Linda Hilton, Michael O. Hilton, and William B. Hilton Jr., the son of Barron Hilton. In addition, Barron Hilton is an emeritus member of the board.

In another effort to safeguard Conrad Hilton's intentions, all Hilton Foundation board members have to sign a contract stating that they have read and understood Conrad Hilton's will and promise to uphold Conrad Hilton's donor intent.

"The Board's 1982 Statement of Purpose held that it considered the Will 'a sacred trust to be honored to the extent possible,'" the Hilton Foundation's official history notes. "All directors formally commit in writing to honor the spirit and sentiment expressed in the Will. The Board has dutifully followed the instructions of its Founder's Will, while the latitude granted in the Will has enabled change and growth with the times."[45]

In December 2014, Steven Hilton sent a memorandum to the Hilton Foundation board on the occasion of Barron Hilton's retirement as an active member of the board:

> With my father's retirement from the Board today and my retirement as President and CEO at the end of next year, I believe it is vitally important to make every effort to preserve donor intent. (It is not unusual to find examples of foundations that gradually strayed away from the donor's intentions of how their charitable funds should be allocated. I reached out to our legal counsel and asked his advice on how best to mandate that future board members stay true to our donors' intent.

The board agreed to add the following clause to Article II of the Hilton Foundation's Articles of Incorporation:

> 1. The corporation shall make distributions and conduct activities in accordance with the philosophy of Conrad N. Hilton, which philosophy includes Conrad N. Hilton's religious, ethical, business, and conservative beliefs. Specifically, the primary purposes of the corporation over which distributions should be made are

to alleviate human suffering, and to aid the distressed, the disadvantaged, and the destitute, without regard to territorial, religious, color, or other discriminating restrictions on the corporation's benefactions; more specifically, as expressed in Conrad N. Hilton's Last Will and Testament, support shall be provided especially to the Catholic Sisters as well as to the needs of children.

2. In addition to making distributions as set forth in subparagraph 1 of this paragraph B, the corporation may make distributions for other purposes as determined by the directors from time to time, but in aggregate, distributions for other purposes shall be minimal, in comparison to distributions for primary purposes.

3. William Barron Hilton, son of Conrad N. Hilton and a significant donor to the Conrad N. Hilton Foundation, confirmed his alignment with his father's philosophies as set forth in subparagraph 1 of the paragraph B, and it is Barron Hilton's desire and request that the corporation provide very modest contributions to the charitable activities of aviation related organizations.

The board also added the following clause to Section 4 of the Hilton Foundation bylaws:

...All current and future Board members must sign an affirmation of principles taken from the provisions in Conrad N. Hilton's Last Will and Testament where Conrad N. Hilton advised future Board members regarding his wishes pertaining to the Foundation and from the 2014 Memorandum of Understanding between Conrad N. Hilton Foundation and William Barron Hilton where William Barron Hilton shared his values and reflections, which are intended to help guide the future directors and staff of the Foundation.

The final document approved by the board in 2014 was a "Memorandum of Understanding between the Conrad N. Hilton Foundation and William Barron Hilton," in which Barron Hilton agreed to donate the two unitrusts to the Hilton Foundation on

300

his death. It also included an article written in 2009 when Barron Hilton was chairman of the Hilton Foundation, listing seven principles that Barron Hilton said guided him throughout his life, including growth, partnership, sustainability, boldness, efficiency, *esprit de corps*, and integrity.

Barron Hilton then agreed to the following four points:

> 1. Barron Hilton believes that the Foundation should in future years continue to adhere to, and carry out the wishes expressed in Conrad N. Hilton's Last Will and Testament and displayed throughout his lifetime, including his religious, business, and conservative beliefs, that have guided the Foundation from its inception to the present.

> 2. As expressed in his Last Will, Conrad N. Hilton felt a moral obligation to alleviate human suffering and aid the disadvantaged, especially children. Barron Hilton shares these goals and desires that his gift to the Foundation align with these goals.

> 3. Conrad N. Hilton requested in his Last Will that the "largest part" of the Foundation's giving be provided to the Catholic Sisters. As a result of the creation and agreed-upon funding of the Conrad N. Hilton Fund for Sisters, Barron Hilton feels that his father's intent in this regard has been fulfilled. Nevertheless, Barron Hilton believes that future boards, at their discretion, should be encouraged to provide additional funding to support the Sisters, whom Barron Hilton also greatly respects and admires.

> 4. It is Barron Hilton's desire and request that a very modest portion of Foundation giving shall support the charitable activities of aviation-related organizations, since Barron Hilton has always had a passion for aviation.

The board members were then asked to sign the changes to the Hilton Foundation articles of incorporation and bylaws, agreeing that, "as a member of the Board of Directors of the

Conrad N. Hilton Foundation, I hereby commit to honor the spirit and sentiment expressed within the Last Will and Testament of Conrad Nicholson Hilton and to honor the spirit and sentiment expressed in the 2014 Memorandum of Understanding between Conrad N. Hilton Foundation and William Barron Hilton."[46]

Donors can only hope, and as the Sisters who shaped Conrad Hilton would add, pray, that their intentions will be honored by future generations of their family with as much integrity as the Hilton family has thus far honored Conrad and Barron Hilton's legacy.

14

The Daniels Fund

In November 2003, the Daniels Fund, a three-year-old Denver-based philanthropy, announced that it would undergo a dramatic downsizing, closing regional offices in three states and sacking 21 employees—a third of its staff. "We have to operate more efficiently," foundation president Hank Brown told the *Denver Post* at the time.[1]

Three months later, the *New York Times* ran a critical story of the upheaval at the Daniels Fund. "Had his ashes—combined at his request with those of his beloved cat, Sydney—not been scattered over the Pacific three years ago, Bill Daniels would probably be turning over in his grave," wrote *Times* philanthropy reporter Stephanie Strom.[2]

"I feel strongly that what has happened is outside the bounds of what Bill Daniels wanted," Daniels' niece, Diane Denish, a Democrat who served as New Mexico's lieutenant governor between 2003 and 2011, told Strom. "There's a difference between bean counting and philanthropy."[3]

Denver Post columnist Susan Barnes-Gelt noted that the Daniels Fund's creator, Robert William "Bill" Daniels, gave millions in his lifetime to the University of Denver to establish courses in business ethics. Daniels was such a generous donor that the university renamed its business school after him.

"Daniels believed that rigorous training in leadership and values were the key to business success," Barnes-Gelt observed. "Meanwhile...the Daniels Fund struggles to emulate the charitable struggles of its namesake. The fund's behavior appears more appropriate to a compliance-based widget factory than a charitable foundation."[4]

"I think there is politics at play here," Georgetown University philanthropy scholar Pablo Eisenberg told the *Chronicle of Philanthropy*. "This is sort of like a right-wing coup."[5]

Yet given Bill Daniels' politics, the Daniels Fund could hardly be "taken over" by the Right. Daniels was a life-long Republican who in 1974 ran for governor of Colorado, losing to John Vanderhoof in the primary. As a donor, Daniels gave six-figure contributions to the Republican Party in at least two presidential contests. In 1991, he hired Neil Bush, son of President George H.W. Bush and brother of President George W. Bush, to work in his company's Houston office for two years. In addition, Daniels held a campaign fundraiser for George Bush in 1987 and in 1990 sponsored a charitable fundraising event hosted by First Lady Barbara Bush and Neil Bush's wife, Sharon Bush.[6]

In 2003, President George H.W. Bush wrote a preface to a biography of Daniels commissioned by his estate. "If one were to ask me to name someone who exemplified the dynamism of America in the twentieth century," former President Bush wrote, "I'd be hard pressed to come up with a better example than my old friend, Bill Daniels."[7]

The true story of the Daniels Fund is one of a foundation that recovered its donor intent. The story of the turmoil surrounding the Daniels Fund shows how to develop strategies to make sure that your donor's intent is respected.

Robert William Daniels was born on July 1, 1920, in Greeley, Colorado. His father was in the insurance business, and like many families, the Daniels home struggled during the Great Depression. "My dad was selling life insurance to farmers then, in Omaha," Daniels told the *Los Angeles Times* in 1986. "Farmers started paying their premiums in chickens and pigs. We lost our house, and moved to Council Bluffs, Iowa, where my grandmother had a home with no mortgage. My brother and I had to scrounge around in the woods in the winter, gathering firewood. We couldn't afford coal."[8]

Daniels was a wild teenager, and his parents scraped up enough money to send him to the New Mexico Military Institute. To help pay the tuition, Daniels worked nights. "I hauled groceries at the market and worked an 8 p.m.-2 a.m. shift cooking burgers in a diner, all through high school," Daniels said in his *Los Angeles Times* interview.[9]

Daniels never attended college; instead he went straight from high school graduation in 1941 into training to be a fighter pilot. Commissioned as a lieutenant in 1942, Daniels spent the war flying several planes—the F4F Wildcat, the F6F Hellcat, the F8F Bearcat, and the Chance Vought Corsair. He learned to fly at night and how to land on an aircraft carrier whose lights had been turned off to avoid detection by the Japanese. Daniels' service included assisting in the invasion of North Africa in 1942 and in the Pacific from 1942-45. He downed 11 enemy planes and was awarded the Air Medal, the Distinguished Flying Cross, and the Navy Cross.

On November 25, 1944, Daniels was serving on the USS *Intrepid* when two kamikaze aircraft crashed into the deck. "I was in the ready room, two decks below flight deck," Daniels later recalled. "The ship was on fire, and one of my squad mates was trapped with his leg half blown off. I had to apply a tourniquet, cut off the rest of his leg, administer morphine, and carry him up two flights to the flight deck for help."[10]

Daniels carried several other wounded sailors through the burning deck to safety. His heroism earned him the Bronze Star.

After World War II, Daniels went back to work in the family insurance business. In 1950, he was recalled to duty for the Korean War. After several missions flying Grumman Panther jets, he returned to the U.S. where he served as a flight instructor. Among his students were pilots who would later become the first members of the Blue Angels, the famous flight demonstration team.

Back in the U.S., Daniels decided to set up a branch of the family insurance business in Casper, Wyoming. While driving from New Mexico to Wyoming, Daniels stopped for a meal at a tavern on South Broadway in Denver. There he had an experience that would change his life.

"The name of the place was Murphy's," Daniels told the *Los Angeles Times*. "And I remember that I had a glass of beer and a corned beef sandwich."

The bar had a television set on it, which was showing "Pabst Wednesday Night Fights." Daniels loved boxing and was a two-time Golden Gloves champion.

"I was shocked," Daniels said. "I'd never seen a television set before. I boxed as a kid, and I couldn't believe I was sitting there watching two guys box in New York or Chicago or someplace. I said to myself, 'Now there is an invention.' I immediately wanted to know how Denver could get television reception but not little places like Casper."[11]

In 1952, the Federal Communications Commission had just lifted a four-year freeze on television licenses. Television was only available in large cities, and Daniels routinely made the trek to Cheyenne or Denver to watch the "Pabst Wednesday Night Fights" or the "Gillette Cavalcade of Sports" on Fridays.

"I began to think there had to be a way to get TV to little towns like Casper," Daniels said. "I discovered there were a lot of rich oil men in Casper who wanted to watch TV. They became my stockholders. I got together with a Denver TV engineer, Tom Morrissey, who showed me what had to be done."

Daniels leased a microwave transmission line from AT&T for $8,500 a month, and raised $125,000 to post as a bond "because the phone company was sure I'd go broke."[12]

Daniels signed up customers for a $150 fee and $7.50 a month. "It was a big hit. Everyone wanted the service. The stockholders loved it."[13] He also offered innovations, including one of the first cable news shows, where a camera was pointed to an Associated Press Teletype.

Daniels soon found himself at the center of a small but steadily growing industry. He first operated his cable business as a sideline to his insurance business, but then in 1958 launched Daniels and Associates to buy and sell cable systems. While not a major investor, Daniels as a broker not only received his commission but also usually acquired a five percent stake in the cable system being bought.

Until the 1970s, cable systems tended to be located in small, isolated towns like Casper that couldn't receive over-the-air broadcasting signals. But cable systems steadily grew. *Business Week* devoted three pages to Daniels in 1962, noting that a million homes received cable and that his business had grown enough that Daniels successfully brokered a $10.7 million deal, earning himself a $93,750 commission. "At 42, Daniels is at the center of this little-known, but whirling industry," *Business Week* noted.[14]

Cable grew slowly. Larger companies began to enter the field. Daniels acted both as someone with an endless source of suggestions, and as a constant source of encouragement to other entrepreneurs frustrated by bureaucracy or the strength of entrenched broadcasters.

John C. Malone, founder of Liberty Media, told Daniels biographer Stephen Singular, "Bill was always the guy who put on the suit of armor and went out to do battle with the industries that were our adversaries, whether it was the broadcasters or the telephone companies or whoever. Bill was always upbeat and always positive."[15]

"Daniels had another trait that was rare in any industry, and he used it to great advantage to build his business," says biographer Stephen Singular. "He genuinely wanted to see others succeed, even when they were competitors. Success for anyone in cable, he realized, ultimately meant success for all."[16]

It took Daniels and his fellow entrepreneurs over a quarter of a century before cable became commonplace. Daniels' persuasive abilities were often tested. In a 1982 profile in *Forbes*, Daniels said, "I've been thrown out of more banks than any man in the country."[17] But these entrepreneurs who struggled through the 1960s and the first half of the 1970s were rewarded by two decisions that substantially improved their business. First, larger cities began to refine rules to allow cable operators to establish franchises, most notably New York City.

A deregulatory policy created by Clay T. Whitehead, who served as director of the White House's Office of Telecommunications Policy between 1970 and 1974, further encouraged the growth of cable. Known as "Open Skies," the proposal allowed cable companies to buy time from any satellite operator willing to launch a satellite and sell their services. Before 1970, anyone who had to broadcast anything from one city to another had to buy transmission time from AT&T, which charged punitive monopoly prices.

In 1972, the FCC adopted Open Skies, and by 1975 satellite operators were launching communications satellites and drumming up business. The dramatic drop in transmission fees resulting from Open Skies made national cable networks financially possible. By 1980 such cable networks as CNN, ESPN, and C-SPAN—which, remember, stands for Cable Satellite Public Affairs Network—were created.[18]

As a broker, Daniels helped create most of the major cable networks and owned small percentages (or "equity positions") in most of them. Sandra Salmans, reporting on Daniels and Associates in a 1983 *New York Times* profile, noted that the firm had conducted deals amounting to $4.2 billion.

"Though a relative unknown outside the business," Salmans wrote, "the short and wiry 63-year-old Mr. Daniels is practically a legend within cable's ranks—and with good reason. Mr. Daniels has probably worked on more cable deals than anyone else in the business."[19]

In a 1985 profile, Randy Welch showed Daniels' importance. According to Welch, Daniels played a role in building the top six cable operators in the U.S.—and eight of the top ten.[20]

The rising tide of cable television success lifted everyone's boats. But Daniels had two major financial successes that made him a billionaire. The first came in 1998, when 24 small cable systems Daniels owned merged with United Artists Communications. Daniels and Associates made $190 million from this deal, and Daniels personally made $100 million.[21]

A second major windfall came because of Daniels' interest in professional sports. Daniels was a close friend of Los Angeles Lakers owner Jerry Buss, and personally owned five percent of the Lakers. In 1985 Buss and Daniels created Prime Ticket, the nation's first sports network controlled by the owners of sports teams, which controlled the television rights to Lakers games and Los Angeles Kings hockey matches. Daniels ended up controlling 82.5 percent of Prime Ticket, which he sold to Tele-Communications Inc. in 1994 for over $200 million.

Los Angeles Times columnist Larry Stewart noted that with the Prime Ticket sale, Daniels had a billion dollars, no children, no wife, and no immediate members of his family except for his brother Jack. "So what's he going to do with all his money?" Daniels "says he doesn't know."[22]

But by this time, Daniels was well on the way to deciding to become a major philanthropist.

℮ Creation of the Daniels Fund

As an employer, Daniels was very generous. For example, in 1989, he hired a French chef to give the staff at Daniels and Associates and Daniels Communications a free lunch every day. "Bill Daniels decided it was not effective to break at noon, get in cars, and go get lunch," Daniels and Associates vice-president Bob Russo told *ColoradoBiz* magazine. By keeping the staff in the office, Daniels made sure that they had opportunities to interact with—and bounce ideas off—colleagues.[23]

At his memorial service, a short film was shown in which Daniels described his philosophy of management. "Treat people decently and you'll be amazed how well they respond," Daniels said. "People don't work for me. They work with me. For a company to become successful, employees shouldn't worry about pleasing the boss. It's the other way around."[24]

As his company prospered, Daniels made sure his employees received some of the wealth. He was also very helpful when dealing with employees who had personal financial crises. "At his memorial service," Shari Caudron observed, "stories were told of employees who received airplane tickets to visit sick family members, clothing for an important event, and rent money during hard times. He even paid for plastic surgery for a receptionist who was very self-conscious because of an eye disorder."[25]

In addition, Daniels frequently rewarded employees who worked hard for him with shares in the cable companies that were Daniels and associates clients. In a 1988 interview with the *Rocky Mountain News*, Daniels said that "if people feel they are part of the company, if they feel they are part of the action, don't you feel they will produce more?"[26]

In 1994, when Daniels sold the pay-cable sports network Prime Ticket, he made sure that $10 million went to 15 senior vice-presidents and department heads while an additional $1-2 million would be divided between 105 less senior employees. "I just want to reward people for a job well done," he told the *Los Angeles Times*.[27]

Daniels was particularly supportive of veterans who worked for him. Vietnam veteran Steve Halstedt began working for Daniels in 1973. Around a decade later, Halstedt came into the office to find a replica of the Vietnam Memorial on his desk with a note from Daniels stating, "Thank you for your service."

"Having been ostracized by my peers when I came back from Vietnam," Halstedt told Stephen Singular, "I realized that this was the first time anyone had ever said, 'Thank you.' I was very touched by that."[28]

Stephen Singular also notes that Daniels was, like many donors, both personally very charitable and very quiet about his anonymous giving. "Often during the winter holidays," Singular writes," he went to poor neighborhoods in Denver and secretly left cash on people's doorsteps or had others do it for him. He worked in soup kitchens, and he handed out food to the indigent so that he could be reminded of all that he had and how little some people got by on. He encouraged everyone who worked for him to be charitable toward the needy."[29]

Daniels' involvement with the work of Denver's Bob Coté was another example of his hands-on commitment to helping the needy. Bob Coté fought poverty in Denver through his nonprofit Step 13 (now called Step Denver) for over three decades until his death in 2013.[30] Coté recalled in an interview shortly before his death that Daniels first introduced himself to him in 1987. "Can I have 15 minutes of your time?" Daniels asked. "You can have a month of my time if you want," Coté replied.[31]

Coté and Daniels immediately hit it off because Coté, like Daniels, had been in the Golden Gloves. After sharing boxing exploits, Daniels took a tour of Step 13. He saw the men watching "a crappy black-and-white Admiral TV." Daniels looked at the cheap television and said, "What is that? Throw it in the Dumpster." Daniels started a fund, which continues today, to supply Step 13 with state-of-the-art TV sets.

Coté recalled two other funds Daniels started. One was the Young Americans Bank. Daniels gave money so that the homeless men struggling to establish themselves at Step 13 would have financial advisors to help them set up bank accounts and save for the future.

When Daniels' mansion, Cableland, was under construction, the building was so large that five existing homes had to be torn down to make way for the new house. The night before construction, Daniels invited Coté and his men to visit the homes about to be torn down and take whatever they wanted. Step 13 was in the process of constructing a new building, and Coté found much of value in the soon to be demolished homes, including a door and accompanying lintel that Coté said would have been priced at $6,000 if he'd bought it commercially.

Daniels did not always follow Coté's advice, however. Daniels regularly gave to Father Woody's Christmas Party, an annual luncheon for poor and homeless people in Denver created by Monsignor Charles Woodrich, a renowned poverty-fighter. Daniels gave money so recipients would be handed a ten-dollar bill when they left. Coté warned Daniels that many of the men staying at his shelter were drunks who would just blow the money on booze at the nine bars within one block of Step 13. Moreover, in those days, the area around Step 13 "was like the Wild West," and the muggers all knew when the drunks had cash. Daniels ignored Coté's advice and continued to hand out money at the party.[32]

Daniels, Coté recalled, was "one of the most generous men I've ever met."[33]

Still, one must separate Daniels' giving from his politics. As we've seen, Daniels was a stalwart Republican. Anyone who visited Cableland would notice his collection of elephants—including two giant ones—which reminded his guests which political party he preferred.[34]

"Remember I am a conservative and want no money going to liberal causes," Daniels wrote in a memo to his philanthropy's board in 1998. "The only thing I have in common with liberals is my concern for the homeless, the poor, and the downtrodden."[35]

During his lifetime, Daniels made two major donations: creating the Young Americans Bank in 1987 and funding business ethics programs at the University of Denver from 1989 onwards.

The bank was part of Daniels' effort to teach young people the importance of free enterprise. In a 1987 interview with *American Banker*, Daniels said that he remembered all the trouble he had persuading banks to loan him money when he was starting out. "I was 24 when I first walked into a bank, and I felt as though I was either going to go on trial for murder or go through major surgery," Daniels said. "Children want their own accounts, they want to learn about banking, and this will teach them the responsibility of earning money."[36] In a 1988 interview, Daniels said that the goal of the bank was to produce "more responsible, productive adults who are better equipped to utilize the options inherent in our free-enterprise system."[37]

Linda Childears, the current Daniels Fund CEO, was hired by Daniels in 1987 to run the Young Americans Bank. She said that these regulators, never having seen such an entity, were worried there was some sort of hidden reason the bank was being created, perhaps as a way to hide some of Daniels' profits. Daniels told the regulators, "Why do you think I'm trying to make money off of kids?"[38]

The Young Americans Bank began operations in 1987 and has thrived ever since as a for-profit entity whose losses are paid for by the Daniels Fund. Daniels also supports the Young Americans Center for Financial Education, a companion nonprofit which holds entrepreneurship classes for young people and operates Young AmeriTowne, a program that goes to fifth- and sixth-grade classes and shows young people what it's like to run a small city.[39]

As for ethics, numerous accounts tell how Daniels insisted on several rules in dealing with clients and staff: Keep a neat desk. Do what you tell clients you are going to do. And, like many veterans, he stressed the importance of punctuality.

Steve Schuck, a developer in Colorado Springs, Colorado, worked with Daniels over the years on several projects. "Bill was the kind of guy who became friends with everyone he met," Schuck said in an interview. "He had this magnetic personality and sincere interest in others. When you met him, you had an immediate sense that he meant what he said."[40]

Daniels' proudest moment in upholding business virtues came in 1975. Daniels loved sports and owned the Utah Stars, an American Basketball Association franchise. But in the mid-1970s Daniels had a financial crisis and couldn't meet the Stars' payroll. The club folded, having played only 9 of the 42 home games in the 1975-76 season.[41]

Five years later, Daniels paid back all of the Stars' season ticket holders and creditors with 8 percent interest, a move that cost him $750,000. "I owned a basketball team in Utah and went bankrupt," Daniels subsequently said. "The banks simply said, 'Bill, you can't go any further.' I had to look myself in the mirror every morning. I had no legal obligation (to pay) but it bugged my conscience."[42]

When Daniels announced his decision to repay season ticket holders in 1980, Charles S. Fox, who had filed a class-action suit seeking partial reimbursement, told the *Salt Lake Tribune* that Daniels' reimbursement plan was "a truly Christian act" that "totally satisfies me."[43]

LaDell Anderson, who coached the Stars for two years when Daniels was owner, told the *Salt Lake Tribune* in 2011 that when Daniels "said something to you, you could take it to the bank. It was very emotional to me to have known a guy like that."[44]

In his 1988 announcement of an $11 million grant to the University of Denver, Daniels said he hoped students would learn the right way to act in the office. "There is virtually no place in the country where young men and women can learn such basic assets as manners, protocol, communication skills, treatment of people, ethics, integrity, respect for others, dress, and all the other qualities that go toward successful business careers for men and women.... In addition, few are taught at a young age the value of giving back to their community and society."[45]

❧ Initial Problems of the Daniels Fund

In the mid-1990s, Daniels spent some time working on the bylaws for the Daniels Fund, which was incorporated in May 1997. In many ways Daniels was quite specific in what he wanted. He stated that his fund would have 11 purposes. Its primary purpose, to which 30 percent of the fund's grants would be budgeted, would be in "providing scholarships and other financial assistance to graduates of high schools" in Colorado, New Mexico, Wyoming, and Utah. The other purposes included supporting "innovative education initiatives," helping the homeless and disadvantaged, helping alcoholics and drug addicts recover, assisting the elderly, funding educational programs "which emphasize ethics and integrity," supporting amateur sports, and specifically supporting the Young Americans Education Foundation and the South Platte River Greenway Fund.[46]

Most of these causes were personal ones. Daniels had for years had to deal with the health problems of his mother, so the Daniels Fund supports programs to help the aged. As a talented amateur boxer, Daniels wanted to support amateur sports. And Daniels was an alcoholic until a horrific night in 1985 when he passed out in a Scottsdale, Arizona, hotel room after drinking two fifths of Scotch. Daniels was flown to the Betty Ford Center where he spent six weeks drying out. Daniels stayed sober for the rest of his life—and wanted to make sure his fund would help other alcoholics in trouble.[47]

Daniels was also emphatic about causes he wasn't interested in. Daniels barred his foundation from supporting "research of any kind." His authorized biography says that this was "probably because he always gave to programs that actively worked to help people, not to programs that analyzed how to prevent problems."[48] Also barred were grants to programs that treated AIDS, because Daniels knew that such grants were the focus of many other foundations.

Finally, the Daniels Fund is prohibited from supporting cultural activities. "Most of my giving does not match with symphonies, art, and opera," Daniels wrote. "I am just not into that. I am into helping people who need help, who are hungry, unclothed, in trouble."[49]

The Daniels Fund is organized in perpetuity. History provides many examples of foundations drifting from a donor's intent once people who knew him died. CEO Childears says that Daniels liked the idea that Daniels scholarships would be awarded for generations. But Childears adds, "I don't think any of us" saw the problems of donor intent of "setting up a foundation this size in perpetuity."[50]

℮ The Years of Crisis

In March 2000, Daniels died[51] and the Daniels Fund began operations. The fund's first president, Phil Hogue, had worked for Daniels and Associates as an executive vice president. Hogue, who died in 2007,[52] decided to ask outsiders for help. Hogue, Linda Childears said, "went to experts to see what should be done.... We went to big foundations and hired people with expertise in grants and scholarships."[53]

Most of these large foundations Hogue visited were firmly on the left. Hogue also consulted Harvard's Hauser Center, whose wealth comes from Gustave Hauser, former chairman of Warner Cable Communications. These experts pointed Hogue towards well-credentialed veteran grantmakers, most of whom were liberals. The Daniels Fund's chief operating officer, Jesse King, for example, came to the fund from the Rockefeller Foundation.

Once these high-ranking officials were hired, they in turn hired program officers who also had impressive résumés. "We hired on credentials," Childears said.[54] But these program officers, too, were also hardline leftists.

"The people we hired were good people, bright people," said Hank Brown, who served as president of the Daniels Fund between 2002-2004. "But they did not share Bill's values."[55]

Two Daniels Fund policies allowed these liberals to get away with quite a lot. Program officers, according to Childears, were allowed to approve grants of up to $100,000 without board approval. Moreover, they were free to award multiple grants of under $100,000 to the same organization without restraint, so that organizations they favored would get several grants of over $90,000 at a time.

Secondly, the board only knew about the grants these program officers had approved. They did not know about grantees that had been rejected.

In 2002, Phil Hogue resigned as president of the Daniels Fund for health reasons, although he remained on the board. Hank Brown, who had formerly been a university president, a congressman, and a senator, succeeded him.[56]

In an interview, Brown said he found that the administrative costs at the fund were spiraling out of control. With the Daniels Scholarships, for example, "we were spending more money on administration than on scholarships."[57] A second problem, according to Childears, was that in 2002 and 2003 the Daniels Fund board kept getting "wake-up calls" from rejections made by program officers using their unlimited veto power. Rejected grantees alerted the board that the program officers' decisions didn't "feel like Bill Daniels."

One decision made by the liberal program officers was to ban all grants to the Boy Scouts because of the Scouts' decision at the time to reject homosexuals from membership. The program officers unilaterally denied the Boy Scouts funding, even though the board had stated that the Daniels Fund was officially neutral on the issue of gays and the Boy Scouts. "Bill *loved* the Boy Scouts," Childears said, and rejecting the Scouts was a firm denial of Daniel's intentions as a donor.

A second rejection, reported by Evan Sparks in *Philanthropy*, was given to the National Air and Space Museum. In 2002 the museum applied to the Daniels Fund for a grant to preserve World War II aircraft for use in an exhibit at the museum. The museum was rejected because, according to the program officer who issued the rejection, it was not the fund's policy to preserve "instruments of war."

The museum wrote back to the fund, saying that it wanted to preserve many of the planes that Daniels flew during the war. The museum received a second rejection, stating that the fund's official policy was not to support preserving objects that "kill people."[58]

Hank Brown notes that the Daniels Fund before 2003 was uninterested in education reform. "Bill was a strong advocate for vouchers and education reform," Brown said, yet "Most of the grants we made were not for education reform, but continued the status quo."[59]

A final deviation from Daniels' intentions came with the administration of the Daniels Scholarships. The program officers proposed selecting potential scholars from a college prep program that the fund would create and administer. Childears told Sparks that while the prep program had found "many great candidates," "there was nothing" to suggest that Bill Daniels had favored such a program.[60]

Ultimately the deviations from donor intent proved to be too much for the board, leading to the November 2003 meeting in which many of the liberal program officers were sacked. The board's decision had only two dissenters—Phil Hogue and Daniels' niece, Diane Denish, a liberal Democrat. In addition, the board slashed overhead costs by $2 million and canceled an expensive conference center that was nearing construction.

"Obviously," Brown recalled, the firings "were painful for everybody, but a majority of the board thought this was what Bill would want. We did provide a very generous severance package."[61]

The program officers who were sacked did not comment on their firing, with one exception. A person who was fired told *Westword* reporter Stuart Steers that among the new programs created by the liberal program officers and terminated by the board was one on fighting homelessness that was "reflecting a modern approach to philanthropy that emphasizes targeting donations to go to the root of problems rather than just high-profile giving."[62]

The anonymous source did not explain how such "root-cause" philanthropy—where donors give money to groups that hire highly credentialed experts to study the poor and issue reports, rather than give money to organizations that help the poor improve their lives—in any way reflected Bill Daniels' more traditional approach to poverty-fighting, which stressed direct aid to persons in need.

❧ Recovering Donor Intent

The Daniels Fund made several reforms after 2003. The privilege of program officers to issue unrestricted rejections and grant approval up to six figures was removed. The Daniels Fund board now approves all grants and sees all rejections.

The rejection of the grant to the National Air and Space Museum was overturned. In 2005, the Daniels Fund approved a $3 million grant to the museum, which has a section of its Sea-Air Operations Gallery detailing Daniels' career.[63] In addition, the fund supports the Medal Of Honor Foundation, which has created a curriculum that teaches students about the virtues of Medal of Honor winners. In 2011, the fund hosted a reception where France's consul general awarded medals to Denver veterans who took part in D-Day operations.

But more needed to be done in order to determine what Bill Daniels wanted the Daniels Fund to do. John V. Saeman, a long-time friend of Bill Daniels who served on the Daniels Fund board for over a decade, explained the problem in a 2010 interview in *Philanthropy*. Saeman explained that while Daniels had "very specific instructions" in some aspects of his giving, such as the percentages that would be given to various causes, "those instructions didn't actually tell us very much about how he saw the world." Saeman said in 1999, the year before Daniels died, he and Daniels' brother Jack Daniels "tried—unsuccessfully—to set up a meeting in which we would sit down and ask Bill questions: 'What do you mean by this? What do you mean by that?' But we never got that opportunity."[64]

So the Daniels Fund staff spent a great deal of time gathering every letter Daniels wrote and sorting them in order to catalogue the donor's intentions.

Take, for example, the clause of the Daniels Fund bylaws that states the fund should provide "financial support to educational organizations that include courses in their curricula which emphasize ethics and integrity, as well as courses which develop skills relating to managerial and societal effectiveness."[65]

What did "ethics" mean in this context? "We went through his files, his letters, and, just as importantly, his actions," Saeman said, taking the story of how Daniels repaid the Utah Stars season tickets owners as an example.

> What kind of man was Bill? What kind of ethical position did he have? The board concluded that Bill was fundamentally a principle-based ethicist. He believed that there are certain principles—man's integrity, honesty—that are inviolable. He believed in the reality of absolute ethical principles, and the need of all people to follow them. He was known for being extremely honest and fair in business. He made business decisions solely on the basis of what he thought was the right thing to do, not what was in the best financial interest of his company.... So the Daniels Fund supports ethics programs—but only if they're principle-based.

If they don't follow the guidelines of a principle-based ethics program, the Daniels Fund won't support them. Period.[66]

In 2012, the board adopted a set of principles to ensure that donor intent is preserved. Every Daniels Fund employee and every member of the board has to sign a statement that declares, "The Daniels Fund is committed to ensuring the mission does not drift from that which Bill Daniels originally intended. You, as Directors and Associates, play the single most critical role in this effort.... You agree to set aside your personal views or preferences when acting on behalf of the Daniels Fund. It is the Board and Associates' responsibility to ensure that the Daniels Fund most effectively fulfills Bill Daniels' intentions and remains true to his ideals." The contract concludes, "Yes, as a Director or Associate of the Daniels Fund, I understand everything I have read above and in this document. I am committed to preserving Bill Daniels' donor intent and I understand the seriousness of this endeavor."[67]

To aid the board and the staff, the fund has come up with many ways to understand donor intent. Kiosks at the Daniels Fund and elsewhere help people understand Daniels' life and ideals. The board commissioned a new biography of Daniels. They incorporated documents expressing Daniels' donor intent as part of the fund's bylaws, particularly ten principles that guided Daniels throughout his life, including loyalty, support for free enterprise, patriotism, and etiquette.

"*It is imperative that Directors, Potential Directors, and Associates understand who Bill Daniels was, the charitable purposes he set for the Daniels Fund, and what motivated him throughout his life,*" the fund wrote in a statement of its donor intent policy.[68]

In an interview, Linda Childears noted two additional ways the board tries to preserve donor intent. Once a year, the primary topic at a board meeting is donor intent—what has been done to preserve Daniels' legacy and what will be done in the future. In addition, all program officers who deal with Daniels Fund programs in New Mexico are made familiar with the New Mexico Military Institute to understand the institution that molded Bill Daniels' character.

The Daniels Fund's strong support for its founder's intentions received praise in 2014 from the liberal National Committee for

Responsive Philanthropy. "The foundation remains unique among larger grantmakers in the seriousness with which it approaches its connection with its founder," noted Kevin Laskowski.[69]

Laskowski added that part of the reason donor intent was successful at the Daniels Fund was Bill Daniels' strong commitment to fighting poverty on multiple fronts, with programs that aid the poor, the old, the disabled, and drug addicts. "The foundation's spread betting [in poverty fighting] represents a responsiveness rare among larger funders," he wrote. "The Daniels Fund is, by many accounts, very responsive to community needs."[70]

Laskowski and his colleagues interviewed many recipients of Daniels Fund grants. One was a "youth development grantee" who explained how powerfully the program had affected him: "I had the great pleasure to attend the awards banquet [of the Daniels Scholars]. At all tables, you were mingled with young people— one going to Harvard, the other going to MIT. They would have never been able to do that if it weren't for the Daniels Fund. Their accomplishments were amazing."[71]

❧ The Daniels Fund Today

The Daniels Fund continues to fund programs in all nine areas of interest to Bill Daniels. Its most recent Form 990, filed for 2015, lists $1.3 billion in assets and grants of $46.7 million and an additional $16.2 million awarded in scholarships.

The largest single grant was to the Young Americans Education Foundation, which received $1.6 million. The fund awarded three other seven-figure grants. The Marketing and Business Administration Research and Curriculum Center received $1.5 million for a program to teach business ethics in high schools. The American Enterprise Institute received $1 million for a program to promote free enterprise on college campuses. The third and fourth largest grants were both for local causes: a million dollars to the Positive Coaching Alliance and a million dollars to the Casper, Wyoming, YMCA for support of a capital campaign.

The Daniels Fund's Rapid Response Fund distributed $307,830 to deal with emergency aid, including 46 grants to help people with their rent and 43 for money for dental problems. Because the foundation can't give money directly to individuals, grants from the fund go to trusted nonprofits.

In 2015 the Daniels Fund spent $16.2 million on 1,204 Daniels Scholarships, with the most scholarships going to students at Colorado State University (123, plus an additional 13 at Colorado State University–Pueblo (129), followed by the University of Denver (121) and the University of Colorado Boulder (103, plus an additional 64 at two other branches of the University of Colorado).

As of May 2017, Daniels Scholars are fulfilling Bill Daniels' prediction that "When these kids graduate … they will go back and help their community. They will go out and mentor the next group, and it will continue on and on and on."

Surveys the Daniels Fund has conducted of 1,700 Daniels Scholars who were graduated from college found that the top three majors were "business and related," education, and engineering. The Daniels Scholars earned 16 percent more than comparable college graduates, and put twice as much money into savings as did their peers. They made 75 percent more charitable contributions than their peers and volunteered 11 percent more often. Over 55 percent were managers.[72]

The one national political issue the Daniels Fund engages in is education reform. It has been a steady contributor to the U.S. Chamber of Commerce's nonprofit affiliate, the National Chamber Foundation. For example, in 2010 the fund paid for a 12-city promotional tour conducted by the Chamber Foundation to promote the documentary *Waiting for 'Superman,'* which exposes many problems with America's government-run schools. The chamber held screenings of the documentary followed by discussions about education reform sparked by the film.[73]

Collaborating with the Walton Family Foundation and other donors, the Daniels Fund paid the legal bills of the Douglas County School District in Colorado in a lawsuit filed against it by the American Civil Liberties Union, Americans United for the Separation of Church and State, and several Colorado organizations. The two national organizations became involved because the proposed Douglas County School District program would include grants from the county to religious schools.

The Daniels Fund pledged support for the lawsuit in August 2011 when it awarded the county $330,000 and an additional matching grant of $200,000. In doing this, Linda Childears said the fund was following the donor intent of Bill Daniels, who "wanted us to fund programs that were really trying new and different ways to accomplish things in education. He specifically mentioned vouchers as a concept that made sense to him, based on his belief in the free market and that parents should have the right to determine the best education for their kids."[74]

This lawsuit, formally known as *Larue v. Colorado Board of Education,* reached the Colorado Supreme Court, which declared in June 2015 that the voucher program was unconstitutional because it conflicted with a clause in the Colorado state constitution that had "broad, unequivocal language forbidding the State from using public money to fund religious schools.... This stark constitutional provision makes one thing clear: A school district may not aid religious schools."

Douglas County School District appealed to the U.S. Supreme Court. As of May 2017, the Supreme Court had not made a decision about whether to accept this case.

In the 2016-17 school year, Douglas County School District attempted to reconstitute the voucher program by excluding religious schools. But in August 2016, Colorado District Judge Michael Martinez ruled against the School Choice Grant Program. Judge Martinez ruled that the second Douglas County School District voucher program was "a continuation" of the earlier program ruled unconstitutional and that "it appears to this court that there is no fundamental difference between the two programs that would warrant exemption under this court's original injunction."[75] After the judge's decision, Douglas County School District rescinded its voucher program.[76]

It should be noted that Bill Daniels' donor intent raised an issue in the 2010 New Mexico gubernatorial race between Republican Susanna Martinez and Democrat Diane Denish, Daniels' niece. In the contest, Democrats bashed Martinez for supporting state-funded vouchers. Republicans responded by noting that Diane Denish, though personally a voucher foe, had served for ten years as a board member at the Daniels Fund, which has long supported school choice as part of the commitment in its bylaws to support "innovative educational systems."

Albuquerque Journal reporter Sean Olson noted that Denish "said she disagrees with voucher programs but could stomach the Daniels Fund donations because they were private money going to other private organizations."

Denish, who lost the race, said that her goal on the board was preserving her uncle's donor intent. "I loved and respected my uncle," Denish said. "We often didn't agree politically, but by serving on the board I accepted the responsibility of carrying out donor intent."[77]

One further way the Daniels Fund supports education reform is with its support of ColoradoSchoolGrades.com, which hired researchers from the University of Colorado (Denver), took education data from state and local education agencies, and converted it into measures of schools in a variety of areas, such as overall performance, academic excellence, and "academic proficiency," an overall index of school improvement. The results, *Denver Post* columnist Vincent Carroll observes, are "concise and compelling evaluations" that give parents a lot of useful information with which to compare schools.[78]

15

A Legal History
of Donor Intent

And besides, what right has the State, or those called upon to administer a charity, to dictate conditions to its founder? Those conditions may seem to us foolish fancies; we may deem ourselves far more competent to establish such as will secure the general object, but it is not ours to say. When we see fit to create such a foundation out of our own fortunes, we shall be at perfect liberty to show our wisdom, but it is out of place in administering the fortunes of others.

— State v. Adams, *Missouri Supreme Court (1869)*[1]

Was John Hiram's will fairly carried out? That was the true question; and if not, was it not his especial duty to see that this was done-his especial duty, whatever damage it might do to his order—however ill such duty might be received by his patron and his friends?

— *Anthony Trollope,* The Warden *(1854)*[2]

The law of donor intent is quite old. The battle between donors and inheritors predates the founding of the United States by several hundred years. Some scholars trace the roots of the conflict to Britain's Charities Act of 1601; others to the mortmain laws of the thirteenth century; and at least one expert, historian H.F. Jolowicz, to the late Roman Empire.

Given that the history of charitable trust law is at least 400 years old, it would take a book (and possibly a bookshelf) to exhaust the subject. This chapter provides a general overview of the legal history of donor intent, including a discussion of the terms often used in legal cases, so that donors will better understand what they can and cannot do in creating a foundation or charitable trust. Donors need to know what mortmain was, why the Rule Against Perpetuities is important, and why the Victorians found the subject of "the dead hand" so controversial.

℮ The Statute of Mortmain

The problems of donor intent begin in medieval England. The English church by this time had grown quite wealthy, as generations of people had willed it land and other property, which it controlled in perpetuity. To limit the church's ability to derive increasing amounts of income from estates, the Statute of Mortmain *(De viris religiosis)* was passed in 1279. (*Mort main* means "dead hand" in French.) This law prohibited the church from buying or receiving property that could be perpetually controlled, ordering that "no one at all, whether religious or anyone else, may presume to buy or sell any lands or tenements, or to receive them from anyone under the colour of gift or lease or any other title whatsoever, or to appropriate them to himself in any other way or by any device or subterfuge, so that they pass into mortmain in any way, under pain of their forfeiture."[3]

As Cambridge University historian Sandra Raban notes, however, after 20 years the church managed to devise ways to avoid the statute, often by acquiring short-term leases to land, which were then constantly renewed. Not until the sixteenth century, when Henry VIII (1491-1547) eliminated most British monasteries and created the Church of England with himself as its head, did mortmain cease to be a problem.

But even after the Church of England was nationalized, thus putting property it acquired under state control, the notion that mortmain was a bad idea persisted. By now, the French term "mortmain" became the English "dead hand," a term that one nineteenth-century historian said was derived from the "resemblance to holding of a man's hand that is ready to die, for what he then holdeth he letteth not go till he be dead. So that an inheritance is supposed to remain in men of religion as long as the house itself continues."[4]

In the fourteenth and fifteenth centuries, "trusts" or "uses" were created, whereby a testator could will land or an estate to a third party and thus avoid punitive death duties. During the same time, the church in England, seeking to avoid mortmain penalties, encouraged donors to will their estates to third parties that would use them to perform good works. By the time of the reign of Elizabeth I (1558-1601), these third parties had evolved into charitable trusts. In the sixteenth century, private charities were created in England that had little to do with religion.

As historian W.K. Jordan notes, such charitable trusts had been evolving for a long time. As early as the reign of Henry V (1413-1422), the British courts had created a commission to encourage donations to support hospitals, and several laws passed between 1530 and 1597 were intended to discourage gifts to religious organizations while encouraging aid to the poor and the sick. The next step was to determine what sort of gifts were and were not charitable. This was accomplished in 1601 by the Statute of Charitable Uses, which defined what organizations were charities. It also established a set of commissioners to ensure charities were properly run.

☙ Cy Pres

How were the wishes of donors who created charities to be upheld? That was the function of the Court of Chancery. During the seventeenth century, judges in this court set a series of precedents that established *cy pres* doctrine. *Cy pres* means "as close as possible" in French, and the courts used it to mean that a donor's wishes should be adhered to as closely as possible in legal proceedings that construe the donor's will. Historians are uncertain how *cy pres* evolved over the centuries, but as Cambridge University's Gareth Jones notes, by the early seventeenth century, it had become "a sophisticated and mature doctrine."[5]

The *cy pres* doctrine in 1600 varied little from today's. The Court of Chancery would not alter a will unless a donor's wishes were illegal, impossible, or indefinite. Consider *Emmanuel College, Cambridge v. English,* a 1617 case. A donor asked his executors to spend £1,000 on land. The income from the land would be given to Cambridge University's Emmanuel College at a rate of £50 a year to support two fellows, to be paid £10 a year each, and six scholars, whose annual salary would be £5 a year.

Emmanuel College objected, saying that no one, even in 1617, could live on £5 a year. Sir Francis Bacon, who was Lord Keeper (chief judge) of the court, ruled that the donor's intentions were impossible to carry out, and declared that the scholars should be paid £5, six shillings, and eight pence a year. Bacon, according to a court report of the era,

> did not intend to alter anything concerning the disposition of the legacy contrary to the will, except it were in that which was impossible to be performed, which might prove a hindrance and inconvenience to the college; and also that, in that which was necessary to be altered in respect of impossibility and inconvenience as aforesaid, he desired to tie himself to come as near as might be to the will and meaning of the testator in the ordering and disposing thereof.[6]

But Bacon's ruling was unusual. In most cases, English judges applying *cy pres* tests did as little as possible to alter a donor's intentions. In a 1682 case, a donor gave money to a Cambridge University college to endow a professorship in divinity, with stipulations that the professor hold a bachelor's degree or a doctorate in divinity, be at least 50 years old, deliver five lectures a term, and deliver legible copies of these lectures to the university once each term. The university asked the courts to alter the will so that the endowed professor be over 40 years old, give three lectures a term, and deliver his copies once a year. The courts rejected the petition, ruling that the donor's wishes were neither illegal nor impossible, and thus should be followed.

Perhaps the best example of the attitude of seventeenth-century English courts was in *Man v. Ballet,* another 1682 case. A donor left money to help the poor, repair local roads, and refurbish the parish church. The trustees petitioned the court to alter the will so that the church would receive nothing, claiming that the trustees' own "greatness and excess" in other worthy affairs absolved them from fulfilling the donor's intentions. Lord Nottingham, the chief judge, denied the petition, charging that if this exemption were made,

> at this rate we should have all persons' charities given away to preaching ministers and lecturers; but they should not think to rob Peter to pay Paul; however, for as much as this money for a long time had been thus

326

promiscuously applied for the time past, they should not be punished for that mis-employment in anything, saving as to what was paid to the parson, for which they should not be allowed one farthing.[7]

ℰ The Rule Against Perpetuities

Another innovation of late seventeenth-century English courts was the Rule Against Perpetuities, intended to prevent estates from using charities as a means to pass wealth through a family. Still the law in England and America, this rule states that only charitable trusts can be continued through successive generations. Other trusts can be passed through only one generation. As an example, consider the fortune of the Rockefellers. The Rockefeller Foundation is immortal, at least until its endowment runs out. But the Rockefeller family fortune must be willed anew by each generation. Further, the Rule Against Perpetuities forbids "mixed trusts," which give money to heirs and to charity. By 1700, the courts repeatedly warned donors that they must divide their estates should they wish to give money to both heirs and charity.

The English Parliament tightened rules regarding donor intent with the Mortmain Act of 1736. Under this act, all gifts of land to charities were illegal unless made at least one year before the donor's death and unless the deed of gift was registered at the Court of Chancery within six months after it was made. Further, such transfers were unconditional and could not be revoked by any later wills the donor might make. The only exemptions were for Oxford and Cambridge universities and three public schools— Eton, Winchester, and Westminster. It is unclear why this law was passed. As historian David Owen notes, the act "was not one of Parliament's more inspired decisions in the charity field, nor, for that matter, one of the more readily intelligible."[8]

The English courts chose to interpret the Mortmain Act of 1736 in a very strict manner. In a series of decisions, they ruled that charities could not acquire land or anything whose income derived from land, such as railway or canal shares, or mortgages for toll roads. Moreover, should a donor die less than a year after preparing a will, and should the will include any enterprise that involved land acquisition, the courts would declare it illegal and nullify donor intent. This was what happened to nineteenth-century philanthropist George Moore, who wished to leave £15,000 for a hospital. Because he died less than a year after making his will, and because land for the hospital had not yet been acquired, the Court of Chancery declared the will illegal.

Interestingly, the English Parliament in the nineteenth century allowed a series of private exemptions to the Mortmain Act of 1736. Some London hospitals could receive land while others could not. It was legal under the Mortmain Act to will the bonds of the Leicester Corporation to charity, but illegal to will the company's stock. Not surprisingly, long-established organizations petitioned the courts to declare that they were not charities in order to exempt themselves from the Act. In 1826 the British Museum (the English equivalent of both the Smithsonian Institution and the Library of Congress) unsuccessfully tried to persuade the Court of Chancery to declare it a non-charitable institution.

Nonetheless, during the first half of the nineteenth century, the Court of Chancery was very strict in maintaining donor intent. Provided a donor followed the Mortmain Act, the courts generally upheld his wishes.

ℰ Donor Intent in Nineteenth-Century Great Britain

The Court of Chancery in the nineteenth century was headed by a series of strict constructionists. None was more uncompromising than Lord Eldon, who headed the court from 1805 to 1828. Eldon ruled that Leeds Grammar School could not teach French and German since the trust that established the school specified that the school's purpose was to teach "learned languages," specifically Greek and Latin. When asked to divert one bequest made to the school to a different purpose, namely, aiding the poor, Eldon refused, saying the Court "must administer" the trust as its original donors intended.[9]

A typical example of Lord Eldon's hard-headedness was *Morice v. The Bishop of Durham*, decided by the Court of Chancery in 1804. Ann Cracherode died in 1801, and left her estate to the Bishop of Durham "to dispose of the ultimate residue to such objects of benevolence and liberality as the Bishop of Durham in his own discretion shall most approve of." Cracherode's heirs sued to break the will on the grounds that Cracherode's intentions were indefinite.

328

Lord Eldon agreed, on the grounds that Cracherode's wishes were "too indefinite to create a trust." Because Cracherode did not precisely define what she wanted done with her wealth, Eldon ruled that the Bishop of Durham should spend Cracherode's wealth immediately on any purpose "not for his own benefit."[10]

The result of such case law was that by 1850, England was filled with charities that were very old, founded by donors with very specific wishes, and functioning in ways that, at least to social reformers, seemed very outmoded. Trustees of the Victorian era were still fulfilling the wishes of a donor named Greene, who wanted to give green clothes to the poor; a donor named Grey, who thought that gray was the ideal color for the poor; and a man named Rose who willed that his town should always have plenty of rosebushes. In Chester, England, a seventeenth-century donor named Owen Jones willed his inheritance to poor members of 23 trading companies (or guilds) in that city. But as income from the endowment grew, funds were given to all guild members without a means test to determine which were in need. By 1869, 369 of 412 members of the Chester trading companies were receiving funds, including some who were soldiers in Australia. Only one of the companies still practiced its trade; the rest were shells that survived solely to receive money.

In enforcing donor intent, Victorian courts did not seek to redistribute income from an endowment if the funds exceeded the amount needed to fulfill a donor's wishes. This led to such cases as that of Christ's Hospital in Durham, England, founded in the twelfth century to help lepers. The hospital's endowment, invested in minerals, land, and mines, grew so that by 1850, it had expenses of £1,700 a year and income of £4,700 a year.[11] Author Anthony Trollope used the Christ's Hospital case and similar examples as the basis for *The Warden,* a novel in which Septimus Harding is paid £80 a year for religious duties and an additional £800 for being warden of Hiram's Hospital. Ultimately, Harding resigns his position as warden, but his real-life counterparts generally preferred to clutch their sinecures.

❧ Sir Arthur Hobhouse's Legacy

These antiquated charities eventually prompted a major debate between the English thinkers John Stuart Mill and Sir Arthur (later Lord) Hobhouse. Mill believed that charities should be subject to state control and modification 50 to 100 years after a donor's death; Hobhouse preferred to entirely eliminate perpetual charitable trusts.

In *The Dead Hand* (1880), Hobhouse explained that what infuriated him were cases such as *Thornton v. Howe,* an 1862 Court of Chancery case that contested an 1843 will by Ann Essam. Essam wanted to publish the writings of Joanna Southcote, a seventeenth-century mystic who believed she was to give birth to a second Messiah. Master of the Rolls Lord Romilly declared the will void, since it involved the transfer of land and thus violated the Mortmain Act of 1736. But Romilly noted that had the estate not included land, "this Court would, in my opinion, have enforced the bequest and regulated the application of it as well as it could."[12]

For Hobhouse, *Thornton* was an example of pernicious donor intent, since Southcote had no followers. But Hobhouse's goal was not to revise the wills of antiquated foundations; he wanted to eliminate foundations entirely. "But of the greater Foundations, will anybody confidently assert that they produce more good than evil?" Hobhouse asked.

> Will any contemporary of mine at Eton assert that the then state of the College was useful or edifying? Will any contemporary of mine at Oxford say that the Foundations of Merton or Waynflete or Chichele were then playing their part in the world? There may be times of awakened conscience and active exertion, but the question is whether rich Foundations derived from private origin do not invariably gravitate towards sloth and indolence? It is difficult to point to one instance of a private endowment for learning achieving great results by itself alone.

> To me, it seems that in this matter of Charitable Foundations we are reaping simply as we have sown. We have committed a vast power to fortuitous and irresponsible hands; and they have used it according to the measure of their goodness and wisdom.... If the plans of our noblest spirits—our Mertons and Wykehams and Colets—are found unsuitable as time runs on, what are we to expect from the easy and self-complacent spirit of the ordinary testator?[13]

While Hobhouse did not expect to entirely eliminate the influence of the dead hand, he did want to end all foundations that a state tribunal would declare as "interfer[ing] with the public welfare." This tribunal would be "charged with the duty of adjusting to new objects all Foundations which have become pernicious or useless." After the tribunal had its way for a period of time, "the living principle of using property so as to benefit mankind would, with the assent of the great majority, prevail over the deadly superstition of blind obedience to the commands of the dead."[14]

Hobhouse's views did not prevail. *Cy pres* rules in Britain were loosened somewhat, and the Mortmain Act of 1736 was partly repealed in 1888 (and totally repealed in 1960 after a government commission found it to serve no useful purpose). The British courts, however, still concerned themselves with trifling details. In a notorious 1939 case, the courts decided that the will of Caleb Diplock, which left £250,000 "for such charitable or benevolent object or objects" as his executors could determine, was void because "benevolent" and "charitable" were not synonymous, and that therefore the will did not meet the *cy pres* test for certainty. (Had Diplock's lawyer used the phrase "charitable and benevolent," the will would have been declared valid.)[15]

❧ The Dead Hand Problem in America

Hobhouse did, however, have a lasting influence in America. Granted, American charities rarely had the dead hand problem; the cases in which a donor's intentions have been completely nullified have been few. But the fear of the dead hand was far more influential than any "dead hand" foundation. This threat was one reason for the rise of community foundations. It was also Julius Rosenwald's main reason for inventing the term limit for charitable trusts. Further, since most major foundations in America were created *after* the idea of the dead hand became common, their vague, amorphous charters ensured that the dead hand was not guiding the foundation and that the donor's living hand was pushed aside at the earliest possible time.

But it took over a century for this to happen. American courts first had to establish what the legal rules were for donor intent. They had to decide whether English precedents would be considered in rulings. Was the Statute of Charitable Uses something to which

American courts were bound? What about *cy pres* doctrine? Was it a principle American courts should adopt?

These questions were debated for decades. As Edith L. Fisch, Doris Jonas Free, and Esther R. Schachter note in their authoritative analysis of the laws regulating charities,

> the new nation vehemently condemned anything reminiscent of English sovereign power or of an aristocratic society as being unfit for a democracy. Not only did some states repeal all English statutes including the Statute of Charitable Uses, but some jurisdictions rejected the notion of *cy pres* because it was mistakenly regarded as being exercisable only by the prerogative power of the king and hence contrary to the spirit of our democratic institutions and in conflict with the doctrine of separation of powers.[16]

One of the states that repudiated English law was Virginia, and it was unclear whether charitable trusts could even be established there. This uncertainty was compounded by the U.S. Supreme Court in the *Hart's Executors* case of 1819, in which the court upheld a Virginia decision nullifying a clause of Silas Hart's will that gave much of his estate to the Philadelphia Baptist Association. The association was unincorporated and, in the court's view, did not legally exist.

The *Hart* decision was quite confusing. Some states interpreted the decision to mean that nearly all charitable trusts were illegal. The Virginia courts, in particular, were very strict. In 1833, the Virginia Supreme Court in *Janey's Executors v. Latane* nullified a provision of a will that left $1,000 to educate poor children in a particular school district because the will did not identify what children should be helped. The Maryland Court of Appeals was also very strict. Only four months after *Hart,* it nullified as vague and uncertain a will intended to benefit "the real distressed private poor of *Talbot* county."[17]

ℰ The Case of Girard College

Only 25 years later, in a case involving the will of Stephen Girard, did the Supreme Court finally declare charitable trusts legal and donor intent constitutional. Girard (1750-1831) was a French immigrant who owned a fleet of ships. He was America's first millionaire and first national philanthropist—the 1820s equivalent of a Rockefeller or Carnegie. Like most of the great philanthropists, he was also very modest. In 1822, a would-be biographer named Stephen Simpson wrote Girard asking for information. Girard declined. "My actions, Mr. Simpson, must be my life," he wrote. "I have no information to give; when I am dead that will speak for itself."[18]

When Girard died in 1831, he left an estate of $6 million—an amount equal to half the federal budget of the time. Some of this was given to the city of Philadelphia (where Girard had spent most of his life) for various good works. But most went to create an orphanage, to be known as Girard College. It was to be endowed by a charitable trust, which would be administered by the city of Philadelphia.

Girard's heirs, who were given small sums, tried to overturn the will on the grounds that the city of Philadelphia could not acquire real estate nor control a private trust. Further, "the objects of the charity were altogether indefinite, vague, and uncertain and therefore the trusts were incapable of execution or of being cognizable in law or in equity."[19]

After several years, the Girard case went to the Supreme Court. Girard's heirs hired Daniel Webster to represent them. Ignoring most of the claims that Girard's intent was uncertain, Webster decided to base his case on the terms by which Girard College was to be created. Clause XXI of Girard's will left very precise instructions, including specifications for the height and length of the college and the placing of windows in buildings.[20] The college was to be open to "as many poor white male orphans, between the ages of six and ten years, as the said income be adequate to maintain."[21] The orphans

> shall be instructed in the various branches of a sound education, comprehending reading, writing, grammar, arithmetic, geography, navigation, surveying, practical mathematics, astronomy, natural, chemical, and experimental philosophy, the French and Spanish languages, (I do not forbid, but I do not recommend the Greek and Latin languages)—and such other learning

and science as the capacities of the several scholars may merit or warrant; I would have them taught facts and things, rather than words or signs.[22]

The orphans were not, however, to be instructed by clergymen. "I enjoin and require," Girard wrote, "that no ecclesiastic, missionary, or minister of any sect whatsoever, shall ever hold or exercise any station or duty whatsoever in the said college; *nor shall any such person ever be admitted for any purpose, or as a visitor, within the premises appropriated to the purposes of the college.*"

> In making this restriction, I do not mean to cast any reflection upon any sect or person whatsoever; but, as there is such a multitude of sects, and such a diversity of opinion amongst them, I desire to keep the tender minds of the orphans, who are to derive advantage from this bequest, free from the excitement which clashing doctrines and sectarian controversy are apt to produce; my desire is, that all the instructors and teachers in the college shall take pains to instil [*sic*] into the minds of the scholars, *the purest principles of morality, so* that, on their entrance into active life, they *may from inclination and habit, evince benevolence towards their fellow creatures, and a love of truth, sobriety, and industry,* adopting at the same time such religious tenets as their matured reason may enable them to prefer.[23]

For Webster this clause, if carried out, would mean that America, a Christian nation, would be using its laws to promote atheism. In a nine-hour speech lasting three days, Webster told the Supreme Court that Girard's will was not even charity, since it would deny Christian teaching to the students of Girard College. "If charity denies its birth and parentage," Webster explained, "if it turns infidel to the great doctrines of the Christian religion— if it turns unbeliever—it is no longer charity! There is no longer charity, either in a Christian sense, or in the sense of jurisprudence, for it separates itself from the fountain of its own creation."

Further, Webster argued that Girard's will was illegal since Pennsylvania was not an "infidel state," but founded on Christian principles. Pennsylvania, he said, "has a Christian origin—a

Christian code of laws—a system of legislation founded on nothing else, in many of its important bearing upon human society, than the belief of the people of Pennsylvania—their firm and sincere belief, in the divine authority and great importance of the truths of the Christian religion. And she should the more carefully seek to preserve them pure."[24]

The Supreme Court unanimously rejected Webster's argument and upheld Girard's will. In *Vidal v. Girard's Executors,* Justice Joseph Story, writing for the majority, ruled that it was impossible to know what Girard's opinions about Christianity were. He noted that Girard did not say that Christianity was not to be taught at Girard College, only that no ministers would be allowed to enter the college. "In cases of this sort," Justice Story wrote,

> it is extremely difficult to draw any just and satisfactory line of distinction in a free country as to the qualifications or disqualifications which may be insisted upon by the donor of a charity as to those who shall administer or partake of his bounty.... In America, it has been thought, in the absence of any express legal prohibitions, that the donor might select the studies, as well as the classes of persons, who were to receive his bounty without being compellable to make religious instruction part of these studies.[25]

ꙮ Establishing *Cy Pres* in America

Vidal not only determined that charitable trusts were legal in America; it was the first major decision to confirm that donor intent was to be part of American law.

Not until the case of *Jackson v. Phillips* did the *cy pres* doctrine become firmly established. In 1867, the Massachusetts Supreme Court considered the case of Francis Jackson, an abolitionist who died in 1861. Jackson willed $10,000 to a board of trustees "for the preparation and circulation of books, newspapers, and delivery of speeches, lectures, and such other means as, in their judgment, will create a public sentiment that will put an end to negro slavery in this country."[26]

The Massachusetts Supreme Court ruled that the Thirteenth Amendment, which outlawed slavery, had nullified Jackson's original plans. But because blacks still faced considerable problems after slavery, the court ruled that *cy pres* applied, and ordered that a master be appointed to assist the trustees in creating an organization to provide general assistance to African-Americans.

Jackson was the first case in which *cy pres* was used to alter donor intent. But the doctrine was not immediately established everywhere. Some states still wrongly believed that *cy pres* was exercised by the English crown rather than English courts, and was therefore a doctrine inapplicable in America. Other courts, even in the late nineteenth century, questioned a will that left funds for a charitable cause rather than to specific individuals. In *Tilden v. Green* (1891), Samuel Tilden, a prominent politician and the Democratic presidential candidate of 1876, willed a portion of his estate to create a library in New York City. The New York Court of Appeals nullified the will since it did not specify what persons would receive the benefit. In 1893, however, the New York legislature overturned the decision, allowing bequests to charities to be made.

According to legal historian Ronald Chester, the changing attitude of the courts to *cy pres* law reflects differing attitudes that generations have had toward private property. By Chester's count, before 1860 fifteen states had considered cases where *cy pres* might be invoked, and in ten states the courts had rejected *cy pres* as unconstitutional. Between 1850 and 1900, Chester says, the courts received the notion of charitable trusts more favorably because they "saw that by encouraging private contributions, they were reducing the costs of government.... The intent of the donor was paramount. Charitable trusts were construed by detailed inquiries into the state of the testator's mind and his wishes at the time of the making of the gift, instead of being seen in light of changing social conditions."[27]

❧ Early Twentieth-century Challenges to *Cy Pres*

In the nineteenth century, courts were reluctant to apply *cy pres* because they wished to do as little as possible to disturb a donor's wishes. Most nineteenth-century judges believed that an estate was private property, and that property was something that must be preserved.

This attitude, however, began to change in the more socialist-minded twentieth century. Some judges eager to modify donor intent cited Andrew Carnegie's belief that his wealth was a public trust for future generations. Other judges followed the views of the Legal Realists, whose leader, Harvard Law School dean Roscoe Pound, firmly opposed donor intent. "No amount of admiration for our traditional system," Pound wrote in 1906, "should blind us to the obvious fact that it exhibits too great a respect for the individual, and for the entrenched position in which our legal and political history has put him and too little respect for the needs of society, when they come in conflict with the individual, to be in touch with the present age."[28]

As Ronald Chester notes, only between 1900 and 1950 did courts begin to use *cy pres* doctrine liberally to divert wills from uses thought insufficient. In *Will of Neher*, a 1938 case, the New York Court of Appeals considered the will of a donor who left land for a hospital which a town could not afford to build. The court ruled that the donor's main intention was to build a memorial to her husband, and allowed the town to construct an administration building instead.

But if the dead hand was loosened, it was not loosened much, as exemplified by the Mullanphy Trust. Created in 1849 "to furnish relief to all poor immigrants and travelers coming to St. Louis on their way, *bona fide,* to settle in the West,"[29] the Mullanphy Trust by 1900 had outlived its purpose. It was cited by everyone from Julius Rosenwald to the organizers of community foundations as an example of outdated charity. But it took no less than seven court cases spanning three decades for the trust to be broken. In *Thatcher v. Lewis* (1934), the Missouri Supreme Court modified the trust, allowing it to become a traveler's aid program.

ℰ Suggestions for Donors, Based on Modern Donor Intent Cases

Will of Neher and *Thatcher* mark the beginning of modern donor intent case law. Nearly all recent cases involve small foundations and estates. Large foundations have generally avoided donor intent problems because donors' intentions, philosophies, and principles are usually ignored when creating them. *Estate of Buck,* discussed in chapter seven above, is unusual in that it involves a large fortune.

(The cases of the Barnes and Robertson Foundations, described in chapters six and eight above, are also unusual donor intent cases because of their size.)

Just as problems relating to wills have generally been seen as a matter of state, not federal, law, most decisions regarding donor intent have been made by municipal and state courts. Justice Hugo Black noted in *Evans v. Abney* (1970), one of the few donor intent cases to reach the Supreme Court, that "the construction of wills is essentially a state-law question."[30]

The rest of this chapter highlights recent court cases involving donor intent. I hope to provide potential donors with a better understanding of how to establish general charitable intent while avoiding the threat of *cy pres* doctrine being used to alter a will. What does it take to establish charitable intent, and what do the three pillars of *cy pres* doctrine—illegality, impossibility, and impracticality—actually mean?

The first rule in creating a charity is to avoid invoking the Rule Against Perpetuities. As noted, perpetual charitable trusts are allowed while non-charitable ones are not. Care should also be taken to ensure that the proposed foundation is, in fact, a charitable institution. While courts have upheld as valid wills that simply give money "to charity" without qualification, a charity must relieve poverty, advance religion, promote education, further public health, serve governmental or municipal purposes, or provide other services that benefit others.

Donors should also not use the word *benevolent* in creating foundations. While there has never been a case in America equivalent to the British case of Caleb Diplock's will, the precedents suggest that *benevolent* is not equivalent to *charitable*, and that using the phrase "charitable or benevolent" at any point in a will or deed of trust will likely be grounds for protracted—and unnecessary—legal action.

❧ *Hardage v. Hardage*

In *Hardage r. Hardage* (1954), a man named J.J. Hardage sought to create an endowment whose income would be used "to defray the hospital and medical expenses of any of my blood relatives who may be in need of such care and who because of poverty, hardship, or old age are unable to properly provide such care out of their own resources." His endowment would also have made "educational loans at not greater than 4% interest to any person of reasonable college age, who is a dependent of any of my blood relatives and has shown by his or her character, mental ability, and desire for education to be deserving thereof."[31]The Supreme Court of Georgia ruled that Hardage's plan was not charity, but a private trust meant to benefit his family. Such a trust violated the Rule Against Perpetuities, and the two clauses establishing the trust were struck down.

❧ *Estate of Scholler*

It is also doubtful that a valid charitable trust can be created that has clauses benefiting a particular class of persons, even if benefits are unrestricted by race or sex. Frederick C. Scholler, the sole shareholder of Scholler Brothers, Inc., created the Scholler Foundation in 1939 to help the poor, promote scientific research, assist people with disabilities, and help hospitals, educational institutions, and churches. But distributions from the foundation were

> not to be limited geographically to the United States of America; (and specifically for the purpose of providing hospitalization, medical care, and educational, literary, and recreational facilities for employees and/or former employees of Scholler Brothers, Inc. and/or Schuller Brothers, Ltd., and/or Trisco Products, Inc. [parts of Scholler Brothers, Inc.] and their families, and/or employees of any other corporation, a majority interest in the voting stock of which is subsequently acquired by The Scholler Foundation, or by Scholler Brothers, Inc., or Scholler Brothers, Ltd., or Trisco Products, Inc.)"[32]

In 1947, the Treasury Department granted the Scholler Foundation charitable status. But Canadian authorities would not consider the foundation a charity under Canadian law unless the clause benefiting Scholler Corp. employees was removed. Scholler did this in 1951 and died six years later. His heirs sued in 1959, saying that the Scholler Corp. employee clause, although it had been removed, was evidence that Scholler sought to create an illegal trust. In 1961, the Pennsylvania Supreme Court rejected the heirs' requests, stating that the Scholler Foundation's revised deed of trust was a valid charity.

After *Estate of Scholler* the law of trusts became clearer. The general rule that emerged was that a donor could create a charitable trust to study particular ideas, and even to glorify himself. But when a donor tried to restrict distributions of a charity to a narrow class of beneficiaries—heirs, associates, former employees—the courts would almost certainly declare it an illegal mixed trust.

❧ *Estate of Carlson*

It *is* legal, however, to have a foundation provide scholarships that benefit particular individuals, provided that they are not limited by race or sex (or possibly religion). It is also legal to create a foundation to aid a particular person, as long as that person uses grants to perform services that benefit an entire community. In *Estate of Carlson* (1961), the Kansas Supreme Court ruled that it was legal to create a charitable trust to send a person to medical school, as long as the person returned to his community after earning his M.D.[33] Similarly, land trusts that preserve a family's home and property are generally legal, provided that the property has "historic worth" and would therefore benefit the community and future generations.[34]

❧ *Register of Wills for Baltimore City v. Cook*

It is also charitable to will money to nonprofit organizations that seek to change the law or public policy. This precedent was established in *Register of Wills for Baltimore City v. Cook* (1966), in which a donor willed money to the National Women's Party, a nonprofit whose main goal was to convince states to ratify the Equal Rights Amendment. The Baltimore register of wills imposed a 7 percent tax on the estate. The estate paid, sued, and won a rebate, which did not apply to gifts made to charitable organizations. The Maryland Court of Appeals ruled that the National Women's Party's goals fell within the definition of a charity:

> Whatever may be the views of individuals, laymen, or
> judges, as to the need or desirability of the passage of

the Equal Rights Amendment or similar legislation, our system of government is not opposed to attempts to secure legislative changes by legal means. Indeed, the channeling of efforts to effect social or political changes to the public discussions involved in proposed constitutional amendments or legislation, rather than by possible violence or subversion, is fundamental to our democracy.[35]

☙ *Shenandoah Valley National Bank v. Taylor*

In 1951, the Supreme Court of Virginia in *Shenandoah Valley National Bank v. Taylor* provided another clarification of what a donor cannot do. A Winchester, Virginia, donor named Charles B. Henry tried to use his $86,000 estate to create the "Charles B. Henry and Fannie Belle Henry Fund." Income would be divided among first-, second-, and third-grade students of an elementary school in Winchester and paid each year on the last school day before Easter and again on the last day before Christmas. The Virginia Supreme Court ruled that while the students would certainly welcome the money (it would "no doubt cause them to remember or think of their benefactor with gratitude and thanksgiving"), the proposed fund did not qualify as a charity, and the will was nullified.[36]

☙ *Estate of Robbins*

Until 1965, courts generally declared a charity illegal if the beneficiaries had to perform illegal actions to receive funds. In *Estate of Robbins* (1962), the Supreme Court of California considered the case of a donor who left money "for the care, comfort, support, medical attention, education, sustenance, maintenance or custody of such minor Negro child or children, whose father or mother, or both, may have been incarcerated, imprisoned, detained, or committed in any federal, state, county or local prison or penitentiary, as a result of a conviction of a crime or misdemeanor of a political nature."[37]

The donor's grandnephew, an heir, tried to void the will, claiming that such a provision might encourage people to commit crimes so that their children could claim benefits. The court rejected the argument, stating that this possibility was "far more remote than that which the Legislature itself may have created by provision for the care of children that extends to those of convicted prisoners."[38]

ℰ Commonwealth of Pennsylvania v. Brown

Courts have been increasingly willing to modify charitable trusts, however, if they contain restrictions based on race and sex. These used to be very common: an 1886 Connecticut Supreme Court case *(Beardsley v. Selectmen of Bridgeport)* upheld a bequest to benefit "worthy, deserving, poor, white, American, Protestant, Democratic widows and orphans residing in the town of Bridgeport, Conn."[39] Precedents regarding race and sex begin with the will of Stephen Girard. As noted, a clause limited entry to Girard College to "poor white male orphans." According to legal historian David Luria, this ensured that Girard's will would be "the most litigated will in American history."[40]

In 1954, in the wake of the Supreme Court's *Brown v. Board of Education* decision, two black orphans sued to be admitted to Girard College, claiming discrimination based on race. The Orphans Court of Philadelphia rejected the request twice, and the Pennsylvania Supreme Court upheld the ruling. In 1957, the U.S. Supreme Court overturned the Pennsylvania decision, ruling that because Girard College's board of trustees was appointed by the city, the city was violating the Fourteenth Amendment clauses against discrimination. In turn, the city of Philadelphia replaced these trustees with private trustees and continued to refuse admission to black orphans. The Pennsylvania Supreme Court upheld the action, and the U.S. Supreme Court refused to consider the case. (Meanwhile, Girard College had modified Girard's will to allow admission of needy boys whose mothers were still alive.)

By 1957, the legal questions regarding Stephen Girard's will seemed to be resolved. But in 1965, another group of black orphans began to sue in federal courts. This time, they won. After five more decisions in district and circuit courts over a three-year period, concluding in *Commonwealth of Pennsylvania v. Brown* (1968), Girard College was required to modify Stephen Girard's will to admit blacks. (As Luria notes, a second modification of the will in 1984 to admit girls "seems to have been accomplished with relatively little litigation or controversy."[41])

One further attempt to modify Stephen Girard's will took place in 2013, when the City Trusts of Philadelphia as administrator petitioned the Philadelphia Orphans Court to alter Girard's will to close the college's high school and end all boarding on campus, which would change the school from a boarding school that served grades K-12 into a day school that ended with the eighth grade.

In August 2014, Judge Joseph D. O'Keefe rejected the City Trusts' petition and upheld Stephen Girard's donor intent. "The design of Girard College as a boarding school, intended to provide a residence, as well as an education, to its students is reflected in the very terms of the will," Judge O'Keefe ruled.[42]

❧ *Evans v. Newton* and *Evans v. Abney*

Other well-established educational institutions had the wills of their founders modified in the 1960s to remove racial restrictions. *Guillory v. Administrators of Tulane University* (1962) eliminated the clause of merchant Paul Tulane's will that required the university to benefit "young white persons." *Coffee v. William Marsh Rice University* (1966) voided the clause of the founder's will saying that the university would educate "white inhabitants of the City of Houston, and State of Texas."

The U.S. Supreme Court considered donor intent and racial discrimination in *Evans v. Newton* (1966) and *Evans v. Abney* (1970). In 1911, Senator Augustus O. Bacon of Georgia willed a piece of land known as Baconsfield to the city of Macon, Georgia, for "a park and pleasure ground" for whites. He believed that "in their social relations the two races (white and negro) should be forever separate."[43]

In the 1960s, the Macon city government said it could no longer enforce discrimination on property it administered. Bacon's heirs sued, charging that Bacon's wishes had been violated and that Bacon's estate was entitled to the land. While the Supreme Court of Georgia ruled in favor of the heirs, the U.S. Supreme Court reversed the decision. Justice William O. Douglas, writing the majority decision, stated that because the state was involved in administering the bequest, and because the park was not like a social club or an academy but was open to everyone, it should continue to operate and be open to all races.

The heirs of Senator Bacon sued again; this time they convinced the Supreme Court of Georgia that because Bacon's wishes for a park for whites only was now impossible, the court should use *cy pres* doctrine to have the land revert back to the estate. In *Evans v. Abney* (1970), the U.S. Supreme Court upheld the lower court ruling. The loss of charitable benefits "such as Baconsfield is part of the price we pay for permitting deceased persons to exercise a continuing control over assets owned by them at death," Justice Hugo Black wrote in his majority decision. "This aspect of freedom of testation, like most things, has its advantages and disadvantages. The responsibility of this Court, however, is to construe and enforce the Constitution and laws of the land as they are and not to legislate social policy on the basis of our own personal inclinations."[44]

❧ Wilson v. Flowers

Joseph L.K. Snyder died leaving a will that said that his trustees should leave 20 percent of what was left from his estate "to such philanthropic causes as my Trustees may select." Snyder's trustees, his next of kin, sued to have the will voided for uncertainty on the grounds that "philanthropic" was a broader term than "charitable." They cited the 1939 British case that voided Caleb Diplock's will because "benevolent" was not synonymous with "charitable."

In 1971, the New Jersey Supreme Court ruled against Snyder's trustees, stating that "it is no longer clear that 'philanthropic' by legal definition is broader than 'charitable' by legal definition" and ordered Snyder's trustees to donate part of Snyder's estate to charity.[45]

❧ Howard Savings Institution v. Peep

In the 1960s, courts began striking down bequests that imposed religious tests. In *Howard Savings Institution v. Peep* (1961), the New Jersey Supreme Court considered the bequest of C. Edward McKinney Jr., an alumnus of Amherst College, who left $50,000 to his alma mater on condition that it be "held in trust to be used as a scholarship loan fund for deserving American-born, Protestant, Gentile boys of good moral repute, not given to gambling, smoking, drinking or similar acts. (It being my thought that if a young man has enough funds to allow the waste of smoking, he certainly does not need help.)"[46] McKinney also left most of his estate to Amherst, provided that it agree to accept his scholarship plan.

Amherst College sued, saying that its charter barred it from discrimination based on religion, and asked the courts to strike down the religious clause in McKinney's will. (Amherst had no difficulty accepting McKinney's restrictions on smokers.) The New Jersey Supreme Court agreed, ruling that because the college's charter prohibited discrimination based on religion, the college could not accept the McKinney bequest as it stood.

But in making the decision, the court warned that recipients could not arbitrarily alter donor intent, and it cited *Connecticut College v. United States* (1960), in which the U.S. Military Academy sued to alter a donor bequest for a new building, saying that it did not fit the academy's expansion plans. The academy wanted to use the funds for an addition to an existing building, rather than build a new one as the donor intended, but the court ruled that *cy pres* could not be invoked "merely because the variation will meet the desire and suit the convenience of the trustee."[47]

So in the end, the court considering the McKinney bequest ruled that the bequest's violation of the Amherst charter meant it had to be modified, but modifications of the donor's intention that would be made simply to ease burdens on Amherst would not be allowed.

❧ *Lockwood v. Killian*

Howard Savings Institution v. Peep is important because it established a precedent courts could follow, particularly when stricter federal anti-discrimination laws were enacted in the 1960s and 1970s. Sometimes the courts upheld restrictions based on religion. In *Lockwood v. Killian* (1979), the Connecticut Supreme Court considered the will of Frank Russell Fuller, who willed his estate to create a "Fuller Scholarship Fund" to benefit boys in Hartford, Connecticut, and its suburbs who were "members of the Caucasian race and who have severally, specifically professed themselves to be of the Protestant Congregational faith." The court ruled that the fund had to be open to women and minorities from other parts of the state. But the court upheld Fuller's limits on aid to Protestants, stating that the restriction should not be considered under the anti-discrimination clauses of the Fourteenth Amendment, but was an exercise of the donor's religious freedom, and thus was constitutionally protected under the First Amendment."[48]

ℰ *Equal Employment Opportunity Commission v. Kamehameha Schools*

The Ninth Circuit's ruling in *Equal Employment Opportunity Commission v. Kamehameha Schools* (1993) may signify a less tolerant attitude toward religious restrictions in wills. The Court upheld a ruling that charged that private schools in Hawaii could not discriminate against non-Protestants when hiring teachers, despite a clause in an 1884 will by Bernice Bishop (which established the schools) specifying that only Protestants should be teachers. The Ninth Circuit ruled that because the schools were not church-affiliated, the religious restriction in Bishop's will violated the Civil Rights Act of 1964. Historian Scott A. Merriman suggests that this case acts as a precedent that donors that are not churches or faith-based organizations will probably have religious restrictions in their wills overturned. "Mere preference, however forcefully stated, for people of one religion does not create a right to hire only those of that religion," he writes.[49]

ℰ *In Re Estate of Wilson*

Courts have generally been more restrictive in upholding bequests that limit funds based on race and sex. In *In Re Estate of Wilson* (1983), the New York Supreme Court considered two scholarship funds created to help boys in a particular school district. In one case (known as the "Wilson Trust"), the school superintendent was to certify who the best students were. In the other (the "Johnson Trust"), the local board of education, acting as trustee, was to pay scholarships to the best students. The school district refused to cooperate, saying that it would be enforcing and approving discrimination.

Lower courts removed the superintendent's certification function in the Wilson Trust and allowed women to apply for the Johnson Trust scholarships. The New York Supreme Court upheld the decision in the matter of the Wilson Trust, but reversed the ruling in the Johnson Trust. Following the precedent of *Shelley v. Kraemer* (1948), which states that the Fourteenth Amendment "erects no shield against merely private conduct, however discriminatory or wrongful," the court ruled that the two trusts were private institutions. Unlike the park considered in *Evans v. Newton,* they had no "indelible public character."[50] The court concluded that it had no jurisdiction in modifying the bequest, except in the case of the Wilson Trust, because the school superintendent refused to honor his obligation under the terms of the trust.

❧ *In Re Certain Scholarship Funds*

In a similar case, however, the Supreme Court of New Hampshire came to a strikingly different conclusion. In *In Re Certain Scholarship Funds* (1990), the court considered two trusts left to the city of Keene, New Hampshire. One was for "some poor ... boy," and the second for "some worthy protestant boy." The city of Keene, acting as trustee, refused to administer the trusts unless they were open to all students, citing a clause in the New Hampshire state constitution that prohibited discrimination by creed or sex.

The New Hampshire Supreme Court noted two precedents to follow: *Matter of Wilson* and *Commonwealth of Pennsylvania v. Brown.* The court ultimately sided with *Brown,* ruling that the trusts had to be modified to remove sex and religious restrictions. "Our society permits discrimination in the private sector in recognizing that the desire of human beings is to associate with, and confer benefits upon, other human beings and institutions of their own choosing," Justice William F. Batchelder wrote in his majority decision. "Such private decision-making is a part of daily life in any society. However, when the decision-making mechanism, as here, is so entwined with public institutions and government, discrimination becomes the policy statement and product of society itself and cannot stand against the strong and enlightened language of our constitution."[51]

Chief Justice David A. Brock, however, wrote a vigorous dissent:

> Freedom of testation is a cherished right which permits a testator to breathe his last, secure in the expectation that

the law will venerate, and not frustrate, his last wishes. A court may, accordingly, replace an unfit or unsuitable trustee as part of its general duties in supervising the administration of a charitable testamentary trust, but the court is not free to rewrite a decedent's will or to attribute to him, posthumously, a desire to spend his bounty for the collective good when the designated and preferred class of beneficiaries has not been exhausted.[52]

❧ In Re Los Angeles County Pioneer Society

Generally, courts have ruled charitable trusts impossible or impracticable for two reasons. In some cases, donors unintentionally leave money to organizations that do not exist. In other cases, bequests are vague, and courts use *cy pres* formulas to assign beneficiaries. In *Estate of Tomlinson* (1976), a donor left funds to a nonexistent "Cancer Research Fund." *Cy pres* doctrine was used to award the gift to the American Cancer Society. *Estate of Bernstrauch* (1981) left money to a nonexistent "Masonic Lodge for Crippled Children." A court awarded the funds to the Shriners Lodge for Crippled Children after discovering that the donor was handicapped but not a Mason.

Courts, however, are more skeptical about efforts to overturn wills because donors made minor mistakes or omissions in naming beneficiaries. In *Vadrnan v. American Cancer Society (1980)*, the American Cancer Society tried unsuccessfully to use *cy pres* to acquire a bequest made to the "National Cancer Foundation" instead of the National Cancer Foundation, Inc.[53] In other cases, donors leave fortunes to organizations that do not exist after their deaths. In *Re Los Angeles County Pioneer Society*, decided by the Supreme Court of California in 1953, centered on the Los Angeles County Pioneer Society, an organization that honored the founders of that city. In 1946, Emma Stoltenberg left $53,000 to the organization, which it used to buy a building for meetings. But membership in the society was falling, and in 1948 it voted to disincorporate, distribute its assets (which totaled $95,243.54) among its members, and continue as an unincorporated association.

The courts ruled that in doing so, the Pioneer Society ceased to be a charitable association and had become a profit-making enterprise. They appointed the Historical Society of Southern

California as trustee of all Pioneer Society assets. The Pioneer Society responded that it still existed, that it still conducted activities, and that Emma Stoltenberg had willed her funds as a personal gift to her friends, not as charity.

The California Supreme Court ruled that Emma Stoltenberg was acting charitably when she made the gift, since she had said before her death that the money was to be used for a new building. The court likewise ruled that the Pioneer Society was no longer a charity, since it reorganized after the Stoltenberg bequest (and two years before it disincorporated) by closing its membership and saying that each member had a proprietary interest in its assets. While Stoltenberg's general charitable intent had been established, the Pioneer Society was no longer a charity, and its assets were held in trust until a suitable recipient was found.[54]

❧ *Freme v. Maher*

Los Angeles County Pioneer Society is very unusual in that a court overturned a bequest because its intended recipient was no longer a charity. Usually, courts will honor gifts to specific charities even if they are failing or bankrupt. In *Freme v. Maher* (1984), a Maine court considered a bequest made in 1976 to Ricker College, a school that went bankrupt several months after the donor's death in 1978. Though Ricker College had sold its buildings and other assets, it still existed as a corporation, and the college trustees asked the court to use the bequest for scholarships for students in Aroostook County, Maine. A court-appointed referee, having established the donor's general charitable intent, sought to use *cy pres* powers to divert the estate and divide it between Bates College, Bowdoin College, and Colby College, three nearby private schools.

The court rejected the referee's request and awarded the estate to Ricker College for scholarships. The court declared that since part of the college bylaws stated that the school existed to "provide an opportunity for a college education at modest cost to great numbers of deserving youths of Aroostook County," providing scholarships was consistent with the donor's intentions, even though the college only had a corporate and not a physical existence. "A resort to *cy pres* would tend to defeat, rather than further, the general charitable intent expressed in the Knox will," the court ruled, "and application of the doctrine under the circumstances of this case was therefore error as a matter of law."[55]

❧ In Re Estate of Crawshaw

Chester Crawshaw, a donor in Salina, Kansas, died on May 4, 1989. In his will, he left 15 percent of his estate to the Salvation Army and 85 percent to Marymount College, to form the "Mary Anne and Chester D. Crawshaw Trust Fund" to benefit students studying nursing. Marymount College went out of business on June 30, 1989, and was succeeded by the Marymount Memorial Education Trust Fund, which awarded scholarships to students planning to be nurses.

The Salvation Army sued to receive the entire $140,000 estate, claiming that Crawshaw's will could not be fulfilled on grounds of impracticability, because Marymount College no longer existed. The Supreme Court of Kansas ruled against the Salvation Army, declaring that Crawshaw's intent was to help potential nurses. Since the Marymount Memorial Education Trust Fund awarded scholarships in many fields, the court ruled that the fund could receive the Crawshaw funds, provided they were restricted to scholarships for nurses.[56]

❧ Carl F. Herzog Foundation v. University of Bridgeport

In 1986, the Carl F. Herzog Foundation made a grant to the University of Bridgeport for nursing scholarships. In 1991, the University of Bridgeport closed the nursing school and added the grant money to its endowment. The Herzog Foundation sued, asking either to recover the grant money or to transfer the grant to the Bridgeport Area Foundation, which was prepared to administer nursing scholarships.

In 1997, the Connecticut Supreme Court ruled in favor of the University of Bridgeport because the Herzog Foundation did not include a reversionary clause in its gift stating that the money should be returned if the funds could no longer be used for their original purpose. The case should remind donors to include such clauses, particularly in the case of gifts that are intended to be in perpetuity.[57]

350

❧ *Smithers v. St. Luke's-Roosevelt Hospital Center*

In 1971, R. Brinkley Smithers, a recovered alcoholic, pledged $10 million to the St. Luke's-Roosevelt Hospital Center in New York City. He stated in his deed of gift of June 16, 1971, that he would continue to supply funds to the hospital provided that the hospital constructed a center separate from the hospital that provided "rehabilitation in a free-standing, controlled, and non-hospital environment." Smithers also stated that "it is understood, however, that the detailed project plans and staff appointments must have my approval."

The hospital purchased a building that formerly housed the Algerian Embassy and opened the Smithers Alcoholism Treatment and Training Center in 1973. Smithers grew increasingly suspicious of the hospital, and only agreed to a substantial final contribution to the hospital provided it was used to create the Smithers Endowment Fund, for which "the income is to be used exclusively for the support of the Smithers Center, to the extent necessary for current operations."

From 1992 onwards, the hospital repeatedly asked Smithers and his wife, Adele Smithers, for more money and for assistance in planning a Silver Anniversary Gala for the Smithers Center scheduled for April 1995. Smithers, before his death in January 1994, persuaded his friends to donate substantial sums for the gala.

In March 1995, the hospital announced it was selling the Smithers Center building and asked Adele Smithers to cancel the fundraiser. In May 1995, after investigations by Adele Smithers's accountants, the hospital told Mrs. Smithers that it had been misappropriating money from the Smithers Endowment Fund. Adele Smithers and the Christopher Smithers Foundation asked the New York State Attorney General to investigate, and the Attorney General found that the hospital took money from the Smithers Endowment Fund and put the money in its general endowment, calling the transfers "loans." The Attorney General ordered the hospital to return $5 million to the Smithers Endowment Fund.

In 1998, the Attorney General's office entered into a settlement with the hospital where the hospital agreed not to take any more money from the Smithers Endowment Fund and to place $1 million into the fund when the Smithers Center building was sold. In 1999, the building was sold for $15 million.

Adele Smithers found these terms unacceptable, and received Special Letters of Administration from the Nassau County, New York, Surrogate's Court appointing her Special Administratrix of Brinkley Smithers's estate. She then sued the hospital and the Attorney General's office seeking to recover the entire $15 million from the sale of the Smithers Center building.

The New York State Supreme Court initially dismissed Adele Smithers's suit, siding with the hospital and the Attorney General's office, which said that Adele Smithers lacked standing to sue. During the appeals process, Eliot Spitzer became New York Attorney General and decided to reverse earlier decisions and side with Adele Smithers.

Adele Smithers won the appeal in 2001, as the court ruled that she did have standing and that "the donor of a charitable gift is in a better position to be vigilant, and, if he or she is so inclined, to enforce his or her own intent." As part of a subsequent settlement, the Smithers Center was renamed the Addiction Institute of New York, and the St. Luke's-Roosevelt Hospital gave $6 million to the Christopher Smithers Foundation and agreed to use the remaining $9 million for the treatment of alcoholism. In 2003, the Nassau County Surrogate's Court ordered the hospital to repay Mrs. Smithers's court costs.

In 2008, thanks to gifts from Adele Smithers and the Christopher Smithers Foundation, the Smithers Alcoholism Treatment and Training Center was opened at St. John's Riverside Hospital in Yonkers, New York.[58]

❧ Home for Incurables of Baltimore City v. University of Maryland Medical System

In 1963 Dr. Jesse C. Coggins died leaving money to four people named in his will. On the death of the last person named in the will, funds were to be left to "the Keswick Home, formerly the Home for Incurables of Baltimore City," to build the Coggins Building, "to house white patients who need physical rehabilitation. If not acceptable to the Keswick Home, then this bequest shall go to the University of Maryland Hospital to be used for physical rehabilitation."

In 1998, Dr. Coggins's widow died, and this clause came into force. The University of Maryland Medical System persuaded a circuit court to award it Dr. Coggins's legacy, on the grounds that the will should be voided for illegality given the racial restriction. In 2002, the Court of Appeals of Maryland (the state's supreme court) reversed the lower court, stating that to comply with *cy pres* doctrine, "The provisions of the will should be administered as if the word 'white' was not contained in the bequest to the Keswick Home."[59]

❧ Summary

The record of American courts in matters of donor intent boils down to a few rules of thumb: Courts tend to uphold donor intent so long as the bequest is fairly small and does not involve restrictions based on race, sex, or religion. But once donors have severed their interests in the philanthropies they have created, either through vague charters or through the actions of trustees, courts have never restored their control.

PART 3

PRACTICAL CONSIDERATIONS

16

The Two Most
Powerful Strategies

Time is not the friend of foundation vigor and effectiveness. In fact, with the passing of years, decay and stagnation are quite common, if not epidemic.
— *historian Waldemar Nielsen[1]*

Money is only useful when you get rid of it. It is like the odd card in 'Old Maid'; the player who is finally left with it has lost.
— *Evelyn Waugh*

As we have seen, disrespect for donor intent often occurs when donors establish perpetual foundations and offer little or no restrictions on how their wealth is to be used. Two of the most powerful strategies to maintain donor intent are (1) to term-limit your foundation, or (2), even more radically, to do your giving while you're living, and if you still have a significant estate at the end of your life, leave it not to a foundation but to charities you trust.

This chapter will examine a few donors who are exemplars of these strategies in American philanthropy. Their stories show that employing these two means often produces giving that is far more powerful—and exciting—than the conventional mediocrity which so many foundations eventually fall into. Term-limiting a foundation, for example, can help a donor and his or her trustees focus tightly on a particular mission, because of the necessity of meeting a final deadline, and have a more powerful impact than diffuse, unfocused giving would produce.

Term-limited foundations can also have more impact because of the larger sums they can invest. A conventional, perpetual foundation typically makes grants of only 5 percent of its assets

357

each year (the legal minimum), while term-limited foundations typically invest two to four times as much of their assets annually, punching far above their weight, as it were.

❧ The Popularity of Term Limits

Term-limited foundations seem to be enjoying increasing popularity. The nation's two richest donors, Warren Buffett and Bill Gates, have in effect created foundations with term limits. Buffett's wealth, except for the funds given to his three children and his first wife, will be turned over at his death to the Bill and Melinda Gates Foundation with instructions that it be paid out within ten years of the final settlement of Buffett's estate. The namesake founders of the Gates Foundation in turn have directed that their foundation is to spend itself out of existence no later than twenty years after the death of Bill or Melinda Gates (whoever survives the longest).[2]

Foundation term limits are not a left/right issue. True, several prominent conservatives, including John M. Olin and William Simon, placed term limits on their foundations, as we shall see. But in all likelihood, liberal donors have sunsetted more foundations than conservative ones, if only because there are far more liberal foundations than conservative ones. The largest foundation to spend down, the Atlantic Philanthropies, is left wing. So too is the foundation run by former New York mayor Michael Bloomberg, who has announced that his foundation will spend itself out after his daughters' lifetimes.[3]

No one knows how many foundations are term-limited, but studies suggest around 10 percent of them are. The Foundation Center and the Association of Small Foundations surveyed 1,074 family foundations in 2008 and found that 12 percent had a term limit, while 25 percent were undecided about whether they should terminate at some point, and the remaining 63 percent intended to exist in perpetuity. The study hinted strongly that donors are wary of perpetuity, however, because foundations with living founders were three times as likely to have a term limit and twice as likely to be undecided, compared to foundations who no longer had a founder to exercise authority over them. Also, the younger a foundation, the more likely it was to have a term limit. Foundations with no endowment were more likely to have limited lives than foundations with an endowment.[4]

Another study by Francie Ostrower, a public policy professor at the University of Texas, surveyed 850 private foundations in 2007 and 2008 and discovered that 8 percent had imposed term limits, while another 15 percent had not made up their minds. The remaining foundations planned to exist in perpetuity. Ostrower noted that her findings were consistent with those of Elizabeth Boris, who surveyed 435 foundations in the early 1980s and found 10 percent had imposed term limits.[5]

The foundations Ostrower surveyed (which were not limited to family foundations) were also more likely to spend down if the founder was still alive. Younger foundations were more likely to have term limits than older ones, as were foundations on the West Coast compared to their East Coast cousins.

"Perhaps the most common argument made by advocates of limiting foundation life is that it promotes adherence to donor intent," Ostrower wrote, "while perpetual life foundations drift away from that intent after the death of their donor. Our findings are consistent with this position. Among limited life and perpetual life foundations whose donors are deceased, a far higher percent of limited life foundations (91 percent) than perpetual ones (65 percent) say that adherence to the founding donor's wishes are very important. These differences endure even with controls for asset size and age."

❧ The Debate over Perpetuity

The first half of the twentieth century saw passionate debates over perpetual foundations. I have written at length on this history in my book *Should Foundations Live Forever?* (available from Capital Research Center, the publisher).[6] For now let us note that these debates were carried on not only by philanthropists, who disagreed on the desirability of perpetual foundations, but also by political activists and politicians, some of whom didn't want large foundations of any kind to be legal in the first place.

The political foes of foundations did not succeed in banning them or even mandating that they be term limited, and I don't think term limits should be set by federal or state law. Yet I do believe that it is best for a donor who does establish a foundation to legally require it to spend down by 25 years after the donor's death. A lucky few foundations have been able to maintain donor intent and be productive for longer than that, but their rarity proves the rule.

At the dawn of the modern philanthropic era, as the nineteenth century ended and the twentieth began, the titans who would launch the vast foundations that still dominate American life did *not* urge perpetuity. It is commonly believed that men like Carnegie and Rockefeller wanted their foundations to exist forever in order to make their names immortal, but little evidence supports this notion. None of the great philanthropists argued that foundations' lives should be immortal; several argued for limited foundation lives.

Carnegie in his "Gospel of Wealth" (1889) warned donors of the danger of giving money without imposing limits. Even by his day, he found that the history of "legacies bequeathed is not calculated to inspire the brightest hopes of much posthumous good being accomplished by them." Donor intent is often "thwarted," he added, and even when it is not intentionally ignored, it regularly fails to be accomplished.

Carnegie's advice was seen as common sense by most of his peers. The first modern philanthropist, industrialist George Peabody, created a foundation in 1867 with a fifty-year term limit. Russell Sage, a well-known investment banker of the 1890s, also favored limits. John D. Rockefeller Sr. rarely committed his views to print, but his grandson, John D. Rockefeller III (1902-1978), testified to Congress that both his father and grandfather opposed perpetual foundations. "As my grandfather once said, 'perpetuity is a very long time.'"[7] Nonetheless, Carnegie, Sage, and Rockefeller ended up endowing massive institutions that were not firmly required to term limit themselves and ended up refusing to do so.

That was a common phenomenon of the time, in fact. Foundations whose donors toyed with the idea of term limits, or even expressly permitted their philanthropies to spend down, ended up giving their wealth to institutions that decided the fun should never end. Such entities were called "optional perpetuities," and the leaders of few to none of them ever chose the option to relinquish the pleasures of job security and power.

Two examples can be found in the John Simon Guggenheim Memorial Foundation, established in 1925, and the Twentieth Century Fund, established in 1919.

Simon Guggenheim, in creating the Guggenheim Foundation, said his trustees could spend the endowment in any way they chose, or spend it down if they desired.[8] "The endowment I am now making," Guggenheim declared, "carries with it the expectation that in the ordinary course it will be kept invested and the income applied to the corporate purposes, so that the work and influence of the Foundation will be continuous and permanent; but no limitation is placed on the lawful authority of the Trustees and their successors to apply the principal of the fund, or any part of it, in case an emergency shall arise which makes a change of policy advisable to the judgment of the Trustees. We are confident that you would not use the power to deplete the principal except in a distinct emergency, and it is our hope that the principal always may be maintained intact."[9]

In 1922, Edward A. Filene donated $417,200 to the Twentieth Century Fund, "the income of which shall be applied to the purposes enumerated in the Certificate of Incorporation or any amendments thereto." A year later, Filene wrote a letter to the Fund's trustees stating that his 1922 gift could be interpreted "to make the Fund perpetual, which is not my wish. It is my desire that after twenty-five (25) years from the date of transfer, that is, on or after March 30, 1947, the Trustees shall have full power at their discretion to use the principal as well as the income of the Fund for the purposes specified, and I modify my gift accordingly by authorizing the corporation to use principal as well as income after March 30, 1947."[10]

Foundation historian M.M. Chambers notes that similar clauses exist in many other foundations of this era, including the Commonwealth Fund, the John and Mary R. Markle Foundation, the A.W. Mellon Educational and Charitable Trust, and the Alfred P. Sloan Foundation. All of these foundations still exist, and none have spent down. The Twentieth Century Fund outlived the twentieth century and is now the Century Foundation.[11]

Perpetual foundations continued to be created in the 1920s. But they were to face their greatest foe in one of America's greatest philanthropists: Julius Rosenwald.

ℰ The Achievements of Julius Rosenwald

The perpetuities, rigidities, and the bureaucracies against which Rosenwald inveighed were in charities whose purposes were too specific and hence likely to become obsolete. But the foundations who dominate the scene these days are extremely general in their

361

purpose. The public dangers that arise from them come precisely from the fact that there is no prospect they will ever become obsolete.
— *Daniel J. Boorstin (1962)[12]*

Julius Rosenwald (1862-1932) was the most important philanthropist to warn about the problems of perpetual foundations. His two most famous essays about the subject, published in the *Atlantic Monthly* in 1929 and 1930, provide valuable advice to today's grantmakers.

Unlike most of the great philanthropists, Rosenwald was not notable for building businesses from scratch but for improving an existing business. His wealth came from Sears, Roebuck, which Rosenwald did not create but ended up heading for many years. In 1895, Alvah Roebuck retired, and Richard Sears began looking for another partner. He found Aaron Nussbaum, who made a small fortune selling ice cream and soda pop to attendees of the 1893 Chicago World's Fair. Nussbaum borrowed the $15,000 he needed to invest in Sears, Roebuck from his brother-in-law, Julius Rosenwald, who joined the famous company.

Rosenwald steadily rose through the department store's ranks, becoming chairman of the board in 1908. His great achievement was to create a way to enable Sears, Roebuck to fulfill orders more efficiently. Working with Sears's chief of operations Otto C. Doering, Rosenwald constructed a 40-acre warehouse on Chicago's West Side that enabled employees to fulfill 100,000 orders a day. The time taken to process orders fell from four months to one day. No one had created such a huge warehouse before, and some historians say Rosenwald and Doering's achievement was an ancestor of Ford Motor's innovative assembly lines.

Rosenwald's active giving began after he read *Up From Slavery* by black leader Booker T. Washington in 1911. Rosenwald and Washington became friends, and Rosenwald began to donate to the South—first to Washington's Tuskegee Institute, later to YMCAs and schools in the South. Following Andrew Carnegie's strategy with libraries, Rosenwald would only contribute to building a school for African-Americans if the states agreed to continue them and if local blacks contributed to the school's construction.

The results of this educational project are one of the greatest achievements in American philanthropy. By the time of Rosenwald's death in 1932, he had donated $4.4 million to build 5,357 schools in the South. This giving leveraged $18.1 million in government funds, $1.2 million from foundations, and $4.7 million from African-Americans.[13]

By the mid-1920s, Rosenwald began his other major philanthropic achievement: warning about the dangers of perpetual foundations. Rosenwald's first substantial statement about the dangers of perpetuity was made in a 1913 address to the American Academy of Political and Social Sciences: "Permanent endowment," Rosenwald warned, "tends to lessen the amount available for immediate needs, and our immediate needs are too plain and too urgent to allow us to do the work of future generations."[14]

But Rosenwald's views did not receive national prominence until 1927. Rosenwald had created the Julius Rosenwald Fund to handle his giving in 1917, but he didn't hire a staff to administer its grants until 1927. As Rosenwald was hiring, he decided to endow the Rosenwald Fund with 20,000 additional shares of Sears, Roebuck stock, boosting the fund's endowment to $20 million. But in making this gift, Rosenwald imposed a condition: the fund must spend itself out within 25 years of his death.

"I am not in sympathy with this policy of perpetuating endowments," Rosenwald wrote in his deed of gift, "and believe that more good can be accomplished by expending funds as Trustees find opportunities for constructive work than by storing up money for long periods of time. By adopting a policy of using the Fund for this generation, we may avoid those tendencies towards bureaucracy and a formal or perfunctory attitude toward the work which almost inevitably develops in organizations which prolong their existence indefinitely. Coming generations can be relied upon to provide for their own needs as they arise."[15]

Rosenwald also decided to take his case to the press, first in a 1929 *Saturday Evening Post* article, then in "Principles of Public Giving," published in the May 1929 *Atlantic Monthly*. This essay is one of the most important in the history of philanthropy.

Rosenwald began by discussing charities that had outlived their usefulness, such as a fund designed to give students at one of Oxford University's colleges half a loaf of bread a day, or the will of late-eighteenth-century donor Robert Richard Randall, which turned his Manhattan farm into a retirement home for sailors. The farm, known as the Sailors' Snug Harbor, was located on prime

Manhattan real estate worth over $30 million in 1929—an amount that "vastly exceeds any reasonable requirement for the care of retired seafarers."[16]

But far worse than old nonprofits ruled by the dead hand, Rosenwald wrote, were living institutions with large endowments whose trustees only spent the interest the endowments created. While serving as a trustee of the University of Chicago, Rosenwald found his fellow board members reluctant to touch the endowment, even for such useful purposes as buying books or aiding professors' research.

"I think it is inevitable that as trustees and officers of perpetuities grow old they become more concerned to conserve the funds in their own care than to wring from those funds the greatest possible usefulness," Rosenwald wrote. "That tendency is evident already in some of the foundations, and as time goes on it will not lessen but increase."[17]

"The cure for this disease is a radical operation," Rosenwald concluded. "If the funds must exhaust themselves within a generation, no bureaucracy is likely to develop around them."[18]

"Principles of Public Giving" created a sensation in the philanthropic world. Rosenwald received hundreds of letters from colleagues who headed foundations and universities—and a surprising number agreed with him. Rockefeller Foundation president George Vincent wrote that the case against "specific permanent endowments" has "been proved over and over again."[19] Edward A. Filene declared that Rosenwald was one of America's ten most important business executives because his "business experience has led him to see through the shams of philanthropy and the pretenses of greatness which so often go with the accidental accumulation of great wealth."[20] Brookings Institution founder Robert Brookings told Rosenwald that the wealth he had given away "was insignificant" compared to "the value of this idea" of term limits for foundations.[21]

Rosenwald did have some imitators. He helped Conrad Hubert, founder of American Ever-Ready (now Eveready Battery), dispose of a $6 million estate in 1929. Maurice Falk, a Pittsburgh industrialist, specifically cited Rosenwald's ideas in his decision to set a term limit on the Maurice and Laura Falk Foundation, which disbursed its endowment on Pittsburgh-based charities and good government organizations until it spent itself out in 1965.

Rosenwald also influenced his own family. The Stern Fund, begun by Rosenwald's daughter Edith Rosenwald Stern and her husband Edgar Stern, was created in 1936 with a fifty-year time limit. It was in many ways a continuation of the Rosenwald Fund, since the Rosenwald Fund's last action in 1948 was to transfer $900,000 and some staff members to the Stern Fund. The Stern Fund spent itself out of existence on schedule in 1986.

Philip Stern, Edgar Stern's son and an investigative journalist, created the Stern Family Fund. It was also created with a term limit and spent itself out in 2005. The fund's president, David Stern, said that "we inherited this belief" in term limits "from my great-grandfather. It has become almost biblical in our family. Foundations become almost more interested in their own preservation than in doing the social change work they were set out to do."[22]

As for the Rosenwald Fund, it spent itself out of existence in 1948, nine years ahead of schedule.[23]

Rosenwald even had an influence on Congress in the 1950s and 1960s, when that body considered changing the laws governing foundations.

The two major Congressional investigations of foundations in the 1950s, chaired first by Rep. Eugene Cox (D-Ga.) and then by Rep. B. Carroll Reece (R-Tenn.), had little effect, although the latter's committee did urge a 25-year term limit on all foundations because that would "avoid the calcification which sometimes sets in on foundations" and "minimize the seriousness of the danger that the foundation might, at some future period, pass into the control of persons whose objectives differed materially from those which the creator of the foundation intended."[24]

The next Congressional critique came from Rep. Wright Patman (D-Texas), a populist who complained in 1967, "The foundations of America, which as a whole make up one of the powerful economic and propaganda forces in modern times, are virtually unregulated."[25] Rep. Patman grounded his criticism on Julius Rosenwald's critique of perpetuity. He quoted Rosenwald and former Rockefeller Foundation president Max Mason, who said, "old man Rockefeller did not set up the foundation, or any of his philanthropic enterprises for that matter, with the idea of everlastingness.... It is clear that numerous foundations violate the spirit of their charters by hoarding rather than giving. They also violate the principle of the era upon which their founders established them."[26]

Rep. Patman, who chaired the House Ways and Means Committee, helped shepherd the Tax Reform Act of 1969 through Congress. The Senate's version of the Act would have imposed a 40-year term limit on foundations' lives, but after a lobbying effort by foundations that historian Thomas C. Reeves calls "the most extensive publicity campaign in their history,"[27] this provision was dropped in conference committee.

The final version of the Act did address perpetuity indirectly in Section 4942[28] by imposing a minimum annual distribution of grant money (six percent of assets, later reduced to five percent). Foundations refer to this as "the payout," and the proper size and nature of the payout has been a source of endless discussion ever since.

Establishing the payout is as close as Congress has come to mandating any sort of term limit on foundations.[29] Although Congress has occasionally threatened other alterations to the laws on foundations, little change has occurred since 1969. That means decisions to limit the lives of foundations are the responsibility of donors and boards of trustees.

☙ Recent Term-limited Foundations

The number of term-limited foundations is now so large they cannot adequately be described in one chapter. Readers who want more such history should consult my book *Should Foundations Live Forever?* (published by the Capital Research Center). Here we will consider what can be learned from a few of the most important limited-life foundations, before we turn to the most radical option for donors, exemplified by George Eastman of Eastman Kodak, who gave his fortune away without the help of a foundation.

Atlantic Philanthropies
The Atlantic Philanthropies is the largest foundation to have a term limit. It ceased active grantmaking in 2016 and will spend itself out by 2020, 38 years after its creation. Its lifetime grants will total $8 billion.

Atlantic is the creation of Chuck Feeney, born in 1931 in a poor Irish Catholic neighborhood in New Jersey. Feeney's wealth came from Duty Free Shoppers or DFS, which he founded with three partners. By the mid-1970s, Feeney's wealth reached $250 million and he pondered what to do. He turned to New York University law professor Harvey P. Dale, who gave him a thick reading list. Feeney was particularly impressed with the advice of Jesus in the Sermon on the Mount and of the great medieval rabbi Maimonides, both of whom taught that the best way to give is anonymously. Feeney was also struck by the view Andrew Carnegie taught in "The Gospel of Wealth": after providing "moderately for the legitimate wants of those dependent upon him," a philanthropist should "consider all surplus revenues which come to him simply as trust funds, which he is called upon to administer…. The man who dies rich, dies disgraced."

The Atlantic Foundation (the philanthropy's original name) was established in 1982 in Bermuda. This was in part to allow it to give money anonymously. Also, under Bermuda law, Feeney could transfer his entire 38.7 percent stake in DFS stock to his charity, something he could not do under American law.

The Atlantic Philanthropies' existence was publicly disclosed in 1996, when DFS was sold to the French company LVMH and Feeney's decision had to be made public. Atlantic's historian, Tony Proscio, says that it was always assumed that the Atlantic Philanthropies would have some sort of term limit, but the decision was not formally made until Feeney, at a 1999 press conference, said that Atlantic's giving would rise to $400 million a year, a pace that would cause the foundation to spend out between 2020-2030. An anonymous trustee told Proscio, "We knew what Chuck wanted to do and there was such reverence for him around the table that there was no way anyone was going to oppose it…. If we kept on making grants at the rate we were making them, the spend-down was going to happen anyway."[30]

After several years of planning, Atlantic's board ultimately settled on the dates of 2016 for an end to new grants and 2020 for shutting down entirely. As Proscio wrote in 2010, most of this large foundation's task for its final decade would be "forecasting, planning, allocating resources, and in relatively few years' time, execution."[31]

John M. Olin Foundation

The John M. Olin Foundation is the most prominent conservative foundation to spend itself out of existence. The foundation's historian, John J. Miller, says that as early as 1975, John M. Olin was given a memo by Frank O'Connell, later to become the foundation's first president, saying that the foundation "should not aim at perpetuity, but rather at liquidation within a given period (perhaps 25 years)—or sooner, in the discretion of the Trustees, should events indicate that to be a necessary or desirable course."

According to Miller, Olin "worried that if it did not cease to exist at some point in the not-too-distant future, the enemies of free enterprise might gain control of the foundation's assets and turn them against their original objective. Moreover, Olin believed that later generations of Americans would be much better able to address the problems they faced than he would be able to anticipate them. Meanwhile, the intellectual defense of capitalism needed all the help it could get as soon as it could get it."[32]

William E. Simon Foundation[33]

William E. Simon (1927-2000) was not only a former Secretary of the Treasury and the man who worked with John M. Olin to shape the John M. Olin Foundation. He was also a successful entrepreneur in his own right, whose leveraged buyout of Gibson Greetings in the early 1980s was the basis of his fortune.[34]

While the Olin Foundation's mission was primarily to influence public policy, the Simon Foundation's primary purpose is poverty fighting. "The main purpose of my foundation is to help the needy by providing the means by which they may help themselves," Simon wrote in his autobiography. He added that he agreed with Andrew Carnegie, who said in "The Gospel of Wealth" that "in bestowing charity," the philanthropist should provide only "part of the means by which those who desire to improve may do so," because it is best "to assist, but rarely or never to do all."[35]

Unlike the Olin Foundation, the Simon Foundation has a fixed term limit; it is to spend itself out within 30 years of Simon's death, or no later than December 31, 2029. In a 2000 interview with *Philanthropy*, Simon stated, "I have asked that the foundation's work be complete within the lives of my sons Billy and Peter, who are in their late forties now." He added that in order to ensure that the foundation spends down on schedule, he had created "a lead trust that will start on the day that I die. There is a very complex process by which my children can recoup part of the trust, but only after all of the foundation's money has been given away."[36]

To ensure that they understand their commitment to helping the less fortunate, Simon Foundation board members can only retain their seats on the board if they perform at least 150 hours a year of volunteer work in helping the poor.[37]

In a 2008 interview with the *Wall Street Journal*, William E. Simon Jr. said he fully supported his father's intention that the Simon Foundation has a hard term limit. "It was something Dad felt strongly about," Simon said, adding, "People's behaviors change…. You have to be targeted in your focus and it's harder to do that as you…get further away from the donor."[38]

ℰ The Power of Giving While Living

> *If a man has wealth, he has to make a choice, because there is the money heaping up. He can keep it together in a bunch, and then leave it for others to administer after he is dead. Or he can get it into action and have fun, while he is still alive. I prefer getting it into action and adapting it to human needs, and making the plan work.*
> — *George Eastman (1923)*[39]

George Eastman (1854-1932) remains the most important philanthropist who never set up a foundation. Although few people today realize just how powerful his achievements were, even a brief sketch of them will make clear that he was an American giant.

During his lifetime, he gave away $125 million. While this was less than Andrew Carnegie, John D. Rockefeller Sr., or John D. Rockefeller Jr., it was enough to put him into the rarefied list of donors of his generation who gave more than $100 million, which includes James B. Duke, Edward Harkness, and Nettie Fowler McCormick.[40]

Eastman never set up a foundation for several reasons, but chief among them was his desire for privacy. Journalist B.C. Forbes, founder of *Forbes* magazine, interviewed Eastman in 1917 for a book of profiles of business leaders of the day. "I could not draw from him one fact about his benefactions." Forbes nonetheless concluded "George Eastman has little use for money except as an instrument for establishing worthy aims."[41]

After perfecting the portable camera, Eastman largely retired from Eastman Kodak at age 45 and spent the rest of his life as a philanthropist. The two chief recipients of his philanthropy were both universities: the University of Rochester, located in Eastman's hometown of Rochester, New York, and the Massachusetts Institute of Technology, which trained many of Eastman Kodak's best engineers. Ultimately the University of Rochester received $35 million during Eastman's lifetime, and an additional $19 million from his estate. MIT received $24 million, and much of Eastman's giving there was anonymous—leading students to a frantic but unsuccessful search to discover who actually was the benefactor the faculty called "Mr. X." Indeed, Eastman saved MIT during a financial crisis. Without his strategic giving at that moment, no one living today might even have heard of MIT.

Although Eastman gave generously to MIT and to African-American institutions in the South, most of his philanthropy went to the city of Rochester, including the city's main hospital, many dental clinics for the poor, and the Eastman Theatre, first home of the Rochester Philharmonic Orchestra. The city of Rochester's chief historian, Blake McKelvey, notes that by 1925 Eastman's donations to Rochester were so great that the city became known primarily as George Eastman's home. The city, McKelvey wrote, had been "made over in Eastman's image."[42]

Eastman's sprawling largesse wins him a place in the Philanthropy Roundtable's donor Hall of Fame, which summarizes some of his grandest achievements:

> Eastman established brand-new campuses for two universities that became among the best of their kind. He established a medical school, and did pioneering work in improving the dental health of children in the U.S. and Europe. He built one of the greatest music schools in the world. And he was the largest contributor to the education of African Americans during the 1920s.[43]

In 1924, Eastman announced that he was giving away $30 million to the University of Rochester, MIT, Hampton Institute, and Tuskegee Institute. (James B. Duke in the same week announced the creation of the Duke Endowment.) The *Boston Globe* declared in an editorial "Few can endow great universities. But many can apply George Eastman's philosophy of giving; invest in your own community and do so while your money can be put to work while you still live."[44]

After giving away the overwhelming majority of his fortune by his death in 1932, Eastman bequeathed the remainder, about $25 million, in his will.

℮ Lessons Learned

As this chapter makes clear, donors have multiple reasons to be wary of creating another perpetual foundation. The dangers of your own foundation eventually betraying your intentions are great, as is the threat of mediocrity that all institutions face over time. In contrast, there are significant advantages to term-limiting a foundation. The limitation often forces a philanthropy to be more focused and effective, and it also causes a foundation to have significantly higher sums each year to invest in good works, compared to a perpetual foundation peer.

But for donors who are especially brave and hardy, and want to maximize their own pleasure in doing good, there is the higher road of giving while living. In this scenario, donors avoid the difficult challenge of ensuring that a long-lived foundation stays on the right path. Instead, they get to enjoy the delight of seeing just how much they have improved the world with their philanthropy.

17

What Donors Can Do

I believe that, after the first generation, inherited wealth loses the spirit and the values of the people who earned that wealth. There comes a disconnection between the funds and the source of the funds.... The culture of those in charge becomes not dissimilar from the culture of the government bureaucracies who dispense funds confiscated from the taxpayers.

— Joseph J. Jacobs[1]

The previous chapters have examined how donor intent became a problem, how the law has addressed the issue, and how foundations, large and small, have either followed or, more often, abandoned the wishes of their founders. This chapter draws general conclusions about the problems of donor intent and outlines principles that donors should consider as they make long-term plans for their giving.

As the earlier parts of this book make clear, there is no iron-clad guarantee that families, friends, and associates will honor one's wishes after one's death. Far too often, the stories of great fortunes begin with heirs who agreed with a donor's intentions when alive, but end with betrayal after the donor's death. Trusted family lawyers have also helped create foundations that betray donors' wishes. John D. MacArthur's lawyer, William Kirby, helped ensure that the John D. and Catherine T. MacArthur Foundation would not fund any cause that John MacArthur supported. John D. Rockefeller's lawyer, Starr Murphy, not only ensured that Rockefeller would have little say in the Rockefeller Foundation's affairs, but that Rockefeller would be kicked out of the foundation by 1920—even though Rockefeller lived until 1937.

The first rule for donors, then, is that in the long run you cannot trust your alma mater, family, friends, colleagues, or staff. The second rule is that you, the donor, are the best judge of your intentions. People intelligent enough to acquire fortunes are smart enough to know what charities or causes they wish to support. Donors should be wary of any advisor who suggests leaving money to vague causes, or who suggests leaving no instructions on how an endowment should be used. But donors must also recognize that they bear a weighty responsibility to think through their intentions, then to document them, and finally to plan how to implement them.

Writing in the *Wall Street Journal,* Adam Meyerson, president of the Philanthropy Roundtable, lists the top practical considerations every donor should consider:

- Clearly define your charitable mission. Write it down in your founding documents. Supplement your mission statement with a long written or oral record about your likes and dislikes in charitable giving.

- Choose trustees and staff who share your fundamental principles. Choose family members, friends, and close business associates such as lawyers, bankers, and accountants *only* if they fit into this category.

- If possible, separate your philanthropic interests from your interests in maintaining control of your company. Donor intent frequently suffers when the two are mixed.

- Give generously while living, and strongly consider a sunset provision for your foundation, perhaps a generation or two after your death.

- If you do establish a foundation in perpetuity, establish procedures for electing future trustees who share your principles, and for encouraging future boards to consider respect for donor intent as part of their fiduciary duty.[2]

This book's histories prove each of Meyerson's practical principles. For example, James Buchanan Duke's philanthropy has stayed true to his principles in large part because he thought through those principles carefully, limited them geographically and by subject area, wrote them down at length, and ensured his successors would confront his intentions regularly (see chapter twelve).

As for choosing trustees and staff with care, we've just recounted lawyers who failed to defend their donors' intent. Or to take another example, Andrew Carnegie's advisors first twisted and then abandoned his flagship project of building public libraries (see chapter three).

The need to keep your corporate concerns distinct from your philanthropic enterprise is the moral of the Ford family story (see chapter two). Although Henry Ford had thoughtful things to say about good and bad charity and achieved a good track record of giving during his life, when his foundation was being established, he let business concerns shunt aside proper planning for his posthumous philanthropy. Henry Ford II would likewise have more care for the family business than the family foundation, until things became so bad at the latter that he felt obliged to resign from the board in disgust.

Giving while living is, as philanthropic giants like George Eastman and Julius Rosenwald show, the best school in which to develop excellence in your philanthropy (see chapter sixteen). You will learn how to give well through practice, and you will also learn what charities you can trust to do the good works you want to support. You can support them while living and leave the bulk of your estate to them as bequests. Or if you want to take a riskier course, you can establish a philanthropy that will outlive you, yet set a time limit on that organization that gives you decent odds of having your intent respected through its entire life cycle. Putting term limits on a philanthropy will also help it focus its giving and, in addition, it will be paying out far more than the conventional 5 percent a year of perpetual foundations, which means it will function as if it were far larger and more powerful than it otherwise would be.[3]

Adam Meyerson's last point is also correct: if you establish a perpetual foundation, you must also carefully establish procedures for electing future trustees who share your principles, and for encouraging future boards to consider respect for donor intent as part of their fiduciary duty. The story of the Daniels Fund is one of the few cases of a turnaround on donor intent, as we saw in chapter fourteen. The Fund's return to its founder's desires only occurred because its board acted boldly to put themselves under the discipline of multiple procedures designed to ensure that seats on the board only go to persons who will respect Bill Daniels' intent.

Another alternative donors can consider for their posthumous giving is to set up a so-called Donor-Advised Fund (DAF) at a nonprofit. When created, such a fund will function as a tax-deductible gift to charity on your taxes, and the DAF-sponsoring organization will legally control your gift, but in practice the organization will write checks to charities that you advise them to support on your behalf, without your having the hassles of setting up and maintaining your own foundation. These funds are offered by charitable offshoots of giant money management firms like Charles Schwab and Vanguard, but also by specialized groups such as DonorsTrust in Virginia, which will never make grants to a left-of-center organization, no matter what your heirs may request. There are also mission-driven DAF providers that specialize in serving Jewish, Protestant, and Catholic donors.

If you're going to plan posthumous giving, there are still more complexities for you to consider: do you want to establish an operating or nonoperating foundation, or perhaps a supporting organization? Do you want to engage third parties in hopes of bolstering your donor intent; say, by allowing them to name some board members or by indicating they have grounds to sue the philanthropy if it betrays your intent?

Personally, I doubt it is wise to alter the law to allow third parties to contest foundation indentures, but some role for third parties may be helpful in some instances. One of the best guides to the debates over these kinds of questions, and to the practical decisions a donor should make in his long-term planning, is Jeff Cain's guidebook for the Philanthropy Roundtable, *Protecting Donor Intent: How to Define and Safeguard Your Philanthropic Principles.*[4] In addition, donors will need legal counsel, and I strongly urge you to find counsel with broad experience in nonprofit law, rather than relying on corporate attorneys.

To reiterate the moral of this book one last time, I say again, the best way donors can ensure that their wishes are fulfilled is by spending funds on projects they prefer within their lifetimes.

Living donors are better able to ensure that their fortunes are appropriately spent than dead ones. If you still end up with a sizable estate, consider leaving it to charities you already trust, rather than taking a gamble by leaving it to a foundation. And if you do create a foundation, consider limiting its life.

Above all, be wary of anyone who argues that the ideas, principles, and passions of donors are unimportant.

Notes

Introduction

1. Cited in Frederick T. Gates, *Chapters in My Life* (New York: Free Press, 1977), p. 212.

2. *Ibid.,* p. 265.

3. Barry D. Karl and Stanley N. Katz, "The American Private Philanthropic Foundation and the Public Sphere 1890-1930," *Minerva,* Summer 1981.

4. Kathleen D. McCarthy, "The Gospel of Wealth: American Giving in Theory and Practice," in Richard Magat, ed., *Philanthropic Giving: Studies in Varieties and Goals* (New York: Oxford University Press, 1989), p. 58.

5. Marvin Olasky, *The Tragedy of American Compassion* (Washington, D.C.: Regnery Gateway, 1992), p. 127.

6. Cited in John M. Glenn, Lilian Brandt, and F. Emerson Andrews, *The Russell Sage Foundation,* 1907-1946 (New York: Russell Sage Foundation, 1947), p. 6.

7. Joseph J. Thorndike Jr., *The Very Rich: A History of Wealth* (New York: American Heritage, 1976), p. 337.

8. *The Russell Sage Foundation, 1907-1946, op. cit.,* p. 7.

9. *Ibid.,* p. 13.

10. *Ibid.,* p. 26.

11. Scott M. Cutlip, *Fund Raising in the United States: Its Role in American Philanthropy* (New Brunswick, N.J.: Transaction, 1990), pp. 206-207.

12. By 1907, Ward and Pierce's whirlwind techniques had been successfully used in Duluth, Dallas, Denver, and St. Paul. Ward and Pierce even went to Australia and New Zealand, but found little enthusiasm for their high-pressure salesmanship. "The smart Yankee 'organizing' secretary of the Victorian Y.M.C.A. is growing monotonous with his glorious schemes for collecting cash," the Sydney, Australia, *Bulletin* editorialized in August 1907, adding that however worthy the Y.M.C.A. might be, "it isn't good enough to justify the eternal importunities of a begging secretary, who presumably draws commission on his 'order' in addition to a fat salary." *Ibid.,* p. 249.

13. *Ibid.,* p. 116.

14. Such appeals, however, were not new. When America's first great philanthropist, Stephen Girard, began making major donations in the 1820s, he was besieged with charitable requests. After giving to Philadelphia's St. Mary's Catholic Church, other churches in Boston, Cincinnati, Annapolis, Maryland, and Perryville, Missouri, begged for loans. Yale University sought a new building; Dickinson College wanted an endowed chair in chemistry; and a man with the pseudonym "Amicus Patriae" insisted that with $800,000 he could start a "University of the United States." Someone from Ohio also wrote Girard, claiming that "the Supreme Being having revealed himself to me for the execution of His purposes on the earth directs me to call on you in His name for $25,000. He will demonstrate His concern in the matter by showing you what must be considered a miracle. For that purpose, when you have perused this letter you must lay it on a table and the Supreme Being will restrain you or

deprive you of the power of touching it for one minute by the exercise of His omnipotency." Girard gave the alleged ambassador from God no money. Harry Emerson Wildes, *Lonely Midas: The Story of Stephen Girard* (New York: Farrar and Rinehart, 1943), pp. 267-271.

15. The study was conducted by the New York Bureau of Municipal Research. Most grantseekers assured Mrs. Harriman that she would never miss the money. "Please do sit down and write a check for one million dollars," one woman wrote. "It will look so small that you will see you'll never miss the sum and make me famous and fortunate." William H. Allen, *Modern Philanthropy: A Study of Efficient Appealing and Giving* (New York: Dodd, Mead, 1912), p. 4. While most recipients wanted unconditional loans or grants, 216 people wanted to sell Mrs. Harriman a total of $8,000,000 in goods, including a farm, magazine subscriptions, old coins, a fire escape, a "crazy patch silk quilt," and a "horn that was taken from the head of a steer that was eat *[sic]* for breakfast by a company of Virginia soldiers." *Ibid.,* p. 29.

16. *Ibid.,* pp. 189-190.

17. *Ibid.,* p. 203.

18. *Ibid.,* p. 204.

19. *Ibid.,* p. 204.

20. *Ibid.,* p. 290.

21. Frederick Goff, a banker who created the Cleveland Foundation, was so preoccupied with the problem of the dead hand, his wife recalled, that his youngest child once "asked in a frightened tone to be told where it was and what it did." Diana Tittle, "Cleveland's Best Idea," *Foundation News,* September/ October 1989.

22. Walter Greenough, "The Dead Hand Harnessed: The Significance of Community Trusts," *Scribner's Magazine,* December 1923.

Chapter 1: The Rockefeller Legacy

1. Herbert N. Casson, "The Rockefeller Foundation," *Munsey's Magazine,* June 1910.

2. John Ensor Harr and Peter J. Johnson, *The Rockefeller Century* (New York: Scribner's, 1988), pp. 24-25.

3. Frederick T. Gates, *Chapters in My Life* (New York: Free Press, 1977), p. 161.

4. Rockefeller was such a prominent donor to the school that when he visited in 1896, he was serenaded by undergraduates, who shouted, "John D. Rockefeller, wonderful man is he/Gives all his spare change to the U. of C." Cited in Gerald Jonas, *The Circuit Riders: Rockefeller Money and the Rise of Modern Science* (New York: Norton, 1989), p. 32.

5. *Ibid.,* p. 27.

6. Ron Chernow, *Titan: The Life of John D. Rockefeller Sr.* (New York: Random House, 1998), p. 468.

7. *Ibid.,* p. 469.

8. Peter Collier and David Horowitz, *The Rockefellers: An American Dynasty* (New York: Holt, Rinehart, and Winston, 1976), p. 3.

9. *Ibid.,* p. 3. Capitalization original. The cartoon was reprinted in the April 13, 1905, *Independent.*

10. James L. Barton, "The Correspondence on the Rockefeller Gift," *Independent,* April 13, 1905.

11. According to historian Ray Eldon Hiebert, in 1884 the president of the University of Rochester wrote to Rockefeller saying that he was writing a paper that would show how Rockefeller's consolidation of the oil industry was resulting in better quality goods at lower prices. Rockefeller refused to cooperate, fearing that the president's reputation would be harmed.

That same year, a woman sought an interview with Rockefeller for articles she was writing on prominent Americans of the day. She believed "it is a good thing for the world to know that the President of the great Standard Oil Company is a Christian, a gentleman, an earnest temperate man, and generous in all good works." Rockefeller's response was that "in accordance with a decision reached some time hence, I have declined to allow anything to be written in the manner as suggested, but I appreciate the kindness of my friends desiring to say something favorable to me and that might be helpful to others." Cited in Ray Eldon Hiebert, *Courtier to the Crowd: The Story of Ivy Lee and the Development of Public Relations* (Ames, Iowa: Iowa State University Press, 1966), pp. 110-111.

After Ida Tarbell published the *History of the Standard Oil Company* in 1904, Standard Oil hired a public-relations specialist. But Rockefeller, who had retired from the company in 1897, did nothing. As a result, notes Hiebert, "few people thought of Rockefeller as a human being, but only as a billion-dollar machine that crushed everything in its path. He was pictured as a stingy old man who would step on anyone to make another dollar. He was commonly described as morose and mean, fearful of being attacked by people he had ruined, and ringed by body guards. When he gave sizable sums to church or charity, it became 'tainted money' with which he was seeking to salve his guilty conscience." *Ibid.,* p. 110.

12. Cited in Raymond B. Fosdick, *John D. Rockefeller, Jr: A Portrait* (New York: Harper, 1956), p. 110. In his memoirs, Gates says that by 1905, "I came to disbelieve altogether in the peculiar tenets of the Baptist Church, or in the doctrines generally held by orthodox Protestants, and to reject the inspiration and inerrancy of the Scriptures.... My religion became, and still is, simply the service of humanity in the Spirit of Jesus. It is the religion of Jesus, of science, and of evolution alike. Creeds, churches, sects, religious organizations, and all the agencies of civilization are to be valued and used only as they are agents to the service of humanity on earth." Gates, *op. cit.,* pp. 206-207.

Rockefeller's fortune dramatically increased in the late 1890s, after gasoline became a common fuel for cars instead of a useless byproduct of refining. An 1897 editorial in the *New Era* calculated that Rockefeller's wealth was increasing at the rate of $55 million a month, equivalent to $972 million today. Ron Chernow estimates that Rockefeller's wealth increased tenfold after 1897. Chernow, *op. cit.,* p. 397.

13. Gates, *op. cit.,* p. 208.

14. *Ibid.,* p. 209.

15. Harr and Johnson, *op. cit.,* p. 83.

16. Allan Nevins, *Study in Power. John D. Rockefeller, Industrialist and Philanthropist* (Westport, Connecticut: Easton Press, 1989), p. 308.

17. Raymond B. Fosdick, *The Story of the Rockefeller Foundation* (New Brunswick, New Jersey: Transaction, 1989), p. 15.

18. Gates, *op. cit.,* p. 234.

19. Fosdick, *Rockefeller Foundation,* p. 16.

20. *Ibid.,* p. 17.

21. Henry F. Pringle, *The Life and Times of William Howard Taft* (New York: Farrar and Rinehart, 1939), pp. 662-663. Other prominent Americans also joined in opposing the Rockefeller charter, including former president Theodore Roosevelt, who said that "of course no amount of charities in spending such fortunes can compensate in any way for the misconduct in acquiring them." American Federation of Labor president Samuel Gompers charged that the most noble act John D. Rockefeller could do was to create a foundation to "help other people see in time how they can keep from being like him." Collier and Horowitz, *op. cit.,* p. 64.

22. Chernow, *op. cit.,* p. 565.

23. Barry Karl and Stanley Katz, "Foundations and Ruling Class Elites," *Daedalus,* Winter 1987.

24. *Ibid.*

25. Robert E. Kohler, *Partners in Science: Foundations and Natural Scientists 1900-1945* (Chicago: University of Chicago Press, 1991), p. 47.

26. Priscilla Long, "Ludlow Massacre," in Mari Jo Buhle, Paul Buhle, and Dan Georgakas, *Encyclopedia of the American Left* (New York: Garland, 1990), p. 441.

27. According to Mackenzie King, "Mother" Jones thought that John D. Rockefeller Jr. was "a man with a thin, hard jaw, who kept his teeth and mouth firmly compressed and his hands clutching out for money all the time." F.A. McGregor, *The Fall and Rise of Mackenzie King, 1911-1919* (Toronto: Macmillan of Canada, 1962), p. 137.

28. "In accepting I had to consider that I was prejudicing my political future for all time to come," King wrote to John D. Rockefeller Jr. "My battles henceforth would not be with the political issues but against the Rockefeller prejudice.... I would not be harangued against as a Liberal politician but as a 'Standard Oil man.' Still I felt I was not going to be governed by prejudice, and had decided on this basis." Harr and Johnson, *op. cit.,* p. 135.

29. H. M. Gitleman, *Legacy of the Ludlow Massacre: A Chapter in American Industrial Relations* (Philadelphia: University of Pennsylvania Press, 1988), p. 222.

30. Graham Adams Jr., *Age of Industrial Violence, 1910-15: The Activities and Findings of the United States Commission on Industrial Relations* (New York: Columbia University Press, 1966), p. 162.

31. *Ibid.,* p. 163.

32. Karl and Katz, "American Private Philanthropic Foundations."

33. McGregor, *op. cit.,* p. 139.

34. Kohler, *op. cit.,* p. 47.

35. *Ibid.,* p. 47.

36. Albert F. Schenkel, *The Rich Man and the Kingdom: John D. Rockefeller, Jr., and the Protestant Establishment* (Minneapolis: Fortress Press, 1995), pp. 59-60.

37. After Mackenzie King returned to Canadian politics in 1917, Harr and Johnson note that John D. Rockefeller Jr. would never again "ask the Foundation to become involved in an activity that had anything to do with a personal or family problem, or for that matter with any highly personal preference of his own as to where money should go." Harr and Johnson, *op. cit.,* p. 145.

38. *Ibid.,* p. 146.

39. *Ibid.,* p. 146.

40. Karl and Katz, "Foundations and Ruling Class Elites."

41. Harr and Johnson, *op. cit.,* p. 147.

42. Edwin R. Embree and Julia Waxman, *Investment in People: The Story of the Julius Rosenwald Fund* (New York: Harper, 1949), p. 31.

43. Julius Rosenwald, "Principles of Public Giving" *Atlantic Monthly,* May 1929.

44. Rosenwald, "The Trend Away From Perpetuities," *Atlantic Monthly,* December 1930.

45. Rosenwald's views did, however, influence his family, including his grandson, Philip Stern (1926-1992), whose Stern Family Fund has been a leading source of grants for liberal nonprofits. Stern's will declared that the Stern Family Fund, which as of January 1994 had assets of $2 million, must spend its endowment by 2017. In an interview, Stern's son David explained that his father imposed this restriction because Philip Stern did "not want the dead hand to rule." Juliet Eilperin, "Phil Stern: Muckraking With Dollars," *Washington City Paper,* January 28, 1994. For more information about Julius Rosenwald's views about perpetuity, see Martin Morse Wooster, *Should Foundations Live Forever? The Question of Perpetuity* (Capital Research Center, 1998).

Chapter 2: The Ford Foundation

1. Cited in Harry S. Ashmore, *Unseasonable Truths: The Life of Robert Maynard Hutchins* (Boston: Little, Brown, 1989), p. 317.

2. Waldemar A. Nielsen, "The Donor's Role in Donor Intent," in *Donor Intent* (Indianapolis: Philanthropy Roundtable, 1993), p. 19.

3. William Greenleaf, *From These Beginnings: The Early Philanthropy of Henry and Edsel Ford, 1911-1936* (Detroit: Wayne State University Press, 1964), p. 7.

4. George Bernard Shaw, "Socialism for Millionaires," *Contemporary Review*, February 1896.

5. *Ibid.*

6. *Ibid.*

7. Ford N. Bryan, *Clara: Mrs. Henry Ford* (Dearborn, Michigan: Ford Books, 2001), pp. 113-114.

8. Greenleaf notes that Ford even received requests from peasants and factory workers in the Soviet Union, who "asked whether it was true that Ford was wealthier than any of the Czars." Greenleaf, *op. cit.,* p. 9.

9. Henry Ford with Samuel Crowther, *Today and Tomorrow* (Cambridge, Massachusetts: Productivity Press, 1978), pp. 179-180.

10. Greenleaf, *op. cit.,* p. 15.

11. By 1942, Ford Motor had 11,163 disabled employees, including 1,208 blind or partially blind employees, 322 with "organic heart ailments," 260 with one crippled arm, 157 with one leg amputated, and 111 deaf mutes. Edsel Ford, "Why We Employ Aged and Handicapped Workers," *Saturday Evening Post,* July 6, 1943.

12. David L. Lewis, *The Public Image of Henry Ford: An American Folk Hero and His Company* (Detroit: Wayne State University Press, 1976), p. 120.

13. Henry Ford with Samuel Crowther, *Moving Forward* (Garden City, New York: Doubleday, Doran, 1930), pp. 97-98.

14: Samuel S. Marquis, *Henry Ford: An Interpretation* (Boston: Little, Brown, 1923), pp. 105-06.

15. *Ibid.*, p. 104.

16. *Ibid.*, p. 111.

17. *Ibid.*, p. 112.

18. Charles E. Sorensen with Samuel T. Williamson, *My Forty Years With Ford* (New York: Norton, 1956), p. 21.

19. *Ibid.*, pp. 21-22.

20. *Ibid*, pp. 22-23.

21. Greenleaf, *op. cit.,* p. 126.

22. "Ford Calls Charity a Barbarous Thing," *New York Times,* May 30, 1932.

23. *Ibid.*

24. Judson C. Welliver, "Mr. Ford Is Interviewed," *American Review of Reviews,* September 1925.

25. Garet Garrett, *The Wild Wheel: The World of Henry Ford* (London: Cresset Press, 1952), pp. 153-154.

26. Allan Nevins and Frank Ernest Hill, *Ford: Decline and Renewal, 1933-1962* (New York: Scribner's, 1963), p. 411.

27. Robert Bendiner, "Report on the Ford Foundation," *New York Times Magazine,* February 1, 1953.

28. Greenleaf, *op. cit.,* p. 185.

29. Nevins and Hill, *op. cit.,* p. 410.

30. Greenleaf, *op. cit.,* p. 188.

31. Lally Weymouth, "Foundation Woes: The Saga of Henry Ford II, Part II," *New York Tunes Magazine,* March 12, 1978.

32. *Tax-Exempt Foundations: Hearings Before the Select Committee to Investigate Tax-Exempt Foundations and Comparable Organizations* (Washington, D.C.: Government Printing Office, 1952), pp. 221-222.

33. See Kate O'Neill, "Model Ts and Do-Si-Dos: Henry Ford and Traditional Dancing," *Michigan History,* January/February 2001. According to O'Neill, lovers of old dances have revived them in recent years using facilities built by Henry Ford.

34. Thomas C. Reeves, *Freedom and the Foundation: The Fund for the Republic in the Era of McCarthyism* (New York: Knopf, 1969), p. 284. In a 1978 interview with Lally Weymouth, Forest Marden, a long-time friend and associate of Henry Ford II, said that in its early years, the Ford Foundation's chief asset was some land in Dearborn, Michigan, which had some apartment buildings. "To everyone in Dearborn then," Marden said, "that land was the Ford Foundation." Weymouth, *op. cit.*

35. Francis X. Sutton, "The Ford Foundation: The Early Years," *Daedalus,* Winter 1987.

36. *Ibid.*

37. Cited in Sidney Hyman, *The Lives of William Benton* (Chicago: University of Chicago Press, 1969), p. 426.

38. Ashmore, *op. cit.,* p. 323.

39. *Ibid.,* p. 330.

40. *Ibid.,* pp. 330-331.

41. "Los Angeles: Pink Ford?" *Time,* July 27, 1953.

42. Weymouth, *op. cit.*

43. *The Fulton Lewis Jr. Report on the Fund for the Republic* (Washington: Special Reports, 1955), p. 9.

44. Weymouth, *op. cit.*

45. Leonard Silk and Mark Silk, *The American Establishment* (New York: Basic Books, 1980), p. 129.

46. Reeves, *op. cit.,* p. 332.

47. *Ibid.,* p. 337.

48. William F. Buckley Jr., "A Letter to Mr. Henry Ford," *National Review,* December 14, 1955.

49. "Ford's Letter on Fund," *New York Herald Tribune,* December 8, 1955.

50. "Robert Hutchins's Platonic Grove," *The Nation,* January 30, 1988. Ferry later became a philanthropist. The *Washington Post* reported in October 1993 that he was a "major benefactor" of the radical Institute for Policy Studies, and was honored by IPS during that organization's 30th anniversary. Hutchins, observed *American Scholar* editor Joseph Epstein, "was never able to attract truly serious people permanently to the Center; despite everything the place offered in the way of luxury and the little it asked for in the way of work, it must have resembled nothing so much as an endless talk show to which no one was tuned in." Joseph Epstein, "The Sad Story of the Boy Wonder," *Commentary,* March 1990.

51. Ben Hibbs, "Mr. Ford's Busy Billions," *Saturday Evening Post,* March 16, 1963.

52. This confusion between the Ford Motor Company and Ford Foundation continued even after the foundation began selling Ford Foundation stock. When the foundation gave a grant in the early 1960s to the Center for Community Change, a nonprofit headed by United Farm Workers organizer Cesar Chavez, California farm owners announced a boycott of Ford trucks. An early 1960s grant to the Mozambique Institute, a nonprofit branch of the Marxist-Leninist revolutionary group FRELIMO, prompted a Portuguese boycott of Ford Motor and some friction in U.S. negotiations over military bases in the Azores Islands. Peter D. Bell, "The Ford Foundation as a Transnational Actor," *International Organization,* Summer 1971.

53. Joe McCarthy, "The Ford Family," *Holiday,* September 1957.

54. Silk and Silk, *op. cit.,* p. 131. Donald David was the only person who wasn't a member of the Ford family who was both on the Ford Motor and the Ford Foundation boards. Hibbs, "Mr. Ford's Busy Billions."

55. For profiles of Heald, see William Barry Furlong, "Heald of the $2.5 Billion Foundation," *New York Times Magazine*, September 30, 1956, and "Philanthropoid No. 1," *Time*, June 10, 1957.

56. *Ibid.*, p. 131.

57. William L. Cary and Craig B. Bright, *The Law and the Lore of Endowment Funds* (New York: Ford Foundation, 1969), p. 17.

58. Peter Collier and David Horowitz, *The Fords: An American Epic* (New York: Summit, 1987), pp. 363-364.

59. These "Kennedy grants" were quite controversial at the time; Senator John J. Williams (R-Delaware) even introduced a bill that would have banned any foundation grants for two years to government officials who left their posts. Senator Albert Gore Sr. (D-Tennessee) argued that supporters of defeated Democratic presidential contender Eugene McCarthy were also entitled to aid, since "they were not only broken-hearted but broken-nosed. They were disappointed and beaten up." See Joseph Goulden, *The Money Givers* (New York: Random House, 1971), pp. 278-279.

In a 1989 interview, Peter Edelman was still defensive about receiving a Kennedy grant. Edelman told *Foundation News's* Roger M. Williams that the grants were "very constructive and important, something the Ford people should be proud of. Instead, they put their tails between their legs and said, 'I'm very sorry.'" Roger M. Williams, "To Each His Own," *Foundation News,* May/June 1989.

60. Weymouth, *op. cit.*

61. Collier and Horowitz, *op. cit.,* p. 397.

62. In 1966, the value of the Ford Foundation's investments was $3,051,000,000; by1977, it had fallen to $2,091,100,000. Professional investors, however, spotted the Ford Foundation's investment problems early. "When assurance of anonymity is given," an *Institutional Investor* article in 1968 observed, "institutional money managers are surprisingly outspoken at ripping away at Ford. The core of their criticism is this: though the Foundation spends freely from capital—$1.2 billion since its inception in 1936, and $308 million in 1966 and 1967—its assets are run as if the organization were wired to live solely off its dividends and interest." "The Problems of Being the Ford Foundation," *Institutional Investor*, November 1968.

These investors were particularly bothered by McGeorge Bundy's call in the 1967 Ford Foundation annual report that colleges and universities place more of their endowments in speculative investments. One of Warren Buffett's first public pronouncements was critiquing Bundy's advice, saying he would stick to the philosophy of value investing that ultimately made him a mega-billionaire. Martin Morse Wooster, "Warren Buffett: A Wealthy Philanthropist With Some Bad Ideas," *Foundation Watch*, November 2011.

63. "Crumbling Foundations," *Time,* October 7, 1974.

64. Waldemar A. Nielsen, *The Golden Donors: A New Anatomy of the Great Foundations* (New York: Dutton, 1985), p. 70. Despite this massive spending spree, the Ford Foundation managed to remain the nation's largest until 1998, when it was superseded by the Lilly Endowment, which in 1998 had $12.7 billion in assets compared to the Ford Foundation's $9.4 billion. Judith Havemann, "Lilly Endowment Is Nation's Top Giver," *Washington Post,* February 15, 1998.

65. Walter Hayes, *Henry: A Life of Henry Ford II* (New York: Grove Weidenfeld, 1990), p. 56.

66. "Excerpts from Henry Ford Letter," *New York Times*, January 12, 1977.

67. Weymouth, *op. cit.*

68. *Ibid.*

69. Jon Pepper, "The Henry Ford II Tapes: Ford Was Main Catalyst for Building Renaissance Center," *Detroit News,* September 21, 1994.

70. Hayes, *op. cit.,* p. 56.

71. Ian Wilhelm, "Michigan Asks Ford Foundation to Show It Is Following Donor's Intentions," *Chronicle of Philanthropy,* April 27, 2006.

72. Daniel Howes, "Bill Challenges Ford Foundation," *Detroit News,* June 7, 2006. See also Ian Wilhelm, "Bill Triggered by Ford Foundation Would Require Funds Set Up in Michigan to Direct Half of Giving Within State," *Chronicle of Philanthropy,* June14, 2006.

73. Thomas Bray, "Raiding the Ford Foundation," *New York Sun,* June 14, 2006.

74. John J. Miller, "Charity Begins at Home, But Must It Stay There?" *New York Times,* May 15, 2006.

75. Chad Livengood, "Ford Foundation to Open Detroit Office After 64-Year Hiatus," *Crain's Detroit Business,* May 30, 2017.

Chapter 3: The Carnegie Corporation of New York

1. Letter from Andrew Carnegie to John D. Rockefeller, February 8, 1903, posted on Carnegie Corporation website.

2. Andrew Carnegie, *Triumphant Democracy, or, Fifty Years' March of the Republic* (New York: Scribner's, 1886), p. 479.

3. *Ibid.,* p. 169.

4. Aileen McLaughlin, "Prenuptial Reveals Carnegie's True Plan," *Glasgow Sunday Herald,* May 1, 2005.

5. Andrew Carnegie, "The Gospel of Wealth," in Joseph Frazier Wall, ed., *The Andrew Carnegie Reader* (Pittsburgh: University of Pittsburgh, 1992), p. 133.

6. *Ibid.,* p. 135.

7. *Ibid.,* p. 135.

8. *Ibid.,* p. 139.

9. Andrew Carnegie, "The Best Use of Wealth," in Burton J. Hendrick, ed., *Miscellaneous Writing of Andrew Carnegie* (Garden City, New York: Doubleday, 1933), p. 206.

10. *Ibid.,* p. 207.

11. Frederick Lynch, *Personal Recollections of Andrew Carnegie* (New York: Fleming H. Revell, 1920), p. 135.

12. *Ibid.,* p. 135.

13. William C. Greenough, *It's My Retirement Money, Take Good Care of It: The TIAA-CREF Story* (Homewood, Illinois: Irwin, 1990), p. 15.

14. Information provided by Gay Clyburn of the Carnegie Foundation for the Advancement of Teaching, in an interview, March 5, 2013.

15. Information provided in emails from Gay Clyburn and Ann Whitfield of the Carnegie Foundation for the Advancement of Teaching, July 24, 2006.

16. Joseph Frazier Wall, *Andrew Carnegie* (Pittsburgh: University of Pittsburgh Press, 1989), p. 881. Historian Larry Fabian describes how one university president courted Carnegie during this period. "I'll tell you how I felt," the president said. "I felt like backing him up in the corner and saying, 'Give it!' And then I kept saying to myself, 'It's his money, it's his money.'" Larry L. Fabian, *Andrew Carnegie's Peace Endowment: The Tycoon, the President, and their Bargain of 1910* (Washington: Carnegie Endowment for International Peace, 1985), p. 22.

17. Michael Rosenthal, *Nicholas Miraculous: The Amazing Career of the Redoubtable Dr. Nicholas Murray Butler* (New York: Farrar, Straus, and Giroux, 2006), pp. 161-62.

18. *Ibid.,* p. 162.

19. For Edwin Ginn's role in the creation of the World Peace Foundation, see Richard Marchand, *The American Peace Movement and Social Reform, 1898-1918* (Ann Arbor, Michigan: University of Michigan Press, 1972), pp. 99-103. The World Peace Foundation is now controlled by Harvard University.

20. Rosenthal, *op. cit.,* p. 167.

21. Fabian, *op. cit.,* p. 41. Carnegie asked Secretary of State Philander Knox to serve on the new endowment's board, and at one point inserted a clause (later removed) saying that the Carnegie Endowment for International Peace could

contribute to political parties if "one party ever stands for measures leading to international peace and the other against this, contributions be made to the former."

22. Philip C. Jessup, *Elihu Root: Volume 2, 1905-1937* (New York: Dodd, Mead, 1938), p. 491.

23. Robert M. Lester, *Forty Years of Carnegie Giving* (New York: Scribner's, 1941), p. 166.

24. Wall, *op. cit.,* p. 883.

25. Burton J. Hendrick, *The Life of Andrew Carnegie* (New York: Harper, 1932), Vol. II, p. 351. Philip C. Jessup observes that Carnegie, while he obeyed Root's decision, disliked it intensely. Root, Jessup wrote, observed many years later that "Carnegie had a distrust of lawyers, regarding them as people who tried to prevent him from doing what he wanted to do." Jessup, *op. cit.,* p. 491.

26. Robert E. Kohler, *Partners in Science: Foundations and Natural Scientists, 1900-1945* (Chicago: University of Chicago Press, 1991), p. 56.

27. Theodore Jones, *Carnegie Libraries Across America: A Public Legacy* (New York: Preservation Press/Wiley, 1997), p. 101.

28. Alvin Johnson, *Pioneer's Progress: An Autobiography* (New York: Viking, 1952), p. 236.

29. *Ibid.,* pp. 236-237.

30. *Ibid.,* p. 238.

31. *Ibid.,* p. 239.

32. Ellen Condliffe Lagemann, *The Politics of Knowledge: The Carnegie Corporation, Philanthropy, and Public Policy* (University of Chicago Press, 1992), p. 27.

33. Jones, *op. cit.,* p. 102.

34. *Ibid.,* p. 66.

35. *Ibid.,* p. 68.

36. According to a 1965 profile in *Fortune,* Gardner became president of the Carnegie Corporation as a result of connections he made serving in the Office of Strategic Services during World War II. Robert P. Elson, "An 'In' Man for the Cabinet," *Fortune,* November 1965.

37. Waldemar Nielsen, *The Golden Donors: A New Anatomy of the Great Foundations* (New York: Dutton, 1985), p. 134.

38. I discuss the role the Carnegie Corporation played in creating public television in Martin Morse Wooster, *Great Philanthropic Mistakes* (Washington, D.C.: Hudson Institute, 2006).

39. Lagemann, *op. cit.,* p. 242.

40. Paul Desruisseaux, "What Would Andrew Carnegie Think About How His Money Is Used Today?" *Chronicle of Higher Education,* August 7, 1985. See also Paul Desruisseaux, "Celebrating the Legacy of Andrew Carnegie's Philanthropy," *Chronicle of Higher Education,* September 11, 1985.

41. *New York Times,* January 22, 1993.

42. Claudia Dreifus, "It Is Better to Give than to Receive," *New York Times Magazine,* December 14, 1997.

43. Patrick Reilly, "Replacing Welfare with Child Care: Foundations Lay Groundwork for Clinton's Costly Proposals," *Foundation Watch,* June 1998.

44. Debra Viadero, "Carnegie Corp. Repeats History With New Library Grants," *Education Week,* June 16, 1999.

45. Tamar Lewin, "Leading Philanthropists Get Carnegie Medals," *New York Times,* December 11, 2001. I discuss Gregorian's role as philanthropic adviser to Walter Annenberg in *Great Philanthropic Mistakes.* For an extended interview with Gregorian, see "A Conversation with Vartan Gregorian," *Humanities,* September 2003.

46. "In His Own Words: A Q&A With Vartan Gregorian," interview posted on Carnegie Corporation of New York website.

47. Caroline Bermudez, "Why Andrew Carnegie Still Matters," *Chronicle of Philanthropy*, June 9, 2011.

48. Leslie Lenkowsky, "The Carnegie Corporation at 100," *Philanthropy*, Winter 2011.

49. "The Centenarians Square Up," *The Economist*, June 9, 2011.

Chapter 4: John D. and Catherine T.
MacArthur Foundation

1. Kiki Levathes, "The Busiest Billionaire: 'My Advice to Youth? Go On Welfare,'" *New York Daily News*, July 13, 1976.

2. Tom Burke, "The Sweeter Options of John D. MacArthur and Truman Capote," *Esquire*, December 1970.

3. Stewart Alsop, "America's New Big Rich," *Saturday Evening Post*, July 17, 1965.

4. T.A. Wise, "The Incorrigible John MacArthur," *Fortune*, July 1958.

5. Kiki Levathes, "The Busiest Billionaire: A Penny Saved is a Billion Earned," *New York Daily News*, July 12, 1976.

6. William Hoffman, *The Stockholder* (New York: Lyle Stuart, 1969), p. 19.

7. "John D. MacArthur of Bankers Life and Casualty," *Nation's Business*, July 1974.

8. Lewis Beman, "The Last Billionaires," *Fortune*, November 1976.

9. Joshua Muravchik, "MacArthur's Millions," *American Spectator*, January 1992.

10. Anne Matthews, "The MacArthur Truffle Hunt," *New York Times Magazine*, June 7, 1992.

11. Richard T. Griffin, "The Feuding MacArthurs," *New York Times*, January 23, 1977.

12. Phyllis Berman with R. Lee Sullivan, "Limousine Liberal," *Forbes*, October 26, 1992. In January 1994, the J. Roderick MacArthur Foundation announced that it was shrinking. Its long-time president, Lance Lindblom, was not replaced when he departed for a professorship at DePaul University, and the foundation's staff was cut from four to one. In addition, the foundation announced that it would no longer consider unsolicited grants, and with the exception of three organizations fighting the death penalty and censorship, would be devoted to the personal philanthropic interests of Rod MacArthur's children, Solange, Gregoire, and John R. "Rick" MacArthur. Charles Storch, "Foundation Shrinks Its Circle of Recipients," *Chicago Tribune*, January 21, 1994. Gregoire "Greg" MacArthur died in 2001 of a heart attack at age 53. His chief political activity was, in 2000, to form a nonprofit called Citizens for Strategic Voting, which bought full-page advertisements in the *New York Times* urging people to vote for the Green Party, stating "A vote for Ralph Nader is not a vote for Bush." For his obituary, see Wolfgang Saxon, "Greg MacArthur, Philanthropist and Green Party Supporter," *New York Times*, December 6, 2001.

13. Alsop, "America's New Big Rich."

14. Burke, "The Sweeter Options of John D. MacArthur."

15. Jon Nordheimer, "Florida's Accessible Billionaire," *New York Times*, June 3, 1973. After John D. MacArthur's death, the Colonnades Hotel steadily deteriorated. The hotel was closed in 1987 after a ceiling beam crashed into the hotel's main dining room. The Colonnades was razed in 1990. Fred Lowery, "Celebrity Days Remembered As Colonnades Hotel is Razed," *South Florida Sun-Sentinel*, February 17, 1990.

16. Ruth Dean, "The MacArthur Foundation," *Foundation News*, March/April 1982.

17. According to T.A. Wise, MacArthur was "thrifty to the point that would embarrass a professional Scot." MacArthur's frugal habits included saving half-smoked cigarettes and refusing collect calls—and then returning them

collect. According to Wise, someone once burnt the baked beans at a Bankers Life picnic. The frugal MacArthur showed up next day in the staff cafeteria with a syrup that he claimed would make burnt baked beans tasty. Wise, *op. cit.*

By 1976, MacArthur looked so poor that Lewis Beman declared that he "looks less like a billionaire than a retired postal clerk whose Social Security check was being stretched too thin." At the time of the interview, the windows in MacArthur's five-year-old Cadillac were broken, and MacArthur's apartment "is furnished with odds and ends that might have been picked up decades ago." Beman, *op. cit.*

At his 80th birthday party in 1977, MacArthur thriftily took some leftover bacon and sausage and put it into a napkin to save for breakfast the next day. Gayle Pallesen, "A Billionaire's Birthday: Even the Icing Was Plaid," *Washington Post,* March 14, 1977.

18. Brenda Shapiro, "Shaking the Foundation," *Chicago,* June 1992.

19. Carol Oppenheim, "Billionaire MacArthur: A Contented Man," *Chicago Tribune,* March 15, 1976.

20. Nancy Kriplen, *The Eccentric Billionaire: John D. MacArthur—Empire Builder, Reluctant Philanthropist, Relentless Adversary* (New York: AMACOM, 2008), p. 158. Kriplen does not give any details as to when this documentary aired.

21. *Ibid.,* pp. 143-47, 178.

22. Christina Robb, "The Foundation Behind the 'Genius Grants,'" *Boston Globe Magazine,* April 13, 1986.

23. Muravchik, *op. cit.*

24. Shapiro, *op. cit.*

25. Muravchik, *op. cit.*

26. Shapiro, *op. cit.*

27. See Martin Morse Wooster, "The MacArthur Fellowships: The Oscars of the Multicultural Elite," *Philanthropy Culture, & Society,* January 1996.

28. Matthews, *op. cit.*

29. Denise Shekerjian, *Uncommon Genius: How Great Ideas Are Born* (New York: Viking, 1990), pp. 97-98.

30. Liz McMillen, "MacArthur Foundation Expected to Review, and Perhaps Revise, Its Grants Program," *Chronicle of Higher Education,* March 8, 1989. However, Daniel Socolow, who became director of the MacArthur Fellows Program in 1997, said that he would like to give MacArthur Fellowships to entrepreneurs. "I'd like to see more entrepreneurs [winning]," Socolow said. "We wouldn't fund Steve Jobs when he had Apple Computer, but maybe when he was in his garage playing with a strange box." Dyan Machan, "Venture Capital for Geniuses," *Forbes,* February 23, 1998.

31. John Leo, "MacArthur Awards More About Gender Than Genius," *New Orleans Times-Picayune,* June 28, 1995. I discuss the MacArthur Fellows program at greater length in *Great Philanthropic Mistakes.*

32. Mark Scheffler, "Genius Grants Don't Pay Off in Literature," *Crain's Chicago Business,* January 24, 2005.

33. Paul Deruisseaux, "MacArthur Foundation Seeks a Narrower, Deeper Focus," *Chronicle of Higher Education,* July 14, 2000.

34. For details of recent MacArthur Foundation grants, see Martin Morse Wooster, "The MacArthur Foundation," *Foundation Watch,* September 2005. See also Neil Hrab, "The MacArthur Foundation on Foreign Policy and Defense," *Foundation Watch,* September 2003.

35. Steve Hendershot, "The 800-lb. Gorilla of Philanthropy," *Crain's Chicago Business,* August 20, 2007.

36. "MacArthur Grants Support Efforts to Ensure Fair Elections, Protect Voting Rights," press release from the MacArthur Foundation dated August 9, 2012.

37. "MacArthur Announces Grant to Lady Gaga's Born This Way Foundation," press release from the MacArthur Foundation dated February 27, 2012.

38. Cheryl L. Reed, "MacArthur Brass Lives Large–Frugal Founder Didn't," *Chicago Sun-Times,* May 23, 2004.

39. Curtis Skinner, "Charity to Invest $75 Million to Reduce U.S. Jail Population," Reuters, February 11, 2015.

40. Alex Daniels, "MacArthur's $50 Million Climate Change Push Aims at Voters," *Chronicle of Philanthropy,* August 19, 2015.

41. "MacArthur Awards $19 Million to Bolster Local Climate Change Solutions," *Philanthropy News Digest,* May 5, 2017.

42. Steve Johnson, "MacArthur Names 8 Semifinalists for $100 Million Grant," *Chicago Tribune,* February 15, 2017. For a profile of one of the semifinalists, the Himalayan Cataract Project, see Martin Morse Wooster, "Restoring Eyesight: A Simple Solution With Huge Consequences," *Philanthropy Daily,* May 11, 2017.

43. Gail MarksJarvis "Benefit Chicago Fund Makes First Round of Loans to Six Small Businesses, Nonprofits," *Chicago Tribune,* May 16, 2017.

44. Alex Daniels, "Inside MacArthur's Rapid Strategic Shift to 'Big Bets,'" *Chronicle of Philanthropy,* January 11, 2016.

45. Sam Worley, "Can The MacArthur Foundation Find Its Mojo?" *Chicago Magazine,* September 2015.

Chapter 5: The Pew Charitable Trusts

1. Scott Allen, "The Greening of a Movement," *Boston Globe,* October 19, 1997.

2. J. Howard Pew, *Governmental Planning and Control as Applied to Business and Industry: A Common Sense Plea by an American Citizen* (Princeton, New Jersey: Guild of Brackett Lecturers, 1938), pp. 9-10.

3. Later renamed Sunoco, Sun Oil retained its independence until 2012, when Energy Transfer Partners acquired the company for $5.3 billion. R. Anderson Pew, the last Pew family member on the Sunoco board, was forced to leave in 2009 when he reached the mandatory retirement age of 72. Michael Armstrong, "For Sunoco, An 'Everything Must Go' Deal at Last," *Philadelphia Inquirer,* May 2, 2012.

4. John C. Schmidt III, "Sun Ship: Vessels of Progress," article posted by the Pennsylvania Center for the Book in the fall of 2010, pabook.libraries.psu.edu/palitmap/SunShip.html. The shipyard was closed in 1989 and demolished in 2005, to be replaced by a horseracing track and casino.

5. August W. Giebelhaus, *Business and Government in the Oil Industry: A Case Study of Sun Oil, 1876-1945* (Greenwich, Connecticut: JAI Press, 1980), p. 207.

6. "The Republican Party: Up From the Grave" *Fortune,* August 1939.

7. Dan Rottenberg, "The Sun Gods," *Philadelphia Magazine,* November 1975. Rottenberg estimates that the Pew family gave about $2.7 million to Republicans during the Roosevelt administration and $600,000 between 1945 and 1972.

8. Nielsen, *op. cit.,* pp. 170-171.

9. Potomacus (pseudonym), "Pew of Pennsylvania," *The New Republic,* May 8, 1944.

10. "J. N. Pew Jr.'s Help to Dewey Scorned," *New York Times,* March 20, 1960.

11. Mary Sennholtz, ed., *Faith and Freedom: The Journal of a Great American, J. Howard Pew* (Grove City, Pennsylvania: Grove City College, 1975), pp. 86-87.

12. Lucinda Fleeson, "How a Foundation Reinvented Itself," *Philadelphia Inquirer,* April 27, 1992.

13. Jack Willoughby, "Putting on Heirs," *Institutional Investor,* March 1997.

14. "Sun Oil," *Fortune,* February 1941.
15. *The Chairman's Final Report to the Members of the National Lay Committee* (New York: National Council of Churches, 1956), p. 169.
16, John Wicklein, "Layman Charges Church Meddling," *New York Times,* March 20, 1960.
17. Carl F. H. Henry, *Confessions of a Theologian: An Autobiography* (Irving, Texas: Word, 1986), p. 156.
18. Arnold Forster and Benjamin R. Epstein, *Danger on the Right* (New York: Random House, 1964), p. 191. Forster and Epstein say the Christian Freedom Foundation's positions included calling Social Security "the older generation stealing from the younger," the income tax as "Communist doctrine," and labor unions as "stemming from Socialism."
19. Nielsen, *op. cit.,* p. 163.
20. *J. Howard Pew Freedom Trust Annual Report 1985* (Philadelphia: Glenmede Trust, 1985), pp. 16-17.
21. Eileen Shanahan, "House Tax Panel Eases Rule on Foundation Spending," *New York Times,* October 14, 1971.
22. Rottenberg, *op. cit.*
23. David Diamond, "The Pews of Philadelphia: The Subtle Control of a Vast Fortune," *New York Times,* October 25, 1981.
24. Fleeson, *op. cit.*
25. Kathleen Teltsch, "Pew Memorial Trust Issues Report, First in 22 Years of Discreet Charity," *New York Times,* June 23, 1980.
26. Lucinda Fleeson, "Little-Known Pew Charities Let Light In," *Philadelphia Inquirer,* February 24, 1987.
27. *Ibid.*
28. Kristin A. Goss, "New Head of Pew Trusts Stirs Strong Passions in Quest for Radical Philanthropy," *Chronicle of Philanthropy,* November 8, 1988.
29. "Reorganization at Glenmede Trust: Philanthropy in the 1980s," *Chronicle of Philanthropy,* January 1988.
30. *Pew Charitable Trusts 1988 Annual Report* (Philadelphia: Pew Charitable Trusts, 1989), p. 13.
After Langfitt left Pew in 1994, he became president of the College of Physicians of Philadelphia. Langfitt died in 2005. For obituaries, see Adam Bernstein, "Pew Trusts Leader Thomas Langfitt Dies at 78," *Washington Post,* August 9, 2005. Gayle Ronan Sims, "Thomas Langfitt; Led Pew Charitable Trusts," *Philadelphia Inquirer,* August 9. 2005.
31. Roger M. Williams, "From Inside Right to Out Front," *Foundation News,* May/June1991.
32. Dan Rottenberg, "The Pew Charitable Trusts: Foundation for the Future," *Town and Country,* December 1991.
33. Lucinda Fleeson, "An Extra $35 Million a Year? Call In The 'Dream Team,'" *Philadelphia Inquirer,* April 26, 1992.
34. Lucinda Fleeson, "Trusts' New Direction Leaves Region Behind," *Philadelphia Inquirer,* April 26, 1992.
35. Fleeson, "How a Foundation Reinvented Itself," *op. cit.*
36. Kathleen Teltsch, "2d-Largest Philanthropy Widens Role," *New York Times,* August 27, 1990.
37. Williams, *op. cit.*
38. Jennifer Moore, "Council on Foundations Hobbled by 'Political Correctness,' Report Charges," *Chronicle of Philanthropy,* May 4, 1993.
39. Letter to the author, dated December 16, 1997.
40. Paul Starobin, "Raging Moderates," *National Journal,* May 10, 1997.
41. Judith Havemann, "Bankrolling an Activist Agenda," *Washington Post,* March 29,1998.

42. Robert Lerner and Althea K. Nagai, "The Pew Charitable Trusts: Revitalizing 'the Spirit of the '60s,'" Capital Research Center, *Alternatives in Philanthropy,* November 1995.

43. *The Pew Charitable Trusts Public Policy Program—1996 Grants.*

44. *The Pew Charitable Trust Environment Program—1996 Grants.*

45. Stephen Salisbury, "Private Money, Public Power: Pew Charitable Trusts Develops a Hands-On Role," *Philadelphia Inquirer,* October 13, 1996.

46. *Ibid.*

47. Dan Rottenberg, "The Agony, the Ecstasy, and the Guidelines," *Philadelphia Style,* March 2004, posted on broadstreetreview.com.

48. Salisbury, *op. cit.*

49. Nathan Gorenstein, "Pew Charitable Trusts Sells Last of Sun Oil Stock," *Philadelphia Inquirer,* August 5, 1997.

50. Richard O'Mara, "Buzzword for Pew: 'Pro-Active,'" *Baltimore Sun,* March 17, 1997.

51. Reichert has worked with J. Howard "Howdy" Pew II, a grandnephew of J. Howard Pew and an ardent conservationist.

52. Starobin, *op. cit.* For an interview with Reichert, see "Forging, Founding, and Funding," *Foundation News and Commentary,* July/August 1994. Pew activities have been denounced by liberals, who perceive its program directors as arrogant. "They're bullies," Beth Daley of the National Committee for Responsive Philanthropy told Paul Starobin. "Some of us were joking around that we should have a Pew liberation front–committed to getting environmental organizations off the Pew dole." Starobin, *op. cit.*

53. Stephen Salisbury, "Private Money, Public Power: Pew Ventures Into New and Unusual Territory," *Philadelphia Inquirer,* October 14, 1996.

54. *Ibid.*

55. Alicia Shepard, "Buying Press Coverage: How Pew's Civic Journalism Movement Put Newspapers, Radio, and Television Stations on the Payroll," *Foundation Watch,* August 1996. G. Bruce Knecht, "Why a Big Foundation Gives Newspapers Cash to Change Their Ways," *Wall Street Journal,* October 17, 1996. Howard Kurtz, "The New Reform School," *Washington Post,* May 12, 1997. For an analysis of the ideas behind the civic journalism movement, see Scott Sherman, "The Public Defender," *Lingua Franca,* April 1998.

56. Edwin Diamond, "Civic Journalism: An Experiment That Didn't Work," *Columbia Journalism Review,* July/August 1997.

57. Lewis A. Friedland, "Open Source Interview: The Evolution of Public Journalism," in Jack Rosenberry and Burton St. John III, eds., *Public Journalism 2.0: The Promise and Reality of a Citizen-Engaged Press* (New York: Routledge, 2010), p. 58.

58. David S. Broder, "Panel Urges Americans to Turn Off TV, Get Involved," *Washington Post,* June 25, 1998.

59. Ben Wildavsky, "Talking the Talk on Social Security," *National Journal,* November 1, 1997.

60. Howard Kurtz, "Adversaries Join Campaign to Improve Coverage of State, Local Politics," *Washington Post,* May 28, 1998. Daniel Le Duc and Charles Babington, "A Call for More TV Time for Campaigns," *Washington Post,* June 18, 1998. Jodie Morse, "Making Dirty Tricksters Behave Themselves," *National Journal,* July 5, 1997.

61. Howard Kurtz, "A Reporter with Lust in Her Hearts," *Washington Post,* July 6, 1998.

62. Rob Gurwitt, "With Strings Attached," *Governing,* April 1998.

63. Annie Groer and Ann Gerhart, "Rap's Social Conscience," *Washington Post,* May 13, 1998.

64. "A Matter of Trust," *Philanthropy,* May/June 2000.

65. Rebecca W. Rimel, "Charity and Strategy: Philanthropy's Evolving Role," accessed at pewtrusts.com, April 13, 2006.

66. "Pew Charitable Trusts Plans to Split From Money-Management Firm," *Philadelphia Inquirer,* July 27, 2003.

67. David Bank, "Pew Casts Itself in Fresh Role as Public Lobby," *Wall Street Journal,* November 6, 2003. See also Marianne D. Hurst, "Pew Seeks Flexibility Through New 'Public Charity' Status," *Education Week,* November 19, 2003, and Stephanie Strom, "Pew Charitable Trusts Will become Public Charity," *New York Times,* November 7, 2003.

68. Rottenberg, "The Agony, The Ecstasy, and the Guidelines."

69. For Alice Goldfarb Marquis article, see *New York Times,* August 9, 1999. For Pew proposals, see David N. Dobryzynski, "Heavyweight Foundation Throws Itself Behind Idea of a Cultural Policy," *New York Times,* August 2, 1999.

70. Douglas Jehl, "Charity is New Force in Environmental Fight," *New York Times,* June 28, 2001. For an analysis of Pew efforts to stop global warming, see Ron Arnold, "The Pew Charitable Trusts: Global Warming Power Nexus," *Foundation Watch,* May 2004.

71. Wendy Tanaka, "Groups Mobilize to Get Nation's Young Adults to Vote," *Philadelphia Inquirer,* September 15, 2004.

72. Ryan Sager, "Buyer 'Reform,'" *New York Post,* March 17, 2005. See also Martin Morse Wooster, "Too Good to be True," *Wall Street Journal,* April 1, 2005, and David Hogberg, "Something Stinks at Pew," *Foundation Watch,* June 2005.

73. *New York Post,* March 25, 2005.

74. Daniel Libit, "Taking the Long View on Green," *Politico,* December 7, 2009.

75. Margaret Kriz, "Going Super-Green," *National Journal,* March 19, 2007.

76. Libit, *op. cit.*

77. Brian Seasholes, "The Green Pipeline," *Green Watch,* October 2012. Other American foundations involved in the anti-oil sands effort include the Moore, Hewlett, and Packard foundations.

78. John Fund, "The Net Neutrality Coup," *Wall Street Journal,* December 21, 2010.

79. Scott Walter, "Pew and the Gang Ride Again: Citizens' Free Speech Still in Danger," *Foundation Watch,* April 2011.

80. William Schambra, "James Q. Wilson and 'Broken Windows' Philanthropy," Philanthropy Daily, March 11, 2012.

81. Rebecca W. Rimel, "A Response to William Schambra," Philanthropy Daily, March 22, 2012. Addressing Schambra's main point, Rimel said that Pew funded the sort of small-scale charity Schambra favored, but that it would also continue to fund larger, "root cause" projects.

Rimel did not state when Joseph N. Pew III made this statement, but in testimony before the Montgomery County, Pennsylvania, Orphans Court in December 2003, about the Barnes Foundation she used a similar statement without attributing it.

82. Helena Andrews, "CEO Who Makes $4 Million a Year Is Auctioning Off Her Record Collection to Employees," *Washington Post,* March 11, 2015. Rick Cohen, "Rebecca Rimel's Millions in Compensation at Pew Charitable Trusts and Elsewhere," *Nonprofit Quarterly,* March 12, 2015.

83. Rebecca W. Rimel and R. Anderson Pew, "Just The Facts," *Town and Country,* June/July 2017.

Chapter 6: The Barnes Foundation

1. Benjamin Forgey, "For Art's Sake," *Washington Post Magazine,* April 11, 1993.

2. *Ibid.*

3. Carl W. McCardle, "The Terrible Tempered Dr. Barnes," *Saturday Evening Post,* March 21, 1942.

4. A.H. Shaw, "De Medici in Person," *New Yorker,* September 22, 1928.

5. Howard Greenfeld, *The Devil and Dr. Barnes: Portrait of An American Art Collector* (New York: Viking, 1987), p. 3.

6. Albert C. Barnes, "Sabotage of Public Education in Philadelphia," in *Art and Education: A Collection of Essays,* 3rd ed. (Merion, Pennsylvania: Barnes Foundation, 1954), p. 276.

7. Greenfeld, *op. cit.,* p. 5.

8. Richard Blow, "The Barnes Collection: Wow!"*Washington Post,* April 29, 1993.

9. Greenfeld, *op. cit.,* p. 27.

10. Henry Hart, *Dr. Barnes of Merion: An Appreciation* (New York: Farrar, Straus, 1963), p. 70.

11. Greenfeld, *op. cit.,* p.31.

12. Edward J. Sozanski, "Barnes at the Pennsylvania Academy: A Scandal in 1923," *Philadelphia Inquirer,* May 4, 2012.

13. Albert C. Barnes, "The Barnes Foundation," *New Republic,* March 14, 1923.

14. Violetta de Mazia, "The Barnes Foundation," *House and Garden,* December 1942 (emphasis in text).

15. Gilbert M. Cantor, *The Barnes Foundation: Reality vs. Myth* (Philadelphia: Chilton, 1963), p. 200.

16. Cynthia Flannery Stine, "My Private War with Dr. Barnes," *Harper's Magazine,* August 1956.

17. Milton Esterow, "Barnes Bars Barr," *Art News,* December 1991.

18. Stine, *op. cit.*

19. McCardle, *op. cit.*

20. Cited in Lois G. Forer, "No Place for the Rabble," *Horizon,* Spring 1964.

21. Quotation from "Dr. Barnes Plans to Desert Merion," *New York Times,* April 16, 1927. See also "Negro Center Plan Incenses Merion," *New York Times,* April 14, 1927, and "Barnes Trust in Merion," *New York Times,* April 20, 1927.

22. Greenfield, *op. cit.,* p. 277.

23. *Ibid.,* p. 281.

24. *Ibid.,* p. 281.

25. Cantor, *op. cit.,* p. 187.

26. *Ibid.,* p. 182-184.

27. *Ibid.,* p. 194

28. Hart, *op. cit.,* pp. 117-18. Hart notes that when Barnes sold the A.C. Barnes Company to American Zonite Corp. for $6 Million in 1929, he promptly invested money in tax-exampts,"a fact people should bear in mind when they think,or say, the Barnes Foundation was created to avoid the payment of taxes."

29. Cantor, *op. cit.,* p. 198, 200.

30. *Ibid.,* p. 209.

31. Dorothy McCardle, "Mrs. Barnes Tells Why Doors Bang Again on Art Treasures," *Washington Post,* August 17, 1952.

32. Cantor, *op. cit.,* p. 145.

33. Forer, *op. cit.* According to Forer, during this era Leningrad University art historian Igor N. Diakonoff applied for admission to the Barnes galleries and was rejected. Diakonoff "declared on the basis of his experience at the Barnes Foundation that America was a police state."

34. Greenfeld, *op. cit.,* p. 290.

35. Lucinda Fleeson, "Lincoln U. To Control $1 Billion Barnes Art Collection," *Philadelphia Inquirer,* September 27, 1988.

36. Fleeson, "Lincoln U. To Control $1 Billion Barnes Art Collection." Franklin Williams died in 1989.

37. Lucinda Fleeson, "Opening Doors," *Philadelphia Inquirer,* June 13, 1990.

38. John Anderson, *Art Held Hostage: The Battle Over the Barnes Collection* (New York: Norton, 2003), p. 93.

39. Carol Vogel, "A Controversial Man in an Eccentric Place," *New York Times,* April 4,1993. Some evidence of the exaggeration about the expenses needed to restore the Barnes Foundation is provided in A.F. Brown, *The Barnes Case X Grand Scam: How the Trustees Faked It* (Broomall, Pennsylvania: A.F. Brown, 1993) Brown's study should be treated with caution, as he engages in relentless hyperbole, such as comparing the Barnes battles to the Dreyfus case.

40. *Washington Post,* May 2, 1993.

41. David D'Arcy, "Barnes Storm," *Vanity Fair;* August 1991.

42. Lucinda Fleeson, "From Crisis to Dilemma The Art-Sale Plan Was Doomed and Dashed," *Philadelphia Inquirer,* July 22, 1991.

43. Dale Russakoff, "A Bitter, Beautiful Legacy: The Bizarre Life—And Afterlife—of Albert Barnes," *Washington Post,* May 2, 1993.

44. "Once is Enough," *Art News,* September 1992.

45. Jennifer Moore, "Barnes Foundation, De Mazia Trust Drop Lawsuits Against Each Other," *Chronicle of Philanthropy,* January 26, 1995.

46. Edward J. Sozanski, "The Bottom Line at the Barnes Foundation: It's Now a Museum," *Philadelphia Inquirer,* November 19, 1995.

47. Lee Rosenbaum, "Masterpieces Back Home, Hung in Same Weird Way," *Wall Street Journal,* November 28, 1995.

48. Leonard W. Rosenberg, "Barnes Foundation Seeks Court Action to Hold Gala," *Philadelphia Inquirer,* October 13, 1995.

49. Leonard W. Rosenberg, "Court Allows Barnes' Guests at Dinner a Feast for Eyes, Too," *Philadelphia Inquirer,* November 9, 1995.

50. Robert W. Fowler, "A Cha-Cha Near a Cezanne? Court Opens Barnes Door," *Philadelphia Inquirer,* September 14, 1996.

51. Kyle York Spencer, "Gallery Is Urged to Stay Shut," *Philadelphia Inquirer,* November 16, 1995.

52. Kyle York Spencer, "Barnes Foundation Ordered to Cut Its Hours," *Philadelphia Inquirer,* December 14, 1995.

53. Anne Barnard, "Barnes to Open for Summer," *Philadelphia Inquirer;* July 3, 1996.

54. Kyle York Spencer, "Two Groups Say L. Merion Board Shows Preference," *Philadelphia Inquirer,* January 19, 1996.

55. Anne Barnard, "Bold Style Was Help and Hindrance to Barnes Chief," *Philadelphia Inquirer,* February 11, 1998, and Anne Barnard, "Barnes, L. Merion Go Back to Court over Zoning Dispute," *Philadelphia Inquirer,* January 28, 1997.

56. Anne Barnard, "L. Merion Files Suit Against Glanton," *Philadelphia Inquirer,* March 5, 1996.

57. Anderson, *op. cit.,* p. 129.

58. Anne Barnard, "Traffic Snarls An Uneasy Relationship," *Philadelphia Inquirer,* April 14, 1996.

59. Anne Barnard. "Countersuit is Filed by L. Merion," *Philadelphia Inquirer,* June 20, 1996.

60. Patrick Kerkstra, "Nearly Broke, the Barnes Foundation Calls for Help," *Philadelphia Inquirer,* September 10, 2000.

61. Anne Barnard, "Lower Merion Countersues Barnes Foundation's Chief," *Philadelphia Inquirer,* November 27, 1996.

62. Anne Barnard, "Court Curtails Barnes' Hours and Admissions," *Philadelphia Inquirer,* August 8, 1997. Ralph Vigoda, "At the Barnes, Court Order Keeps Visitors Out," *Philadelphia Inquirer,* September 4, 1997.

63. Anne Barnard, "Judge Throws Out Barnes Lawsuit Against Lower Merion Township," *Philadelphia Inquirer,* September 27, 1997.

64. Anne Barnard, "2 Montco Judges Affirm Zone Board, Barnes a Museum," *Philadelphia Inquirer,* November 3, 1997.

65. Anne Barnard, "Bold Style Was Help and Hindrance to Barnes Chief."

66. Shannon P. Duffy, "Federal Judge Rules Barnes Must Pay Fees to Neighbors," *Legal Intelligencer,* July 20, 2006. The case was effectively concluded in

March 2001, when the Third Circuit Court of Appeals ruled against the Barnes Foundation. "We must conclude that the Barnes cynically brought this frivolous action to capitalize on its minority status to achieve its goal of alleviating its parking problems," noted Judge Morton I. Greenberg. "The Barnes's representatives and the Barnes staff should have recognized that persons may controvert their views without being racists." Negotiations continued for another five years over whether the Barnes Foundation should pay damages, and if so, how much it should pay.

67. Bernard, *Ibid.* The best analysis of the Rome suit is Shannon P. Duffy, "Rome Sues Glanton, Barnes," *Philadelphia Legal Intelligences,* July 30, 1996. See also Michael Janofsky, "Italians Sue the Barnes Because Show Didn't Go to Rome," *New York Times,* July 31, 1996.

68. See 1998 stories in the *Philadelphia Inquirer:* Larry King, "A Quiet Man Taking the Reins at Barnes," February 11, 1998. Rich Henson, Stephanie A. Stanley, and Julia M. Klein, "Barnes Hires Interim Manager," February 11, 1998. Anne Barnard and Peter Dobrin, "Barnes Switches Course," February 15, 1998.

69. Rich Henson, Stephanie A. Stanley, and Julia M. Klein, "Barnes Foundation Appoints an Interim Manager," *Philadelphia Inquirer,* February 13, 1998.

70. Stephanie A. Stanley, "Town to Govern Building Usage," *Philadelphia Inquirer,* June 15, 1998.

71. Edward J. Sozanski, "Glanton's Tenure: A Mission to Alter Albert Barnes' Dream," *Philadelphia Inquirer,* February 18, 1998.

72. Russakoff, *op. cit.*

73. Eric Gibson, "Barnes Storming," *Washington Times,* April 30, 1992.

74. Cited in Lawrence Osborne, "Are a Donor's Wishes Sacred?" *National Law Journal,* July 3, 1995.

75. "The Barnes Foundation Receives Permission to Remain Open During the Summer Months," *PR Newswire,* August 5, 1998.

76. Kerkstra, "Nearly Broke, The Barnes Foundation Calls for Help."

77. Jeffrey Toobin, "Battle for the Barnes," *New Yorker,* January 29, 2002.

78. Joann Loviglio, "Former Lincoln University President Suing Former Barnes Chief," Associated Press, July 30, 2001. "Former Lincoln President's Suit Against Former Counsel Dismissed," Associated Press, August 1, 2001.

79. Patricia Horn, "Pennsylvania Governor-Elect Offers Help in Battle Over Art Collection's Move," *Philadelphia Inquirer,* January 17, 2003.

80. This document, called "Agreement," was made part of the court record in *In Re Barnes Foundation.* It is available on the Friends of the Barnes Foundation website, barnesfriends.org.

81. *Ibid.,* p. 15.

82. *Ibid.,* p. 56-57. As part of the cross-examination, Rimel was asked, "If there was a provision in the trust of the Pew Charitable Trusts, for example, that represents the donors' intent, you would adhere to the intent of the donor?" Judge Ott said that Rimel did not have to answer the question because Rimel was "not the one that will be overseeing the adherence to the intent" of the Barnes Foundation. Rimel did say that she thought it was "the responsibility of the board that's charged with the stewardship of the institution to determine that and carry it out." *Ibid.,* pp. 68-69.

83. Patricia Horn. "Philadelphia-Area Museum Fights Student Petition, Hopes to Move Collection," *Philadelphia Inquirer,* October 31, 2002. John L. Pulley, "Barnes Foundation Seeks to Cut Lincoln U.'s Role," *Chronicle of Higher Education,* November 1, 2002.

84. Jennifer Batchelor, "Foes of Barnes Foundation Move Answered by Art Foundation's Lawyers," *Legal Intelligencer,* November 19, 2002. David R. Caruso, "Barnes Foundation Claims Its Creator Planned to Sever Ties With Lincoln U.," Associated Press, November 19, 2002.

85. Don Sternberg, "Bill Would Let University Veto Art Collection's Move to Philadelphia," *Philadelphia Inquirer,* November 30, 2002.

86. Patricia Horn, "Lincoln University in Pennsylvania Can Participate in Art Collection Trial," *Philadelphia Inquirer,* February 13, 2003.

87. Patricia Horn, "Pennsylvania Judge Wants Art Foundation to Explain Refusal to Disclose Audit," *Philadelphia Inquirer,* March 12, 2003. During this period, Barnes Watch placed billboards in African-American neighborhoods with Barnes' portrait captioned, "A MAN'S WILL SHOULD NOT BE BROKEN." Kendra Hamilton, "A Battle of Wills," *Black Issues in Higher Education,* July 17, 2003.

88. Ralph Blumenthal, "Release of Audit Roils Trust Fight at the Barnes," *New York Times,* May 5, 2003.

89. Patricia Horn, "Pennsylvania Attorney General Requests Changes to Art Museum's Petition," *Philadelphia Inquirer,* May 29, 2003.

90. Patricia Horn, "Pennsylvania Art Museum Board Members Raise Concerns Over Proposed Expansion," *Philadelphia Inquirer,* June 4, 2003.

91. Don Sterberg, "Philadelphia's Barnes Foundation Was in Chaos, Audit Shows," *Philadelphia Inquirer,* July 2, 2003. Ralph Blumenthal, "Audit Sharply Criticizes Art Institution's Dealings," *New York Times,* July 2, 2003.

92. "Chester County, Pa. University Disagrees With Foundation over Audit Findings," *Philadelphia Inquirer,* July 13, 2003.

93. Don Sternberg, "Chairman of Pennsylvania Art Collection Says Bankruptcy May Be in Future," *Philadelphia Inquirer,* September 4, 2003.

94. Patricia Horn and Don Sternberg, "Petition to Move Art Collection to Philadelphia May be Abandoned," *Philadelphia Inquirer,* September 3, 2003.

95. Patricia Horn, "Philadelphia-Area Foundation Clears Way for Proposed Move of Art Collection," *Philadelphia Inquirer,* September 13, 2003. Patricia Horn, "Chester County Pa. University Board Accepts Smaller Role in Foundation," *Philadelphia Inquirer,* September 21, 2003.

96. Patricia Horn. "J. Paul Getty Trust Backs Moving Art Collection to Philadelphia," *Philadelphia Inquirer,* October 10, 2003.

97. Patricia Horn, "Judge Agrees to Let Students Take Part in Art Collection Case in Philadelphia," *Philadelphia Inquirer,* October 30, 2003.

98. John Anderson, "Will the Pew's Fine Print Determine the Fate of the Barnes Collection?" *Wall Street Journal,* December 9, 2003. Patricia Horn, "Pew Charitable Trusts, Not Barnes Foundation, Could Control $150 Million," *Philadelphia Inquirer,* November 20, 2003. Don Sternberg, "Philadelphia-Area Foundation Begins Process of Trying to Move its Art," *Philadelphia Inquirer,* December 7, 2003.

99. Patricia Horn and Don Sternberg, "Foundation Head Testifies in Case Concerning Philadelphia-Area Art Collection," *Philadelphia Inquirer,* December 9, 2003. Patricia Horn, "Philadelphia-Area Foundation Had No Money for Feasibility Study, Director Says," *Philadelphia Inquirer,* December 10, 2003. Patricia Horn, "Judge Expresses Doubt About Art Foundation's Proposal to Move to Philadelphia," *Philadelphia Inquirer,* December 11, 2003.

100. Patricia Horn, "Trial Concerning Art Collection's Proposed Move to Philadelphia Ends Early," *Philadelphia Inquirer,* December 12, 2003.

101. Patricia Horn and Don Sternberg, "Foundation Allowed to Expand Board Over Philadelphia-Area Art Collection," *Philadelphia Inquirer,* January 30, 2004. Asher Hawkins, "Barnes Move Delayed Pending Look At Fund-Raising Options," *Legal Intelligencer,* January 30, 2004.

102. Patricia Horn and Matthew P. Blanchard, "Foundation Attorneys Say Art Collection Can't Stay in Lower Merion, Pa.," *Philadelphia Inquirer,* September 22, 2004.

103. Patricia Horn, "Consultant Says Philadelphia Arts Foundation's Fund-Raising Goal is Workable," *Philadelphia Inquirer,* September 24, 2004.

104. Patricia Horn, "Selling Philadelphia School's Artwork is OK, Expert Says," *Philadelphia Inquirer,* September 25, 2004.

105. Blanchard, "Merion Pa. Resists Push to Move Barnes Art Museum."

106. Patricia Horn, "Philadelphia-Area Foundation Offers $100,000 to Keep Art Gallery in Township," *Philadelphia Inquirer,* September 30, 2004.

107. Melissa Nann Burke, "Barnes Foundation Wins OK to Move to Phila.," *Legal Intelligencer,* December 14, 2004.

108. Patricia Horn, "Judge Amends Ruling Concerning Pennsylvania Art Museum," *Philadelphia Inquirer,* December 22, 2004.

109. Patricia Horn, "Barnes Foundation's Planned Move to Philadelphia Will Face Court Appeal," *Philadelphia Inquirer,* March 10, 2005. For a profile of Jay Raymond, see Amy Donohue Korman, "The Handyman vs. the Billionaires," *Philadelphia Magazine,* September 2005.

110. Asher Hawkins, "State High Court Ends Barnes Appeal," *Legal Intelligencer,* April 28, 2005.

111. "Philadelphia's Foundations, Corporations, Citizens Contribute $150 Million to Relocate Barnes Foundation Gallery," *U.S. Newswire,* May 15, 2006.

112. Debra Blum, "Court Ruling Could Influence Restrictions," *Chronicle of Philanthropy,* January 6, 2005.

113. Leslie Lenkowsky, "A Risky End to the Barnes Case," *Wall Street Journal,* December 16, 2004.

114. Tom L. Freudenheim, "Intentions Be Damned!–Donors of Art Often Find Themselves Betrayed," *Wall Street Journal,* December 31, 2005.

115. Robert Zaller, "A Manufactured Offer: Is the Barnes Foundation Really in Trouble?" posted on broadstreetreview.com, February 24, 2006.

116. Jeff Shields, "Commissioners Plan Suit to Keep Barnes in Merion," *Philadelphia Inquirer,* June 8, 2007. Mari A. Schaefer, "Montco Floats New Proposal to Keep Barnes," *Philadelphia Inquirer,* June 13, 2007.

117. Michael Rubinkam, "Philly Suburbs in Last Ditch Effort to Keep Barnes Art," Associated Press, June 25, 2007.

118. Tom Infield, "Neighbors Sue to Keep Barnes From Moving," *Philadelphia Inquirer,* August 29, 2007.

119. Mark McDonald, "At Last a Deal Is Reached on Youth Center," *Philadelphia Daily News,* November 30, 2007. Jeff Shields and Dwight Ott, "West Phila. To Get Youth Study Center," *Philadelphia Inquirer,* November 30, 2007.

120. Carolyn Davis, "Phila.'s New Youth Detention Center Dedicated," *Philadelphia Inquirer,* December 22, 2012.

121. Amaris Elliott-Engel, "Barnes Foundation Court Fight Heats Up Again," *Legal Intelligencer,* March 12, 2008.

122. Derrick Nunnally, "Judge Again Rejects Foes of Barnes Move," *Philadelphia Inquirer,* May 16, 2008.

123. Amaris Elliott-Engel, "Montgomery County Won't Appeal Barnes Ruling," *Legal Intelligencer,* June 17, 2008.

124. Derrick Nunnally, "Fight to Halt Move of Barnes Foundation Ends," *Philadelphia Inquirer,* June 19, 2008.

125. "Commonwealth of Pennsylvania, City of Philadelphia, Pew Charitable Trusts Announce Extensive Improvements For Ben Franklin Parkway and Development," press release from the city of Philadelphia, July 17, 2008.

126. Christopher K. Hepp, "Protesters Gather to Keep Barnes in L. Merion," *Philadelphia Inquirer,* January 3, 2011.

127. Kristin E. Holmes, "Ivory V. Nelson, Lincoln University President, Announces Retirement," *Philadelphia Inquirer,* January 6, 2011.

128. Cited in "Friends of the Barnes Foundation Answers Pew's Frequently Asked Questions," barnesfriends.org/files/pew_FAQ.html. This document is a response to a "Frequently Asked Questions" list issued by the Pew Charitable Trusts about their role in the Barnes Foundation move and why they refused to cooperate with the producers of *The Art of the Steal.*

129. Joann Loviglio, "Barnes Foundation Move Opponents Go Back to Court," Associated Press, February 17, 2011.
130. Stephen Salisbury, "Pa. and Barnes Must Explain Why Relocation Case Should Not Be Reopened," *Philadelphia Inquirer*, March 30, 2011.
131. Stephen Salisbury, "Barnes Funds Top $200 Million," *Philadelphia Inquirer*, June 29, 2011.
132. Stephen Salisbury, "Judge Rejects Group's Petition to Stop the Barnes Move," *Philadelphia Inquirer*, October 7, 2011.
133. Chris Mondics, "Opponents of the Barnes Move Soldier On," *Philadelphia Inquirer*, May 30, 2012.
134. Chris Mondics, "Barnes Collection's Move Is Now Grist for Law Schools," *Philadelphia Inquirer*, January 21, 2013.
135. Kimberly Camp, "Thoughts on the New Barnes Foundation," kimberlycamp.com/index.php?option+com_content.
136. Joseph DiStefano, "Barnes Ex-Boss: 'We Never Said We Were Bankrupt.' Really?" *Philadelphia Inquirer*, July 2, 2012.
137. Jed Perl, "A House Is Not a Home," *New Republic*, September 13, 2012.
138. Peter Dobrin, "Barnes Move to Parkway is Progress, But a Quirky Something Has Been Lost," *Philadelphia Inquirer*, May 21, 2012.
139. James Panero, "Outsmarting Albert Barnes," *Philanthropy*, Summer 2011.
140. Peter Van Allen, "Neubauer To Lead Barnes Foundation Board," *Philadelphia Business Journal*, February 24, 2014. For a profile of Neubauer and his philanthropy, see Jeff Gammage, "Aramark Chairman Quietly Calls It A Career," *Philadelphia Inquirer*, December 3, 2014.
141. Randy Kennedy, "Barnes Foundation Recruits Director From Miami," *New York Times*, January 8, 2015.
142. Virginia A. Smith, "Other Barnes Treasure—Its Arboretum— Now Easier to Visit," *Philadelphia Inquirer*, June 23, 2014.
143. Stephen Salisbury, "Barnes and De Mazia Foundations to Merge," *Philadelphia Inquirer*, April 16, 2015.
144. "New Barnes Documentary Tells Foundation's Side of the Story," *Philadelphia Daily News*, January 19, 2015.
145. Hilarie M. Sheets, "A Wink at the Quirks of a Famed Collector," *New York Times*, March 6, 2015.
146. Ted Loos, "Barnes Foundation's Director Aims to 'Unpack the Ideas' In The Art," *New York Times*, October 28, 2016.
147. Kenneth Hilario, "$5.8M In Upgrades Coming to Barnes Foundation: Additional Education Space, Restaurant Changes," *Philadelphia Business Journal*, January 20, 2017.
148. "Lincoln University Unveils Historic Partnership With the Barnes Foundation," press release issued April 10, 2017.
149. Natalie Kostelni, "Was Moving the Barnes Worth It?" *Philadelphia Business Journal*, March 2, 2017.
150. Robert Zaller, "The Theft of the Barnes After Five Years," *The Triangle*, May 26, 2017.

Chapter 7: The Buck Trust

1. Vanessa Laird, "Phantom Selves: The Search for a General Charitable Intent in the Application of the *Cy Pres* Doctrine," *Stanford Law Review*, April 1988. The case has achieved a certain notoriety. It was used as the basis of an episode of *L.A. Law*, in which crusading lawyers at Mackenzie, Brackman pondered whether or not a trust willed "for the poor of Beverly Hills" could be used to benefit the Los Angeles area.

2. Aaron Wildavsky, "Exchange Versus Grants: The Buck Case as a Struggle Between Equal Opportunity and Equal Results," *University of San Francisco Law Review,* Summer 1988.

3. Superior Court of the State of California, County of Mann, *In the Matter of the Estate of Beryl H. Buck, Deceased: Statement of Decision,* filed August 15, 1986, p. 5. (Referred to hereafter as "Decision.")

4. Douglas Bartholomew, "The Battle for the Buck," *Los Angeles Times Magazine,* December 21-28, 1986.

5. Ted Holdrich, "Widow's Request Spawns Marin County Headache," *Los Angeles Times,* February 1, 1986.

6. Decision, *op. cit.,* p. 10.

7. *Ibid.,* p. 15.

8. *Ibid.,* p. 12.

9. Peg Brickley and Fred Powledge, "Mann County Legacy, or the Curse of the Buck Bucks," *The Nation,* May 14, 1983.

10. Memorandum from Wayne Lamprey to Robert C. Harris, dated July 24, 1979.

11. *Ibid.,* p. 12.

12. Decision, *op. cit.,* p. 21.

13. *Ibid.,* pp. 25-26.

14. Michael Cieply, "The Lotus-Eaters," *Forbes,* July 19, 1982. According to an article in the *Los Angeles Times Magazine,* Public Advocates employees claimed they had thought up the notion of breaking the trust. In a 1982 interview in *Forbes,* Public Advocates partner Robert Gnaizda said that breaking the Buck Trust would be an important precedent. "If the court allows his group to intervene on Buck, he says, the precedent could lead to greater public scrutiny of such private foundations as 'Kresge, Rockefeller, Ford, you name it.'"

15. See "The Buck Trust," an article written by New York University law professor Harvey Dale, available on Dale's website at nyu.edu/projects/hdale/.

16. "California Case Challenges Donors' Rights," *Organization Trends* (Washington, D.C.: Capital Research Center, January 1986).

17. *Ibid.*

18. Robert B. Buck, "Attack on Bay Area Foundation Could Hit Charitable Groups," *Sacramento Union,* December 26, 1985.

19. Roger M. Williams, "When the Buck Stopped," *Foundation News,* November/December 1988.

20. Paul Desruisseaux, "A Foundation Grapples With the Meaning of a 'Magnificent Gift," *Chronicle of Higher Education,* March 27, 1985.

21. California Attorney General's petition to the court, p. 5.

22. Katy Butler, "Trial Starts Today over Buck Trust," *San Francisco Chronicle,* February 3, 1986.

23. *Marin Independent Journal,* February 12, 14, and 20, 1986.

24. *Marin Independent Journal,* March 15, 1986.

25. *San Francisco Chronicle,* May 6, 1986.

26. Williams, *op. cit.*

27. *San Francisco Chronicle,* May 6, 1986.

28. From Martin Paley speech in The Commonwealth, June 1986.

29. Decision, *op. cit.,* pp. 110-111.

30. "Text of Agreement," *Marin Independent Journal,* July 26, 1986.

31. John G. Simon, "American Philanthropy and the Buck Trust," *University of San Francisco Law Review,* Summer 1987.

32. *San Jose Mercury News,* February 11, 1990.

33. Jim Wood, "The Buck Is Growing," *Marin Magazine,* September 2011.

34. Marin Community Foundation Newsletter, Spring 1989.

35. Marin Community Foundation, 1997 annual report.

36. Peter Fimrite, "S.F. Supervisors Lack Faith in Trust," *San Francisco Chronicle,* March 5, 2002.

37. Richard Halstead, "Measurable Impact: Marin Community Foundation's New Course," *Marin Independent Journal,* December 1, 2007.

38. Richard Halstead, "New Funding Priorities, Policies for Marin Community Foundation Debated," *Marin Independent Journal,* October 13, 2006.

Chapter 8: The Robertson Foundation

1. "Mrs. Marie H. Reed Engaged to Marry," *New York Times,* October 7, 1936.

2. *Composite Certificate of Incorporation of the Robertson Foundation,* p. 1.

3. *Ibid.,* pp. 3-4.

4. *Memorandum of Points and Authorities in Support of Plaintiffs' Motion for Partial Summary Judgment Re Fiduciary Duties and Business Judgment Rule,* submitted by Saul Ewing LLP to Superior Court of New Jersey, Chancery Division, Mercer County, January 2006, p. 32. Gen. Goodpaster said he became involved with the Robertson donation in 1960, when he served as President Eisenhower's staff secretary. President Goheen, Gen. Goodpaster recalled, asked him to talk to Charles Robertson about "what Princeton could do to…support the kind of foreign policy and security policy that Eisenhower was carrying out as president." *Ibid,* p. 32.

5. *Ibid.* p. 15.

6. Cited in "Interpreting the Mission of the Robertson Foundation," Princeton University press release, issued June 2, 2003. Goheen served as Princeton president from 1957 to 1972 and died in 2008. For his obituary, see "Robert F. Goheen, President of Princeton University, Dies At Age 88," Princeton University press release, issued March 31, 2008.

7. "$35 Million Given to Princeton for Government Services School," *New York Times,* August 6, 1961.

8. "Wilson School Endowers Identified as a L.I. Couple," *New York Times,* June 14, 1973.

9. Letter from Charles Robertson to William Robertson, July 3, 1962 (exhibit P-607).

10. *Memorandum of Points and Authorities,* p. 17.

11. *Ibid.* p. 17.

12. Robertson Foundation IRS Form 4023, submitted to the IRS August 20, 1970 (Document D-1333).

13. *Memorandum of Points and Authorities,* p. 19. [Underlining removed]

14. Letter from Charles S. Robertson to William Bowen dated November 18, 1972 (exhibit P-4). [Underlining in original removed.]

15. William Bowen, *Lessons Learned: Reflections of a University President* (Princeton, New Jersey: Princeton University Press, 2011), p. 124.

16. *Memorandum of Points and Authorities,* p. 27.

17. *Ibid.* p. 31.

18. Susan Warner, "Thriving in a World in Crisis," *New York Times,* December 23, 2001.

19. The number of plaintiffs fell to four when John Robertson died in an accident in February 2003. Daniel Lipsky-Karasz, "Robertson Suit May Be Delayed by Injury to Judge," *Daily Princetonian,* February 3, 2003.

20. Maria Newman, "Princeton University is Sued Over Control of Foundation," *New York Times,* July 18, 2002. See also Kelly Heyboer, "Heirs Sue Princeton Over Endowment—College Is Accused of Misusing A&P Gift," Newark *Star-Ledger,* July 19, 2002. "Follow the Money," *Wall Street Journal,* July 19, 2002. Silla Brush, "Donors Allege Misuse of Woodrow Wilson School's $550 M Endowment," *Daily Princetonian,* September 11, 2002. Jeffrey O. Nelson, "Donor Beware," *National Review Online,* October 3, 2002.

21. "Princeton-Appointed Trustees and the University File for Dismissal of Robertson Lawsuit," Princeton University press release, issued November 4, 2002.

22. Silla Brush, "Princeton Files to Dismiss Robertson Suit," *Daily Princetonian*, November 5, 2002.

23. "New Evidence Displays Princeton's Arrogance in Treating $500 Million Foundation as University 'Piggy Bank,'" Robertson family press release, issued February 4, 2003. See also Daniel Lipsky-Karasz, "Robertsons File Response to Notion to Dismiss Lawsuit," *Daily Princetonian*, February 5, 2003.

24. Daniel Lipsky-Karasz, "Wilson School Defends Use of Endowment," *Daily Princetonian*, March 25, 2003.

25. Jeff Linkous, "Judge Asked to Dismiss Suit Alleging Princeton Misused Endowment," Associated Press, June 5, 2003.

26. John J. Miller, "Giving, and Taking Away: A Controversy at Princeton Offers Broad Lessons," *National Review*, September 29, 2003.

27. Michael Powell, "At Princeton, Feeling Failed: Family Seeks Return of $525 Million, Saying University Has 'Abused' Gift," *Washington Post*, October 8, 2003.

28. Zachary A. Goldfarb, "PRINCO to Advise WWS Endowment," *Daily Princetonian*, November 6, 2003.

29. William Robertson, "It's National Philanthropy Day—Do You Know Where Your Money Is?" *Christian Science Monitor*, November 14, 2003.

30. Joyce Howard Price, "Princeton Sued for Funds Misuse: A&P Heirs Say Money 'Diverted,'" *Washington Times*, June 20, 2004. Erin Strout, "New Complaint in Lawsuit Alleges That Princeton U. Misused Donors' Money," *Chronicle of Higher Education*, July 2, 2004.

31. Raj Hathiramani, "How A Memo Became a Symbol of Contention," *Daily Princetonian*, October 11, 2004.

32. Raj Hathiramani, "Robertson Family Seeks to Amend Complaint," *Daily Princetonian*, September 13, 2004.

33. John Covaleski, "Fraud Count Added to Donors' Suit That Princeton Misused Endowment," *New Jersey Law Journal*, November 8, 2004.

34. Kelly Heyboer, "Big Stakes as Donor's Heirs Fight Princeton—Suit to Regain Gift Could Spark Others," Newark *Star-Ledger*, November 28, 2004. The largest lawsuit in Princeton's history prior to the Robertson affair was a 1990 case in which an undergraduate won an out-of-court settlement after nearly electrocuting himself after a drinking binge. Raj Hathirimani, "Robertson Lawsuit Most Expensive in U. History," *Daily Princetonian*, November 19, 2004.

35. Chanakya Sethi, "University Files New Claims in Suit," *Daily Princetonian*, February 3, 2005. See also "University Seeks Resolution of Key Issues in Robertson Lawsuit," Princeton University press release, issued February 2, 2005.

36. "Princeton 'Donor Intent' Lawsuit Gathers Steam," Philanthropy News Network Online, June 18, 2005.

37. Chanakya Sethi, "Resignation Sparks Fracas," *Daily Princetonian*, September 21, 2005.

38. Zogby America Poll conducted November 20-22, 2005.

39. "University Seeks Summary Judgment on Three Key Robertson Litigation Issues," Princeton University press release, issued January 9, 2006.

40. Viola Huang, "University Seeks Ruling on Robertson Case," *Daily Princetonian*, January 13, 2006.

41. John Hechinger and Daniel Golden, "Poisoned Ivy: Fight at Princeton Escalates Over Use of a Family Gift," *Wall Street Journal*, February 7, 2006. For more about the McGuire report, see Joyce Howard Price, "Princeton Faulted on Foundation Funds Use," *Washington Times*, February 16, 2006.

42. "Princeton Responds to Feb. 7 WSJ Article," Princeton University press release, issued February 7, 2006.

43. Robert K. Durkee, "Robertson Funds Not Diverted," *Times of Trenton*, February 17, 2006.

44. "Scholars in the Nation's Service," *Princeton Weekly Bulletin*, March 7, 2006.

45. Charles Forelle, "Princeton, Amid Donor Flap, Sets Government Scholarship," *Wall Street Journal*, February 27, 2006.

46. Katherine Hamilton, "University Claims it Underbilled Foundation," *Daily Princetonian*, March 16, 2006. See also John Hechinger, "Princeton Claims it Undercharged Donor Foundation," *Wall Street Journal*, March 16, 2006.

47. Jennifer Epstein, "Princeton Dean Unfazed by Family's Suit," *Daily Princetonian*, October 19, 2006.

48. Erin Strout, "Princeton U. Returns $782,000 to Robertson Foundation as Legal Battle With Heirs Continues," *Chronicle of Higher Education*, March 13, 2007. See also Charles Toutant, "Princeton, Sued for Alleged Misuse of Trust Funds, Gives a Little Back," *New Jersey Law Journal*, March 12, 2007, and John Hechinger, "Princeton Reimburses Donors' Foundation," *Wall Street Journal*, March 13, 2007.

49. John Hechinger, "Ruling May Cost Princeton Millions if Heirs Win Case," *Wall Street Journal*, October 28, 2007. Charles Toutant, "Stage Set for Trial on Heirs' Claim That Princeton Misused Donation, *New Jersey Law Journal*, October 26, 2007. Erin Strout, "Judge Issues Mixed Rulings in Lawsuit vs. Princeton," *Chronicle of Higher Education*, November 2, 2007.

50. Ann McClure, "Spin Control," *University Business*, December 2007.

51. Matt Westmoreland, "Judge for Princeton Lawsuit to Step Down," *Daily Princetonian*, February 29, 2008.

52. "Court Confirms Trial Date of Oct. 1 in Princeton Case," Princeton University press release issued March 7, 2008.

53. Matt Westmoreland, "Trial Date Over Princeton Foundation Endowment Pushed Back," *Daily Princetonian*, June 27, 2008.

54. "N.Y. Appeals Court Orders Insurer to Pay Princeton $9.6 M in D&O Case," *Best's Insurance News*, June 9, 2008.

55. Linda Stein, "Retired Judge Gets Case of Princeton Endowment," *Times of Trenton*, October 24, 2008.

56. Matt Westmoreland, "Retired Judge to Decide Robertson Lawsuit," *Daily Princetonian*, November 3, 2008.

57. W. Raymond Ollwerther, "Robertson Lawsuit Settled," *Princeton Alumni Weekly*, January 28, 2009.

58. Ben Gose, "Princeton to Pay $90 Million to Settle Dispute With Donors' Heirs," *Chronicle of Higher Education*, December 11, 2008.

59. Maureen O'Connor, "Princeton Mourns 'Tragic' Loss of Glorious Moneybags," ivygateblog.com, posted December 10, 2008.

60. "'I'm Enormously Pleased,'" *Princeton Alumni Weekly*, January 28, 2009.

61. Kathryn Masterson, "What Colleges Can Learn from 'Robertson v. Princeton,'" *Chronicle of Higher Education*, December 11, 2008.

62. Naomi Schaefer Riley, "A Conservative Philanthropist Looks to the Future," *Wall Street Journal*, December 27, 2008.

63. Doug Lederman, "Unsettling Settlement Over 'Donor Intent,'" insidehighered.com, December 11, 2008.

64. Neal B. Freeman, *The Robertson v. Princeton Case: Too Important to Be Left to the Lawyers* (Washington, D.C.: Hudson Institute, 2009), p. 8. Freeman's paper is followed by comments from several people, including the author.

Chapter 9: The Packard Foundation

1. David A. Kaplan, *The Silicon Boys and Their Valley of Dreams* (New York: Morrow, 1999), p. 33.

2. In 2015, Hewlett-Packard split into two companies: HP, which makes printers and personal computers, and Hewlett-Packard Enterprise, which has the

remaining Hewlett-Packard divisions. Richard Waters, "HP Split is Latest Twist in Rehabilitation Saga," *Financial Times*, November 2, 2015.

3. "Stanford Research Park: Self Guided Tour," produced by Stanford University in March 2010. Frederick Terman's biography is C. Stewart Gillmor, *Fred Terman at Stanford: Building a Discipline, a University, and Silicon Valley* (Stanford, California: Stanford University Press, 2004). For Terman's obituary, see Wolfgang Saxon, "Frederick Emmons Terman, Stanford Engineer, Dies at 82," *New York Times*, December 21, 1982. Terman was also an early investor in Hewlett-Packard, and served on the company's board of directors from 1957-73. His investment paid off handsomely,

4. "David Packard of Hewlett-Packard," *Nation's Business*, January 1974.

5. "Reluctant Tycoons," *Time*, January 25, 1963.

6. "David Packard of Hewlett-Packard."

7. George Anders, *Perfect Enough: Carly Fiorina and the Reinvention of Hewlett-Packard* (New York: Portfolio, 2003), p. 12.

8. *Ibid.*, pp. 3-4.

9. Interview with Peter Flanigan, December 12, 2012.

10. Interview with Christopher DeMuth, December 14, 2012.

11. Tom Perkins, *Valley Boy: The Education of Tom Perkins* (New York: Gotham Books, 2007), p. 75.

12. *Ibid.*, p. 56.

13. This total includes funds Packard contributed for the Terman Engineering Center, a $9.2 million project funded by Hewlett, Packard, and other donors, which was opened in 1977 and which Stanford tore down in 2011. Kathleen J. Sullivan, "Excavator Tears Down Walls, Ceilings, and Floors of Terman Engineering Center," *Stanford Report*, October 18, 2011.

14. Joan O'C. Hamilton, "David Packard: Silicon Valley's Class Act," *Business Week*, April 8, 1996.

15. Lawrence E. Davies, "Stanford's Drive Tops $109 Million," *New York Times*, January 17, 1964.

16. Cited in Irving Louis Horowitz and William H. Friedland, *The Knowledge Factory: Student Power and Academic Politics in America* (Chicago: Aldine, 1970), p. 316.

17. Fred Cohen, Gini Linsley, and David Pugh, "Insurrection at Stanford," article in the April 24, 1969 *New Left Notes* available at http://www.1960s-counterculture.org/sds-new-left-notes/4-24-1969.

18. W. Glenn Campbell, *The Competition of Ideas: How My Colleagues and I Built the Hoover Institution* (Ottawa, Illinois: Jameson Books, 2000), p. 143.

19. Marylin Bender, "Curb Asked on Gifts to Colleges," *New York Times*, October 18, 1973.

20. Cited in G.W.B., "Mr. Packard Turns the Clock Back," *Change*, Winter 1973/74.

21. Bender, "Curb Asked on Gifts to Colleges."

22. I discuss this battle at greater length in *Games Universities Play* (Raleigh, North Carolina: Pope Center, 2011).

23. Leonard Sloane, "Flexible Education Aid Backed," *New York Times*, November 3, 1973.

24. Gene I. Maeroff, "College Vs. Business: The Versus Declines," *New York Times*, January 25, 1974.

25. "Not for Sale," *New York Times*, October 29, 1973.

26. McGeorge Bundy, "The Art of Giving: It Requires Practice, Concern, and Trust," *New York Times*, January 16, 1974.

27. "Mr. Packard Turns The Clock Back."

28. Michael S. Malone, *Bill & Dave: How Hewlett and Packard Built The World's Greatest Company* (New York: Portfolio, 2007), p. 311.

29. Dennis Kelly, "$77.4 Million Building Gift Largest in Stanford University," *USA Today*, October 13, 1994.

30. Jean Merl, "Stanford President, Beset by Controversies, Will Quit," *Los Angeles Times*, July 30, 1991. See also "The Cracks in Stanford's Ivory Tower," *Business Week*, March 10, 1991.

31. Bill Workman, "David Packard Says Hearing Was 'A Sad Day for Stanford,'" *San Francisco Chronicle*, March 15, 1991.

32. Karen Grossmuck, "What Happened at Stanford: Mistakes at Crucial Times in a Battle With the Government Over Research Costs," *Chronicle of Higher Education*, May 15, 1991. Donald Kennedy was a member of the Packard Foundation board from 2005 to 2014.

33. David Binder, "Group Warns of Soviet Expansion," *New York Times*, April 4, 1977. For a profile of the Committee for the Present Danger, see Linda Charlton, "Groups Favoring Strong Defense Making Gains in Public Acceptance," *New York Times*, April 4, 1977. Other signers of the report included former Secretary of the Treasury Henry Fowler, AFL-CIO secretary-treasurer Lane Kirkland, and former Secretary of State Dean Rusk.

34. Interview with Christopher DeMuth.

35. Claude Witze, "In Procurement, The New Look Looks Old," *Air Force Magazine*, January 1971.

36. George Shultz, "His Inquiring Mind Was Always Trying to Learn Something," *San Jose Mercury News*, March 30, 1996. "I've seen him at ease," Shultz said. "I've seen him under great pressure. He was always David Packard, the same guy, whether he was talking to the president of the United States or to any of us."

37. "David Packard Oral History," interview with Daniel S. Morrow for the Computerworld Honors Program International Archives, April 19, 1995.

38. William Beecher, "Packard Charges Politics Bars Big Defense Savings," *New York Times*, December 14, 1971.

39. Tom Perkins, *Valley Boy*, pp. 83-84.

40. "The 'Cronies' Ford Turns To When He Wants to Relax," *U.S. News and World Report*, September 29, 1975. Other members of the "kitchen cabinet" included former Secretary of Defense Melvin Laird, former Pennsylvania Governor William Scranton, and Sen. Robert Griffin (R-Michigan).

41. James M. Naughton, "Head Fund-Raiser for Ford Resigns," *New York Times*, November 1, 1975. Warren Weaver Jr., "New Law Balked Ford Fund-Raiser," *New York Times*, November 2, 1975.

42. Margot Hornblower, "Gold-Plated Panel Set to Raise, Spend Millions for Reagan," *Washington Post*, July 10, 1980.

43. Susan Heller Anderson and David W. Dunlap, "Briefing: The Reagan Foundation," New York Times, February 18, 1986.

44. "Executives For Clinton Have Blundered," *San Jose Mercury News*, September 17, 1992.

45. Packard was also on the Hoover board from 1956 to 1969, but was an *ex officio* member in those years while he served on the Stanford board. Email from Denise Elson of the Hoover Institution, January 20, 2013.

46. Oral History Interview with David Packard, conducted by Raymond Henle for the Herbert Hoover Presidential Library and the Hoover Institution on War, Revolution and Peace, September 20, 1967, in Herbert Hoover Oral History Program Interviews, Box 17, Hoover Institution Archives, p. 22.

47. For more information, see Palo Alto Stanford Heritage website, http://pasthistory.org/articles/LHHooverMF.html (accessed 12/11/14).

48. George H. Nash, *Herbert Hoover and Stanford University* (Stanford, California: Stanford University Press, 1988), p. 126.

49. *Ibid.*, p. 143.

50. *Ibid.*, p. 139.

51. His full name was John Ewart Wallace Sterling, but he did not use his first two names, signing his letters "J. E. Wallace Sterling."

52. Nash, *Herbert Hoover and Stanford University*, p. 139.

53. "Additional Matters," summary of Stanford trustees meeting of November 20, 1958, cited in Bernice Miller, *Mr. Hoover's Twelve-Year Fight*, Herbert Hoover Papers, Herbert Hoover Presidential Library, pp. 169-170. This manuscript was written by Herbert Hoover's long-time assistant, Bernice Miller, in 1963-64 and describes the conflict between Herbert Hoover and Stanford University. It was never published.

54. David Packard Oral History, Hoover Institution Archives, p. 15.

55. Mr. Hoover's Twelve Year Fight—Correspondence—David Packard (Henceforth cited as David Packard Correspondence, Herbert Hoover Presidential Library), Herbert Hoover Papers, Herbert Hoover Presidential Library.

56. *Ibid.*

57. Letter from Herbert Hoover to Wallace Sterling, April 4, 1959. "Mr. Hoover's Twelve Year Fight," Herbert Hoover Presidential Library, p. 250.

58. Letter from Wallace Sterling to Herbert Hoover, April 11, 1959, "Mr. Hoover's Twelve-Year Fight," Herbert Hoover Presidential Library, pp. 251-52.

59. Letter from David Packard to Herbert Hoover, April 17. 1959, David Packard Correspondence, Herbert Hoover Presidential Library.

60. Letter from Morton Blumenthal to Herbert Hoover, May 18, 1959, David Packard Correspondence, Herbert Hoover Presidential Library.

61. *Mr. Hoover's Twelve-Year Fight*, pp. 209-210.

62. Special Committee of the Hoover Institution report to the Stanford University Board of Trustees, May 20, 1959, David Packard Correspondence, Herbert Hoover Presidential Library.

63. The best source for biographical information about Kemp is the short biography in the introduction to the Arthur Kemp Papers, which are at the Hoover Institution.

64. Letter from David Packard to Herbert Hoover, August 21, 1959, David Packard Correspondence, Herbert Hoover Presidential Library.

65. Letter from Herbert Hoover to David Packard, August 26, 1959, David Packard Correspondence, Herbert Hoover Presidential Library.

66. Bernice Miller, "Mr. Hoover's Twelve-Year Fight," Herbert Hoover Presidential Library, p. 254.

67. The dossier is in "Mr. Hoover's Twelve-Year Fight," Herbert Hoover Presidential Library, p. 255.

68. Letter from Wallace Sterling to Herbert Hoover, *Mr. Hoover's Twelve-Year Fight*, Herbert Hoover Presidential Library, pp. 257-58.

69. Memoranda in *Mr. Hoover's Twelve-Year Fight*, Herbert Hoover Presidential Library, pp. 259-261.

70. Letter from Herbert Hoover to David Packard, December 20, 1959, David Packard Correspondence, Herbert Hoover Presidential Library.

71. Special Committee of the Hoover Institution Report, May 20, 1959.

72. Craig Murray, "Interview With New Hoover Director Shows Revised Goals of Institution," *Stanford Daily*, March 29, 1960, *Mr. Hoover's Twelve-Year Fight*, Clipping File, 1960-61, Herbert Hoover Presidential Library.

73. "A Note of Regret," *Stanford Daily*, March 29, 1960, *Mr. Hoover's Twelve-Year Fight*, Clipping File, 1960-61, Herbert Hoover Presidential Library.

74. Steve Friedberg, "Interview With Sterling," *Stanford Daily*, March 30, 1960, *Mr. Hoover's Twelve-Year Fight*, Clipping File, 1960-61, Herbert Hoover Presidential Library.

75. Raymond Lawrence, "Freedom at Stanford," *Oakland Tribune*, April 1, 1960, *Mr. Hoover's Twelve-Year Fight*, Clipping File, 1960-61, Herbert Hoover Presidential Library.

76. Letter from David Packard to Herbert Hoover, May 27, 1960, David Packard Correspondence, Herbert Hoover Presidential Library.

77. Letter from Herbert Hoover to David Packard, June 2, 1960, David Packard Correspondence, Herbert Hoover Presidential Library.

78. Nash, *Herbert Hoover and Stanford University*, p. 157. In his 1995 memoir *The HP Way*, Packard said "I spent considerable time trying to reconcile Hoover's insistence that the Hoover Institution had to fight the evils of Communism with the idea of academic freedom. "We finally solved the problem. The donor, President Hoover, had a right to say what he wanted his institution to do. At the same time research should be broad and objective without any preconceived outcome." David Packard, *The HP Way: How Bill Hewlett and I Built Our Company*, edited by David Kirby with Karen Lewis (New York: Harper, 1995), p. 170.

79. Frank Taylor, "Stanford and the Man With the Midas Touch," *Saturday Evening Post,* December 3, 1960.

80. Letter from David Packard to Herbert Hoover, January 24, 1961, David Packard Correspondence, Herbert Hoover Presidential Library.

81. Letter from John K, Stewart to David Packard, February 8, 1961, David Packard Correspondence, Herbert Hoover Presidential Library.

82. Letter from Herbert Hoover to David Packard, June 7, 1961, David Packard Correspondence, Herbert Hoover Presidential Library.

83. Nash*, Herbert Hoover and Stanford University*, p. 165. This "Hoover Foundation" should not be confused with the Herbert W. Hoover Foundation, which is the family foundation created by the founder of the Hoover vacuum cleaner fortune.

84. Letter from Herbert Hoover to David Packard, April 21, 1964, David Packard Correspondence, Herbert Hoover Presidential Library.

85. Nash, *Herbert Hoover and Stanford University*, p. 230.

86. Campbell, *The Competition of Ideas*, pp. 123-24. Campbell adds that the Scaife money came with a string—that Charles Luckman, who oversaw construction of some Scaife buildings in Pittsburgh, be hired as architect. Campbell says that Herbert Hoover protested that Luckman designed the Lever Building in Manhattan, which Hoover called "that glass monstrosity on Park Avenue." When Campbell said that Luckman was a salesman and not an architect, Hoover said, "that for $750,000 the Scaifes were entitled to select the architect." *Competition of Ideas,* p. 124.

87. Letter from David Packard to Herbert Hoover, April 28, 1964, David Packard Correspondence, Herbert Hoover Presidential Library.

88. Telegram from Herbert Hoover to David Packard, May 6, 1964, David Packard Correspondence, Herbert Hoover Presidential Library.

89. Campbell, *Competition of Ideas*, p. 153.

90. Alvin P. Sanoff, "Matters Over Minds," *Regardie's,* January 1987.

91. *Ibid.*

92. Interview with Christopher DeMuth, December 14, 2012. DeMuth recalls that Packard's gift was $400,000.

93. Interview with Christopher DeMuth.

94. Rushworth M. Kidder, "David Packard," *Christian Science Monitor,* November 21, 1986.

95. Anders. *Perfect Enough*, p. 109.

96. *Perfect Enough*, p. 110.

97. Kathleen Teltsch, "Groups Launch Effort to Curb Third World Population Growth," *New York Times,* September 5, 1988.

98. Kidder, "David Packard." Packard also said that "unfortunately" the best solution to America's energy needs was nuclear power, and "we're going to have to come to some form of nuclear power sooner or later—and I think we're going to have to do that during the 21st century."

99. Wallace Turner, "Environmental Group Progresses in Acquiring Land," *New York Times,* November 15, 1981.

100. "New Wildlife Foundation Established by Clark," Associated Press, January 22, 1985. According to the foundation's website (nfwf.org), the major foundation donors to this organization no longer include the Packard Foundation, but do include the Houston Endowment, the Gordon and Betty Moore Foundation, and the Walton Family Foundation.

In 2012 the National Fish and Wildlife Foundation was awarded a five-year, $2.3 billion grant from BP, as part of the $4 billion fine BP was required to pay for conservation measures as a result of a court settlement after the 2010 Gulf of Mexico oil spill. Juliet Eilperin, "BP Settlement a Boon to Conservation Group," *Washington Post,* December 17, 2012.

Also in 2012, the Justice Department required Gibson Guitar to donate $50,000 to the National Fish and Wildlife Foundation as part of a settlement alleging that the guitar company had illegally imported valuable wood from India and Madagascar. John Fund and Hans van Spakovsky, "The Justice Department's Green Raid on America," *Green Watch,* October 2014.

In 2016 the National Park and Wildlife Foundation bought the 7,139-acre Flying M Ranch in Nevada from Barron Hilton for $18.9 million, with a proviso that Hilton could continue to live on the ranch during his lifetime. Benjamin Spillman, "Conservation Group Nabs Nevada's Iconic 'Hilton Ranch,'" *Reno Gazette-Journal,* August 26, 2016,

101. Robert Lindsey, "Huge Ocean-Front Aquarium to Open in Steinbeck's Monterey," *New York Times,* October 20, 1984.

102. "David Packard Oral History."

103. Interview with Christopher DeMuth.

104. Anders, *Perfect Enough,* p. 108.

105. *Perfect Enough,* p. 108.

106. "2016 Packard Fellowships in Science and Engineering Awarded to Eighteen Researchers," Packard Foundation press release, October 15. 2016.

107. Jon Cohen, "Philanthropy's Rising Tide Lifts Science," *Science,* October 8, 1999. Marina Dundjerski, "Packard Pours $1.6 Billion Into Humanities Institute," *Chronicle of Philanthropy,* July 29, 1999.

108. "A Conversation with Cole Wilbur," *Foundation News and Commentary,* March/April 1999.

109. Marina Dundjerski and Holly Hall, "The Packard Way," *Chronicle of Philanthropy,* January 29, 1998.

110. For profiles of David W. Packard, see Tom Sabulis, "Silicon Cash, Silver Screen Love," *San Jose Mercury News,* July 2, 1989 and Mick LaSalle, "A Rich History Worth Saving (With Millions)," *San Francisco Chronicle,* August 13, 2000.

111. Valerie Richardson, "The New Packard," *Philanthropy,* November/December 2000.

112. For an article about the Packard Humanities Institute's efforts in Herculaneum, see Joshua Hammer, "The Fall and Rise of Pompeii," *Smithsonian,* July 2015.

113. Richardson, "The New Packard."

114. Interview with Christopher DeMuth, December 14, 2012. Hoover information from email from Denise Elson of Hoover, January 20, 2013.

115. Jennifer Reese, "Susan Packard Orr on Philanthropy," *Stanford Business,* December 1997.

116. Nancy Gibbs, Ann Blackman, and Dick Thompson, "The Pill Arrives," *Time,* October 9, 2000.

117. Anders, *Perfect Enough,* p. 309.

118. Anders' *Perfect Enough* is the best account of the battle. See also Molly Williams and Gary McWilliams, "Family Affair: H-P Deal's Fate Rests With Skeptical Heirs of Company Founders," *Wall Street Journal,* December 6, 2001, and Steve Lohr with Chris Gaither, "A Family's Struggle, A Company's Fate," *New York Times,* December 2, 2001. Hewlett-Packard subsequently fired Carly Fiorina in 2005. She ran for the Senate as a Republican, but lost a bid to

unseat Sen. Barbara Boxer in 2010. In 2015 she launched a bid for the Republican presidential nomination, which failed in 2016.

119. Elizabeth Greene, "Cutting the Losses," *Chronicle of Philanthropy*, March 20, 2003. Roger M. Williams, "Rollercoaster at Packard," *Foundation News and Commentary*, July/August 2003. For the Center on Budget and Policy Priorities, see Elizabeth Schwinn, "Packard's Spending Cuts Cause Budget Woes for a Budget Expert," *Chronicle of Philanthropy*, March 20, 2003. The center subsequently made up some of the Packard cuts through additional grants from the Annie E. Casey Foundation. In 2014 the Packard Foundation awarded the center two grants totaling $690,000.

120. Kevin Starr, "Foundation of a New Kind of Governance?" *Los Angeles Times*, January 4, 2004.

121. Sara Hebel, "The Hard Birth of a Research University," *Chronicle of Higher Education*, April 1, 2005. The William and Flora Hewlett Foundation also contributed $2 million to the land-buying effort.

122. Charlotte Allen, "Boondoggle U," *Weekly Standard*, April 23, 2012.

123. "Local Donations to Presidential Campaigns," *Palo Alto Online*, August 12, 2012, paloaltoonline.com/news/story_print.php/story_id=26450.

124. "Super PAC: Planned Parenthood Votes," elections.nytimes.com/2012/campaign-finance/pac/planned-parenthood-votes.

125. "A Vibrant and Responsive Democracy," mission statement on California Forward website, cafwd.org/pages/democracy-reforms.

126. "Endorsements: No On the Well-Intentioned Proposition 31," *Sacramento Bee*, September 10, 2012.

127. Wyatt Buchanan, "Prop. 31: Budget Overhaul Defeated," *San Francisco Chronicle*, November 7, 2012.

128. "Population and Reproductive Health: United States," mission statement on packard.org website.

129. "Expanding Access to Reproductive Health Care," packard.org website.

130. "Teaching Schools to Teach About Sex," Packard.org website.

131. Nishant Sinha, "Condoms at Petrol Pumps, Stores Now," *Times of India*, May 13, 2011.

132. "Democratic Women of Monterey County Honoring Nancy Burnett and Julie Packard," press release on Democratic Women of Monterey County website (dw-mc.org).

133. "Monterey Bay Aquarium Director Julie Packard Unleashes Sea of Change," *Monterey County Herald* article on Monterey Bay Adventures website, montereybayadventures.com/canneryrow/ci_15742228, 2010.

134. *Design to Win: Philanthropy's Role in the Fight Against Global Warming* (San Francisco: California Environmental Associates, 2007), p. 35.

135. From the Resources Legacy Fund website.

136. Brian Maffly, "Groups Donate $1.5M to Bears' Ears 'Engagement' Fund," *Salt Lake Tribune,* January 13, 2017.

137. Brian Seasholes, "The Green Pipeline," *Green Watch*, October 2012.

138. Peter O'Neil, "Enbridge Points to 'Curious' Funding of Pipeline Opposition by U.S. Charities," Postmedia News, December 5, 2011.

139. Vivian Krause, "Packard's Push Against B.C. Salmon," *Financial Post,* January 26, 2011.

140. Christina Blizzard, "Taking Charities Out of Politics," *Toronto Sun,* April 18, 2012.

Chapter 10: The JM Foundation

1. Clarence R. Wharton, *Gail Borden, Pioneer* (San Antonio: Naylor, 1941), p. 193.

2. "The Quiet Milbank Millions," *Fortune,* May 1959. When the railroad reached South Dakota, a town first used as a maintenance stop was renamed Milbank.

3. *Ibid.* Elizabeth Milbank Anderson ensured, however, that the "palace" did not serve hard liquor, which she fiercely opposed.

4. For Jeremiah Milbank's obituary, see "Jeremiah Milbank, A Financier Who Aided the Crippled, Dead," *New York Times,* March 23, 1972.

5. John Briggs, *The Face of a Family* (Greenwich, Connecticut: The JM Foundation, 1992), p. 27.

6. "Red Cross to Open School for Cripples," *New York Times,* January 20, 1918.

7. "600 Cripples Guests of Jeremiah Millbank," *New York Times,* July 20, 1929.

8. Cited in "The Quiet Milbank Millions," *op. cit.*

9. Jeremiah Milbank with Grace Fox Perry, *Turkey Hill Plantation* (Ridgeland, South Carolina: Cypress Woods Corporation, 1966), p. 102.

10. Scott Eyman, *Empire of Dreams: The Epic Life of Cecil B. DeMille* (New York: Simon and Schuster, 2010), p. 214.

11. "Money Votes," *Time,* July 30, 1928.

12. Briggs, *op. cit.,* p. 43.

13. *Ibid.,* p. 75.

14. *Ibid.,* p. 1.

15. *Ibid.,* p. 2.

16. *Ibid.,* p. 2.

17. "The Quiet Milbank Millions," *op. cit.*

18. *Turkey Hill Plantation, op. cit.,* preface. The preface is by Perry alone.*

19. Jeremiah Milbank, "Will Giver Get Hand Bitten after Giving?" *Leaders,* Fourth Quarter, 1984. Jeremiah Millbank Jr. was also active in Republican politics. In 1962, he and J. William Middendorf II agreed to donate enough money to keep the "Draft Goldwater" offices operating until after the 1962 mid-term elections, at which time other donors pledged their support. Milbank and Middendorf were such efficient fund-raisers that they were nicknamed "The Brinks Brothers." Lee Edwards, "The Unforgettable Candidate," *National Review,* July 6, 1998.

20. John J. Miller, "Jeremiah Milbank Jr.," *Philanthropy,* September/October 2007. See also Douglas Martin, "Jeremiah Milbank Jr., Donor and G.O.P. Official, Dies at 87," *New York Times,* August 19, 2007.

21. William F. Buckley Jr., "Jeremiah Milbank R.I.P.," *National Review,* September 10, 2007.

22. Lindsey Uniat, "Donation to Expand Palliative Care," *Yale Daily News,* January 18, 2013.

23. Miller, *op. cit.*

Chapter 11: Lynde and Harry Bradley Foundation

1. John Gurda, *The Bradley Legacy: Lynde and Harry Bradley, their Company, and their Foundation* (Milwaukee: Lynde and Harry Bradley Foundation, 1992).

2. *Ibid.,* p. 41

3. *Ibid.,* p. 98.

4. *Ibid.,* p. 120.

5. *Ibid.,* p. 115.

6. *Ibid.,* p. 112.

7. *Ibid.,* p. 116.

8. *Ibid.,* p. 117.

9. *Ibid.,* pp. 115-116.

10. "Harry Bradley, R.I.P.," *National Review,* August 24, 1965.

11. Gurda, *op. cit.,* p. 124.

12. *Ibid.,* p. 121.

13. *Ibid.*, p. 125.

14. Harvey W. Peters, *America's Coming Bankruptcy: How the Government Is Wrecking Your Dollar* (New Rochelle, New York: Arlington House, 1973), p. 118.

15. *Ibid.*, p.121.

16. Jane Bradley Pettit died in 2001 at age 83, leaving most of her wealth to the Jane Bradley Pettit Foundation, which primarily funds nonprofits in Milwaukee. For an obituary, see "Jane Pettit Was Philanthropist Beyond Compare," *Milwaukee Business Journal,* September 16, 2001. Pettit also owned 14 percent of the Milwaukee Brewers and contributed $1 million to the construction of Miller Park.

Pettit's two children both formed foundations. Lynde Uihlein formed the Brico Fund and David Uihlein Jr. created the David and Julia Uihlein Charitable Foundation.

17. "Bradley Foundation Gets New Chairman," *Milwaukee Journal Sentinel,* June 9, 2000. For Rader's obituary, see Jason Gertzen, "Industrialist Was Catalyst for a Company: I. Andrew 'Tiny' Rader, 1914-2003," *Milwaukee Journal Sentinel,* February 15, 2003.

18. Rick Henderson, "Art Pope Named Chairman of the Bradley Foundation," *Carolina Journal,* April 6, 2017.

19. Daniel Bice, "Hacked Records Show Bradley Foundation Taking Wisconsin Model National," *Milwaukee Journal Sentinel,* May 7, 2017.

20. Gurda, *op. cit.*, p. 157.

21. Steven Schindler, "Case 62: School Choice: Vouchers in Milwaukee," in Joel E. Fleishman, J. Scott Kohler, and Steven Schindler, *Casebook for The Foundation* (New York: PublicAffairs, 2007), pp. 161-162.

22. Charles Storch, "Money Talks," *Chicago Tribune,* March 4, 1993.

23. James A. Barnes, "Banker with a Cause," *National Journal,* March 6, 1993.

24. Cited in Brian D. Willats, "Restoring Donor Intent: The Philanthropy Roundtable," *Philanthropy, Culture & Society* (Washington, D.C.: Capital Research Center, February 1993).

25. Eric Alterman, "The 'Right' Books and Big Ideas," *The Nation,* November 27, 1999.

26. Shawn Zeller, "Conservative Crusaders," *National Journal,* April 26, 2003.

27. Alan Borsuk, "Bush Stresses Faith-Based Efforts," *Milwaukee Journal Sentinel,* July 3, 2002.

28. For a report of a 2005 Bradley Center conference, see Thomas B. Edsall, "Now in Power, Conservatives Free to Differ," *Washington Post,* February 20, 2005. I have edited transcripts of Bradley Center conferences.

29. For an account of the 2005 Bradley Prizes, see Jennifer Frey, "For Bradley Prize Winners, a Conservative Celebration," *Washington Post,* February 17, 2005. Andrew Ferguson, "The Right Stuff," *Weekly Standard,* March 7, 2005, provides a skeptical account of the Bradley Prizes.

One of the 2006 Bradley Prize winners, Fouad Ajami, had previously been a MacArthur Fellow.

30. Among the more important tributes to Michael Joyce were James Piereson, "Michael Joyce, 1942-2005: The Godfather of Conservative Philanthropy," *Weekly Standard,* March 20, 2006, and William A. Schambra, "Michael Joyce's Mission: Using Philanthropy to Wage a War of Ideas," *Chronicle of Philanthropy,* March 9, 2006.

31. "Staying the Course," *Philanthropy,* July 2003.

32. Daniel Bice, Bill Glauber, Ben Poston, "From local roots, Bradley Foundation builds conservative empire," *Milwaukee Journal Sentinel,* November 19, 2011.

33. *Ibid.*

34. Daniel Bice, "Hacked Records Show Bradley Foundation Taking Its Wisconsin Model National," *Milwaukee Journal Sentinel*, May 5, 2017.

35. John J. Miller, "The Right's Venture Capitalist," *National Review*, October 10, 2016.

36. Daniel Bice and Bill Glauber, "GOP Insider Rick Graber To Head Bradley Foundation," *Milwaukee Journal Sentinel,* June 23, 2016.

37. Bill Glauber, "Rick Graber puts imprint on Bradley Foundation," *Milwaukee Journal Sentinel,* May 17, 2017.

Chapter 12: The Duke Endowment

1. Cited in Joe Maynor, *Duke Power: The First Seventy-Five Years* (Albany, New York: Delmar, 1980), p. 44.

2. Patrick G. Porter, "Origins of the American Tobacco Company," *Business History Review*, Spring 1969.

3. Cited in Watson S. Rankin, *James Buchanan Duke (1856-1925): A Great Pattern of Hard Work, Wisdom, and Benevolence* (New York: Newcomen Society, 1952), p. 9.

4. In April 1994, British-American Tobacco (now known as B.A.T. Industries) acquired American Tobacco.

5. While Southern Power System president, Duke continued his thrifty ways. In her memoirs, Cordelia Drexel Biddle, who married Benjamin Duke's son, Tony Duke, recalled that sometime around 1920, James Duke decided to teach his nephew the family trade and took him on a tour of Southern Power System facilities. At one hotel, James Duke found that Tony had booked two rooms. "You'll get nowhere in business wasting money like that," James Duke said. "Give us that room with the double bed that Ben and I always slept in."
According to Biddle, Tony Duke "never recovered from the fact that one of America's richest men was worrying about saving a dollar a night in a primitive country hotel. However, his admiration for Mr. Duke has never wavered. 'After a day on the trail with that wonderful old man,' says Tony, 'I was so tired that I could just as easily have slept with a cobra.'" Cordelia Drexel Biddle, as told to Kyle Crichton, *My Philadelphia Father* (Garden City, New York: Doubleday, 1955), p. 195.

6. For an analysis of Duke's role in turning waterpower into electricity, see Christopher F. Manganiello, "Hitching the New South to 'White Coal': Water and Power, 1890-1933," *Journal of Southern History*, May 2012.

7. Cited in Robert F. Durden, *The Dukes of Durham, 1865-1929* (Durham, North Carolina: Duke University Press, 1975), pp. 97-98. Duke University Press published a sequel by Durden, *Lasting Legacy to the Carolinas, The Duke Endowment, 1924-1994*, in 1998.

8. *Ibid.*, p. 97.

9. Earl W. Porter, *Trinity and Duke, 1892-1924: The Foundations of Duke University* (Durham, North Carolina: Duke University Press, 1964), p. 80.

10. James B. Duke, "Politics and Prosperity," *North American Review*, April 9, 1915.

11. Arthur Pound and Samuel Taylor Moore, eds., *They Told Barron: Conversations and Revelations of an American Pepys in Wall Street* (New York: Harper, 1930), p. 54.

12. *Ibid.*, p. 55.

13. "Duke Calls Power Good in Wealth," *New York Times*, December 16, 1924.

14. "Politics and Prosperity," *op. cit.*

15. William E. King, *If Gargoyles Could Talk: Sketches of Duke University* (Durham, North Carolina: Carolina Academic Press, 1997), p. 33.

16. William King, "Washington Duke and the Education of Women," Duke University Libraries website, accessed 5/4/17.

17. *Ibid.*, pp. 34-35.

18. Durden, *op. cit.*, p. 113.

19. Robert H. Woody, ed., *The Papers and Addresses of William Preston Few, Late President of Duke University* (Durham, North Carolina: Duke University Press, 1941), pp. 90-91. Benjamin Duke gave Trinity College $120,000 between 1898 and 1901. He also ensured that his children attended the school. His son Angier was graduated with the 1905 class and his daughter Mary was a 1907 alumnus.

20. Porter, *op. cit.*, p. 150.

21. Durden, *op. cit.*, p. 163.

22. Woody, *op. cit.*, p. 93.

23. *Ibid.*, p. 104.

24. *Ibid.*, p. 93.

25. *Ibid.*, p. 93.

26. *Ibid.*, p. 94.

27. *Ibid.*, pp. 94-95.

28. Durden, *op. cit.*, p. 214.

29. Woody, *op. cit.*, p. 135.

30. *Ibid.*, p. 105.

31. Cited in Robert F. Durden, *The Launching of Duke University, 1924-1949* (Durham, North Carolina: Duke University Press, 1993), p. 22.

32. *Ibid.*, p. 22.

33. James F. Gifford Jr., *The Evolution of a Medical Center: A History of Medicine at Duke University to 1941* (Durham, North Carolina: Duke University Press, 1972), p. 36.

34. Gifford, *op. cit.*, p. 39.

35. Durden, *Dukes of Durham*, p. 227.

36. *Ibid.*, p. 229.

37. Woody, *op. cit.*, p. 106.

38. *The Duke Endowment Indenture of Trust* (Charlotte, North Carolina: Duke Endowment, n.d.), pp. 10-11.

39. Porter, *op. cit.*, p. 62.

40. *The Duke Endowment Indenture of Trust, op. cit.* p. 12

41. *Ibid.*, p. 14.

42. *Ibid.*, p. 14.

43. *Ibid.*, p. 17.

44. *Ibid.*, p. 17.

45. *Ibid.*, pp. 17-18.

46. *Ibid.*, p. 18.

47. *Ibid.*, pp. 18-19.

48. *Ibid.*, p. 19.

49. "Duke Calls Power Good in Wealth," *op. cit.*

50. *Ibid.*

51. Ned Glascock, "Slug! Slug! Slug!" *Raleigh News and Observer*, August 11, 1996.

52. "The Goose Step and the Golden Eggs," *The New Republic*, December 24, 1924.

53. Rankin, *James Buchanan Duke,* p. 9.

54. Durden, *Dukes of Durham*, p. 239.

55. Gifford, *op. cit.*, pp. 43-44.

56. "Texan Enlivens Duke Will Trial," *New York Times*, March 17, 1928.

57. "Right to Texas Fund Denied Duke Girl," *New York Times*, May 22, 1928.

58. Tom Valentine and Patrick Mahn, *Daddy's Duchess: The Unauthorized Biography of Doris Duke* (Secaucus, New Jersey: Lyle Stuart, 1989), pp. 13-14.

59. John K. Winkler, *Tobacco Tycoon: The Story of James Buchanan Duke* (New York: Random House, 1942), p. 317.

60. Elsa Maxwell, "Mr. and Mrs. James H.R. Cromwell," *Ladies Home Journal*, December 1938.

61. Karen Garloch and Jack Horan, "Their Mission: Give Away $41 Million," *Charlotte Observer*, November 13, 1988.

62. *Ibid.*

63. Stephanie Mansfield, *The Richest Girl in the World: The Extravagant Life and Fast Times of Doris Duke* (New York: Putnam, 1992), p. 260.

64. *Ibid.*, p. 260.

65. Cited in Ted Schwarz with Tom Rybak, *Trust No One: The Glamorous Life and Bizarre Death of Doris Duke* (New York: St. Martin's Press, 1997), pp. 262-263. While this book is a useful guide to legal documents, the authors make many claims unsupported by evidence, including allegations that James Duke was murdered by his wife Nannaline and that James Duke in 1917 (when he was no longer in the tobacco business) suppressed research that showed that cigarette smoking causes cancer.

66. Stephanie Mansfield, "Billionaire's Heir Out of Place," *Washington Post*, March 7, 1993. Duke biographer Schwarz notes that it is unclear whether Duke could legally annul her adoption of Heffner, even though it is clear that Heffner could be disinherited. Schwarz, *op. cit.*, p. 263.

67. Schwarz, *Trust No One*, pp. 262-63.

68. Paul Lieberman and John J. Goldman, "Doris Duke's Will Evolves into Ultimate Probate Fight," *Los Angeles Times*, January 1, 1996.

69. Catherine Clabby, "Duke University President, Liz Taylor Get Chance to Dole Out Heiress' Charity," *Raleigh News and Observer*, August 30, 1994.

70. John J. Goldman and Robert J. Lopez, "Police to Investigate Death of Heiress," *Los Angeles Times*, January 25, 1995.

71. James C. McKinley Jr., "Los Angeles Police Begin Inquiry into Heiress's Death, "*New York Times*, January 27, 1995.

72. John J. Goldman and Paul Lieberman, "Former Employees of Heiress Contest Legality of Will," *Los Angeles Times*, February 25, 1995.

73. Schwarz, *op. cit.*, p. 255.

74. John J. Goldman and Paul Lieberman, "New Legal Twist Entangles Heiress's Will," *Los Angeles Times*, March 3, 1995. Surrogate Preminger's uncle was Otto Preminger, the film director.

75. See Paul Lieberman's *Los Angeles Times* stories: "Nurse Who Said Heiress Was Slain Held in Theft," April 2, 1995 (with Stephanie Simon); "Heiress Duke's Nurse Charged in Thefts," May 25, 1995 (with John J. Goldman); "Nurse Admits Thefts from Rich Patients," October 14, 1995 (with John J. Goldman); and "Doris Duke Nurse Gets Eight Years in Theft," February 29, 1996.

76. See James C. McKinley, "Judge Removes the Executors of Duke Estate," *New York Times*, May 23, 1995; Margaret A. Jacobs, "U.S. Trust and Butler Dismissed as Co-Executors," *Wall Street Journal*, May 23, 1995; Cristina Merrill, "Unseemly Case of the Bank, the Butler, and the Billionaire," *American Banker*, June 12, 1995; and David Stout, "Bernard Lafferty, the Butler for Doris Duke, Dies at 51," *New York Times*, November 5, 1996. James C. McKinley Jr., "Stakes in the Duke Case: A Long Reputation and a Lot of Dollars," *New York Times*, May 31, 1995.

77. James C. McKinley Jr., "Judge Blocks Replacement of Executors in Duke Case," *New York Times*, June 2, 1995, and McKinley, "Ousting of Doris Duke Executors Is Upheld," *New York Times*, October 11, 1995.

78. George James, "More Than $65 Million for Adopted Duke Daughter," *New York Times*, December 30, 1995.

79. Joseph P. Fried, "Court Reverses the Removal of Duke Estate's Executors," *New York Times*, January 12, 1996, and Goldman and Lieberman, "N.Y. Court Rejects Ouster of Duke Estate's Executor," *Los Angeles Times*, January 12, 1996.

80. Don Van Natta Jr., "Settlement May Be Reached in Battle Over Duke Estate," *New York Times*, January 25, 1996, and Van Natta, "Lawyers in Duke Estate Case Ask the Judge to Step Aside," *New York Times*, January 30, 1996.

81. Katharine Fraser, "Chemical and Bank of N.Y. Challenge U.S. Trust for Control of Duke Estate," *American Banker*, January 29, 1996.

82. See April 11, 1996 stories in the *New York Times, Raleigh News and Observer, American Banker,* and *Los Angeles Times*.

83. Susan Kaufman, "Judge Gives Blessing to Settlement in Doris Duke Estate Battle," *Raleigh News and Observer*, May 16, 1996, and Don Van Natta Jr., "Accord Clears the Last Will of Doris Duke for Probate," *New York Times*, May 16, 1996.

84. See stories in *Los Angeles Times*, July 25, 1996, and *Raleigh News and Observer*, November 5, 1996.

85. Salvatore Arena, "Judge Slashes Fees 14M in Heiress Estate Case," *New York Daily News*, May 2, 2000.

86. Susan Kaufman, "Duke University Honors an Heiress," *Raleigh News and Observer*, October 1, 1996.

87. John J. Goldman and Paul Lieberman, "Hoping to End Wrangles, Duke Charity Picks President," *Los Angeles Times*, January 29, 1997, and Susan Kaufman, "As Troubles Recede, Doris Duke's Largesse Poised to Flow," *Raleigh News and Observer*, January 29, 1997.

88. Judith M. Dobrzynski, "Confronting a $1.4 Billion Blank Page," *New York Times*, November 10, 1998.

89. Marina Dundjerski, "At Long Last, a Legacy," *Chronicle of Philanthropy*, December 11, 1997.

90. Stephanie Strom, "Not All of Helmsley's Trust Has to Go to Dogs," *New York Times*, February 25, 2009.

91. Susan Kaufman, "Doris Duke's Charity Flows," *Raleigh News and Observer*, December 10, 1997.

92. Joyce Mercer, "Colleges Watch for Signals on Priorities of Doris Duke's Charitable Foundation," *Chronicle of Higher Education*, March 13, 1998.

93. Brian K. Sullivan, "Harvard Begins Project to Replace Kyoto Protocol," Bloomberg, July 6, 2007.

94. Application from Duke Farms to the National Trust for Historic Preservation, received by the Office of New Jersey Heritage, May 5, 1987.

95. Letter from Gregory A. Marshall to Andras Fekete, June 12, 1987.

96. Anne Raver, "Transformation Involves Sacrifice," *New York Times*, May 8, 2008. See also Jane Garmey, "Duke's Storied Gardens Are No More," *Wall Street Journal*, May 28, 2008.

97. Jim Wright, "Duke Farms is a Birder's Paradise," *The Record*, July 6, 2012. See also Heather Haddon, "Duke Estate Reopens," *Wall Street Journal*, May 2, 2012, and Kate Zernike, "An Oasis, Once Gilded, Now Greened," *New York Times*, May 3, 2012.

98. Mark Di Ionno, "Grand Irony: Doris Duke Legacy Being Erased With Her Own Money," Newark *Star-Ledger*, March 20, 2016. See also Mark Di Ionno, "A Bird's-Eye View of the Duke Estate," Newark *Star-Ledger*, March 31, 2016. A book about the battle over Doris Duke's home, including interviews with long-time employees of Duke Farms, is Rikki Lynn Hauss, *The Duchess of South Somerville* (Totowa, New Jersey: Lightning Press, 2017).

99. Dave Hutchinson, "N.J. Supreme Court Rules Duke Mansion Can Be Abolished," *Newark Star-Ledger*, March 21, 2016.

100. Louis Graves, "Benevolent Water Power," *World's Work*, December 1931.

101. Durden, *Launching of Duke University*, pp. 58-59.

102. Walter L. Lingle, "Endowment Aids Davidson," *Charlotte Observer*, April 26, 1937.

103. Robert F. Durden, "James B. Duke Wins and Loses: The Partial Collapse of His Grand Design for Perpetual Philanthropy in the Carolinas," *North Carolina Historical Review*, January 1997.

104. *Ibid.*

105. *Ibid.*

106. Dan Chapman, "Endowment Selling 60% of Duke Shares," *Charlotte Observer*, March 3, 1994.

107. *The Duke Endowment 1991 Annual Report* (Charlotte, North Carolina: Duke Endowment, 1992), p. 3. Semans died in 2012. For an obituary, see "Philanthropist, Arts Supporter Mary Semans Dies in N.C.," *Palm Beach Daily News*, January 27, 2012. See also "A Life Remembered," press release on Duke Endowment website, dukeendowment.org/about-us/mary-d-b-t-semans-a-life-remembered. For a tribute to Semans, see "A Remarkable Life," *Duke Magazine*, March/April 2012.

108. *Ibid.*, pp. 4-5.

109. *Ibid.*, p. 5.

110. *Ibid.*, p. 4.

111. Stephanie Strom, "Fees and Trustees, Paying the Keepers of the Cash," *New York Times*, July 10, 2003.

112. "Duke Plans To Become Carbon Neutral by 2024," Duke University press release issued October 20, 2009.

113. Jessica Lichter, "Duke Endowment Gives $50M to DUMC," *Duke Chronicle*, April 5, 2008. "$80 Million Gift From Duke Endowment Will Remake Duke's Student Union, Other Landmark Facilities," Duke University press release issued March 7, 2011. April Bethea and David Perlmutt, "Duke Endowment Gives $35 Million to JCSU," *Charlotte Observer*, October 12, 2011. Mark Price, "Duke Endowment Gives Davidson College $45 Million for Construction, Renovation," *Charlotte Observer*, October 12, 2012.

114. Mark Prince, "Duke Endowment Hits $3 Billion Mark for Grants," *Charlotte Observer*, January 3, 2013.

Chapter 13: The Conrad N. Hilton Foundation

1. Meyer Berger, "Conrad Hilton, Collector of Hotels," *New York Times Magazine*, October 30, 1949.

2. Jeffrey Gitomer, "50 Years Later, Hilton's Customer Service Skill Offers Lessons," *Business Press*, August 20, 1999.

3. Tom Furlong, "Barron Hilton on Hot Seat," *Los Angeles Times*, April 2, 1990.

4. *The Hilton Legacy: Serving Humanity Worldwide* (Los Angeles: Conrad N. Hilton Foundation, 2009), p. 18.

5. Whitney Bolton, *The Silver Spade: The Conrad Hilton Story* (New York: Farrar, Straus, 1954), pp. xii-xiii.

6. *Ibid.*, pp. xiii-xiv.

7. Conrad N. Hilton, "'The Face of America,'" *Vital Speeches of the Day*, January 15, 1962.

8. "Hilton Gets Prize for Brotherhood," *New York Times*, November 22, 1950.

9. Conrad N. Hilton, "The Uncommitted Third," *Vital Speeches of the Day*, May 15, 1957.

10. *Ibid.*

11. Conrad N. Hilton, "The Face of America," *op. cit.*

12. Joel F. Olesky, "Conrad Hilton's International Shoestring," *Dun's Review and Modern Industry*, April 1965.

13. "Notes on People," *New York Times*, April 20, 1972. The Mayo Foundation was named in Hilton's will as a beneficiary and received the balance of the pledge from Hilton's estate. *The Hilton Legacy, op. cit.*, page 33.

14. Joan Cook, "Conrad Hilton, Founder of Hotel Chain, Dies at 91," *New York Times*, January 5, 1979.

15. Al Delugach, "Bates Vows to Protect Hilton Estate," *Los Angeles Times*, May 9, 1985.

16. "Daughter Contests Conrad Hilton's Will," *Los Angeles Times*, March 13, 1979.

17. Myrna Oliver, "Effort to Break Conrad Hilton Will Fails," *Los Angeles Times*, March 29, 1980.

In a 2008 *Los Angeles Times* profile, Robert W. Welkos said that Francesca Hilton was "not bitter" about her father's decision to disinherit her when she contested his will. "You can't live in the past," Francesca Hilton said. "That was his decision." Robert W. Welkos, "She Just Has To Laugh," *Los Angeles Times,* August 3, 2008. Francesca Hilton died in 2015. For an obituary, see Kurtis Lee, "Francesca Hilton, Daughter of Zsa Zsa Gabor and Conrad Hilton, Dies at 67," *Los Angeles Times*, January 8, 2015.

18. Al Delugach, "Bates Vows to Protect Hilton Estate," *Op. cit.*

19. Eileen White, "Claims to Big Hilton Estate Are Heating Up," *Wall Street Journal*, February 20, 1986.

20. *Ibid.* See also Al Delugach, "Head of Hilton Trust Refuses to Step Aside," *Los Angeles Times*, January 31, 1986.

21. David Johnston and Al Delugach, "IRS Says Hilton Estate Can Keep Controlling Block of Stock," *Los Angeles Times*, February 10, 1986, and Johnston and Delugach, "Fight Over Conrad Hilton Estate Gets Increasingly Bitter," *Los Angeles Times*, March 4, 1986.

22. Marcia Chambers, "The Hilton Will in Court: Heir Fights Foundation," *New York Times*, June 16, 1986.

23. *Ibid.*

24. *Ibid.*

25. Information from emails from Pat Modugno of the Hilton Foundation, April 17, 2013 and June 20, 2017.

26. Al Delugach, "Barron Hilton Wins Battle for Chain," *Los Angeles Times*, November 26, 1988. See also Anne Lowrey Bailey, "Hilton Fund Gets Over $500 Million in Accord, But Charities Disappointed," *Chronicle of Philanthropy*, December 6, 1988.

27. Ricki Fuhman, "Hilton Foundation, Heir Share Interests," *Pensions and Investments*, April 20, 1998. Information on the Barron Hilton Charitable Remainder Unitrust from an email from Patrick Modugno of the Conrad N. Hilton Foundation, dated August 16, 2006.

28. *Conrad N. Hilton Foundation Annual Report 1992-1993* (Reno, Nevada: Conrad N. Hilton Foundation, 1993), pp. 4-5.

29. *Ibid.*, p. 1.

30. *Ibid.*, preface.

31. Email from Pat Modugno of the Hilton Foundation, June 23, 2017.

32. *Conrad N. Hilton Foundation Annual Report 1992-1993, op. cit.,* preface.

33. *Ibid.*, p. 8. For more information about the Hilton/Perkins Program, see Donald H. Hubbs, "Helping the Multi-Handicapped Blind," *Philanthropy*, June 1995.

34. "An Interview With Steve Hilton, Chairman—Conrad N. Hilton Foundation," posted on fadica.org, December 2015. For a history of the Hilton Foundation's involvement with the Perkins School, see *The Hilton Legacy: Saving Humanity Worldwide*, pp. 61-71. Steven Hilton also discusses the Hilton Foundation's involvement with the Perkins School in an interview with the Bridgespan Group conducted in December 2013, available on the Bridgespan website.

35. Peter Panepanto, "Once a Wanderer, Hotel Heir is at Home in the Family Foundation," *Chronicle of Philanthropy*, November 24, 2005.

36. Anne Riley-Katz, "Steven Hilton Started in the Hotel Business, Then Switched to Philanthropy Through the Foundation Established by his Father Conrad," *Los Angeles Business Journal,* January, 2006.

37. Elizabeth Olson, "A Hilton In The News (And It's Not Paris)," *New York Times,* December 30, 2007.

38. Lauren Foster, "Living Donors Top US Charity List for First Time," *Financial Times,* January 14, 2008.

39. Information from emails from Pat Modugno of the Hilton Foundation, April 17, 2013 and June 20, 2017.

40. Paul Harasim, "Hilton Heir Announces Effort to End Hunger in LV Valley," *Las Vegas Review-Journal,* June 6, 2007.

41. Corey Levitan, "Filling Bellies Focus of Three Square Food Bank," *Las Vegas Review-Journal,* March 28, 2010.

42. Scott Wyland, "Medical Clinic in Park Gets Nod From County," *Las Vegas Review-Journal,* June 3, 2009.

43. "Conrad N. Hilton Foundation Kicks Off 5-Year Drive to End Chronic Homelessness in Los Angeles With $13 Million in Grants," Hilton Foundation press release issued December 1, 2010.

44. Abt Associates, *Evaluation of the Conrad N. Hilton Foundation Chronic Homelessness Initiative Phase I Final Report,* October 2016.

45. *The Hilton Legacy, op. cit.,* p. 41-42.

46. Memorandum from Steven M. Hilton to the Conrad N. Hilton Foundation board of directors, November 18, 2014.

Chapter 14: The Daniels Fund

1. Andy Vuong, "Daniels Fund Nixes New Center," *Denver Post,* November 21, 2003.

2. Stephanie Strom, "Turmoil Hits Charity Fund Over Its Handling of Money," *New York Times,* February 14, 2004.

3. *Ibid.*

4. Susan Barnes-Gelt, "The Daniels Dilemma," *Denver Post,* February 25, 2004.

5. Ben Gose, "Rocky Times at Colorado Foundation," *Chronicle of Philanthropy,* February 5, 2004.

6. Narcy Gordon, "Neil Bush's New Boss Says He Will Continue Fight for Cable Industry," Associated Press, July 15, 1991. Marcy Gordon, "Neil Bush Working for Cable Consulting Firm," Associated Press, October 5, 1992.

7. Stephen Singular, *Relentless: Bill Daniels and the Triumph of Cable TV* (New York: James Charlton Associates, 2003), preface.

8. Earl Gustkey, "The King of Cable," *Los Angeles Times,* December 8, 1986.

9. *Ibid.*

10. *The Life and Legacy of Bill Daniels* (Denver: Daniels Fund, 2012), pp. 22-23.

11. Gustkey, "The King of Cable."

12. *Ibid.*

13. *Ibid.*

14. "Brokerage House for TV Systems," *Business Week,* September 1, 1962.

15. Singular, *Relentless,* p.145.

16. *Ibid.,* p. 150.

17. Steven Flax, "Prime Time for Captain Video," *Forbes,* May 10, 1982.

18. Christopher DeMuth, "Open Skies and Open Spectrum—The Occasional Power of Simple Ideas," *National Review,* July 15, 2013. DeMuth notes that one reason why the Nixon Administration supported Open Skies was because they "were excited at the prospect of diverse local TV stations independent of the evil empire of ABC, CBS, and NBC. For their part, the networks were excited

at the prospect of distributing programs with their own satellites, freed of their costly dependence on Ma Bell."

C-SPAN founder Brian Lamb served as an assistant to Whitehead during the Nixon Administration. Lamb recalled that his first impression of Daniels around 1971 was that Daniels was "short, well-dressed, and a fast talker." Singular, *Relentless,* 153.

19. Sandra Salmans, "The Cable Industry's #1 Deal Maker," *New York Times,* October 16, 1983. A plain-spoken man with a Western twang, whose favorite adjective is 'helluva" (as in 'it's a helluva good business'), Mr. Daniels seems to have stepped out of a John Wayne movie," Salmans wrote.

In 2006, RBC Capital, a division of the Royal Bank of Canada, acquired Daniels and Associates. Mike Farrell, "Canadian Bank Buys Daniels," *Multichannel News,* November 27, 2006.

20. Randy Welch, "The Builder of Cable Empires," *Channels of Communications,* January/February 1985.

21. *Life and Legend of Bill Daniels,* p. 39.

22. Larry Stewart, "With Daniels, You Find That Nice Guys Needn't Finish Last," *Los Angeles Times,* May 27, 1994.

23. M. Eastlake Stevens, "Companies' Perks Get Creative," *ColoradoBiz,* April 2001.

24. Mike McPhee, "Friends Recall Daniels' Legacy," *Denver Post,* March 16, 2000.

25. Shari Caudron, "Remembering a Good Boy," *Workforce,* May 2000.

26. Michael Romano, "Best Boss?" *Rocky Mountain News,* September 18, 1988.

27. Stewart, *op. cit.*

28. Singular, *Relentless,* pp. 194-95.

29. *Ibid,* p. 151.

30. For an appreciation, see Vincent Carroll, "Bob Coté's Legacy: A Tough-Love Approach to Homelessness," *Denver Post,* October 15, 2013.

31. Interview with Bob Coté, September 24, 2013.

32. Coté interview. The Daniels Fund continues to support Father Woody's Christmas Party, but now pays for the food at the luncheon (which served 4,500 people in 2012), rather than handing out cash. Megan Mitchell, "A Sense of Family," *Denver Post,* December 17, 2012. The area surrounding Step 13 has been considerably gentrified since the 1980s.

33. Coté interview. For a profile of Coté, see Scott Walter, "Rocky Mountain Sheriff," *American Enterprise,* November 2002.

34. Cableland was willed to the city of Denver after Daniels's death to become the official residence for the mayor of Denver. The giant elephants remained outside until they were removed during a 2012 renovation. Suzanne P. Brown, "Cableland Gets a Makeover to Be A Better Place to Entertain," *Denver Post,* October 26, 2012. The giant elephants now reside at the Denver Zoo.

35. Sally Beatty, "Preserving a Donor's Intent," *Wall Street Journal,* October 6, 2006.

36. Mark Tatge, "Banking on Children," *American Banker,* April 2, 1987.

37. Brendan Cooney, "Small Business at Kids' Banks," *American Banker,* August 4, 1988.

38. Interview with Linda Childears, September 5, 2013. For a profile of Childears, see Will Shanley, "New Daniels CEO Proved Worth at Bank," *Denver Post,* May 15, 2005.

39. For more about Young AmeriTowne, see Brad Smith, "Young AmeriTowne Teaches Kids Age-Old Lessons," *Colorado Business,* December 1993.

40. Interview with Steve Schuck, August 6, 2013.

41. For a contemporary account, see Paul L. Montgomery, "Team's Owner Unable to Pay the Players," *New York Times,* December 2, 1975.

42. Cathy McKittrick, "Friends Say Daniels Showed Character and Heart," *Salt Lake Tribune,* October 20, 2011.

43. Lex Hemphill, "Daniels Plans to Repay Stars' Ticket Holders," *Salt Lake Tribune*, July 9, 1980.

44. McKittrick, "Friends Say Daniels Showed Character and Heart."

45. Life and Legend of Bill Daniels, p. 60.

46. Amended and Restated Bylaws of the Daniels Fund, May 2009.

47. For details of Daniels's alcoholism, see "Is Business Bungling Its Battle With Booze?" *Business Week*, March 25, 1991.

48. *Life and Legend of Bill Daniels*, p. 72.

49. *Ibid.*, p. 72.

50. Childears interview.

51. For an obituary, see Nick Ravo, "Bill Daniels, 79, Innovator in Cable Television Industry," *New York Times*, March 9, 2000.

52. For an obituary, see Renee McGaw, "Banker Phil Hogue Dies," *Denver Business Journal,* February 21, 2007.

53. Childears interview.

54. Childears interview.

55. Interview with Hank Brown, October 5, 2013.

56. For an interview with Brown, see "Diamonds in the Rough," *Philanthropy,* November/December 2002.

57. Brown interview.

58. Evan Sparks, "Back to Bill," *Philanthropy,* Fall 2011.

59. Brown interview.

60. Childears interview.

61. Brown interview.

62. Stuart Steers, "The Cable Guy," Westword, February 19, 2004.

63. Will Shanley, "Businessman and Aviator Honored by Smithsonian," *Denver Post*, November 9, 2005.

64. "Philanthropic Integrity: Interview With John V. Saeman," *Philanthropy*, Winter 2010. For a profile of John and Carol Saeman, see Sabrina Arena Ferresi, "The Power of Generosity," *Legatus Magazine*, November 2009.

65. Daniels Fund Bylaws.

66. "Philanthropic Integrity."

67. "Statement of Commitment and Understanding: Preserving Donor Intent," issued by the Daniels Fund.

68. "Donor Intent Policy," issued by the Daniels Fund, August 2012 (italics in text).

69. Kevin Laskowski, *Daniels Fund: How Can This Colorado Grantmaker Fuse Donor Vision With Community Needs for Greater Impact?* (Washington, D.C.: Philamplify/National Committee for Responsive Philanthropy, 2014), p. 7.

70. Laskowski, *Daniels Fund*, p. 14.

71. Laskowski, *Daniels Fund,* p. 18.

72. Daniels Scholarship Program fact sheet issued by the Daniels Fund, May 2017.

73. "'Waiting for Superman' Raises Awareness of Need for Education Reform," press release issued by the Daniels Fund, October 22, 2010.

74. Eric Gorski, "Colorado Supreme Court Rejects Douglas County Voucher Program," *Denver Post*, June 29, 2015.

75. John Aguilar, "Judge Orders Halt to Douglas County's Newest Voucher Program," *Denver Post*, August 3, 2016.

76. Email from Michael Bindas of the Institute for Justice, May 3, 2017.

77. Sean Olson, "Denish Clarifies Ties to Vouchers," *Albuquerque Journal*, September 3, 2010.

78. Vincent Carroll, "Telling the Truth About Our Schools," *Denver Post*, February 6, 2013.

Chapter 15: A Legal History of Donor Intent

1. Cited in Vanessa Laird, "Phantom Selves: The Search for a General Charitable Intent in the Application of the Cy Pres Doctrine," *Stanford Law Review*, April 1988.

2. Anthony Trollope, *The Warden* (New York: Oxford University Press, n.d.), p. 36.

3. Cited in Sandra Raban, *Mortmain Legislation and the English Church*, 1279-1500 (Cambridge: Cambridge University Press, 1982), p. 1.

4. Cited in Edith L. Fisch, Doris Jonas Freed, and Esther R. Schachter, *Charities and Charitable Foundations* (Pomona, New York: Lond, 1974), p. 19.

5. Gareth Jones, *History of the Law of Charity, 1532-1827* (Cambridge: Cambridge University Press, 1969), p. 74.

6. *Ibid.*, p. 74.

7. *Ibid.*, p. 73.

8. David Owen, *English Philanthropy, 1660-1960* (Cambridge, Massachusetts: Harvard University Press, 1964), p. 87.

9. Ian Williams, *The Alms Trade: Charities, Past, Present, and Future* (London: Unwin Hyman, 1989), p. 23. Eldon was also opposed to expanding the notion of charity to include political activism. In *De Themmines v. De Bonneval* (1828), he ruled that political organizations were not included in the Charities Act of 1601, and thus could not be considered charities. As late as 1978, this decision was used in Britain to declare that Amnesty International was not a charity.

10. Elias Clark et al., *Cases and Material on Gratuitous Transfers: Wills, Intestate Succession, Trusts, Gifts, Future Interests and Estate and Gift Taxation*, fourth edition (St. Paul, Minnesota: West, 1999), pp. 563-570.

11. Owen, *op. cit.*, p. 206.

12. Southcote, Lord Romilly continued, "was in my opinion, a foolish, ignorant woman, of an enthusiastic turn of mind, who had long wished to become an instrument in the hand of God to promote some great good on earth.... In the history of her life, her personal disputations and conversations with the devil, her prophecies and her inter-communings with the spiritual world, I have found much that, in my opinion, is very foolish, but nothing which is likely to make persons who read them either immoral or irreligious. I cannot, therefore, say that this devise of the testatrix is invalid by reason of the tendency of the writings of Joanna Southcote." Cited in George Gleason Bogert, Dallin H. Oaks, H. Reese Hansen, and Claralyn Martin Hill, *Cases and Text on the Law of Trusts*, 6th ed. (Westbury, New York: Foundation Press, 1991), p. 226.

13. Sir Arthur Hobhouse, *The Dead Hand: Addresses on the Subject of Endowments and Settlements of Property* (London: Chatto and Windus, 1880), pp. 42-44.

14. *Ibid.*, pp. 121-122.

15. Owen, *op. cit.*, p. 546.

16. Fisch, *op. cit.*, p. 21.

17. Howard S. Miller, *The Legal Foundations of American Philanthropy, 1776-1844* (Madison, Wisconsin: State Historical Society of Wisconsin, 1961), pp. 25-26.

18. Harry Emerson Wildes, *Lonely Midas: The Story of Stephen Girard* (New York: Farrar and Rinehart, 1943), p. 277.

19. *Ibid.*, p. 306.

20. *The Will of the Late Stephen Girard, Esq., Procured from the Office for the Probate of Wills, with a Short Biography of His Life* (Philadelphia: Thomas Desilver, 1848), p. 17. In the building's cellar, Girard called for windows to be placed "one half below, the other half above the surface of the ground."

21. *Ibid.*, p. 21.

22. *Ibid.*, p. 22.

23. *Ibid.*, pp. 22-23.

24. Hon. Daniel Webster, *A Defence of the Christian Religion and of the Religious Instruction of the Young. Delivered in the Supreme Court of the United States, February 10, 1844, in the Case of Stephen Girard's Will* (New York: Mark H. Newman, 1844), pp. 20-21.

25. Cited in Edith Abbott, *Some Pioneers in Social Welfare: Select Documents with Editorial Notes* (New York: Russell and Russell, 1963), pp. 85, 87.

26. Cited in Eugene F. Scoles and Edward C. Halbach Jr., *Problems and Materials on Decedents' Estates and Trusts,* 4th ed. (Boston: Little, Brown, 1987), p. 546.

27. C. Ronald Chester, "*Cy Pres*: A Promise Unfulfilled," *Indiana Law Journal,* Spring 1979.

28. Fisch, *op. cit.,* p. 27.

29. Cited in "Trusts-Cy Pres-Construction of Purpose to Permit Aid of Other than Designated Beneficiaries," *Columbia Law Review,* March 1935.

30. Cited in John Ritchie, Neill H. Alford Jr., and Richard W. Effland, *Cases and Materials on Decedents' Estates and Trusts* (Mineola, New York: Foundation Press, 1982), p. 710.

31. Bogert, *op. cit.,* pp. 210-211.

32. Cited in John T. Gaubatz, Ira Mark Bloom, and Lewis D. Solomon, *Estates and Trusts: Cases, Problems, and Materials* (New York: Matthew Bender, 1989), p. 768.

33. Cited in Jesse Dukeminier and Stanley M. Johanson, *Wills, Trusts, and Estates,* 4th ed. (Boston: Little, Brown, 1990), p. 588.

34. However, the courts have ruled that political parties are not charities. The National Woman's Party, despite its name, did not actively contest elections or nominate candidates. Ritchie, *op. cit.,* p. 710.

35. Bogert, *op. cit.* p. 220.

36. Ritchie, *op. cit.,* p. 673.

37. *Ibid.,* pp. 689-690.

38. *Ibid.,* p. 691.

39. David Luria, "Prying Loose the Dead Hand of the Past: How Courts Apply *Cy Pres* to Race, Gender, and Religiously Restricted Trusts," *University of San Francisco Law Review,* Fall 1986.

40. *Ibid.*

41. *Ibid.*

42. Martha Woodall, "Judge: Girard Must Remain A Boarding School, Keep High School Program," *Philadelphia Inquirer,* August 26, 2014.

43. Scoles, *op. cit.,* p. 534.

44. Ritchie, *op. cit.,* p. 712.

45. Thomas P. Gallanis, *Family Property Law: Cases and Materials on Wills, Trusts, and Future Interests,* fifth edition (New York: Foundation Press, 2011), p. 550-551.

46. Bogert, *op. cit.,* p. 549.

47. *Ibid.,* p. 550.

48. See Paige Lescure, "Lockwood v. Killian: Connecticut *Cy Pres* and the Restrictive Charitable Trust," *Connecticut Law Review,* Winter 1980.

49. Joan Biskupic, "Court Won't Let 2 Hawaii Schools Hire Only Protestant Teachers," *Washington Post,* November 9, 1993. Scott A. Merriman, *Religion and the Law In America: An Encyclopedia of Personal Belief and Public Policy* (Santa Barbara, California: ABC-CLIO, 2007), p. 206.

50. Gaubatz, *op. cit.,* p. 789.

51. Bogert, *op. cit.,* p. 304.

52. *Ibid.,* p. 307.

53. Bogert, *op. cit.,* pp. 572-573.

54. Ritchie, *op. cit.,* pp. 718-725.

55. Scoles, *op. cit.* p. 551.

56. Valerie J. Wollmar, Amy Morris Hess, and Robert Whitman, *An Introduction to Wills and Estates* (St. Paul, Minnesota: Thomson/West, 2003), pp. 1030-1039.

57. Jesse Dukeminier, Robert Sitkoff, and James Lindgren, *Wills, Trusts, and Estates,* eighth edition (New York: Aspen/Wolters Kluwer, 2009), p. 776.

58. *Ibid.*, p. 776-785. For an obituary of Adele Smithers, see Sam Roberts, "Adele Smithers, Who Empowered Charity Benefactor, Dies at 85," *New York Times,* February 15, 2017.

59. Gallanis, *op. cit.*, p. 566-567.

Chapter 16: The Two Most Powerful Strategies

1. Waldemar A. Nielsen, *Inside American Philanthropy* (Norman, Oklahoma: University of Oklahoma Press, 1996), pp. 246-47.

2. Quoted in Frank J. Hanna III, *What Your Money Means (And How to Use It Well)* (New York: Crossroad, 2008), p. 232.

3. Jia Lynn Yang, "Buffett to Gates: Spend It!" *Fortune,* March 2, 2007.

4. Andrew Jack, "A New Kind of Giving," *Financial Times,* April 30, 2013.

5. Loren Renz and David Wolcheck, *Perpetuity or Limited Lifespan: How Do Family Foundations Decide?* (New York: Foundation Center, 2009), pp. 1-6.

6. Francie Ostrower, *Limited Life Foundations: Motivations, Experiences, and Strategies* (Washington, D.C.: Urban Institute, 2009), p. 2. Boris's research can be found in "Creation and Growth: A Survey of Private Foundations," in Teresa Odendahl, ed., *America's Wealthiest and the Future of Foundations* (New York: Foundation Center, 1987), pp. 65-126.

7. *Ibid.*, p. 5.

8. Martin Morse Wooster, *Should Foundations Live Forever?* (Washington, D.C.: Capital Research Center, 1998).

9. *Tax-exempt Foundations: Hearings before the Select Committee to Investigate Tax-exempt Foundations and Comparable Organizations* (Washington, D.C.: Government Printing Office, 1953), p. 568.

10. I discuss the history of the Guggenheim Foundation in Martin Morse Wooster, "The Guggenheim Foundation's Slide into Irrelevance," *Foundation Watch,* March 1997.

11. Cited in M. M. Chambers, *Charters of Philanthropies: A Study of Selected Trust Instruments, Charters, By-Laws, and Court Decisions* (New York: Carnegie Endowment for the Advancement of Teaching, 1948), p. 138.

12. *Ibid.*, p. 217

13. *Ibid.*, p. 32. I discuss the Century Foundation in "The Century Foundation: The Little-Known Liberal Stalwart," *Foundation Watch,* February 2006. The Mellon Charitable Trust reorganized into the Mellon Foundation in the late 1960s.

14. Daniel J. Boorstin, "Transforming the Charitable Spirit: From Conscience to Community," in *The Julius Rosenwald Centennial* (Chicago: University of Chicago Press, 1963), pp. 30-31.

15. The most recent look at Rosenwald's efforts to aid African Americans is Stephanie Deutsch, *You Need a Schoolhouse: Booker T. Washington, Julius Rosenwald, and the Building of Schools in the Segregated South* (Evanston, Illinois: Northwestern University Press, 2011). For a critical look at Rosenwald's philanthropy, see Eric A. Larson and Alfred A. Moss Jr., *Dangerous Donations: Northern Philanthropy and Southern Black Education, 1902-1930* (Columbia, Missouri: University of Missouri Press, 1999).

16. M.R. Werner, *Julius Rosenwald: The Life of a Practical Humanitarian* (New York: Harper, 1939), p. 323.

17. Edwin R. Embree and Julia Waxman, *Investment in People: The Story of the Julius Rosenwald Fund* (New York: Harper, 1948), p. 31.

18. Julius Rosenwald, "Principles of Public Giving," *Atlantic Monthly*, May 1929. The Sailors' Snug Harbor still exists as a nonprofit. In Rosenwald's day, the sailor's home was in Staten Island. In 1972, the home was moved to North Carolina where it operated until 2005. The Manhattan properties Randall owned were not completely sold until 1980. The organization still gives grants to destitute sailors, but does not run a home. The Staten Island buildings are now the Snug Harbor Park, an artists' colony. For details, see TheSailorsSnugHarbor. org.

19. *Ibid.*

20. *Ibid.*

21. Cited in Julius Rosenwald, "The Trend Away From Perpetuities," *Atlantic Monthly*, December 1930.

22. Edward A. Filene, "Ten Key Men of Business," *North American Review*, April 1930.

23. Werner, *op. cit.*, p. 326.

24. Vincent Stehle, "Here and Now or Forevermore?" *Foundation News and Commentary*, January/February 2005. This article is excerpted from the National Center for Family Philanthropy's *Investment Issues for Family Funds: Managing and Maximizing Your Philanthropic Assets*. I edited Philip Stern's last book, *Still the Best Congress Money Can Buy*.

25. Alfred Perkins, Edwin Rogers Embree: *The Julius Rosenwald Fund, Foundation Philanthropy, and American Race Relations* (Bloomington, Indiana: Indiana University Press, 2011), p. 249-250. For an analysis of the Rosenwald Fund, see John R. Thelin and Richard W. Trollinger, *Time is of the Essence: Foundations and the Policies of Limited Life and Endowment Spend-Down* (Washington, D.C.: Aspen Institute, 2009), pp. 4-10.

26. *Tax-Exempt Foundations: Report of the Special Committee to Investigate Tax-Exempt Foundations and Charitable Organizations* (Washington, D.C.: Government Printing Office, 1954), p. 214.

27. Rep. Wright Patman, "The Free-Wheeling Foundations," *The Progressive*, June 1967.

28. *Ibid.*

29. Thomas C. Reeves, *Foundations Under Fire* (Ithaca, New York: Cornell University Press, 1970), p. 33.

30. Section 4941 stated that a foundation could not own more than 20 percent of the stock in a corporation, which played a crucial role in the creation of the Hilton Foundation.

31. For a discussion of the debate over Section 4942, see William H. Smith and Carolyn P. Chiechi, *Private Foundations: Before and After the Tax Reform Act of 1969* (Washington, D.C.: American Enterprise Institute, 1974), pp. 58-64.

32. Tony Proscio, *Winding Down the Atlantic Philanthropies: The First Eight Years, 2001-2008* (Durham, North Carolina: Sanford School of Public Policy, Duke University, 2010), p. 6. This report and its sequel, *Winding Down the Atlantic Philanthropies: Beginning the Endgame, 2009-2010* (Durham, North Carolina: Sanford School of Public Policy, Duke University, 2012) are well written, thoughtful, and very informative.

33. Tony Proscio, *Beginning the Endgame*, p. 48. The literature on Chuck Feeney is extensive, but a good starting place is Conor O'Clery's authorized biography, *The Billionaire That Wasn't* (New York: PublicAffairs, 2007). An hour-long documentary on Feeney was produced by the Irish broadcaster RTE in 2009 and is available on YouTube. I discuss Feeney and the Atlantic Philanthropies in "The Atlantic Philanthropies: Right—and Wrong—Ways to Give," *Foundation Watch*, June 2011.

34. John J. Miller, *A Gift of Freedom: How the John M. Olin Foundation Changed America* (San Francisco: Encounter Books, 2006), p. 185.

35. *Ibid.*, p. 189.

36. *Ibid.*, p. 206. For more information on the Olin Foundation's spending down practices, see James Piereson, "The Insider's Guide to Spend Down," *Philanthropy*, March/April 2002, and Roger M. Williams, "Sustaining Ideas on the Right," an interview with Piereson in *Foundation News and Commentary*, January/February 2006. Piereson was the last president of the John M. Olin Foundation.

37. I have received one small grant from the Simon Foundation to write a short article.

38. Justin Torres provides a good introduction to Simon's life in the Philanthropy Hall of Fame on the Philanthropy Roundtable website.

39. William E. Simon with John M. Caher, *A Time for Reflection: An Autobiography* (Washington: Regnery, 2004), pp. 273-4.

40. "Simon Says," *Philanthropy*, January/February 2000. When asked if Congress should require foundations to spend down, Simon said "absolutely not. You pass a law, and the bureaucrats at IRS and Treasury go to work on it, and pretty soon nobody can understand it."

41. Torres, *op. cit.*

42. Naomi Schaefer Riley, "The Weekend Interview with Bill Simon: A Conservative Philanthropist Looks to the Future," *Wall Street Journal*, December 27, 2008.

43. Arthur Gleason, "A Man Who Has Fun with His Wealth," *Hearst's International*, September 1923.

44. For more information about Harkness, see my biographical entry on him in the "Philanthropy Hall of Fame," at PhilanthropyRoundtable.org.

45. B.C. Forbes, *Men Who Are Making America* (New York: B.C. Forbes, 1917), pp. 91-92.

46. Blake McKelvey, *Rochester: An Emerging Metropolis, 1925-1961* (Rochester, New York: Christopher Press, 1961), p. 2.

47. George Eastman, Philanthropy Hall of Fame, at http://www.philanthropyroundtable.org/almanac/hall_of_fame/george_eastman.

48. Quoted in "Given Away—The Duke and Eastman Millions," *Literary Digest,* Dec. 27, 1924. I discuss Eastman at greater length in *Should Foundations Live Forever?*, pp. 15-22. The primary source for information about Eastman's life is Elizabeth Brayer, *George Eastman: A Biography* (Baltimore, Maryland: Johns Hopkins University Press, 1996).

Chapter 17: What Donors Can Do

1. Joseph J. Jacobs, *The Compassionate Conservative: Seeking Responsibility and Human Dignity* (Lafayette, Louisiana: Huntington House, 1996), p. 287. I provided research for *The Compassionate Conservative.* For more on Jacobs and his foundation, see my *Should Foundations Live Forever?* (Washington, D.C.: Capital Research Center, 1998), pp. 37-41.

2. Adam Meyerson, "When Philanthropy Goes Wrong," *Wall Street Journal,* March 9, 2012.

3. For a valuable description of one foundation's accomplishments when it spent down, see this article by a former president of the now-closed Whitaker Foundation: Miles J. Gibbons Jr., "Going for Broke," *Philanthropy*, May/June 2001, available at http://www.philanthropyroundtable.org/topic/excellence_in_philanthropy/going_for_broke.

4. Jeff Cain, *Protecting Donor Intent: How to Define and Safeguard Your Philanthropic Principles* (Washington, D.C.: Philanthropy Roundtable, 2012); also available at http://www.philanthropyroundtable.org/file_uploads/Protecting_Donor_Intent_Guidebook.pdf.

Index

441

About the Author

Martin Morse Wooster, a senior fellow at the Capital Research Center in Washington, D.C., has written extensively on the history of philanthropy. In addition to the three previous editions of this book, Wooster is the author of *Great Philanthropic Mistakes* (Hudson Institute), *By Their Bootstraps: The Lives of Twelve Gilded Age Social Entrepreneurs* (Hudson Institute), *Games Universities Play: And How Donors Can Avoid Them* (Pope Center for Higher Education Policy), *The Foundation Builders: Brief Biographies of Twelve Great Philanthropists* (Philanthropy Roundtable), *Should Foundations Live Forever: The Question of Perpetuity* (Capital Research Center), and *Return to Charity: Philanthropy and the Welfare State* (Capital Research Center). He has also contributed articles on the history of philanthropy to *The Encyclopedia of Civil Rights*, *The Encyclopedia of Philanthropy*, *The Encyclopedia of the Victorian Era*, and *Notable American Philanthropists*. In addition, he is the author of *Angry Classrooms, Vacant Minds: What's Happened to Our High Schools?* (Pacific Research Institute).

A graduate of Beloit College with a degree in history and philosophy, Wooster has been an editor at *Harper's*; the *Wilson Quarterly*; *Philanthropy*; *Reason*; *strategy+business*; and the *American Enterprise*; as well as a columnist for the *Washington Times*. His articles have also appeared in the *Wall Street Journal, Washington Post, Esquire, Reader's Digest, Elle, Spin, Air and Space, Policy Review, Public Opinion,* the *American Spectator,* and *Washingtonian.* He lives in Silver Spring, Maryland.

About the Capital Research Center

The Capital Research Center (CRC) was founded to be a resource for donors and to serve as a watchdog on the nonprofit world—both grantmakers and grant-seekers. Now in our fourth decade as a think tank based in Washington, D.C., we continue to publish books, magazines, and reports that reveal how donors and charities operate. We also maintain multiple websites. Our main website is CapitalResearch.org, and we supply additional information on specific public charities and private foundations at InfluenceWatch.org.

Our Center for Strategic Giving, headed by a long-time senior staffer from the Bradley Foundation described in Chapter 11 of this book, offers customized advice and insights on ways that donors can affect public policy.

CRC studies the nonprofit world with a special focus on reviving the American traditions of charity, philanthropy, and voluntarism. The growth of government has increasingly supplanted the voluntary action and community-based problem-solving that makes America an exceptional nation. CRC critiques donors and nonprofit groups that promote the growth of the welfare state, and also identifies private alternatives to government programs.

We accept no government funds. Our work is supported entirely by individual donors, foundations, and corporations.

How to Order

Qualified donors who want to share this book with family, friends, and staff are welcome to request free physical and electronic copies of this book. Please write Contact@CapitalResearch.org or call 202.483.6900.

This book is also available through online channels such as Amazon.com. It is published in cooperation with the AmP Publishers Group, whose website offers a 20 percent discount. Please visit AmPPubGroup.com.